THE PEOPLE BESIDE PAUL

Society of Biblical Literature

Early Christianity and Its Literature

David G. Horrell, Editor

Warren Carter
Amy-Jill Levine
Judith M. Lieu
Margaret Y. MacDonald
Dale B. Martin

Number 17

THE PEOPLE BESIDE PAUL

THE PHILIPPIAN ASSEMBLY
AND HISTORY FROM BELOW

Edited by

Joseph A. Marchal

SBL Press
Atlanta

Library of Congress Cataloging-in-Publication Data

The people beside Paul : the Philippian assembly and history from below / edited by Joseph A. Marchal.
     p. cm. — (Early Christianity and its literature ; Number 17)
    Includes bibliographical references and index.
    ISBN 978-1-62837-096-6 (pbk. : alk. paper) — ISBN 978-1-62837-098-0 (ebook) — ISBN 978-1-62837-097-3 (hardcover : alk. paper)
    1. Bible. Philippians—Criticism, interpretation, etc. 2. Philippi (Extinct city)—Church history. 3. Philippi (Extinct city)—Civilization. I. Marchal, Joseph A., editor.
    BS2705.52.P46 2015
    227'.6067—dc23   2015030957

Contents

Acknowledgements

For almost as long as I can remember, I have been working beside many others: at first with my sisters, then my neighbors, then along an assembly line, and then in landscaping crews (before beginning my graduate studies). To properly acknowledge how this more recent work was completed requires further reflections on both memory and collaboration. If memory serves, much of the planning for the early phases of this project began ten years ago this summer over a meeting I had with Dick Horsley and Valerie Abrahamsen in western Massachusetts. It is only fitting, then, that their contributions to this project begin and end this volume.

Among other steering committee members of the Paul and Politics group, Dick championed the idea of having smaller, interactive working groups, each focusing on the particular communities that received Paul's letters, places like Thessalonike, Corinth, Galatia, and of course Philippi. Having just completed my dissertation on Philippians at the time, I was grateful for the opportunity to coordinate the Philippians' working group (and have been for most of the intervening years). Over those years we spent the Fridays before the annual meeting collaborating and more directly responding to and interacting with engaging papers prepared by colleagues from a wide range of perspectives and approaches. It was a collegial and generative environment for those of us lucky enough to present our work in progress on the letter to the Philippians or on Philippi in general. I am certain that my own work (among other presenters') was much improved for the careful, critical, and candid discussion this group has provided. My acknowledgements on this occasion, then, are an extension of those I have and have not remembered to make in the past.

Thus, I cannot fail to note that many other scholars, friends, and colleagues presented, responded to, or discussed the papers that preceded and then led to those crafted into chapters for this volume. What this volume contains, then, at times only dimly reflects much wider circles of engagement and influence from and alongside of colleagues like Efraín

Agosto, Sean Burke, Neil Elliott, Susan (Elli) Elliott, Steven Friesen, Brigitte Kahl, Cynthia Briggs Kittredge, John Lanci, Davina Lopez, David Lull, Justin Meggitt, Jorunn Økland, Ray Pickett, David Rhoads, Luise Schottroff, Elisabeth Schüssler Fiorenza, Abraham Smith, James Walters, Demetrius Williams, and Sean Winter (among others I am sure I am not recalling). Our debts to these sorts of colleagues, both named and unnamed, those who work beside us, are always hard to measure.

The stakes and shapes of the arguments in the chapters to follow have been clarified by all these colleagues, and many more besides, even as the responsibilities for any shortcomings are those of the authors and ultimately myself as their editor. The volume's appearance in this series is due to the gracious and patient work of Gail O'Day and the entire Early Christianity and Its Literature (ECL) editorial board, including the new series editor, David G. Horrell. Certainly, its contents were further improved by the helpful feedback provided by Gail and ECL's anonymous reviewers. The entire team at SBL Press (Bob Buller, Billie Jean Collins, Kathie Klein, Heather McMurray, and Nicole Tilford) has once again capably shepherded this project through its final stages and into production.

Most importantly, however, this volume would not be possible without the collective patience and persistence of all of its contributors: with this project, with each other, with the collaborative process, and with the editor. The process took longer than some of us would have liked, while others preferred still more time with this work, but this volume manages to reflect some of the variety and vitality of this working group, about which all of us should be proud. The contributions cover an impressive array of topics, providing multiple points of entry for our peers to consider and engage in the days still to come. I know that my own (albeit limited) contributions to these conversations were quite concretely made possible by my partners and companions, those who "eat by me" in the days already past—especially Tascha, Liam, Jarvis, and July. But the final acknowledgements and dedication for this volume belong to all of the contributors and to those assembled around them who serve as their collaborators and companions, however they are defined, wherever they have been assembled, whenever they have been "beside" each other.

ABBREVIATIONS

PRIMARY SOURCES

1 Apol.	Justin, *Apologia i*
1 Clem.	1 Clement
1 En.	1 Enoch (Ethiopic Apocalypse)
3 Cor.	3 Corinthians
3 Macc.	3 Maccabees
Abr.	Philo, *De Abrahamo*
Ann.	Tacitus, *Annales*
Ant.	Josephus, *Jewish Antiquities*
Att.	Cicero, *Epistulae ad Atticum*
Aug.	Suetonius, *Divus Augustus*
AUC	Livy, *Ab urbe condita*
Bell. civ.	Appian, *Bella civilian*
Bibl. hist.	Diodorus Siculus, *Bibliotheca historica*
Brut.	Plutarch, *Brutus*
Caes.	Plutarch, *Caesar*
Chaer.	Chariton, *De Chaerea et Callirhoe*
Cher.	Philo, *De cherubim*
Cic.	Plutarch, *Cicero*
Claud.	Suetonius, *Divus Claudius*
Clem.	Seneca, *De clementia*
Contempl.	Philo, *De vita contemplativa*
Cor.	Tertullian, *De corona militis*
Curios.	Plutarch, *De curiositate*
Cyr.	Xenophon, *Cyropaedia*
Daphn.	Longus, *Daphnis and Chloe*
Def. orac.	Plutarch, *De defectu oraculorum*
Deipn.	Athenaeus, *Deipnosophistae*
Demon.	Lucian, *Demonax*

Dial. mort.	Lucian, *Dialogi Mortuorum*
Diatr.	Epictetus, *Diatribai*
Dig.	Digesta
Disc.	Dio Chrysostom, *Discourses*
Dom.	Suetonius, *Domitianus*
Ench.	Epictetus, *Encheiridion*
Ep.	*Epistulae*
Eph.	Ignatius, *To the Ephesians*; Xenophon of Ephesus, *Ephesiaca*
Fam.	Cicero, *Epistulae ad familiares*
Flacc.	*In Flaccum*, Philo
Fug.	Tertullian, *De fuga in persecutione*; Lucian, *Fugitivi*
Git.	Gittin
Haer.	Hippolytus, *Refutatio omnium haeresium*
Hag.	Hagigah
Hist.	*Historiae*
Hist. eccl.	Eusebius, *Historia ecclesiastica*
Hist. Rom.	Cassius Dio, *Historia Romana*
Hom. Phil.	John Chrysostom, *Homiliae in epistulam ad Philippensis*
Idol.	Tertullian, *De idolatria*
Il.	Homer, *Ilias*
Ind.	Lucian, *Adversus indoctum*
Iul.	Suetonius, *Divus Iulius*
Ios.	Philo, *De Iosepho*
I.Priene	inscription from Priene
Juv.	John Chrysostom, *In Juventinum et Maximum martyres*
Legat.	Philo, *Legatio ad Gaium*
Leuc. Clit.	Achilles Tatius, *Leucippe et Clitophon*
Lives	Diogenes Laertius, *Lives of Eminent Philosophers*
LXX	Septuagint
Mart.	Tertullian, *Ad martyras*
Mart. Pal.	Eusebius, *De martyribus Palaestinae*
Mart. Paul	Martyrdom of Paul
Mart. Perpt.	Martyrdom of Perpetua
Metam.	Apuleius, *Metamorphoses*
Metam.	Ovid, *Metamorphoses*
Migr.	Philo, *De migratione Abrahami*
Mor.	Plutarch, *Moralia*
Nat	Pliny the Elder, *Naturalis historia*
Nat.	Tertullian, *Ad nationes*

Noct. att.	Aulus Gellius, *Noctes atticae*
Onir.	Artemidorus Daldianus, *Onirocritica*
Or.	*Orations*
Pan.	Epiphanius, *Panarion* (*Adversus haereses*)
Peregr.	Lucian, *De morte Peregrini*
Phaed.	Plato, *Phaedo*
Phaedr.	Plato, *Phaedrus*
Phil.	Polycarp, *To the Philippians*
Pisc.	Lucian, *Piscator*
Plant.	Philo, *De plantione*
Pol.	Aristotle, *Politica*
PSI	Papyrus Istanza al beneficiaries del Prefetto
P.Oxy	*Papyrus* Oxyrhynchus
P.Yale	Papyrus from the Yale Collection
Sat.	*Satirae*; Petronius, *Satyricon*
Spec.	Philo, *De specialibus legibus*
Strom.	Clement, *Stromata*
Ter.	Terumot
Theog.	Hesiod, *Theogonia*
Tib.	Suetonius, *Tiberius*
Tox.	Lucian, *Toxaris*
Tusc.	Cicero, *Tusculanae disputationes*
Verr.	Cicero, *In Verrem*
Vit. Apoll.	Philostratus, *Vita Apollonii*
Vit. auct.	Lucian, *Vitarum auctio*
y.	Jerusalem Talmud

SECONDARY SOURCES

AB	Anchor Bible
ABD	*Anchor Bible Dictionary.* Edited by David Noel Freedman. 6 vols. New York: Doubleday, 1992.
AJP	*American Journal of Philology*
ANTC	Abingdon New Testament Commentary
Arch	*Archaeology*
BA	*Biblical Archaeologist*
BCH	*Bulletin de correspondance hellénique*
BibInt	*Biblical Interpretation*

BDAG	Danker, Frederick W., Walter Bauer, William F. Arndt, and F. Wilbur Gingrich. *Greek-English Lexicon of the New Testament and Other Early Christian Literature*. 3rd ed. Chicago: University of Chicago Press, 2000.
BDF	Blass, Friedrich, Albert Debrunner, and Robert W. Funk. *A Greek Grammar of the New Testament and Other Early Christian Literature*. Chicago: University of Chicago Press, 1961.
BNTC	Black's New Testament Commentaries
BWANT	Beiträge zur Wissenschaft vom Alten und Neuen Testament
BZNW	Beihefte zur Zeitschrift für die neutestamentliche Wissenschaft
CBQMS	Catholic Biblical Quarterly Monograph Series
CIL	*Corpus inscriptionum latinarum*
CJ	*Classical Journal*
CP	*Classical Philology*
CSJH	Chicago Studies in the History of Judaism
ConBNT	Coniectanea biblica: New Testament Series
EPRO	Etudes préliminaires aux religions orientalies dans l'empire romain
ExpTim	*Expository Times*
GBS	Guides to Biblical Scholarship
GPBS	Global Perspectives on Biblical Scholarship
GRBS	*Greek, Roman, and Byzantine Studies*
HCS	Hellenistic Culture and Society
HNT	Handbuch zum Neuen Testament
HTR	*Harvard Theological Review*
HTS	Harvard Theological Studies
HUT	Hermeneutische Untersuchungen zur Theologie
ICC	International Critical Commentary
IG	*Inscriptiones graecae*
Int	*Interpretation*
JBL	*Journal of Biblical Literature*
JFSR	*Journal of Feminist Studies in Religion*
JHS	*Journal of Hellenic Studies*
JJS	*Journal of Jewish Studies*
JPS	Jewish Publication Society
JSJ	*Journal for the Study of Judaism in the Persian, Hellenistic, and Roman Periods*
JSNT	*Journal for the Study of the New Testament*

JSNTSup	Journal for the Study of the New Testament Supplement Series
JSOTSup	Journal for the Study of the Old Testament Supplement Series
JSPSup	Journal for the Study of the Pseudepigrapha Supplement Series
KEK	Kritisch-exegetischer Kommentar über das Neue Testament (Meyer-Kommentar)
LCL	Loeb Classical Library
LSJ	Liddell, Henry George, Robert Scott, and Henry Stuart Jones. *A Greek-English Lexicon*. 9th ed. with revised supplement. Oxford: Clarendon, 1996.
LIMC	*Lexicon iconographicum mythologiae classicae*. Edited by H. C. Ackerman and J. R. Gisler. 8 vols. Zurich, 1981–1997.
NASB	New American Standard Bible
NewDocs	*New Documents Illustrating Early Christianity*. Edited by G. H. R. Horsley and S. Llewelyn. North Ryde, N.S.W., 1981.
NICNT	New International Commentary on New Testament
NIGTC	New International Greek Testament Commentary
NKZ	*Neue kirchliche Zeitschrift*
NovT	*Novum Testamentum*
NovTSup	Novum Testamentum Supplement Series
NRSV	New Revised Standard Version
NTApoc	*New Testament Apocrypha*. Revised ed. Edited by Wilhelm Schneemelcher. English trans. ed. Robert McL. Wilson. 2 vols. Philadelphia: Westminster, 1963–1966.
NTD	Das Neue Testament Deutsch
NTS	*New Testament Studies*
P. Polit. Jud.	*Urkunden des Politema der Juden von Herakleopolis*. Edited by J. M. S. Cowley and K. Maresch. Papyrologia Coloniensia 29. Wiesbaden: Westdeutscher Verlag, 2001.
PRSt	*Perspectives in Religious Studies*
RB	*Revue biblique*
ResQ	*Restoration Quarterly*
RGG	*Religion in Geschichte und Gegewart*. Edited by Hans Dieter Betz. 4th ed. Tübingen: Mohr Siebeck, 1998–2007.
RSV	Revised Standard Version

SB	*Sammelbuch griechischer Urkunden aus Aegypten*. Edited by Friedrick Preisigke et al. Vols. 1–21. Wiesbaden: Harrassowitz, 1915–2002.
SBL	Society of Biblical Literature
SBLDS	Society of Biblical Literature Dissertation Series
SemeiaSt	Semeia Studies
SIG	*Sylloge inscriptionum graecum*. Edited by Wilhelm Dittenberger. 4 vols. 3rd ed. Leipzig: Hirzel, 1915–1924.
SNTSMS	Society for New Testament Studies Monograph Series
THKNT	Theologischer Handkommentar zum Neuen Testament
TynBul	*Tyndale Bulletin*
WBC	Word Biblical Commentary
WUNT	Wissenschaftliche Untersuchungen zum Neuen Testament
ZNW	*Zeitschrift für die neutestamentliche Wissenschaft und die Kunde der älteren Kirche*
ZPE	*Zeitschrift für Papyrologie und Epigraphik*

Philippian (Pre)Occupations and Peopling Possibilities: An Introduction

Joseph A. Marchal

Occupy Philippi?

This volume addresses several questions. How can we begin to imagine what ancient assembly communities were like "on the ground" or "from the bottom up"? In what ways can scholars conceptualize and describe the everyday Philippians or, more simply, people other than Paul? Are there any ancient or even more recent resources for helping us focus upon different people or even some of the usual suspects differently? Indeed, recent events have an odd way of making these questions urgent in new and more specific ways.

The working group that produced this collection of essays had been meeting and working together since 2005, but began moving toward the versions one will find here in years marked by a range of popular uprisings and populist demonstrations, including the Arab Spring abroad and the Occupy movement in the United States and beyond.[1] While one will see little to no direct reflection or explicit connection of these more recent events within the chapters to follow, this contemporary context provides a striking, if limited, analogue for the concerns embodied by this collection. More than anything else these movements have exposed the exclusions and inequalities embedded within a range of current-day cultures. In

---

1. On the former, see Hamid Dabashi, *The Arab Spring: The End of Postcolonialism* (London: Zed Books, 2012); on the latter, see Janet Byrne, ed., *The Occupy Handbook* (New York: Back Bay Books, 2012); and Writers for the 99%, *Occupy Wall Street: The Inside Story of an Action That Changed America* (Chicago: Haymarket Books, 2012). By many accounts, the actions in Cairo's Tahrir Square inspired the first Occupy actions in and around New York's Wall Street.

turn, they have sought to foreground the perspectives of those who are not benefitting from the economic system, those who lack influence in both local and larger political systems. Generally speaking, the perspectives preserved in the texts and artifacts of the ancient Mediterranean world are predominantly those of the privileged few, rather than the masses at various distances, both spatially and practically, from centers of economic and political power. Such concerns echo throughout this collection. Indeed, most of the people who lived and died in the Greco-Roman world, in places like ancient Philippi, are not represented by the classical texts for studying this world. The accounts given in those texts represent the perspectives of an extraordinarily small sample of the population, those contending at the very apex of power. Those who are marginalized or simply excluded within these resources comprise the vast majority of the people; their numbers even approach an ancient analogue to the contemporary slogan, "we are the 99%!"

However, I have my reservations about the choice to use the term "Occupy" for such efforts, considering the situation of peoples living, both historically and currently, under occupations of various sorts. It is a strikingly imperial and colonial term to reuse, though perhaps its redeployment constitutes a significant enough resituation or even reclamation to counter such forces. Certainly, a number of interpreters find similar modes of resistance and reclamation for imperial terms at work in Paul's letters.[2] Further, "Occupy" has already been paired with and applied to Christian theology as well as the biblical texts themselves.[3] However, this strategic bit of diction still troubles me, in general, but especially when I try to approach the people in first century Philippi. The experiences of many residents of Philippi were likely to reflect or at least approximate these kinds of historical, political, and economic conditions. A survey of Philippi's history running up to this period shows that various invading,

---

2. See, for instance, the three volumes edited by Richard A. Horsley: *Paul and Empire: Religion and Power in Roman Imperial Society* (Harrisburg, PA: Trinity Press International, 1997); *Paul and Politics: Ekklesia, Israel, Imperium, Interpretation; Essays in Honor of Krister Stendahl* (Harrisburg, PA: Trinity Press International, 2000); *Paul and the Roman Imperial Order* (Harrisburg, PA: Trinity Press International, 2004). See also the chapters in this volume by Standhartinger and Brawley.

3. Joerg Rieger and Kwok Pui-lan, *Occupy Religion: Theology of the Multitude*, Religion in the Modern World (Lanham, MD: Rowman & Littlefield, 2012); Susan B. Thistlethwaite, *#OccupytheBible: What Jesus Really Said (and Did) about Money and Power* (New York: Astor + Blue, 2012).

colonizing, and settling efforts were not, in fact, undertaken for the benefit of the vast majority of Philippi's residents, despite the best efforts of ruling elites to cast them in such terms.

What apparently drew some of the earliest settlers from Thracia and then the island of Thasos to this location were the valuable silver mines in the mountains that created a border for the area to the north and north-east of the region (see, for example, Herodotus, *Hist.* 7.112). Mentioned as early as 490 BCE, this site comes to the attention of most historians when Philip II of Macedonia "settled" a fight between the Thasians and Thracians by taking the settlement for himself in 356 BCE (see Diodorus Siculus, *Bibl. hist.* 11.70.5; 12.68.1–3; 16.3.7; and 16.8.6–7). Of course, this was how the city received its more familiar name, when Philip named it (as humbly as most conquerors and kings would) after himself. With control of Philippi came not only control over these mines, but also the strate-gic protection and control of an important west-to-east trade route, given Philippi's location between those mountains to the north and swamps to the south.[4] Philip colonized the entire region and fortified Philippi as a city, building its walls and establishing a military stronghold. The Mace-donian line of kings would rule Philippi and the region until the Romans defeated them in 168 BCE (see Polybius, *Hist.* 31.29; Livy, *AUC* 45.29.5–9) and subsequently annexed the region as a province in 146 BCE.[5] When the

---

4. Surveys of this history offer different evaluations of the ongoing productivity of these mines. Some follow Diodorus Siculus and depict Philip as so exploiting the mines that he exhausted their resources and Philippi soon fell in utility and promi-nence. On the relative unimportance of "precolonial" Philippi, see Lilian Portefaix, *Sisters Rejoice: Paul's Letter to the Philippians and Luke-Acts as Received by First-Century Philippian Women*, ConBNT 20 (Stockholm: Almqvist & Wiksell, 1988), 60; Lukas Bormann, *Philippi: Stadt und Christengemeinde zur Zeit des Paulus*, NovTSup 78 (Leiden: Brill, 1995), 19–20; and Craig S. de Vos, *Church and Community Conflicts: The Relationship of the Thessalonian, Corinthian, and Philippian Churches with Their Wider Civic Communities*, SBLDS 168 (Atlanta: Scholars Press, 1999), 235. The prob-lem is the relative silence of our sources for the period in between Philip II and the rise of the Romans. Thus, both Oakes and Marchal have cautioned against arguing too strenuously for Philippi's "obscurity" from this silence. See Peter S. Oakes, *Philippians: From People to Letter*, SNTSMS 110 (Cambridge: Cambridge University Press, 2001), 19–24; and Joseph A. Marchal, *Hierarchy, Unity, and Imitation: A Feminist Rhetorical Analysis of Power Dynamics in Paul's Letter to the Philippians*, Academia Biblica 24 (Atlanta: Society of Biblical Literature, 2006), 100–104.

5. The assumption that this annexation and colonization brought benefits to the city of Philippi also rests on the assumption that Philippi was in a state of decline

Romans built the Via Egnatia highway, Philippi was a strategic location on the route that connected the ports of the Adriatic Sea in the west to Byzantium and Asia Minor in the east.

Whenever biblical scholars provide a historical or political contextualization for Philippi (and the letter of Paul sent to the community there), their most common starting point comes after these settlements and changes.[6] The events surrounding the Roman civil wars typically have pride of place in these pictures of Philippi, likely because biblical and classical studies are in many ways close cousins. The western plains just outside of Philippi were key sites in these conflicts, including the decisive battle in 42 BCE between the forces of Brutus and Cassius (two of the key liberators or conspirators, who had assassinated Julius) and those of Marc Antony and Octavian. The victorious Antony and Octavian settled veterans there after this battle, and Octavian settled more once he defeated his former ally and consolidated his power in 31 BCE. The second victory and settlement would give this Roman colony a title that reflects Octavian's own changed title to Augustus: Colonia Iulia Augusta Philippensis.[7]

In short, the story that has been told as the historical, political, and occasionally economic background to the letter to the Philippians has been a story about the 1 percent, those various elite Roman imperial males contending for supremacy at the top of their pyramidally arranged society. But from what perspective were these considered "civil wars"? While it was not a fight among most of the residents of Philippi—these were *Rome's*

---

previous to 42 BCE. As noted above, however, this assumption is based upon an argument from silence. Since one hears little of Philippi in the sources for the Hellenistic period, one assumes Philippi declined. However, Roman tendencies in colonization seem to negate such an assumption about the relative state of Philippi. Sites for colonization were primarily selected on the basis of the city or town's already-established prosperity and fertility. See, for instance, Lawrence Keppie, *Colonisation and Veteran Settlement in Italy: 47–14 B.C.* (London: British School at Rome, 1983), 1, 128.

6. This predominant tendency regarding starting points is reflected even in my own work, for example, in *Hierarchy, Unity, and Imitation*, 99–112; see also 53–64.

7. Two helpful overviews of these contexts can be found in Chaido Koukouli-Chrysantaki, "Colonia Iulia Augusta Philippensis," in *Philippi at the Time of Paul and after His Death*, ed. Charalambos Bakirtzis and Helmut Koester (Harrisburg, PA: Trinity Press International, 1998), 5–35; and Eduard Verhoef, *Philippi: How Christianity Began in Europe; The Epistle to the Philippians and the Excavations at Philippi* (London: Bloomsbury, 2013), 1–13.

civil wars after all—it certainly had an impact upon their lives.[8] Too often, however, scholars have not asked careful enough questions about these people and the effects of these events on those people besides the elites contending at the top. Paul's correspondence with the Philippians presents a potentially different perspective on these dynamics; yet scholars have frequently presumed that these colonizing efforts provided a set of uncomplicated benefits for the recipients of this letter. This presumption has been challenged recently, indicating that many interpreters have been too optimistic about the effects of colonization (particularly if one follows the economic profile constructed by Peter Oakes in this volume).[9]

Even Paul, treated as a sanctified authority later, looks different in the light of these forces. As the doubts about his potential status as a citizen of this empire have increased (see, for instance, Angela Standhartinger's contribution in this volume), scholars recall how Paul's place as an ancient Jew locates him within a distinctly marginalized and colonially dominated group, even before considering how he proclaimed a message focused on a crucified criminal from this same racial/ethnic group.[10] To some, such a contextualization of Paul or of the people beside Paul might reflect dated concerns or even a Marxist bent. Yet such lines of interpretation have seldom been pursued in the past of biblical scholarship, even if such an approach remains controversial in larger circumstances to this day. Just in my own localized context, the governor recently tried to ban Howard Zinn's *A People's History of the United States* at the state's universities (one

---

8. For suggestions about the relevance of military events and images for understanding the letter, see especially Edgar M. Krentz, "Paul, Games, and the Military," in *Paul in the Greco-Roman World: A Handbook*, ed. J. Paul Sampley (Harrisburg, PA: Trinity Press International, 2003), 344–83; Timothy C. Geoffrion, *The Rhetorical Purpose and the Political and Military Character of Philippians: A Call to Stand Firm* (Lewiston, NY: Mellen, 1993); and Marchal, "Military Images in Philippians 1–2: A Feminist Rhetorical Analysis of Scholarship, Philippians, and Current Contexts," in *Her Master's Tools? Feminist and Postcolonial Engagements of Historical-Critical Discourse*, ed. Caroline Vander Stichele and Todd Penner, GPBS 9 (Atlanta: Society of Biblical Literature, 2005), 265–85.

9. See also Oakes, *Philippians*, 55–76.

10. For two different, illuminating considerations of Paul in light of dynamics of race/ethnicity (his own and others'), see Davina C. Lopez, *Apostle to the Conquered: Reimagining Paul's Mission*, Paul in Critical Contexts (Minneapolis: Fortress, 2008); and Tat-Siong Benny Liew, *What Is Asian American Hermeneutics? Reading the New Testament* (Honolulu: University of Hawai'i Press, 2008), 75–114.

of which just so happens to be my employer).[11] That the same governor (ironically and potentially unethically) went on to become president of one of these (other) universities indicates how much doing (something like) a people's history very much remains a loaded task.[12] Still, it does lead one to ask exactly *who* is being discussed when one is trying to do a people's history.

Who Are the People in This Ancient Neighborhood?

Within a general readership, among scholars and others, there is growing interest in the theme of "people's history" or "history from below." A multivolume set on "People's History of Christianity" has been published, while individual titles by Diana Butler Bass and Sarah Ruden have also turned (or at least alluded), in a general way, to "the people" in order to redescribe some of the figures in Christian histories (including some less well-known figures).[13] There is even a "people's" version of and *Peoples' Companion to the Bible* now.[14] But who are "the people" in these people's histories or peoples' companions?

---

11. Howard Zinn, *A People's History of the United States* (New York: Harper & Row, 1980); see also Zinn and Anthony Arnove, *Voices of a People's History of the United States* (New York: Seven Stories Press, 2005).

12. For some of the coverage of these (conjoined) controversies, see Tom LoBianco, "Mitch Daniels Wanted to Replace Historian's Teachings in Favor of Bill Bennett's Conservative Review," Indystar.com, http://www.indystar.com/ story/news/education/2013/08/18/mitch-daniels-wanted-to-replace-liberal-historians-teachings-in-favor-of-bill-bennetts-conservative-review/2669093/; Allen Mikaelian, "The Mitch Daniels Controversy: Context for the AHA Statement," American Historical Association, https://www.historians.org/publications-and-directories/perspectives-on-history/september-2013/the-mitch-daniels-controversy-context-for-the-aha-statement; Scott Jaschik, "Daniels vs. Zinn, Round II," Inside Higher Ed, http://www.insidehighered.com/news/2013/07/18/mitch-daniels-renews-criticism-howard-zinn#sthash.CUFSIof5.dpbs.

13. See the multiwork series edited by Denis R. Janz on *A People's History of Christianity*, 7 vols. (Philadelphia: Fortress, 2005–2008); Diana Butler Bass, *A People's History of Christianity: The Other Side of the Story* (New York: HarperOne, 2009); and Sarah Ruden, *Paul among the People: The Apostle Reinterpreted and Reimagined in His Own Time* (New York: Image Books, 2010).

14. *The Peoples' Bible: New Revised Standard Version, with the Apocrypha* (Minneapolis: Fortress, 2008); and *The Peoples' Companion to the Bible* (Minneapolis: For-

The variety of answers to this kind of question presents the challenges, but also the occasions, for an attempt to do a history from below for the first or the twenty-first century. For Bass, the people are simply those who are not part of the "the usual story" and can be cited in the construction of an alternative history.[15] Bass, however, explicitly contrasts her work with that of Zinn's—whose people are consistently those not among the political and economic elite (including workers, slaves, women, indigenous peoples, African-Americans, among others)—admitting that her work includes many well-known, even elite Christians.[16] While Ruden's study is focused upon the letters of Paul, the people that Paul is "among" are none other than those who are represented in the classical Greek and Roman sources—elite and mostly male.[17] Ruden's aim is to discuss how these other people thought at Paul's time in order to discern what is special about Paul.[18] While this ancient context is described as primarily exploitative, even abusive by Ruden, polytheism in particular seems to be the bogeyman in order to account (even apologize) for how Paul is better by comparison.

Despite the title, *Paul among the People*, then, Ruden's work is not actually trying to present a people's history kind of approach to Paul, his letters, or their recipients. Indeed, few interpreters have attempted this for populations in the ancient Mediterranean world. One exception, however, would be Michael Parenti's reconsideration of Julius Caesar.[19] Parenti

---

tress, 2010); both of which are edited by Curtiss Paul DeYoung, Wilda C. Gafney, Leticia A. Guardiola-Sáenz, George "Tink" Tinker, and Frank M. Yamada.

15. See Bass, *People's History*, 4–16.

16. Ibid., 15.

17. Ruden contextualized Paul's letters primarily in terms of the Greek and Latin texts that have been the focus of her classical studies. See the discussion in Ruden, *Paul among the People*, 3–7; and her previous translational work: *The Aeneid: Virgil* (New Haven: Yale University Press, 2008); *Homeric Hymns* (Cambridge, MA: Hackett, 2005); *Aristophanes: Lysistrata* (Cambridge, MA: Hackett, 2003); and *Petronius: Satyricon* (Cambridge, MA: Hackett, 2000).

18. In certain ways Ruden's study is not so different from traditional classical scholarship, yet in simply setting the letters and these texts next to each other, the work consistently fails to contextualize either in relevant cultural settings.

19. Another potential exception could be Robert Knapp, *Invisible Romans* (Cambridge: Harvard University Press, 2011). Knapp even weaves in discussions of materials from Acts and Paul's letters; however, such discussions are rarely circumspect about the rhetoricity of these texts (often treating them as "direct" and therefore straightforward sources, for instance, on *Invisible Romans*, 321).

provides an explicit definition for this kind of approach: "any history that deals with the efforts of the populace to defend itself from the abuses of wealth and tyranny is people's history."[20] Parenti even recognizes the dual difficulties of proceeding with such people in mind: the real dearth of sources for antiquity and the way historical analysis itself has been structured against such efforts.[21] These difficulties mean that people interested in history from below must learn to read against the grain of both the texts and the traditional understanding of them.[22] In terms of Parenti's own analysis, however, he tends to trust those sources that confirm the picture he seeks: the first Caesar as a populist champion of the Roman people (or at least of a certain kind of reformist tendency among some citizens). As with those "civil wars" already discussed in light of Philippi, Parenti's story is focused upon a struggle between different parties at the top of an exploitative society and system. Most distressingly for those considering sites besides the city of Rome (like Philippi), Parenti ignores that Rome was also an empire and that Julius was a main player in their military imperialism (Julius was a military victor, first, and derived most of his power from his campaigns in Gaul). In this light the more meaningful conflict to consider is not between *optimates* and *populares*—different shades of the same ruling elite—but between the rulers and the ruled, the Roman imperial forces and their various subject peoples, including Paul and those in and around Philippi.

These examples indicate, then, that terms such as "the people" are plagued by their vague indeterminacy. After all, if figures such as Julius Caesar or other elites can be depicted as representative of these people, then what makes people's history so different? Can anyone and everyone be counted among the people, or are they *everyone but* the elite? If so, what kind of elite? Are the people the poor, the uneducated, the subordinate, and/or the subaltern?[23] While these groups do overlap, they are far

---

20. Michael Parenti, *The Assassination of Julius Caesar: A People's History of Ancient Rome* (New York: New Press, 2003), 10.

21. Thus, Parenti (ibid., 11) argues: "A people's history should be not only an account of popular struggle against oppression but an exposé of the *anti*-people's history that has prevailed among generations of mainstream historians" (emphasis original).

22. Ibid., 10.

23. See, for example, Peter Burke's questions on this matter in "Overture: The New History; Its Past and Its Future," in *New Perspectives on Historical Writing*, ed. Peter Burke, 2nd ed. (University Park: Pennsylvania State University Press, 2001), 1–24, especially 9–10.

from identical. A history from below requires weighing a range of differentiating factors and their various impacts. Indeed, scholarship in popular culture and social history has generally struggled to develop comprehensive definitions of "below," "the people," or "popular," because of this variety and complexity.[24] Concepts or categories like "below" look rather different if one chooses to focus upon class rather than gender or race.[25] In the chapters to follow, this volume most certainly discusses dynamics of economy and poverty (particularly in chapters by Oakes and Noelle Damico and Gerardo Reyes Chavez), but it is hardly limited to those topics and those angles on people beside Paul. The problems with defining these terms, then, demonstrate the necessity of specifying both approach and focus within people's histories or histories from below.

Happily, Richard Horsley, as the editor of the first people's history of Christianity volume (focused upon Christian origins), specifically defined the opposition between rulers and ruled as the basic division for people's history to consider.[26] This opposition also helps to define who "the people" are (at least in that volume): ordinary people and popular movements, in contrast to and often arrayed against the ruling elites and elite culture.[27] This definition of "the people"—not the elite—provides a broad but abstracted categorization defined more by way of elimination than specification. However, Horsley's introduction to this volume does provide a helpful, if still initial, overview of the import and the difference a people's

---

24. Jim Sharpe, for example, notes: "The fundamental reason for this is that 'the people', as far back as the sixteenth century at least, were a rather varied group, divided by economic stratification, occupational cultures and gender. Such considerations render invalid any simplistic notion of what 'below' might mean in most historical contexts" (Jim Sharpe, "History from Below," in Burke, *New Perspectives on Historical Writing*, 25–42, 28). See also Burke, "Overture," 10. Here Sharpe is referring especially to the work of Burke, including Burke, *Popular Culture in Early Modern Europe* (London: Harper & Row, 1978), 23–64.

25. For instance, as Sharpe admits about the history from below: "'Below' in this context was originally conceived of in terms of a class structure or some other cognate form of social stratification: obviously, writing history from the perspective of women, or indeed, of children, would give different insights into what subordination might entail" (Sharpe, "History from Below," 36).

26. Richard A. Horsley, "Unearthing a People's History," in *Christian Origins*, vol. 1 of *A People's History of Christianity*, ed. Richard A. Horsley (Minneapolis: Fortress, 2005), 1–20 (4).

27. Ibid., 4–5.

history approach makes. People's history departs from "standard history" in a number of ways, not the least of which is the focus on people besides the elites, the so-called "great men" who were the shapers of human history.[28] This change in focus contests the idea that nonelites are insignificant in history, leading to a reexamination of the scope and the sources for historiography. With one's historical perspective shifted to one "from below," the scholar must consider all aspects of life and look in interdisciplinary ways at a wider range of source materials.[29] These forms of historiography developed as responses to the way history had been written; they represented an attempt to do the opposite of Rankean history.[30]

In the past, "kings and wars" were the most common aspects recounted in historical narratives.[31] This is one of the potential problems with Parenti's reconsideration of ancient Rome and indeed even my brief overview about the city and colony of Philippi (above)—both remained focused upon the usual suspects and topics, caesars and civil wars. If kings and wars are what count as history, then by way of analogy, what has counted as religious, or early Christian, history were apostles, evangelists, and bishops and their conflicts about doctrine, made concrete by church councils and creeds.[32] This is a problematic, even anachronistic frame for approaching the assembly community at ancient Philippi. Under the influence of this model for history, as well as later Christian traditions and authorities, debaters such as Paul became saints, small communities were churches, their leaders bishops, and their debates centered on doctrinal matters like Christology.

From Below, Against the Grain?

These problems with historical approaches, though, are closely tied to problems of sources. After all, there are plenty of sources focused on

---

28. Ibid., 1–5. See especially p. 5, where Horsley specifically draws upon an overview by Burke in developing two tables that highlight the differences between people's history and standard history, or as Burke describes them "new" and "old" history. See Burke, "Overture," 3–6.

29. Horsley, "Unearthing a People's History," 5.

30. As Peter Burke highlights for defining what makes this new kind of history "new," it is often easier to say what it is not. See Burke, "Overture," 2–3. Burke also refers here to the paradigmatic role of nineteenth century historian Leopold van Ranke in setting the terms for history as a discipline in the West.

31. Horsley, "Unearthing a People's History," 5.

32. Ibid., 2.

kings and the wars they fought—or forced others to fight—because, simply, they were created and preserved by those kings. This problem is only compounded when one is dealing with the period of this project: Greco-Roman antiquity. Unlike Zinn and others working on more recent periods, students of the ancient world have fewer resources and, thus, a much more limited archive. Whether one is working in the classical or biblical areas (or their intersections), one is also dealing with layers of tradition within this archive, layers expressing the interests of various elites. Within these texts nonelite people often only appear when they are cast as pests or problems, a tendency that potentially troubles any reflections upon a crucified Jesus or an imprisoned Paul (the latter of which Standhartinger adeptly treats in this volume).[33] This problem of sources plagues many efforts in biblical studies, including attempts to do people's history.[34]

If interested in more than the usual suspects, then, one must proceed with care when dealing with dominant or elite sources. As noted above, Parenti stressed the need to read against the grain of such texts, a technique that has been effectively applied by feminist historians to a range of texts and artifacts, particularly within biblical studies.[35] At times both Parenti's and Horsley's descriptions of people's history borrow heavily from feminist approaches to history.[36] Indeed, for the last two to three decades, feminist biblical scholars have been developing and refining just such critical approaches to interpreting problematic "source" materials like the letters of Paul.[37] Recognizing that these letters are not transparent windows to

---

33. For a similar point about when the people "make the papers," as it were, see ibid., 11.

34. See, for instance, the discussion in ibid., 14–16; and Steven J. Friesen, Sarah A. James, and Daniel N. Schowalter, "Inequality in Corinth," in *Corinth in Contrast: Studies in Inequality*, ed. Steven J. Friesen, Sarah A. James, and Daniel N. Schowalter, NovTSup 155 (Leiden: Brill, 2014), 1–13. Horsley titles an entire section on this problem, while the editors of *Corinth in Contrast* note, "The examination of ancient inequalities, however, faces a particular challenge, because these differentials affected not only ancient lives but also our access to those ancient lives. Those with less on any of these scales—political, religious, cultural, economic, etc.—tend to be the ones for whom we now have very little data" ("Inequality in Corinth," 2).

35. Parenti, *Assassination of Julius Caesar*, 10–11.

36. Horsley is slightly more explicit about this borrowing than Parenti. See, for instance, Horsley, "Unearthing a People's History," 1, 15, 17–18.

37. Here the methodological innovations of Elisabeth Schüssler Fiorenza, Antoinette Clark Wire, and Elizabeth Castelli come most directly to mind. See, for instance,

the past, Elisabeth Schüssler Fiorenza, in particular, has repeatedly argued for a critical "reading against the grain" of the kyriarchal texts of this time period.[38] In order to practice historical remembrance of women, one must recognize that these texts are not descriptive of a first-century reality but are attempts to be prescriptive of a reality they are seeking to construct.

Feminist scholars have also been perceptive critics of the patterns of scholarly identification, even among those aiming to do empire-critical or people's history kinds of work. Schüssler Fiorenza notes that "the rhetoric of Pauline interpreters continues not only to identify themselves with Paul but also to see Paul as identical with 'his' communities, postulating that Paul was the powerful creator and unquestioned leader of the communities to whom he writes."[39] For scholars interested in the people beside Paul, both patterns of identification need to be recognized and unwound from their interpretation and analysis. Indeed, the depiction of a heroic Paul persists in the brief examples already discussed: Bass, Ruden, and Horsley identify in a variety of ways with those who have been cast as Christian heroes, like Paul, and want the reader to identify with him and his efforts as well.[40] Despite a range of feminist suggestions for how to decenter Paul in the study of these letters and their recipients, he is rarely ever displaced

---

Elisabeth Schüssler Fiorenza, *But She Said: Feminist Practices of Biblical Interpretation* (Boston: Beacon, 1992); *Rhetoric and Ethic: The Politics of Biblical Studies* (Minneapolis: Fortress, 1999); and *Wisdom Ways: Introducing Feminist Biblical Interpretation* (Maryknoll, NY: Orbis, 2001); Antoinette Clark Wire, *The Corinthian Women Prophets: A Reconstruction through Paul's Rhetoric* (Minneapolis: Fortress, 1990); and Elizabeth A. Castelli, *Imitating Paul: A Discourse of Power*, Literary Currents in Biblical Interpretation (Louisville: Westminster John Knox, 1991).

38. Schüssler Fiorenza's hermeneutical innovations extend back to and through a range of her works, including: *In Memory of Her: A Feminist Theological Reconstructions of Christian Origins*, 10th anniversary edition (New York: Crossroad, 1994), 3–95; *But She Said*, 53–62; and (particularly with regard to Paul's letters) *Rhetoric and Ethic*, 31–55 and 105–94.

39. Schüssler Fiorenza, "Paul and the Politics of Interpretation," in Horsley, *Paul and Politics*, 40–57, 44.

40. In line with some of the arguments made in Schüssler Fiorenza, "Paul and the Politics of Interpretation," there are some helpful (if not always entirely accurate) observations on the persistence of this tendency in Melanie Johnson-DeBaufre and Laura Nasrallah, "Beyond the Heroic Paul: Toward a Feminist and Decolonizing Approach to the Letters of Paul," in *The Colonized Apostle: Paul through Postcolonial Eyes*, ed. Christopher D. Stanley, Paul in Critical Contexts (Minneapolis: Fortress, 2011), 161–74.

or simply even placed as one among many active, leading coworkers in the assembly communities. Several of the chapters in this volume attempt to proceed from such a reorientation, while others only manage to nudge him to the side or just side-by-side with other people.

Feminist scholars have also demonstrated different methods for dealing with the rhetoric of these letters. Referring, for instance, to the work of Antoinette Clark Wire, Horsley admits that "we have recently become more critically aware that we cannot read the history of a Pauline Christianity directly off the pages of Paul's letters."[41] Indeed, these letters are not transparent windows onto historical situations, in either the location of its composition or reception. Rather, Wire's efforts to find out about one group of recipients—the Corinthian women prophets—demonstrates how one must "factor" for the effects of the persuasive function of the letter as just one part of a rhetorical exchange if one wants to postulate historical information about Paul or other people. Wire elaborates: "Nothing he [Paul] writes can be considered reliable unless it serves his purpose of persuasion. In other words, everything spoken as description or analysis is first of all an address to the intended readers."[42] One must distinguish between rhetorical and historical situation, because one must work through the rhetoric to get any kind of historical perspective.[43]

Any direct reflections on particular figures in a letter, then, can be helpful, if measured or "factored" in terms of its argumentative aims. Paul might be basing a claim on a presumed agreement between the audience and himself, yet letters, of course, reveal other purposes than confirming agreement. Indeed, given the effort and resources needed to compose and send a letter, one should imagine that there were particular concerns that would cause someone like Paul to send a letter. Wire's observations about another Pauline letter and context are helpful in this regard as well: "On whatever points Paul's persuasion is insistent and intense, showing he is

---

41. Horsley, "Unearthing a People's History," 17.

42. Wire, *Corinthian Women Prophets*, 9.

43. Cynthia Briggs Kittredge (*Community and Authority: The Rhetoric of Obedience in the Pauline Tradition*, HTS 45 [Harrisburg, PA: Trinity Press International, 1998], 56, 62–65, 101–10), for instance, stresses that there is a difference between the rhetorical situation inscribed within the letter to the Philippians and the historical situation at Philippi. For the difference between rhetorical and historical situation, see Schüssler Fiorenza, *Rhetoric and Ethic*, 109, 115–22, 138–42. On rhetorical situation generally, see Lloyd F. Bitzer, "The Rhetorical Situation," *Philosophy and Rhetoric* 1 (1968): 1–14.

not merely confirming their agreement but struggling for their assent, one can assume some different and opposite point of view in Corinth from the one Paul is stating."[44] Wire suggests that, if one reads the letter's arguments carefully, one can "see" some audience perspectives in the letter. Through a process compatible with reading against the grain, Wire maintains that "those in clear disagreement with Paul should be the ones most accessible through his rhetoric."[45]

The potential importance of feminist scholarship on Paul's letters is hard to overstate for a project like a people's history approach. Feminist work helps interpreters reorient their approach to these letters in creative and self-reflexive ways. When Horsley, for instance, takes this work more seriously, he recognizes that these letters are "sources for various voices than can be heard, however faintly, through Paul's arguments aimed at persuading them to agree with his own point of view."[46] When Paul is resituated as one among many, it becomes harder to imagine his letters as automatically authoritative, theological treatises, instead of ad hoc efforts "from the field" of various assembly communities, efforts that show rather clear signs of difference and even conflict within the movements that cross and connect these communities. These differences reflect the variety and complexity of those who subsisted below, including the people within the ancient assembly community at Philippi.

Variety and Complexity: Particular Philippians

Scholars interested in those "from below" in these ancient contexts, then, must find ways to examine and analyze the specificities within and between these people. Failure to do so risks the homogenization and even a romanticization of "the people," obscuring relevant ethical and political challenges within both the first and the twenty-first centuries.[47] This

---

44. Wire, *Corinthian Women Prophets*, 9.

45. Ibid., 4. This is likely the case because, as Wire notes, "Paul expects controversy—provokes it in fact" (11).

46. Horsley, "Unearthing a People's History," 18.

47. For a similar concern about the homogenization of the poor in liberation hermeneutics, see R. S. Sugirtharajah, "Convergent Trajectories? Liberation Hermeneutics and Postcolonial Biblical Criticism," in *Postcolonial Criticism and Biblical Interpretation* (Oxford: Oxford University Press, 2002), 103–23. On previous occasions, I have explicitly reflected upon the foundations for people's/popular history approaches and interrogated the elisions, ambiguities, and outright conflicts in these

is why each contribution to this volume attends to one set of contextual particularities for these people, while simultaneously placing them in wider settings. The problem of many previous attempts in people's history often lies in the broad sweep they attempt to enact; there is very little time or space for focusing in a detailed way on some of the particular ways in which people besides "the great men" of history participated in their movements. Each of these previous works sacrifices the specific cultural context and the particular insights a tighter but also deeper focus can bring. By beginning with one site and one time frame—Philippi in antiquity—this collection clearly aims to mitigate these problems. In doing so, it provides an opportunity for rare insights and pushes "history from below" beyond bland idealisms or facile generalizations. Not all ancient "Christian" communities were the same; the forms their practices, interactions, and impacts took were shaped by localized contexts. Even if the communities that received Paul's letters were all somehow "Paul's communities," the letters still reflect their differences, differences that Pauline specialists now increasingly admit. This is also why it is important to attend to dynamics that are materially, historically, and rhetorically specific to places like Philippi (and, in turn, others).[48]

If one is interested in highlighting and describing particular people or particular factors from the underside of the Roman imperial world, one needs an approach that can attend to such particularities while simultaneously placing them in a wider context. Further, even from within specific localized contexts, there are differences within and between the different participants in these communities (including gender, ethnic, economic, imperial, and cultic identifications and impacts). By engaging with a wide range of "mainstream" and more "minoritized" issues, then, this volume

---

approaches for any who seek more than a specifically gendered and racialized working class. See Joseph A. Marchal, *The Politics of Heaven: Women, Gender, and Empire in the Study of Paul*, Paul in Critical Contexts (Minneapolis: Fortress, 2008), 26–33.

48. Collections for other sites that received Paul's letter(s) have been published in recent years, but they tend to emphasize the more technical (and, thus, less accessible) aspects of material culture, without addressing the range of topics this volume does by starting with a perspective "from below." See, for example, Steven J. Friesen, Daniel N. Schowalter, and James C. Walters, eds., *Corinth in Context: Comparative Studies on Religion and Society* (Leiden: Brill, 2010); and Laura S. Nasrallah, Charalambos Bakirtzis, and Steven J. Friesen, eds. *From Roman to Early Christian Thessalonike: Studies in Religion and Archaeology*, HTS 64 (Cambridge: Harvard University Press, 2010).

addresses the variety and specificity that would characterize communities composed of such people. In doing so, the contributions connect different elements of biblical and early Jewish and Christian studies to consider a different kind of historical horizon. Thus, the volume has many "points of contact" for scholars attending to a range of interests: archaeology and economy, slavery and sexuality, imprisonment and imperial colonies, among several others.

In order to get to specific kinds of people, one needs to take specific angles on the available materials. Though the following chapters take different angles, the narrowed focus on one site and one time period nets a newly complicated picture of the people in the assembly community at Philippi. Through a common focus and a variety of angles, the contributors reimagine and (re)present these "people beside Paul" in at least three different ways: (1) through other people, the people *other than* Paul in the assembly community "in Christ" at Philippi; (2) through people situated *alongside* Paul, often through careful examination of Paul's letters, particularly his to the Philippians; and/or (3) *through* Paul primarily, as alongside and among the people in this movement, making hymns and managing suffering and imprisonment. While some chapters consider figures from Philippi named in Paul's letters and other ancient remains, others focus on those still unnamed but often labeled "opponents," and still others mostly envision Paul in solidarity with the Philippians. In what follows these people include both females and males, the imprisoned and the enslaved, Jews and other religious groups. The conditions for all of these people reflect the mixing and contact between Jews and non-Jews, assembly members and their surroundings, and occasionally even later Christians and non-Christians.[49]

---

49. In focusing on both specific kinds of people and their conditions of contact with others, this volume also mitigates some of the potential problems with aspirations to reconstruct a "typical" view of a peasant or a poor woman in places such as Corinth, Galatia, or Philippi. If the goal is to construct the "common people," commonalities are likely reinforced and reinscribed, erasing the differences within and among these people and white-washing a complex picture into a monochromatic representation. Such a potential goal in people's history likely also marginalizes the particular, the challenging, the fascinating, the strange, even the queer within these communities, dulling the rich possibilities of historical reconstructive efforts. For an initial description of queer approaches to Paul's letters, see Joseph A. Marchal, "Queer Approaches: Improper Relations with Paul's Letters," in *Studying Paul's Letters: Contemporary Perspectives and Methods*, ed. Joseph A. Marchal (Minneapolis: Fortress, 2012), 209–27;

Fortunately yet paradoxically, Paul's letters present both the common difficulties and the distinct opportunities for doing histories from below. On the one hand, scholars have limited perspectives on the exchange between Paul and the Philippians; there are, after all, no surviving letters from these Philippians to Paul (or others). We have only the perspective of Paul, or, to put it even more precisely, we have only the perspective Paul carefully crafts and constructs through the arguments preserved in his letter to the Philippians. On the other hand, this letter presents a rare opportunity to listen in on one half of an exchange between nonelites. Here, Horsley is characteristically enthusiastic about the potential utility of New Testament texts for investigations into these people, for they are

> highly unusual, almost unique among ordinary people in antiquity, for having left texts that survive in writing. Insofar as the communities and movements that they represent or address had not yet developed a hierarchy that stood in power over the membership, most New Testament and related texts … provide more or less direct sources for these people's movements.[50]

Though several of the contributions in this volume would tend to view Paul's letter as less than direct, they also recognize that the letter reflects an interaction between these people and, therefore, can provide glimpses of people beside Paul. As Richard S. Ascough's response to the first set of chapters highlights, the historical claims that scholars can make about these people might need to be modest. Yet, even as such measured claims offer sometimes partial, dimly glimpsed factors, these glimpses are important, particularly because we know that there is more than the standard stories that have been told, more than the perspective of the 1 percent. Despite the way these letters were treated later as icons and exemplars of high culture, they do provide distinct, if still difficult entry points for thinking about and tracing the practices and positions of "everyday people" in places like Philippi.[51]

---

for some queer reflections specifically on Philippians, see Marchal, *Philippians: Historical Problems, Hierarchical Visions, Hysterical Anxieties*, Phoenix Guides to the New Testament 11 (Sheffield: Sheffield Phoenix, 2014), 69–92.

50. Horsley, "Unearthing a People's History," 15.

51. This would be especially true for this time and place if one also agreed with Horsley's claim: "For in the period of their origins, the communities and movements

Approaching ancient Philippi through this letter and other surviving materials requires degrees of caution and creativity. Of course, all acts of historical (re)construction develop out of creatively reimagining scenarios and rearranging the relations between materials. Each of the chapters in this volume pursues such scenarios and rethinks these relations, but it will become clear that these chapters offer no single method or model (and, I would argue, that is one of their collective strengths). What unites them is a common aim to ask different questions and seek different people, to explore people beside Paul and the various social forms and forces that would affect them. This volume pursues these questions by innovating with methods and materials, putting traditional versions of both to new uses, within different settings. In doing so, some explicitly adapt feminist approaches (Valerie Abrahamsen, Joseph A. Marchal, Damico and Reyes Chavez), and some reflect upon the letter as an example of what James C. Scott calls a "hidden transcript" (Standhartinger, Robert L. Brawley, Damico and Reyes Chavez).[52] They begin well before or after the time of the letter (Abrahamsen and Eduard Verhoef, respectively) or explicitly start with quite modern, but rather problematic uses of the letter (especially Mark D. Nanos). As a whole, then, this volume provides different specifications of "the people," pursuing historical questions differently, either in light of more people or atypical concerns about them.

When Horsley described what a people's history of this time could do, he highlighted at least three activities: "looking again at less familiar sources, questioning old assumptions, and working critically toward new conceptual tools more appropriate to how ordinary people made history."[53] Each of these is reflected in this volume. Many are likely to be unfamiliar with the ancient Samothrakiasts, the more recent Campaign for Fair Food, or some of the material remains addressed here. Common assumptions

---

that were later called Christianity consisted of nothing but people's history" (Horsley, "Unearthing a People's History," 2).

52. James C. Scott, *Domination and the Arts of Resistance* (New Haven: Yale University Press, 1990). For one set of attempts to apply Scott's work to biblical texts, see *Hidden Transcripts and the Arts of Resistance: Applying the Work of James C. Scott to Jesus and Paul*, ed. Richard A. Horsley, SemeiaSt 48 (Atlanta: Society of Biblical Literature, 2004). For two particular cautions about this methodology, though, see Kittredge, "Reconstructing 'Resistance' or Reading to Resist: James C. Scott and the Politics of Interpretation," in Horsley, *Hidden Transcripts*, 145–55; and Marchal, *Politics of Heaven*, 18–19.

53. Horsley, "Unearthing a People's History," 5.

about Jews or "Judaizers," about veterans and economic privilege, about prisons and the custody of Paul, and about slavery and manumission are heartily interrogated. In doing so, the contributors develop new economic profiles and utilize alternative ideas about hidden transcripts, wo/men, and unmen to reconceptualize and recontextualize the letter. Several of the authors make their political and hermeneutical commitments explicit, where others leave them implicit. A few aim to read against the grain of texts; others read along it; and still others try to read between the lines. In short, this volume does not propose a discrete new methodology. Rather, it reflects a constellation of approaches that focus on one site and one time frame (Philippi in antiquity) and aim toward a common goal: knowing more about people beside Paul.

The methodological pluralism of this volume reflects some of the shifting conditions of biblical scholarship. Though the guild is still predominantly conditioned by its mostly Eurocentric, heteronormative, pale male past (and present), it has become increasingly hard to ignore the critiques and counterconstructions developed by feminist, race-critical, postcolonial, and queer approaches to these materials. Often (though perhaps not often enough), these approaches were indications of a change in the kinds of scholarly readers and interpreters. Yet, the corresponding changes in approach did not necessarily stem from contained and cohesive methodologies: what African-American scholars, for instance, tend to share is not a single method, but a difference in starting point and an overlapping set of goals.[54] A people's history approach can be somewhat parallel to these kinds of approaches, even (or especially) as it overlaps or otherwise draws upon these changes in approach. Indeed, works like *The People's Companion to the Bible* reflect the way some corners of biblical scholarship have increasingly considered the difference a difference in social location makes.[55] The contemporary landscape of biblical scholarship has changed

---

54. For just one indication of the variety and complexity of the study of the Bible by, about, as, or with African-Americans, see Vincent L. Wimbush with Rosamond C. Rodman, eds., *African-Americans and the Bible: Sacred Texts and Social Structures* (New York: Continuum, 2000).

55. See, for example, the introductory materials and part 1 in Young et al., *Peoples' Companion*, xvii–xxxii and 3–89. This trajectory of interpreting from within (and critically reflecting upon) one's social location is exemplified by Fernando F. Segovia and Mary Ann Tolbert, eds., *Reading from This Place*, vol. 1: *Social Location and Biblical Interpretation in the United States*, and vol. 2: *Social Location and Biblical Interpretation in Global Perspective* (Minneapolis: Fortress, 1995).

as the kinds of readers and interpreters have expanded (even as very few of
the norms of such scholarship have been altered for the majority).

This also indicates that in order to do something different, one does
not need to start from scratch. Indeed, one of the strengths of scholarship
in this moment is that one has a range of alternative imaginaries on which
to draw in trying to pursue different people and different questions. Kwok
Pui-lan and Joerg Rieger argue in a similar way in their examination of
the relations between the recent Occupy movement and religious practices
of the past and the present. The variety of liberationist practices and the-
ologies present opportunities for unified action with and through (not in
spite of) differences.[56] As a result, Kwok and Rieger propose, "in contrast
to the term 'the people,' which often tends to describe a unified group, 'the
multitude' allows for and welcomes differences among various members."[57]
Given the potential multitude-in-relation within the assembly community
at Philippi—a group that was assembled, but also marked by a range of
differences, it might even be essential to take various angles on the people
beside Paul there (as this volume aims).[58] The possible resonances between
past and present movements need not end there, though, since the leader-
less Occupy movement's use of decentralized networks distantly echo the
assemblies that received Paul's letters.[59] As one will see in the final contribution to this volume, the Campaign for Fair Food similarly recognizes
that it is harder to destroy a decentralized movement when it is populated
by many, "leaderfull" participants. Damico and Reyes Chavez, in turn, use
these experiences of a present-day people's movement to reframe the significance of Paul and the people in Philippi.

In creating some uncommon scholarly space for these kinds of analyses, this volume is less (exclusively) focused upon material remains than

---

56. See Rieger and Kwok, *Occupy Religion*, 59.

57. Ibid., 61, adapting Michael Hardt and Antonio Negri, *Multitude: War and
Democracy in the Age of Empire* (New York: Penguin, 2004).

58. Rieger and Kwok, however, are perhaps a bit too optimistic about using Paul's
letters for an alternative practice now (see, for instance, *Occupy Religion*, 67, 77, 124).

59. See ibid., 121. Kwok and Rieger will also argue that this style of organizing
specifically resonates with the opening verses of the hymn found in Phil 2:6–7: "It
seems to us that these new ways of life are teaching us something about the 'form
of God' as well: emptying oneself of top-down power and reclaiming other sorts of
power may be more God-like than we had ever suspected" (81). While this could be
true for the kenotic image that opens the hymn, it becomes harder to see an interroga-
tion of top-down power in the latter half of the hymn (Phil 2:9–11).

other recent volumes on the urban communities that received Paul's letters. Some of this difference is simply reflecting our respective disciplinary specializations, but I submit that it also stems from a conviction that the letter itself could represent an important, if still rhetorical artifact that can shed light on people beside Paul. Once more, this is also the strength of a volume that tries to pursue several different angles on a common combination of people, place, and time frame. As a whole, the volume may not present a completely cohesive picture of Paul, the assembly community at Philippi, their relations, or their impacts, but it also seems rather unlikely that all of these cohered with each other in the first place.

This volume should help to explain how and why each contribution attends to one set of contextual particularities for these people, while simultaneously placing them in wider settings. Broadly, the whole traces an arc from larger material contexts to more focused rhetorical and historical analyses of the letter and increasingly to receptions and uses of this letter (communal, interpretive, and activist). Collectively, the contributions offer crucial insights into "mainstream" questions—about the letter's hymn and audience, Paul's "opponents," and the sites of the community and of Paul's imprisonment—as well as more "marginalized" topics and groups—including women, slaves, Jews, and members of localized cults. In the end, they manage to cover an impressive and important array of matters: archaeology and architecture, economy and ethnicity, prisons and priestesses, slavery, syncretism, stereotypes of Jews, and the colony of Philippi and a range of communities—there and then, but also here and how (including contemporary people's campaigns).

The chapters of this volume provide multiple points of entry, thus presenting many different ways to proceed through them (besides in order, from front to back). The opening chapters, for instance, have a stronger material emphasis than those that follow them. Abrahamsen's "Priestesses and Other Female Cult Leaders at Philippi in the Early Christian Era" provides essential context to the first generations of members in the Philippian assembly by examining women and especially female functionaries in various cultic activities at Philippi. Starting centuries prior to the letter, Abrahamsen explains the many references in literature to the variety and prominence of women through the archaeology of Philippi, particularly at the acropolis and imperial complexes. Such dynamics not only situate the early Christ cult at Philippi in its opening centuries, but also account for women's roles within the Philippian assembly community. Abrahamsen helpfully (re)introduces a range of sites and roles for women's prominent involvement in cultic life in Philippi. Oakes's contribution, "The Economic Situation of the Philippian Christians," constructs and critically analyzes the economic situation of the assembly community at Philippi. Disputing many previous views about their status, Oakes provides a socioeconomic and comparative analysis of the evidence, particularly given Philippi's role as an urban locale and a *colonia*. Indeed, Oakes comes to different conclusions about women's economic influence than Abrahamsen.[60] In composing a socioeconomic profile of the members of the Philippian assembly community, Oakes traces a precarious situation, where economic status is tied to dynamics of ethnicity, labor, gender, and empire. This analysis accounts for the social patterns and suffering reflected in traditions about this assembly community. Verhoef's "Collaboration of 'Samothrakiasts' and Christians in Philippi" situates the early Christ-followers at Philippi as a minoritized group among adherents within other religious communities. Verhoef considers the meaning of that Christian community "growing up" alongside other cultic groups, particularly the Kabeiric mystery cult of Samothrace, by examining material remains like the shrine of Euephenes alongside later Christian buildings. Starting centuries after the letter, Verhoef explains how the Christians ended up with a basilica in the center of the city in spite of their economic vulnerability. The material domain, then, ends up reflecting the likely positively syncretistic interaction and traffic between these local practices, where adaptation and collaboration explains their practical utility and physical proximity.

When the chapters turn more directly to the letter to the Philippians to consider the dynamic between rhetoric and history, they also contextualize the letter's argumentation in distinct imperial settings. Standhartinger, in "Letter from Prison as Hidden Transcript: What It Tells Us about the People at Philippi," reexamines the letter in light of the living conditions in ancient prisons and the ways people survived and negotiated these conditions. Standhartinger goes beyond typical resources for Paul's imprisonment (including Acts) by focusing upon Roman custody and the dangers of letter-writing, for both senders and recipients, in such contexts. This analysis accounts for the ambiguity of the letter, more helpfully considered as a hidden transcript to a disguised community in resistance. Marchal

---

60. For a third angle on this overlapping set of dynamics, see also the new study on women's socioeconomic status in these communities (specifically in Asia Minor), Katherine Bain, *Women's Socioeconomic Status and Religious Leadership in Asia Minor in the First Two Centuries C.E.*, Emerging Scholars (Minneapolis: Fortress, 2014).

("Slaves as Wo/men and Unmen: Reflecting upon Euodia, Syntyche, and Epaphroditus in Philippi") complicates the picture of the community by focusing upon three of the figures from Philippi named in the letter and their probable status as enslaved or manumitted figures. Situating them within the particularly gendered and sexualized aspects of slave systems specifies some of the glimpses of the historical context of those people often defined by their lack of (imperial) masculinity. This setting affects Paul's arguments, especially when they reflect continuities with enslaving ideologies, but also offers a new vantage point on three particular people moving around the lower rungs of Roman imperial, slave-owning society.

Even as the next chapters keep the focus on the letter, they increasingly reflect upon different receptions and uses of it within different present-day communities or within ancient Philippi itself. Nanos's "Out-Howling the Cynics: Reconceptualizing the Concerns of Paul's Audience from His Polemics in Philippians 3" interrogates the scholarly saw that "dogs" was a distinctly Jewish insult of Gentiles, thus reconsidering all of Paul's arguments in the letter about the apparent "opponents." Nanos demonstrates that there is no literary evidence for dogs as a specifically Jewish slur of non-Jews and shows, rhetorically, that most of Phil 3 would not make sense within such a negative view of first-century Judaisms (within which Paul was still operating). The references to dogs, evil workers, and mutilation could apply generally to a number of groups, but Cynics make an attractive option, particularly if community members are dealing with problems with peers at Philippi and their objections to their new way of life as Gentiles in a Jewish, Christ-based subgroup. Brawley, in "An Alternative Community and an Oral Encomium: Traces of the People in Philippi," presents the letter as a reflection of the community's self-construction as an alternative to the Roman imperial system. Since Philippi was an ancient *colonia*, Brawley situates the community within the context of imperial dominance as a way to account for their difficulties. Their suffering is incorporated into identity arguments, as the letter dramatized the social roles generated in this reality. The letter and the hymn in particular perform the communal life conditioned by suffering and beneficence that they have in Christ Jesus. Damico and Reyes Chavez, in "Determining What Is Best: The Campaign for Fair Food and the Nascent Assembly in Philippi," use their experience as organizers and participants in a contemporary people's social movement (the Campaign for Fair Food) led by poor working people to clarify and qualify how scholars might look at approaches "from below." This chapter highlights vivid connections between the conditions of Immokalee, Florida and Philippi, where people from many cultures have come together, but face violence and intimidation, surveillance and infiltration. Damico and Reyes Chavez suggest that the potential presence of those who were conflicted about or sympathetic to imperially-aligned parties explains the way Paul's arguments aim toward hyperbolic irritation and exposure of those sympathizers. Such conditions can also account for the anxiety and adaptability of messages transmitted.

This volume also features three helpful responses to these three sets of chapters by Ascough, Wire, and Horsley, respectively. While each response is insightful in its own right, all three together complement, complicate, qualify, and extend the arguments within these chapters. They model, in an initial fashion, how we might hope the volume as a whole will be received: people will take up, consider, critique, fill out, reformulate, and otherwise pursue people beside Paul, too.

Priestesses and Other Female Cult Leaders at Philippi in the Early Christian Era

Valerie Abrahamsen

A people's history of Philippi must, of necessity, include an examination of women. Recent work on Philippi, the region of Macedonia, sociological contexts, and related topics has greatly expanded our knowledge of women in antiquity, their status in the culture, their independence (or lack thereof), their family connections, their contributions, and their limitations. Examination of women at Philippi in the first centuries of the Roman Empire can expand our knowledge of the "people beside Paul."

In the patriarchal and imperial Greco-Roman culture of Philippi, women at all levels of society—slave, free, and freed—suffered certain degrees of oppression and marginalization. At the same time, women, especially those from elite families or slaves who were able to purchase their freedom, also had a certain degree of influence and renown, notably through their roles as priestesses and other cultic leaders. Recent scholarship in several fields, drawing on both literary and archaeological evidence, has shown the extent of, and limits to, women's participation in the administration of Greco-Roman cities in the imperial era. Influential and highly respected women, generally in conjunction with the men in their lives, used their wealth, status, and influence in ways that can be seen in the record. Upper-status women carried out many obligations similar to those of men in both religious and civic spheres, and evidence for the lives of slave women, while remaining more difficult to find, can be detected in voluntary associations and other settings. Thus, one can now paint a more nuanced picture of gender roles and a "history from below" than one could just a generation ago.[1]

---

1. See, for instance: Richard S. Ascough, *Paul's Macedonian Associations: The*

In this study, we will attempt to incorporate these expanded understandings into a picture of the roles of both named and unnamed women at Philippi. Building on the foundations of this scholarship, we will examine in particular the women leaders at Philippi as well as evidence from voluntary associations in the first centuries of the Christian era. The cults of Artemis/Diana, Dionysos, and Isis had a high level of female involvement and leadership at Philippi and the surrounding region, and women had roles in the emperor cult. Like many voluntary associations in antiquity, the Jesus groups could also include both women and men in leadership positions.[2] In addition to examining women of the elite levels of society, we will also attempt to describe the ways in which slaves and freedwomen participated in various groups and contributed to society.

Specifically, we will examine the following:

- the cult of Livia, especially the monument built in her honor in the Philippi forum and the named priestesses on that monument as well as their possible families of origin;
- the imperial cult at Philippi as illustrated by the forum temples to Faustina the Younger and her husband, Marcus Aurelius, and any female cult participants involved in these cults;
- the role of priestesses in pagan cults at Philippi, especially cults such as Artemis/Diana, Dionysos, and Isis that had female leaders;
- demographic traits of pagan and early Christian priestesses and other cult officials as far as can be determined, for example, socioeconomic status; slave, free, or freed; single, married, or widowed; and so on;

Social Context of Philippians and 1 Thessalonians, WUNT 2/161 (Tübingen: Mohr Siebeck, 2003); Riet van Bremen, *The Limits of Participation: Women and Civic Life in the Greek East in the Hellenistic and Roman Periods*, Dutch Monographs on Ancient History and Archaeology (Amsterdam: Gieben, 1996); and Joan Breton Connelly, *Portrait of a Priestess: Women and Ritual in Ancient Greece* (Princeton: Princeton University Press, 2007).

2. See especially the following: Ascough, *Lydia: Paul's Cosmopolitan Hostess*, Paul's Social Network: Brothers and Sisters in the Faith (Collegeville, MN: Liturgical Press, 2009); Joseph A. Marchal, *The Politics of Heaven: Women, Gender, and Empire in the Study of Paul*, Paul in Critical Contexts (Minneapolis: Fortress, 2008); and Peter Oakes, *Philippians: From People to Letter*, SNTSMS 110 (Cambridge: Cambridge University Press, 2001).

- examples of named women in the early Christian record—Lydia, Euodia, and Syntyche—and discussions of women by Bishop Polycarp; and
- the extent of early Christian and Byzantine devotion to Jesus and Mary, especially by women.

Our knowledge of Paul will be enhanced and deepened through knowledge of the women he would have encountered at Philippi, of their probable roles and lifestyles, and of their influence on him.

The Cult of Livia

Early in the excavations at Philippi, a monument base for seven large statues was discovered in the forum.[3] The base was situated along the length of the road that borders the northern side of the paved square in immediate proximity to the eastern temple,[4] which was dedicated to the empress Faustina the Younger. The base of the monument is approximately 7.7 meters (25 feet) long. It honors the deified Livia, wife of Augustus and mother of Tiberius. Its inscriptions name four priestesses of Livia, including Maecia C. F. Auruncina Calaviana, who paid for the monument; another name is illegible but probably belonged to a fifth priestess.[5] Maecia is named on the monument twice as both priestess and donor.[6] Maecia and her sister, Julia Auruncina, were daughters of one Caius. Also named are Julia Modia, daughter of someone whose name is not extant, and Octavia Polla, daughter of Publius.[7] According to Michel Sève and Patrick Weber, Maecia's brother, [..l]turius C. f. Vol. Crispus, was honored on a statue base in the forum. However, the other female honorees remain completely unknown except that the name Modius is attested during the reign of Marcus Aurelius as a magistrate who had supervised the construction of the forum temples.[8] There does not seem

---

3. Paul Collart, "Inscriptions de Philippes," *BCH* 57 (1933): 360–62.

4. Michel Sève, "Un monument honorifique au forum de Philippes," *BCH* 112 (1988): 467–79.

5. Ibid.

6. Ibid., 470.

7. Peter Pilhofer, *Philippi I: Die erste christliche Gemeinde Europas*, WUNT 87 (Tübingen: Mohr Siebeck, 1995), 241–43.

8. Sève, "Monument honorifique au forum de Philippes," 470.

to be an overt connection between these people and Livia or the imperial household. While Claudius introduced the cult of Livia in 44 CE, a fact that would likely have been known by Paul and the people of Philippi, the monument was most likely erected in the second half of the first century under the reign of Domitian or slightly before.[9]

Unfortunately, we know little else about the priests and priestesses named on the Philippi monument. Several important things can be learned from the structure, however.

As was the case throughout the Mediterranean in the Hellenistic and early imperial eras, elite families erected honorific monuments and statues in city agoras, and women were included in the honors.[10] The building of such honorific monuments was a long-standing tradition in the Greek East since at least Hellenistic times, undertaken for reasons including civic responsibility, "the preservation of status, political ambitions, and even ideological developments."[11] With regard to statues of priestesses in the Greek world, "by the time that Pausanias traveled through Greece in the second century AD, he encountered images of priestesses at a host of shrines.... Images of priestesses, benefactresses, and women magistrates had become so plentiful in the Greek East that M. Porcius Cato Maior found it necessary to complain publicly about the excessive numbers of female statues crowding cities and sanctuaries."[12]

---

9. Ibid., 472. See also Chaido Koukouli-Chrysantaki, "Colonia Iulia Augusta Philippensis," in *Philippi at the Time of Paul and after His Death*, ed. Charalambos Bakirtzis and Helmut Koester (Harrisburg, PA: Trinity Press International, 1998), 16. She quotes Gertrude Grether, "Livia and the Roman Imperial Cult," *AJP* 67 (1946): 222–52, and states that the cult was introduced in 44 CE, but, without citing a specific page number in the article, that date is uncertain. On page 246, Grether states, "her deification, therefore, did not take place until 41 AD," and on page 247, "at the time of Livia's consecration, in 41 AD." Anthony A. Barrett, *Livia: First Lady of Imperial Rome* (New Haven: Yale University Press, 2002), in his list of significant events, agrees with the date of 41 CE. For a fuller treatment of the Livia monument at Philippi, see Valerie Abrahamsen, "The Honoring of Livia at Philippi" (paper presented for discussion in the Philippi/Philippians Working Group, Society of Biblical Literature Annual Meeting, Washington, DC, 17 November 2006).

10. Bremen, *Limits of Participation*, passim; see especially examples listed in appendices 1 and 2.

11. Ibid., 299.

12. Connelly, *Portrait of a Priestess*, 118.

Women functioned as priestesses in the imperial cult, sometimes along with their husbands or other male relatives.[13] Therefore the Philippi monument of priestesses of the cult of Livia, deified wife of Augustus, falls within this line of tradition. It mainly remains to be determined, if possible, what specifically may have occasioned the construction of the monument and statues, but it is certain that priestesses performing roles in the cult of the emperor would have been part of the culture at the time of Paul's letter to the Philippians.

Despite the fact that women exercised leadership roles in religious groups, their roles generally remained fixed within legal and social limits. Women held a wide variety of roles in the religious and cultic sphere, roles parallel to those of men, but were prohibited from holding civic offices. Women "never had direct and formal access to any of the civic bodies or magistracies which entailed (at least in theory) voting, deliberating, decision-making, the supervision of the market place, of buildings, of food-provision or the keeping of public order; nor did they serve their cities as ambassadors."[14] Thus the Philippi monument reflects the family underpinnings of the tradition as well as the active role of women in the religious activities of the town, the importance of which should not be underestimated, as will become more apparent below.

What in particular may have prompted the construction of the Livia monument, while speculative, can help put it and the priestesses' roles in context. The life of Livia helps to set the stage. Born Livia Drusilla in Rome in 58 BCE, she ultimately became the wife of Augustus. Augustus, who had only one blood child, his daughter Julia, agreed to raise Livia's two children by her first marriage, Tiberius and Drusus. Tiberius would be the future emperor. Drusus, unfortunately, died in 9 BCE.[15]

For all intents and purposes, "Livia played the role of a loving, dutiful and even old-fashioned wife."[16] However, she exercised her power

---

13. Bremen, *Limits of Participation*; see especially 117–25.

14. Ibid., 56.

15. Donna Hurley, "Livia (Wife of Augustus)," *De Imperatoribus Romanis: An Online Encyclopedia of Roman Emperors*, http://www.roman-emperors.org/livia.htm. See also Barrett, *Livia*, appendix I, "Sources," 229–302 for annotated primary literature, as well as 34–39.

16. Hurley, "Livia (Wife of Augustus)," See also Barrett, *Livia*, 234–38, who cites Seneca the Younger, Pliny the Elder, Suetonius, and Cassius Dio as presenting generally favorable portraits of Livia but Tacitus as "most skillful at presenting information that, while strictly accurate, created a damaging effect" (240).

and influence both inside and outside the imperial family. She some-times traveled with Augustus abroad and served as his confidante and advisor, ignoring his relationships with other women.[17] She launched some men's careers, arranged marriages, sponsored charities, and inter-ceded politically.[18]

The ancient sources are not in agreement about her involvement in the deaths of several people, ostensibly in order to see her son Tiberius crowned emperor.[19] The main dilemma "necessitating" these deaths and the intrigue they engendered, it seems, was a problem of succes-sion. Augustus's adopted grandsons, Gaius and Lucius, died in 4 and 2 CE, respectively; his daughter Julia was exiled for adultery in 2 CE; and Tiberius exiled himself to Rhodes in 6 BCE, leaving no one in line for the imperial throne. To remedy this, Augustus adopted Tiberius in 4 CE after making certain that Tiberius in turn adopted Germanicus, Drusus's son. The stage was now set for Tiberius to succeed Augustus,[20] a fortunate development for Livia.

Augustus died in 14 CE. Whether or not Livia had anything to do with his death, she was widely viewed as powerful, influential, and intelligent, even after his death. In an unusual move, Augustus had bequeathed to her one-third of his estate (with two-thirds going to Tiberius). Augustus's will also stipulated that Livia would be adopted into the *gens Iulia* and be given the honorific *Augusta*; she thereafter became known as Julia Augusta. Additionally, she was appointed a priestess in the new cult to the deified Augustus and given a seat with the Vestal Virgins in the theater.[21]

Early in the reign of Tiberius, both he and Livia signed all public doc-uments; likewise, documents were addressed to both of them. She did not appear in person in the senate or the various assemblies, which would have broken with tradition, but otherwise acted as a ruler.[22] Livia's image

---

17. Hurley, "Livia (Wife of Augustus)." See also Barrett, *Livia*, 42–46.

18. Hurley, "Livia (Wife of Augustus)"; and Barbara McManus, "Livia: *Princeps Femina*," *Augustus and Tiberius: Historical Background*, http://www.vroma.org/~bmcmanus/livia.html. Barrett, *Livia*, discusses this in depth, especially pages 186–214.

19. For a comprehensive review of the literary sources and their assessment, see Barrett, *Livia*, 229–47.

20. Hurley, "Livia (Wife of Augustus)."

21. Ibid.

22. Elise Boulding, *The Underside of History*, rev. ed. (Newbury Park: Sage, 1992), 308–9.

does not appear on Roman coins during the lifetime of Augustus, but her image seems to have been subtly introduced into imperial coinage during Tiberius's reign.[23]

The relationship between Livia and Tiberius gradually deteriorated. Just as the senate was poised to award Livia a number of honors, Tiberius moved his court from Rome to Capri, leaving her behind (an alternative interpretation was that Livia forced Tiberius to move to Capri). He turned to others for advice, and Livia was politically isolated until her death in 29 CE at age eighty-six.[24] It was only in 42 CE under the emperor Claudius, her grandson, that she was proclaimed "diva" and other honors bestowed on her.[25]

Along with the literary evidence, statues, coins, gems, paintings, inscriptions, and monuments to and of Livia provide insight into her influence and how nonelites may have perceived her. This in turn helps to postulate some reasons for the construction of her monument at Philippi approximately two generations after her death. During the early impe-rial era, Roman emperors, their wives, and sometimes other members of their families were honored after death and considered deified, usually due to good works they had done for the community or the empire during their lifetime. The surviving ruler or a wealthy benefactor, male or female, would erect a statue or other monument to the deceased, to which citizens would bring offerings as part of their imposed duty.[26]

Numerous individuals were aided by Livia.[27] "She gave financial help to the victims of fires ... [and helped] families that had fallen on hard

---

23. Susan Wood, "Diva Augusta: Images of Imperial Women in Roman Art," in *Text for Exhibition*, Sackler Museum (Cambridge: Harvard University, 1986), 2. See also Barrett, *Livia*, 297–98; it is possible, however, that this coin was actually issued shortly after Livia's death.

24. Boulding, *Underside of History*, 309; and Hurley, "Livia (Wife of Augustus)." Barrett, *Livia*, 251–58, helpfully cites all literary attestations about Livia; it is particu-larly in the writings of Tacitus (*Annales*), Suetonius (*Divus Augustus* and *Tiberius*), and Marcus Aurelius (*Meditations*) that the tensions between Livia and Tiberius are spelled out.

25. J. Rufus Fears, "Ruler Worship," in *Civilization of the Ancient Mediterranean: Greece and Rome*, ed. Michael Grant and Rachel Kitzinger (New York: Scribner, 1988), 2:1009–25, especially 1014–16; Hurley, "Livia (Wife of Augustus)"; Barrett, *Livia*, 21–519.

26. Fears, "Ruler Worship," 1015.

27. Barrett, *Livia*, 108–9 and passim.

times."[28] She saved the lives of many senators and had many women friends.[29] Scores of benefactions are described in the ancient literature, with examples from the Bosporus, Aphrodisias, southern Etruria, Jerusalem, Caesarea, Alexandria, Egypt, and Boeotia.[30] Closer to Philippi, one Antonia Tryphaena married Cotys, king of Thrace.

> The whole of Thrace was temporarily placed under a Roman official.... [Tryphaena] made her way eventually to the prosperous city of Cyzicus, where she settled down and became a benefactress of the city. She held the position of priestess of Livia and dedicated a statue ... to her patron in the Temple of Athena Polias in Cyzicus.[31]

In addition to these honors, Livia was equated with various deities, and she in fact began to be revered as a goddess during her lifetime.[32] A first-century CE cult statue of Livia represents her as Ops holding a sheaf of wheat and a cornucopia,[33] and a colossal statue from Leptis included a dedicatory inscription to Ceres Augusta, perhaps in the early first century CE.[34] A shrine of Concordia, dedicated to marital concord and harmony, resides in the Portico of Livia in Rome, and a cameo shows her wearing the mural crown of Kybele, holding stalks of wheat in one hand (symbolizing Ceres) and a bust of the divine Augustus in the other.[35] At Samos, two inscriptions were recently discovered in the Heraeum; two statues of Livia were dedicated to Hera, one before 27 BCE, the other after. Interestingly, in these cases she is called Drusilla.[36]

Festivals were held at Corinth, where poems "to the goddess Julia Augusta" were recited.[37] She received divine honors on at least one coin

28. Ibid., 108.
29. Ibid., 109–10.
30. Ibid., 195, 197, 205–6.
31. Ibid., 196.
32. Ibid., 194–96.
33. Rolf Winkes, *Livia, Octavia, Iulia: Porträts und Darstellungen*, Archaeologia Transatlantica 13 (Louvain-la-Neuve: Département d'archéologie et d'histoire de l'art Collège Erasme, 1995).
34. Barrett, *Livia*, 208–9.
35. McManus, "Livia."
36. Barrett, *Livia*, 198.
37. Ibid., 208.

from Thessaloniki, dated to 21–19 BCE, and was the object of a cult in Athens in the 20s (along with Julia).[38]

A significant building, perhaps a wool market, uncovered at Pompeii is that of Eumachia, daughter of Lucius. An inscription found over one of its two entrances reads: "Eumachia, daughter of Lucius, priestess of the people, in her own name and in that of her son Numistrius Fronto, built this entrance hall, a cryptoporticus and a portico with her own money, and dedicated them to the honor of Augustan Concord and Piety."[39] The building boasted a two-story colonnade and lavish decoration and would have displayed statues of Tiberius and Drusus.[40] Damaged during the earthquake of 62, it was rebuilt during the time of Tiberius.[41] The statue of Concordia Augusta holding a cornucopia is a personification of Livia and represents "the emotional union between her and her son Tiberius, after her illness of 22." The statue can be seen as Eumachia's statement of loyalty to the emperor and Livia and of Eumachia's modeling her life after the tight mother-son relationship. In addition, Eumachia may have "celebrated the cult of this Livia-Ceres figure."[42]

It was in this context that the Livia monument base was constructed. Since there is not, to my knowledge, any ancient literature about the Livia monument or cult at Philippi,[43] we must consider several possible reasons for its construction. The families of the Livia priestesses erected the honorific statues in the forum. Did they look to the past and remember some benefaction Livia had bestowed on the city? Did they equate her with a beneficent goddess and erect the monument at the urging of the people or city rulers so that people could leave thank-offerings? Perhaps we will never know, but Livia's reputation would have been "in the air" at Philippi during the time of Paul, with the imperial cult a political, social,

---

38. Ibid.

39. Robert Etienne, *Pompeii: The Day a City Died*, Discoveries Series (New York: Abrams, 1992), 86; Piemme D'Orta and Enrika D'Orta, *Together in Pompeii* (Pompeii: Falanga Edizioni Pompeiane, 1985), 13. An alternate translation of the first phrase reads "Eumachia daughter of Lucius public priestess [of Venus], etc." (D'Orta and D'Orta, *Together in Pompeii*, 13).

40. Etienne, *Pompeii*, 86–87.

41. D'Orta and D'Orta, *Together in Pompeii*, 13.

42. Etienne, *Pompeii*, 88.

43. Barrett, *Livia*, does not mention a cult or the monument at Philippi, and Grether, "Livia," only mentions in passing the fact that "epigraphical evidence for a cult of Livia as *Diva* is found" at Philippi (249).

and theological backdrop to the ministry of Paul and his fellow Christ-followers. The significance of this reputation could also be reflected in the construction of the temples to Marcus Aurelius and Faustina the Younger that were constructed near the Livia monument eighty to ninety years later or in the supervision of this construction by Modius (implied as a family member in one of the monument's inscriptions). From this, we can draw further conclusions as to the meaning of these cults for nonelite women (and perhaps men).

Faustina the Younger and Empress Cult

Interesting parallels can be found between Livia and Faustina the Younger, daughter of Antoninus and the elder Faustina and wife of Marcus Aurelius. Faustina the Younger held the title of Augusta from her birth in 147 CE until her death in 175 and was honored on coins for most of that time.[44] As mentioned above, she was also honored by a Corinthian temple in the northeast corner of the Philippi forum, in close proximity to the Livia monument, which would already have stood there.[45]

What were Faustina's attributes, how might they inform our discussion of Livia and her influence, and what can these two empresses tell us about the roles of women at Philippi? First, among Faustina's major accomplishments was bearing at least thirteen children by Marcus Aurelius. As an obviously fertile empress, she was honored on coins as a mother.[46] Despite the fact that Livia and Augustus had no children together, Livia was revered throughout the empire and long after her death as "mother of the empire" because of Tiberius.[47] At Philippi and elsewhere, Diana/Artemis—a primary deity at Philippi—was worshiped as the protector of children and women in childbirth, so it is possible that a mother figure such as Faustina could have been regarded at Philippi as an object of worship by mothers praying to deliver safely and bear numerous offspring.

Also, emperors and their wives traveled through the city, and Faustina often accompanied her husband on his campaigns; it is possible that Faustina and Marcus Aurelius traveled to Philippi.[48] Similarly, the literature

---

44. Wood, "Diva Augusta," 6.
45. Sève, "Monument honorifique au forum de Philippes," 467–79.
46. Wood, "Diva Augusta," 6.
47. Grether, "Livia," 251; see also Hurley, "Livia," 6.
48. Wood, "Diva Augusta," 7.

attests that Livia had accompanied Augustus to Sparta, Samos, Delphi, Asia Minor, Pergamum, Ilium, Gaul, and Spain,[49] so it is not beyond the realm of possibility that Livia had traveled to Philippi with or without Augustus and bestowed benefactions on the city. Even if she never officially visited Philippi, she may have had a fondness for the colony because of her father's death there in 42 BCE.[50]

Another attribute of Faustina is *salus* (health), an association with Livia as well, especially after her recovery from a serious illness. Health and healing were already very important aspects of the religious atmosphere of Philippi: the goddesses Diana/Artemis and Isis, as well as the native cult of the Thracian Horseman, the early Christ cult, and others were intimately associated with healing. Thus both Livia and Faustina may have been further symbols of health and healing for the Philippians.[51] Much later in the early Byzantine era, at Philippi and surrounding areas, goddess cults were still centers of healing.[52]

Moreover, the deified and revered empresses became equated with Philippi's city goddesses, Diana then Isis, who watched over the city and its people in very powerful ways.[53] The phenomenon of city deities is, of course, repeated throughout the empire; Artemis of the Ephesians and Athena at Athens come most readily to mind.

By the time of Marcus Aurelius and Faustina the Younger, elite couples throughout the Mediterranean routinely took their marriage oath near the statues of Augustus and Livia and made offerings to them.[54] The priestly office in the cult was always held by women (although there were male priests earlier, as can be seen in the Livia monument); the priestess was called *flaminica* or *sacerdos*; and municipal priests and priestesses were elected by the *ordo decurionum* (at least in the West). Apparently the priestesses and priests were not paid but, conversely, sometimes "promised certain largesses, such as spectacles and games."[55] This is not out

49. Barrett, *Livia*, 34–39.

50. Ibid., 14.

51. Valerie Abrahamsen, *Women and Worship at Philippi: Diana/Artemis and Other Cults in the Early Christian Era* (Portland, ME: Astarte Shell, 1995), 129–50.

52. See Abrahamsen, *Women and Worship at Philippi*, 137–38.

53. Paul Collart, *Philippes: Ville de Macedoine depuis ses origines jusqu'à le fin de l'époque romaine*, Travaux et Mémoires 5 (Paris: École Française d'Athènes, 1937), 451.

54. Grether, "Livia," 242, n. 121, citing Dio, 58.2, 3.

55. Grether, "Livia," 249–50.

of the ordinary, since it was standard practice throughout the Mediterranean for members of wealthy, elite families to make such donations to their communities.[56]

This continuity shows that Livia remained important to people in some parts of the empire for centuries after her death. While her *cult* may have lapsed by the end of the second century, her influence had not. The Christian poet Prudentius, writing in the late fourth century, vehemently attacked Livia for her marriage to Augustus while pregnant by her first husband and for her identification with goddesses. "Clearly ... five centuries after Livia's own lifetime, her name was still a potent force among a broad section of the populace, and she remained a figure widely revered and admired."[57]

Therefore, from examining the Livia and Faustina cults at Philippi, we can conclude several things about its people: (1) Elite families, including women, erected buildings and monuments in the empresses' honor. These activities served many purposes, including keeping the family names public, announcing the families' largess, and providing a prominent focal point for cultic activities. (2) People at all levels of society were compelled to honor the deified imperial couple. They also looked to them for help and favors as if they were divine and repaid them with honors and thank-offerings. (3) While the evidence is only circumstantial, it is possible that the empresses Livia and Faustina the Younger were seen to have bestowed favors or benefactions on the people of Philippi. (4) Elite women served as priestesses in the cults, with some if not all of the related responsibilities and authority that came with such roles. On the positive side, this means that women, while lacking autonomy, absolute control over their own funds and political power exerted some influence in the community.[58]

Female Leadership in Traditional Greek and Roman Cults

The worship of Artemis/Diana, Dionysos, and Isis at Philippi illustrates the involvement of women at several levels of each cult going back centuries, if

---

56. Bremen, *Limits of Participation*, 57 and passim; Connelly, *Portrait of a Priestess*, passim.

57. Barrett, *Livia*, 223–25.

58. There is also evidence for slave women accumulating some wealth, becoming freed, and using their funds for similar purposes. See below regarding devotees to Dionysos at Philippi and Ascough, *Paul's Macedonian Associations*, 52–54.

not millennia. As Christianity grew in the late first century and as the imperial cult matured, women at Philippi continued their oftentimes ancient practices in more traditional religious organizations. Artemis—the Roman Diana and Thracian Bendis—was worshiped at Philippi and in the general vicinity since prehistoric times. Similarly, the cults of Dionysos and the Egyptian goddess Isis were also popular among women. Because evidence from the first century CE is somewhat limited (in part due to the fact that the Philippi forum was reconstructed in the mid-second century, the material remains of which are visible at the site today), the continuity of veneration from prehistory through classical times, the Hellenistic era, and into the Roman and imperial eras becomes important. The Artemis/Diana and Dionysos cults did not die out during or immediately after the time of Paul and the community who would have received the letter. In fact, these cults were alive and well after the reconstruction of the forum, as we shall see,[59] and the cult of Isis, expanded later, was similarly influential.

In *Portrait of a Priestess*, Joan Breton Connelly presents extensive archaeological and literary evidence for a high level of female involvement and leadership in ancient cults for centuries. The evidence clearly shows the following:

- Female cult agents were public office holders "with a much broader civic engagement than was previously recognized."[60]
- The religious "positions of leadership held by priestly women were primary, not peripheral to the centers of power and influence."[61]

---

59. For general references on Philippi, see Valerie Abrahamsen, "Christianity and the Rock Reliefs at Philippi," *BA* 51 (1988): 46–56; Abrahamsen, "Women at Philippi: The Pagan and Christian Evidence," *JFSR* 3 (1987): 17–30; Lukas Bormann, *Philippi: Stadt und Christengemeinde zur Zeit des Paulus*, NovTSup (Leiden: Brill, 1995); Pierre Ducrey, "The Rock Reliefs of Philippi," *Arch* 30 (1977): 102–7; Holland L. Hendrix, "Philippi," in *ABD* 5:313–17; Demetrios Lazarides, "Philippi," in *Princeton Encyclopedia of Classical Sites*, ed. Richard Stillwell (Princeton: Princeton University Press, 1976), 704–5; Lazarides, "Philippoi," *Archaeologikon Deltion* 16 (1960): 218–19; Oakes, *Philippians*; "Philippi," *The Oxford Classical Dictionary*, ed. N. G. L. Hammond and H. H. Scullard, 2nd ed. (Oxford: Clarendon, 1970), 816; Pilhofer, *Philippi I*; and Lilian Portefaix, *Sisters Rejoice: Paul's Letter to the Philippians and Luke-Acts As Received by First-Century Philippians Women*, ConBNT 20 (Stockholm: Almqvist & Wiksell, 1988).

60. Connelly, *Portrait of a Priestess*, 3.   •

61. Ibid., 5.

- The religious and the secular were intimately connected for the ancients, as were the public and the private. Temple rituals mirrored household rituals, which involved women to a high degree. Since in Attica alone during the classical era there were approximately 2,000 cults in operation and 170 festival days a year, the "organization and performance of cult activities was a widely shared experience within the citizen body," making women's involvement vitally important.[62]
- Priesthood was more often than not temporary, rather than lifelong, and offered the opportunity to participate in public life.

The evidence generally reflects priestesses from elite families, as we have noted above; "in the case of Greek priesthoods, pedigree, wealth, or both were basic requirements for attaining office." Therefore, while slave women may not usually be represented in the ranks of priestesses, there is overwhelming evidence for broader participation of women in public life, their influence, their prestige, and their visibility than has been previously acknowledged. As Connelly states,

> Knowledge of ritual practice, local myths, and ancestral traditions invested priestly women with a cultural capital that made them invaluable to their communities.... The accumulated prestige of priestesses, in leading public processions, overseeing polis festivals, sitting in reserved seats at the theater, and having their images erected in sanctuaries, guaranteed them a symbolic capital that must not be underestimated in a world in which status carried long-lasting power.[63]

What further becomes evident concerning female leadership in the traditional religious groups is the part played by wealth and family connections (primarily the man or men in a woman's life—father, husband, brothers, sons, or guardians). Riet van Bremen demonstrates that priesthoods and other leadership positions in groups throughout the Hellenistic and Roman periods, especially in the Greek East, were intimately tied to a woman's family heritage:

---

62. Ibid., 3–10.
63. Ibid., 24.

Family traditions of office-holding and their claims to certain titles mattered crucially in determining a woman's own civic titles. Equally, the involvement of a woman's family—and, to a lesser extent, that of her husband—on the level of provincial office-holding very directly determined her own position and activities.... The public roles of women were the result of a two-way process (as, of course, were those of men): family circumstances and strategies on the one hand; the demands of the city on the other.[64]

Thus, for all intents and purposes, the religious sphere was "the only appropriate one for a woman's philanthropy."[65] But despite this seeming absence of autonomy and the fact that the majority of strictly *political* offices were off-limits to women, "many of the offices ... accessible to women were, in fact, among the most prestigious in Greek cities.... It is not the case, then, that women were fobbed off with insignificant, empty, ceremonial jobs: ceremonial many may well have been, but they were prestigious first and foremost."[66]

Below we shall examine how this might have played out at Philippi as Christianity developed.

Artemis/Diana/Bendis

Little is known about the early, temple cult of this Olympian goddess at Philippi. The only remains excavated at Philippi, to my knowledge, have been part of a temple of Artemis and Apollo Komaios directly behind the forum, which dates to the second half of the fourth century BCE. Apparently the temple cult fell out of favor, or at least declined, by the first or second century CE, when the evidence for Artemis shifts to the rock reliefs on the acropolis hill (see below).[67]

However, we can learn more about the nature of Artemis worship for the first century by examining evidence from the nearby island of Thasos, just off the coast of Neapolis (today's Kavalla), the port city of Philippi. Several inscriptions were found in an ancient Artemis sanctuary in the agora

---

64. Bremen, *Limits of Participation*, 82–83.

65. Ibid., 26–27.

66. Ibid., 56–57.

67. Abrahamsen, *Women and Worship at Philippi*, 48; and Lazarides, "Philippi," 704.

of ancient Thasos, which dates from the sixth century BCE or earlier.[68] An inscription from the first century BCE relates that a woman dedicated the restoration and construction of the propylon of the temple to Artemis Eileithyia and to the people.[69] This woman, Epie, was the daughter of one Dionysios; she had served twice as *neokoros* of Athena and, when "none of the wealthy women in the likely pool of candidates took on the expensive and nonpaying priesthood of Zeus Euboulos, [she] accepted this post [to Athena] as well ... for life, except in years when someone else could be found to accept the job."[70] We know further that Epie had also several times taken on the position of *neokoros* of Aphrodite.

This illustrates several important aspects of women's involvement in cults, including that of Artemis, near Philippi in the era immediately preceding the advent of Christianity. Epie, like many of her peers, was financially able to underwrite a large portion of building activity in the town; Philippians—in the form of the council and the assembly, who issued the decrees—were grateful to her for doing so;[71] it was not unheard of, though it was unusual, for a woman to serve in the cult to Zeus; and one person could serve multiple deities. The Epie inscription further shows that there was apparently a formal rota system on Thasos whereby wealthy women were expected to take on these cultic roles and could also refuse them (presumably if they could persuasively argue that their finances were limited or on other grounds).[72]

Later evidence for Artemis/Diana worship at Philippi comes from the unique rock reliefs carved on the acropolis hill around 200 CE.[73] Even though the temple cult may have receded, the worship of Artemis appears to have at least continued, if not revived, well after the time of Paul and his letter to the Philippians. The reliefs exhibit a female to male ratio of seven

---

68. Abrahamsen, *Women and Worship at Philippi*, 48; and Ecole Française d'Athènes, *Guide de Thasos* (Paris: Editions E. de Boccard, 1968), 39.

69. Abrahamsen, *Women and Worship at Philippi*, 48; and Ecole Française d'Athènes, *Guide de Thasos*, 39.

70. Connelly, *Portrait of a Priestess*, 193. See also Bremen, *Limits of Participation*, 26 n. 56.

71. Bremen, *Limits of Participation*, 26.

72. For additional information on the Artemis cult on Thasos, see Christiane Dunant and Jean Pouilloux, *Recherches sur l'histoire et les cultes de Thasos*, vol. 2 (Paris: Ecole Française d'Athènes, 1958), 123–26, and 179.

73. See Abrahamsen, *Women and Worship at Philippi*, for a comprehensive analysis of Philippi and the rock reliefs.

to one (see table below). The figure portrayed most frequently is Artemis/ Diana, followed closely by unidentified priestesses. It is highly probable that women themselves carved most of the reliefs.[74] The hill appears to be an open-air sanctuary and is not a cemetery. The worship of Artemis/ Diana at Philippi and elsewhere was linked to her roles as protector of children and of women in childbirth, goddess of healing, and guardian of the afterlife.

Table 1: Proportion of Female to Male Figures on the Philippian Acropolis Hill

Female		Male	
Artemis/Diana	90	Horseman	7
Women	40	Jupiter	5
Minerva	2	Man and Male Heads	4
Kybele	3	Centaur	1
Lunar deity	3	Phallus	1
		Man and altar	1
TOTAL:	138		19

Further, healing with regard to the community is linked to the worship of Artemis as city protector. Artemis in an uncommon guise (shown with her torso covered with breasts or possibly testicles[75]) was the protector of the city of Ephesus, another locus of early Christian activity; this statue, now in the Louvre, shows the goddess wearing a city wall as a crown on her head. While a comparable statue has not been found at Philippi, it is possible that Artemis/Diana functioned in this way there: her sanctuary dominated the acropolis hill, and no other deity appears as influential in the community at this point in time (with the possible exception of the Thracian Horseman).

---

74. Ibid., 103–27.

75. Christine M. Thomas, "On Not Finding Small Finds: Spatial Discourse in Early Christianity at Ephesos and Elsewhere" (paper presented at the Annual Meeting of the Society of Biblical Literature, Boston, 23 November 1999).

A final piece of evidence for the worship of Artemis/Diana at Philippi was discovered in the so-called "bishops' palace" in 1979.[76] A marble relief depicting a goddess surrounded by two signs of the zodiac—the bull and the twins—has tentatively been dated to the third century CE.[77] As reconstructed, it would show a goddess, probably Artemis/Bendis,[78] with a crescent and the point of a spear behind her head and twelve zodiac symbols around her. Its reconstructed diameter would be 0.35 meters (14 inches).[79] While Bendis was uppermost in the creator's and probably the user's mind, the overall religious context suggests that she was revered at the same time that many Philippians, perhaps even the plaque's owner, were also worshiping Jesus the Christ. The bishop in whose chambers the relief was found almost certainly worshiped Jesus and the Christian God.

Dionysos/Bacchus, Liber, Libera, and Herakles

Dionysos (Roman Bacchus) was worshiped at Philippi in conjunction with a trio of deities—the male god Liber, the female deity Libera, and the male god Herakles (the trio abbreviated hereafter LLH)—in a complex south of the forum.[80] The cult of Dionysos provides some of the best epigraphic evidence for cultic worship from the first century CE, the era of the letter to the Philippians, which enables us to see more clearly who honored whom and in what way. Five inscriptions to these three deities were discovered during excavations of the public baths at Philippi:[81]

- One inscription was given by a thiasus of maenads, who "bequeath[ed] a water conduit in honour of" the deities;

---

76. See Valerie Abrahamsen, "Evidence for a Christian Goddess: The Bendis-Zodiac Relief at Philippi," *Forum* 3 (2007): 97–112.

77. Anna Tsitouridou, "Ena anaglupho apo tous Philippous me parastaseis apo to zodiako kuklo," *Résumés des communications* (Thessaloniki: Xe Congres International d'Archéologie Chrétienne, 1980), 97.

78. Charalambos Bakirtzis, private communication, 1983.

79. Tsitouridou, "Ena anaglupho," 97. For a detailed discussion of the Bendis-zodiac relief, see Abrahamsen, "Evidence for a Christian Goddess," 97–112.

80. Hendrix, "Philippi," 5:315.

81. For the following inscriptions, see Portefaix, *Sisters Rejoice*, 100–01, quoting Collart, *Philippes: Ville*, 414.

- A second inscription to LLH mentions Pomponia Hilara, possibly "a noble female of the Pomponians or a liberated bondswoman who had been given the name of her mistress";
- A third inscription to LLH mentions Salvia Pisidia, who offered a sestertia to Liber Pater;
- A fourth inscription to LLH refers to Pisidia Helpis, who appears to dedicate a statue;
- And a fifth inscription to LLH refers to Marronia Eutychia, mentioned with her husband, who may have come from the town of Marroneia on the Via Egnatia.

Three women with names derived from geographic locations—Marronia Eutychia, Salvia Pisidia, and Pisidia Helpis—may have been liberated slaves.[82] Portefaix's conclusion that these five inscriptions demonstrate that the women who created or commissioned them "had a remarkable degree of economic independence"[83] should now be somewhat tempered by Bremen's and others' conviction that "independence" is almost never an economic or social reality for women in antiquity. However, it is still significant that freedwomen were able to act in ways similar to women from traditionally elite families if they had acquired the financial resources.

The links between these deities and their connection with women are several. For one, the water system of the sanctuary to LLH at Philippi was dedicated by a thiasus of maenads, devotees of Dionysos.[84] Second, excavators identified several acropolis rock reliefs portraying Dionysos/Bacchus,[85] and two phalluses were carved in the acropolis rock. Furthermore, the ancient Greek historian Herodotus reported that the Thracian people worshiped Dionysos (*Hist.* 5.7),[86] which is borne out in the sixth–fifth centuries BCE with the depiction on coinage of Silenus, satyrs, and centaurs raping nymphs.

---

82. Portefaix, *Sisters Rejoice*, 101, quoting A. Heubeck, "Personennamen (A)," in *Lexikon der Alten Welt*, ed. C. Andresen et al. (Zürich: Artemis, 1965), 2268.

83. Portefaix, *Sisters Rejoice*, 101.

84. Abrahamsen, *Women and Worship at Philippi*, 13; Hendrix, "Philippi," 315.

85. Collart, *Philippes: Villes*, passim; Collart, "Philippes," 712–42; Charles Picard, "Les dieux de la colonie de Philippes," *Revue de l'histoire des religions* 86 (1922): 159–72. See also Portefaix, *Sisters Rejoice*, 98.

86. As referred to in Picard, "Dieux," 159.

The Philippian countryside also provided evidence for the existence of Dionysiac mysteries in the area and women's involvement in them. One example is an inscription from the village of Podgora dated to the early third century CE, which relates that a man bequeathed 120 denarii on behalf of himself, his wife, and their children to the mysteries of Dionysos for roses to be burnt annually at the grave by cult members.[87] Roses have a long history of involvement with funerary rites.[88]

A second inscription more explicitly speaks of female ecstatics and participants. Found in a church in Doxato, a village near Philippi, the inscription, also dated to the third century CE, is dedicated to a young boy who had apparently been initiated into the Dionysiac mysteries (although there is no explicit mention of Dionysos in the inscription). The dedication, written in Latin, mentions "basket-bearing Naiads" and "tattooed women initiated into the mysteries of Bromios."[89] The inscription also mentions torches, suggesting that the dancing rites occurred in darkness, under the light of the moon.[90]

A large part of the allure of Dionysos for Thracians and Philippians, perhaps especially for women, stemmed from his mythology, with which Philippians would have been well acquainted. At least one version of Dionysos's story starts with Zeus, king of the Olympian gods and goddesses. Zeus had an affair with Semele. Zeus's wife, Hera, was jealous, disguised herself, and went to Semele. Hera advised Semele to test Zeus's divinity by transforming himself into his true form. Since Zeus had promised Semele to grant her whatever she asked, he turned himself into a thunderbolt, which caused Semele's death when she was pregnant with Dionysos. Zeus took the unborn child and sewed it into his thigh until being born.[91]

---

87. Portefaix, *Sisters Rejoice*, 104–5; Paul Perdrizet, "Inscriptions de Philippes: Les Rosalies," *BCH* 24 (1900): 304–5; Collart, *Philippes: Ville*, 417 and n. 1; and Anne-Françoise Jaccottet, *Choisir Dionysos: Les Associations Dionysiaques ou La Face Cachée du Dionysisme* (Zurich: Akanthus, 2003), 2:64–65.

88. For a discussion of the *rosalia* festival in Philippi, Macedonia, and Thrace, in relation with voluntary associations, see Ascough, *Paul's Macedonian Associations*, 26–28.

89. Portefaix, *Sisters Rejoice*, 105; *CIL* 3.868, B1233; Collart, *Philippes: Ville*, 419.

90. Jaccottet cautions that this inscription may point more toward a local cult to Liber rather than to Dionysos per se (*Choisir Dionysos*, 66–68). Both, however, reflected a popular use of associations concerned with funerary rites.

91. Miriam Robbins Dexter, *Whence the Goddesses: A Source Book*, The Athene

Subsequently, the child Dionysos was reared by nymphs at Nysa, a place possibly located on Mount Pangaion, near Philippi.[92] When Dionysos became a young man, he wandered all over the world, teaching people the culture of the vine and the mysteries of his worship. During his wanderings, he met Ariadne, the princess of Crete, who had been abandoned on the island of Naxos. Dionysos rescued and married her—Ariadne was sometimes identified with Libera, further linking the three deities, as at Philippi.[93] When Dionysos arrived at Thebes to establish his cult there, he was accompanied by women dancing and singing exultant songs behind him, waving ivy-wreathed wands and appearing mad with joy. King Pentheus was enraged by Dionysos and his companions and ultimately had him dismembered. In the lower world, he not only rescued Semele but also joyfully rose again, giving assurance to his worshipers of life after death.[94]

Many aspects of Dionysos's mythology would have appealed to Philippians. For those who lost a young child, parents could hope that he or she would reside forever in the "flower-bearing meadows of the Satyrs," as was stated in the above-mentioned epitaph from Doxato. The connection with Semele may have been particularly attractive to women. Semele, associated with the myths around Mount Pangaion, could have been seen by Philippian women as a neighbor and mortal woman who gained immortality by bearing Dionysos and being raised by him and who, by her death, was a metaphor for death in childbirth.[95] The nymphs who attended Dionysos in his adventures became the maenads of the cult; their ecstatic, wild behavior was justified by the joy of bringing new life into the world—the fertility aspects of the vine—and of resurrection—Dionysos's being raised from the dead.

As Richard S. Ascough points out, "voluntary associations in Macedonia [which would include thiasoi to Dionysos] were composed of people of mixed social rank or lower social rank (freepersons, and especially freed-

---

Series (New York: Pergamon, 1990), 41–42, quoting Ovid, *Metam.* 3.261–263; and Hesiod, *Theog.* 942.

92. Portefaix, *Sisters Rejoice*, 107.

93. Edith Hamilton, *Mythology: Timeless Tales of Gods and Heroes* (Chicago: Mentor, 1942), 56; and Portefaix, *Sisters Rejoice*, 108.

94. Hamilton, *Mythology*, 59–62.

95. Portefaix, *Sisters Rejoice*, 109–10.

persons and slaves).["96] Many associations operated by the collection of membership dues, as well as patronage and donations from more wealthy members,[97] which suggests that male and female members of Dionysiac and other groups had at least some funds at their disposal, no matter what their social level. This in turn suggests a certain degree of choice and influence in the disposal of their wealth, though probably again, for women, still under the stricture of the law (that is, their funds would still have been partially controlled by the men in their lives).

Furthermore, Anne-Françoise Jaccottet in her comprehensive study of the cult of Dionysos, discovers several important and surprising facts from examining primarily epigraphic evidence. For one, "there are almost no associations composed entirely of women."[98] Rather, the gender-mixed nature of the associations follows traditional forms, with women having the vital *religious* duties while the men had the usual social and honorary responsibilities. This parallels social mores, as we have seen: "Men cannot be involved in orgiastic practices, for such activities are incompatible with their social and civic roles."[99] The findings at Philippi and its environs further remind us that the religious aspects of funerary and other associations well into the early Christian era, dominated by women, were important to the community in many ways.

Isis

The powerful Egyptian goddess Isis had been introduced to Macedonia as early as the third century BCE, possibly by merchants from Alexandria and Asia Minor.[100] Most of the evidence for her cult at Philippi dates to the third through fifth centuries CE; her temple from this era, from which were discovered a number of artifacts, was located on the acropolis hill near several other cult complexes.[101]

Isis, her husband Serapis/Osiris, and their son Harpocrates/Horus eventually became some of the most popular deities in the Roman

---

96. Ascough, *Paul's Macedonian Associations*, 53.

97. Ibid., 64 and passim.

98. Jaccottet, *Choisir Dionysos*, 334 (English summary translated by Martine Roulin and Kristine Gex).

99. Ibid.

100. Portefaix, *Sisters Rejoice*, 70; Collart, *Philippes: Ville*, 253–54.

101. Portefaix, *Sisters Rejoice*, 117–19.

Empire, both among commoners and the elites of society, but not without sporadic government suppression. Of the three deities in this trio, it was Isis, the mother, who became the most popular when the cult was finally sanctioned in the empire, and it was she who ultimately became the most prevalent deity at Philippi and nearby cities. At Amphipolis, Apollonia, Verroia and Thessaloniki,[102] statues and inscriptions attest to the popularity of her cult, including two Latin inscriptions to "Queen Isis."[103]

For Egyptians, the association between Isis and a queen was logical. Her name meant "throne," and she functioned as the divine king-maker. The worship of Isis also included a wide range of divine female manifestations, chief of which was Hathor, a name that literally meant "house of Horus" or "womb of Horus." Temple dancers used a particular type of necklace with a counterpoise along with a rattle worship of Isis-Hathor. Both ancient Egyptian symbols had associations with the celestial voyage into the afterlife.[104]

The Isis cult, both at Philippi and throughout the Greco-Roman world, consisted of several standard elements. At daily services, the shrine was opened and the statue awakened and clothed. Congregational singing and praise, sacred dances, processions, and initiations for chosen members were all part of the religious praxis; water, believed to be holy water from the Nile, played a large role. Most Isis temples were large complexes that housed professional clergy and temporarily lodged devotees.[105] Both men and women participated in and were officials of the cult, which survived in various parts of the Roman Empire through the mid-sixth century CE.[106]

At Philippi, the cult complex on the acropolis hill consisted of five contiguous rooms on one side and one large room opposite them. The

---

102. Rex Witt, "The Egyptian Cults in Ancient Macedonia," in *Ancient Macedonia*, ed. B. Laourdas (Thessaloniki: Institute for Balkan Studies, 1970), 329.

103. Paul Collart, "Le sanctuaire des dieux égyptiens à Philippes," *BCH* 53 (1929): 82–87.

104. Sheldon L. Gosline, *Archaeogender, Studies in Gender's Material Culture*, Marco Polo Monographs 2 (Warren Center, PA: Shangri-La, 1999), 126–30. See also Barbara G. Walker, *The Woman's Dictionary of Symbols and Sacred Objects* (San Francisco: Harper & Row, 1988), 105, 107, and 121.

105. See Apuleius, *Metam.* 11.9, 19; and the discussion in Sharon Kelly Heyob, *The Cult of Isis among Women in the Graeco-Roman World* (Leiden: Brill, 1975), 59, 96. For details of temple worship, see also Robert Wild, *Water in the Cultic Worship of Isis and Sarapis* (Leiden: Brill, 1981), 19–20; and Gosline, *Archaeogender*, 116–32.

106. Witt, "Egyptian Cults in Ancient Macedonia," 328.

five rooms served as housing for the divinities and people; the one large chamber was used as a gathering room where initiates celebrated a communal, ritual meal. Judging from the inscriptions found in the complex, the sanctuary dates to the third century CE, although it could have been constructed in the second century.[107]

That it was Isis, and not Serapis, who was the dominant member of the pair in Thrace and Macedonia implies not only her overall popularity in the region but also the propensity of the general populace toward a female deity and the influence of her proselytizers in the promotion of her qualities. Her healing and apotropaic promises, along with her many other attributes, would have constituted serious competition to local deities and to Christianity as it matured. Her supporters not only promoted her as queen, but also chose to construct an elaborate worship center in close proximity to the Diana and Sylvanus sanctuaries, one that was attractive to a broad cross-section of Philippians.

A final important artifact to Isis, an altar, was found near the city gate of Philippi. Probably dating to the third century, it contains an inscription in which she is addressed as "Queen Isis." Significantly, a dove and cross, Christian symbols, were carved on one side, yet nothing was defaced. The altar had been moved to its find spot sometime in antiquity. Since moving it would have required tremendous planning, strength, and perhaps money, it was probably accomplished in the face of some impending doom such as an invasion or an earthquake. With this altar and inscription, the Philippians seem to be appealing to Isis for the protection of their city.[108]

Demography and Worship Patterns

Notwithstanding the long tradition of goddess worship and women's involvement in religion at Philippi, the colony was as patriarchal and hierarchical as most other imperial-era cities. Epigraphic evidence shows that its civic officials were male, as was the case throughout the empire, and one of its main shrines, dating to the Hellenistic era and situated in the middle of the city, was the tomb of a young male hero and city founder.[109] Philippi's main Christian witnesses were Paul and Timothy, and as

---

107. Collart, "Dieux," 69–100.

108. Ibid.; Abrahamsen, *Women and Worship at Philippi*, 185–87.

109. Stylianos Pelekanides, "Kultprobleme im Apostel-Paulus-Oktogon von Philippi im Zusammenhang mit einem älteren Heroenkult," in *Atti del IX Congresso*

the imperial cult grew, Philippians honored emperors and their wives just as most other cities did.

Peter Oakes has carefully analyzed Philippi's demography and provided important data that can inform our investigation of women's roles in the religious makeup of the colony in the Roman imperial period. Oakes asserts that, around the time of Paul, the size of the territory was approximately 1900 square kilometers, with a population density about the same as that of Pompeii. This results in an estimated population of 46,000 people. About a third lived in Philippi proper. The elite of the town were probably at 3 percent. The poor—those living at subsistence level and almost always in want—would be about 20 percent and, due to the nature of colonization, predominantly Greek ethnically. Slaves crossed several strata of society except those owned by the poor—they would be poor as well—and comprised roughly 20 percent of the population. Slaves living in town were generally domestic servants or fellow workers with their owners. Peasant colonist farmers commuted between their property (owned or rented) and the city and numbered around 20 percent of the population. Oakes postulates a 50/50 split between farmers who owned their own land and those who rented. The largest sector of the population, at about 37 percent, would be service workers—craftworkers as well as a "cashier, hunter, town-crier, head of a troupe of actors, stage-manager, and doctor" are all attested epigraphically.[110]

Furthermore, according to Oakes, some 40 percent of Philippi's population was Roman citizenry, with 60 percent being Greek-speaking non-citizens. By the middle of the first century CE, veterans who had originally settled in Philippi would have died out and passed their property on to their descendants. Other veterans may have settled there in the intervening years, making it plausible that 5–10 percent of "colonist households … may have been headed by a veteran." Elite or farming colonists comprised about 23 percent of the population living in the town. If heads of household were about six percent of that, then 10 percent of households would only lead to 0.6 percent being veteran. Oakes concludes, significantly, that "the exegetical assumption that a substantial group of the hearers [of the letter to the Philippians] were likely to have been veterans seems com-

---

Internazionale di Archeologia Cristiana (Rome: Pontificio Istituto di Archeologia Cristiana, 1978), 2:393, 396. See also Abrahamsen, *Women and Worship at Philippi*, 159, 169–70.

110. Oakes, *Philippians*, 42–49.

pletely indefensible."[111] In addition, the majority of Philippians in the town were most likely neither Romans nor citizens but rather Greeks in the service economy.[112]

Oakes then goes on to provide a model for the makeup of the *church* at Philippi around the time of Paul, concluding the following: "43 percent service community, 25 percent poor, 16 percent slaves, 15 percent colonist farmers, 1 percent elite landowners." The church most likely consisted of service groups and their slaves and the poor—57 percent service groups, 31 percent poor, and 12 percent slaves. If Romans comprised a third of the service groups and a quarter of the poor, 27 percent in the church would be Romans and 73 percent Greeks. (Note that "Romans" could be freedmen or freedwomen in citizenship categories rather than ethnic Romans, and "Greeks" may have included some slaves who were not native Greeks.) Since most Thracians lived in the countryside and the bulk of Christians were town dwellers, the church most likely had few Thracians among its members.[113]

In a different type of demographic analysis, Lilian Portefaix, writing in the mid-1990s, sketched the religious environment of Philippi of the first century CE. When the Romans arrived to colonize the area in the first century BCE, native Thracian and Greek cults to Thracian Bacchus, the Thracian horseman, Bendis, Dionysos, Artemis, Ares, Zeus, Apollo, Herakles, and the Egyptian gods were present. Traces have also been found of the worship of Jupiter, Juno, Minerva, Mercury, and Liber Pater.[114] This is the atmosphere that Paul would have encountered on his missionary visit to Philippi.

Additional archaeological evidence for the worship of these other deities at Philippi, even though it dates to later centuries, supports the argument that women from several strata of society had some wealth and influence, at least in their religious practice. In addition, evidence from the Dionysos, Libera, and Demeter/Persephone cults suggest the existence of several groups of women at Philippi, perhaps even secret groups, who participated in religious rites such as the Thesmophoria.[115] Portefaix also makes the provocative point that the later rock reliefs to Diana (perhaps

---

111. Ibid., 52–53.
112. Ibid., 54.
113. Ibid., 60–63.
114. Portefaix, *Sisters Rejoice*, 70–71.
115. Ibid., 97.

carved to depict a deceased woman's deification after death) may have been carved to give hope to women that they could "become sharers of her independent life—a way of living unattainable to them in this mortal life."[116]

In addition, Ascough's recent work on ancient voluntary associations also provides information to inform our study (as noted above). Slave women and freedwomen (and their male counterparts) were members of religious associations along with upper-strata women and men and thus participated in association activities, even if they did not function as leaders. There is evidence for slaves and masters belonging to the same groups, which could cause tensions, and some associations were comprised solely of lower-strata people.[117]

This evidence provides a crucial backdrop to the work of Paul and other early Christians in and around Philippi, especially with regard to women. Women from a wide range of socioeconomic strata participated in and led cults and cultic activities, apparently without censure and for a long period of time. Like men and children from the subsistence level of the social scale, women led difficult lives. Their involvement in voluntary associations, including religious cults, provided a measure of camaraderie and social support. Some groups also assured members that they would have a funeral at death, and others may have included a belief system of reunification with a deity after death.

The Christian Trajectory of Women's Roles

Evidence for women's involvement in early Christianity at Philippi comes primarily from three literary sources: Paul's letter to the Philippians; Acts of the Apostles; and Polycarp's letter to the Philippians. In addition, the growing devotion to Mary, the mother of Jesus, as found in both literary and material evidence, also played a role. We will take each of these in turn.

Euodia and Syntyche

> I entreat Euodia and I entreat Syntyche to agree in the Lord. And I ask you also, true yokefellow, help these women, for they have labored side by side with me in the gospel together with Clement and the rest of my fellow workers, whose names are in the book of life. (Phil 4:2–3, RSV)

---

116. Ibid., 96.
117. See Ascough, *Paul's Macedonian Associations*, 59–61.

These are the only verses in the Bible that mention Euodia and Syntyche. In the past, commentators have glossed over them quickly, preferring to investigate the identity and importance of the (male?) "true yokefellow."[118] However, in recent years, much insight has been gleaned about the status of these two women in the community, their possible social location, and their relationship to Paul. Elisabeth Schüssler Fiorenza has described Euodia and Syntyche as "outstanding women missionaries" whose authority was such that any dissension between them could do great damage to the Philippian Christian community.[119] Mary Rose D'Angelo considers them a missionary couple, possibly working independently of Paul.[120]

D'Angelo, Cynthia Briggs Kittredge, and Joseph A. Marchal have developed the theory, contrary to most traditional studies, that the two women "seem to be working together, not in a conflict with each other."[121] This is significant: they work with Paul, yet he asks them to "agree in the Lord." Marchal asserts that there existed an "alternating, ambiguous dynamic between hierarchical contact and separation" between Paul and his coworkers in his travels.[122] Paul wrote to the Philippians from prison, and others of his coworkers endured imprisonment and other forms of punishment by imperial authorities (Epaphroditus in Phil 2:25–30; Prisca and Aquila in Rom 16:3–4). Thus, suggests Marchal, if Euodia and Syntyche worked together in spreading the gospel, as seems likely, they may also have been working against the empire, a dangerous endeavor.

A further dynamic at work is that Paul was an authority figure at a more privileged social level than these two women. It is possible, on the one hand, that his stance was in fact or could have been viewed by the letter's recipients as coercive: Christians in the Philippian community should think and behave like Paul or suffer unfortunate consequences. On the other hand, Euodia and Syntyche may have willingly agreed, ultimately,

---

118. For examples, see Abrahamsen, *Women and Worship at Philippi*, 83 nn. 73–75.

119. Elisabeth Schüssler Fiorenza, *In Memory of Her: A Feminist Theological Reconstruction of Christian Origins* (New York: Crossroad, 1983), 170.

120. Mary Rose D'Angelo, "Women Partners in the New Testament," *JFSR* 6 (1990): 76.

121. Marchal, *Politics of Heaven*, 102. See also Cynthia Briggs Kittredge, *Community and Authority: The Rhetoric of Obedience in the Pauline Tradition*, HTS 45 (Harrisburg, PA: Trinity Press International, 1998), 105–8.

122. Marchal, *Politics of Heaven*, 100.

with Paul's directives. But if they were freed slaves, this willingness could have been entwined with patronage obligations. [123]

Whatever the dynamic might have been between Paul and the two women, we can draw several conclusions about the Christian women of first-century Philippi. At least two named women, Euodia and Syntyche, were leaders in the Philippian Christianity community and designated coworkers with Paul. If as is likely they were not from the elite classes of the city, they mirror other women involved in the religious groups and voluntary associations of the same era, whom we have met earlier. The women represented in the Artemis/Diana and LLH inscriptions cited above appear to be both freed slaves and from the ruling group. Being women, they too lived in an imperial "contact zone," navigating both their own world and that of upper-strata men—speaking both languages, as it were. The contact zone meant that, within the context of an imperial colony that oppressed them in many ways, there were behavioral constraints at the same time they simultaneously played active roles in society through their religiosocial institutions on behalf of themselves, their families, and their communities and in concert with and over against empire. In Marchal's words, "women with some position [could be viewed] as both resistant and complicit, both colonized and colonizing."[124] All of these factors must be held in tension as we search for a "people's history" of Philippi.

Lydia

Another woman from early Christian literary sources is Lydia the purple-seller from Acts 16. Purple dye was used primarily for the clothing of royalty, the wealthy, and governing officials, making the dye precious and valuable. There is also evidence that the dye was used for festive women's dresses and as rouge for cheeks and lips.[125] Luke describes Lydia as being from Thyatira, a Macedonian colony in Asia Minor known for its dye industry. The dye produced there was derived from the madder root, not from the more expensive murex shells used by the Phoenicians.[126] The

---

123. Ibid., 103–4; following Craig S. de Vos, *Church and Community Conflicts: The Relationships of the Thessalonian, Corinthian, and Philippian Christians with Their Wider Civic Communities*, SBLDS 168 (Atlanta: Scholars Press, 1999), 25–26.

124. Marchal, *Politics of Heaven*, 108.

125. Portefaix, *Sisters Rejoice*, 171.

126. John Bowker, *The Complete Bible Handbook* (New York: DK Publishing, 1998), 370.

city was an important center of commerce in antiquity; the archaeological evidence mentions "wood and leather workers, tanners, potters, bronze-smiths, … slave traders [and] linen workers and dyers."[127]

Because many of the guilds were under the patronage of pagan deities, conflicts arose for Christians (as well as Jews) working in these trades. The situation is outlined in Rev 2:18–30—the letter to the Christians at Thyatira. The guilds periodically sponsored idolatrous feasts, and Jezebel attempted to bridge this gap by "practicing immorality" and eating food sacrificed to idols while still remaining a Christian prophet. The author of Revelation condemns her: "I will throw her on a sickbed, and those who commit adultery with her I will throw into great tribulation, unless they repent of her doings; and I will strike her children dead" (Rev 2:22–24a, RSV). Since Revelation was written toward the end of the first century CE and Acts at the beginning of the second century, it is quite possible that the mention of Thyatira in Acts could have resonated with Luke's readers/listeners in a significant way: Jezebel from Thyatira as an example of a Christian woman *not* to follow, while Lydia from Thyatira at Philippi, who opens her home to Paul and his fellow missionaries, as a positive example of a Christian woman.

Ascough has made a convincing argument for Lydia's participation and even patronage in the Philippian Christian group. Ascough, using historical, archaeological, literary, sociological, and epigraphic evidence, postulates that Lydia "was involved in financial transactions as a cloth dealer and had oversight of a household," most likely as a widow who had borne three or four children who survived childhood.[128] With money from either her (deceased) husband or inherited from her father's estate, she was the head of a household in which she provided hospitality to Paul and through which she and Paul most likely had a complex patronage relationship, with both providing benefits to the other.[129]

Polycarp

The letter to the Philippians from Polycarp of Smyrna, written about 110 CE, provides insight into the structure of the Christian community in the early second century, especially with regard to women. Polycarp admon-

---

127. Ibid., 370–71.
128. Ascough, *Lydia*, 45.
129. Ibid., 52–55.

ishes a number of groups about their behavior. Among women, wives and widows appear to be groups with specific social roles. Wives were expected to "cherish their own husbands in all fidelity, and to love all others equally in all chastity, and to educate their children in the fear of God" (Polycarp, *Phil.* 4.2).[130] Widows "should be discreet in their faith pledged to the Lord, praying unceasingly on behalf of all, refraining from all slander, gossip, false witness, love of money," et cetera (Polycarp, *Phil.* 4.3). Virgins or unmarried women, who did not seem to have specific social roles like wives and widows, were to walk with a blameless and pure conscience (Polycarp, *Phil.* 5.3); however, this imperative may well have resonated in the context of Artemis/Diana worship.[131]

Others in the community addressed by Polycarp further show the structure of the group. Deacons are also admonished to be blameless, "not slanderers, or double-tongued, not lovers of money, temperate in all matters" (Polycarp, *Phil.* 5.2); "younger ones" likewise must be blameless, cut themselves off from things of the flesh, and be obedient to the presbyters and deacons (5.3); and presbyters themselves "must be compassionate, ... looking after the sick, not neglecting widow or orphan or one that is poor, ... refraining from all anger, partiality, unjust judgment," and the like (6.1).

While the Philippian Christian group addressed by Polycarp has "an established organization for charity inside the community,"[132] in which he hopes to bolster and increase pure, charitable behavior, his letter also suggests concerns about reputation and future group survival. He urges the community to refrain from occasions of scandal and false brethren (Polycarp, *Phil.* 7.1–2) and to live their lives in a manner "above reproach from the heathen, so that you may receive praise for your good works and the Lord may not be blasphemed on your account" (10.2). He is further very disturbed by the dishonest and greedy actions of Valens, a presbyter, and his wife (11), urging the community to "reclaim them as suffering and straying members" (11.4).

In the face of continuing disregard from the wider society, including sporadic persecution, it is not surprising that a leader of the wider church such as Polycarp would take the opportunity to promulgate specific advice that he felt would strengthen the nascent community. It is in

---

130. Translation from Cyril C. Richardson, ed., *Early Christian Fathers* (New York: Macmillan, 1978).

131. Portefaix, *Sisters Rejoice*, 183.

132. Ibid., 181.

this light that we can better understand his attempt to discourage female asceticism.[133] The overall message of Polycarp to Philippi's Christian women was to behave, to be submissive, and to be obedient to the men of the community. The question of asceticism, addressed in *Phil.* 5.3, shows that the celibate lifestyle was a possible option in the Christian community at Philippi, implied by the fact that the group had apparently asked Polycarp's opinion on the matter. Polycarp did not condemn asceticism, but he did not encourage it either, just as other Christian communities were practicing it, as reflected in the Acts of Paul and Thecla, the Acts of John, and the Acts of Thomas.[134] The important issue for the bishop appears to be *female* asceticism, not male. If elite women left their homes to join other types of living situations, it could threaten the basic family structure that supported communities. Thus Polycarp seems to have felt the need to urge women to remain in their traditional roles supportive of the status quo.

While not pointedly addressed in the letter, Polycarp probably knew of the cult of Livia; the monument base and statues would have been standing in the forum by the time of his letter. Interestingly, the cultic adoration of Augustus's wife, who embodied traditional Roman values, could have worked to bolster Polycarp's admonitions to the Philippian Christians. Polycarp—a high-status male leader—was reflecting imperial mores while at the same time attempting to both preserve the unity of the Christian group and raise its reputation in the wider community. If the Philippian Christian sect in the early second century was still composed of a mixture of elites, slaves, and freedpersons, as it had been earlier, it is possible that some among the women addressed by Polycarp were leaders of, participants in, or donors to the Livia cult. Since emperor worship was imposed on the populace, and since, as we have seen, the very fabric of a city like Philippi depended upon the pagan socioreligious structure, there would not have been much Polycarp could do to dissuade women (and men) from participating in a cult such as that of Livia. In fact, in *Phil.* 12.3, he specifically asks the Philippians to "pray also for emperors and magistrates and rulers" and for "those who persecute and hate you."

Therefore, what Polycarp *could* do to strengthen the group and enhance its reputation was to make the behavioral path for women as

---

133. See Abrahamsen, *Women and Worship at Philippi*, 84–85.
134. Ibid., 85 and 98 n. 87.

narrow as possible. As in the example of Euodia and Syntyche above, Polycarp attempts to keep the marginalized groups at Philippi marginalized, ostensibly for theological, social, and survival reasons. We also know, however, that much of the early church fathers' stances are proscriptive, not prescriptive: they would not have had to argue against a certain behavior if it had not already been occurring.

It is thus an interesting exercise to imagine the Philippian Christian community in 110 CE as being composed of strong women—wives, widows, and "virgins"—who were perceived by the bishop (or accused by enemies of the Christian religion) as impure gossips about to leave their husbands or shun marriage and join a powerful all-female group on the fringes of accepted society. While it is certainly acceptable for a leader to admonish members of a group under his charge to behave in a blameless, upstanding way, Polycarp's admonitions are striking due to what we know of the context at Philippi—strong female participation and leadership in non-Christian groups and the emperor cult; the probability that Euodia and Syntyche, though marginalized, were highly-respected leaders perhaps moving in a different theological direction than Paul (and taking others with them); the long-standing persistence of pagan groups well after the time of Polycarp; and the threat of heresies such as Docetism.

Jesus and Mary

By the late first century, gospel accounts, various apocryphal acts of the apostles, and other early Christian literature were circulating widely and could have been familiar to the people of Philippi. This literature included stories of women around Jesus—his mother Mary, Mary Magdalene, Martha, Salome, and others. Early on, these women seemed to play minor roles, but as time passed, their stature in tradition and legend increased. In the second century, the cult of Mary, mother of Jesus, began.[135] Significantly, the dates of the publication and circulation of the Infancy Gospel of James, which focuses more on Mary than on Jesus, were nearly identical to the birth and death dates of Faustina the Younger: the Infancy Gospel of

---

135. Ignatius of Antioch mentions her in his letters of the early second century; see Raymond E. Brown, Karl P. Donfried, Joseph A. Fitzmyer, and John Reumann, eds., *Mary in the New Testament* (Philadelphia: Fortress, 1978), 253; see also 262, 265.

James was written and published between 140 and 170 CE[136] and Faustina held the title of Augusta from her birth in 147 CE until her death in 175.[137]

We can begin to see the importance of the Mary stories contained in the Infancy Gospel of James when they are juxtaposed with the life of Faustina; as outlined above, Faustina had an important temple at and thus a connection with Philippi. The Mary stories may well have resonated especially with nonelite women. Mary's parents, though certainly not highborn, were yet holy and chosen; Faustina's were equally "chosen"—Antoninus Pius and Faustina the Elder.[138] Mary was a chosen woman from the beginning of her life, as was Faustina; Mary was given to the temple until puberty, and Faustina was the daughter of one emperor, wife of another, and mother of a third. Mary married a righteous man, Joseph, who provided for and protected her, while Faustina's husband, Marcus Aurelius, was not only emperor but also an accomplished Stoic philosopher and author of the *Meditations*, thereby earning him a generally favorable reputation as ruler.[139] Moreover, according to growing Christian lore and the Infancy Gospel of James, Mary gave birth to the savior of the world; early in her husband's reign, Faustina bore twins, including the future emperor Commodus.[140]

What may have been particularly attractive to nonelite women was the exaltation in the stories of the humble Mary to Mother of God. While it is impossible to say that the Infancy Gospel of James was written and understood to counter claims of Faustina's and her husband's divinity, it is not impossible to believe that it was written to counter claims of imperial divinity in general and to exalt Mary alongside Jesus. The fact that Faustina's life coincided with the circulation of the Infancy Gospel of James may have served to make the book that much more popular as her husband persecuted Christians (probably sporadically) for failing to give homage to the royal couple. While there is no specific evidence for persecution at

---

136. See Oscar Cullmann, "Infancy Gospels," *NTApoc* 1:363–401; and Ronald F. Hock, "Infancy Gospels," in *The Complete Gospels*, ed. Robert J. Miller (Sonoma, CA: Polebridge, 1994), 367–96, both of whom date the Infancy Gospel of James in the mid-second century.

137. Wood, "Diva Augusta," 2.

138. "Marcus Aurelius," *Encyclopaedia Britannica* (Chicago: Encyclopaedia Britannica, 1963), 14:870; and Wood, "Diva Augusta," 5.

139. "Marcus Aurelius," 871.

140. Ibid., 870.

Philippi under Aurelius, stories of martyrdom would certainly have been familiar—Stephen, Peter, Paul, and Ignatius. After Bishop Polycarp wrote to the Philippians around 110 CE, he may have been martyred during Aurelius's reign,[141] an incident that could have had a strong impact on the faithful. It may also be significant that several Christian writers wrote Apologies to Aurelius, even though he may not have read any of them.[142]

A final connection between Philippi and Mary can be seen in the Heidelberg Coptic Papyrus version of the Acts of Paul and Thecla, dated to the late second century.[143] In a small section on Philippi, a debate rages in Corinth over the humanity of Jesus, including the belief that Jesus was not born of Mary. The papyrus fragment states that Paul was in jail at Philippi when the Corinthian debate was occurring. In his letter to the Corinthians, as reported in Acts of Paul and Thecla, Paul asserts that God "sent the [Holy] Spirit [through fire] into Mary the Galilean, who believed with all her heart, and she received the Holy Spirit in her womb that Jesus might enter into the world."[144] Such a tradition may also have been familiar to Philippian Christians and become part of the growth of veneration to Mary.

Despite the seeming health of the Philippian Christian community in the first century and the growth of interest in, if not also cultic activity to, Mary in the second century, Christianity did not grow and mature exponentially to the point that it became the prominent religious group in the colony by the time of Constantine. The pagan traditions retained their hold, as attested in the early Byzantine era by two important archaeological artifacts found near the city gate of Philippi, along with the altar to Isis mentioned above.

First, an inscription was found that reads, "(Lord Jesus Christ, born of the) Virgin Mary, crucified (for us, help) this city always to remain, (and protect) those who live in it for (your) glory." Dating to the fifth or sixth century,[145] it asks *Jesus* for protection for the city, much as earlier Philippians had invoked the aid of Artemis/Diana and Isis. Since the Jesus petition

141. "Polycarp, St.," in *The Oxford Dictionary of the Christian Church*, ed. F. L. Cross and E. A. Livingstone, 3rd ed. (Oxford: Oxford University Press, 1997), 1306.

142. "Marcus Aurelius," 1035. The article cites Athenagoras, perhaps Theophilus of Antioch, as well as Miltiades, Claudius Apollinarius, and Melito.

143. Wilhelm Schneemelcher, "Acts of Paul," *NTApoc* 2:322–90, esp. 325.

144. Schneemelcher, "Acts of Paul," 373–76.

145. Denis Feissel, *Recueil des inscriptions chrétiennes de Macédoine, du IIIe an*

also mentions Mary, albeit formulaically, the supplications to Jesus and Isis were also tied to devotion to Mary.

Second, a copy of the popular yet spurious correspondence between King Abgar of Edessa and Jesus further attests to people's appeal to Jesus as city protector during times of duress. Dating between the fifth and sixth centuries, the two letters describe Abgar seeking Jesus's help with a medical ailment and Jesus replying that he cannot come himself but will send someone after his ascension. The significant sentences in Jesus's reply refer to help for Abgar's city: "After my ascension I will send you one of my disciples that he may obtain for you and your city and those with you eternal life and peace. And I will make your city strong so that none of your enemies will have power over you, nor will they ever prevail."[146] This further suggests Philippians' appeal to both their ancient goddesses—Artemis/Diana and Isis—and to the new deities—Jesus and his mother—for protection for their city.[147]

At approximately the same time that the Jesus inscription and Abgar-Jesus correspondence were being created and used, women at Philippi were exercising some level of authority in the growing church. Epigraphic evidence from the early Byzantine basilicas for two female deacons—Agatha, buried with her husband John, a treasury official and linen-weaver, and Posidonia, buried with a canoness named Pancharia—suggests a consecrated order of virgins or widows, while the role of deacon could be held by both men and women.[148]

Although there is no direct evidence, to my knowledge, of a specific cult to Mary at Philippi, it is interesting to note the phenomenon of the Collyridians. By the fourth century, Bishop Epiphanius of Salamis (315–403 CE) was ordering the faithful not to worship Mary but only the Father, Son, and Holy Spirit, suggesting that such activity had been transpiring for a while.[149] It was also Epiphanius who condemned the

---

VIe siècle (Paris: de Boccard, 1983), 189–91; Abrahamsen, *Women and Worship in Philippi*, 187–88.

146. It should be noted that the letters on Jesus's response are larger and more widely spaced than those of Abgar's letter.

147. See Charles Picard, "Un texte nouveau de la correspondance entre Abgar D'Osroène et Jésus-Christ gravé sur une porte de ville, à Philippes (Macédoine)," *BCH* 44 (1920): 41–69; and Abrahamsen, *Women and Worship in Philippi*, 179–91.

148. Abrahamsen, "Women at Philippi," 23, 26.

149. Barbara G. Walker, *The Woman's Encyclopedia of Myths and Secrets* (San Francisco: Harper & Row, 1983), 603.

Collyridian sect (*Pan.* 79) which, according to him, originated in Thrace and was composed primarily of women who sacrificed cakes to Mary in a possible parallel to the cult of Ceres (Demeter) or Artemis.[150] Epiphanius betrays his misogyny in *Pan.* 79.1, "For who should it be that teach thus but women? For the race of women is slippery, fallible, and humble-minded." He goes on to explain the difference between Mary being worthy of veneration and worthy of actual worship: "Yea, verily, the body of Mary was holy, but was surely not God. Verily, the Virgin was a virgin, and was honoured, but was not given to us to worship." The Collyridian sect may have lasted for as long as one hundred years, between 350 and 450 CE, which is not insignificant.

Therefore, we can see that women played important roles in the religious groups at Philippi and thus in the community at large for centuries. Philippian women (and men) at all levels of society continued to revere their ancient deities into the early Byzantine era, while seeming also to incorporate veneration of both Jesus and his mother as time went on. Women like Euodia, Syntyche, and Lydia were paramount in the mission of Paul, and Mary later became equated with traditional goddesses such as Artemis/Bendis and Isis. The syncretistic worship of Dionysos with Liber, Libera, and Herakles further shows the diversity of worship patterns and the inclusion of female objects of devotion and women's leadership. In this dynamic time, one challenged by internal and external threats, it appears that most Philippians, pagan and Christian, elite and marginalized, revered and served all of these—Artemis/Diana/Bendis, Jesus, Isis, Mary, and Dionysos—in order to obtain help, protection, social support, and identity. Women's roles, especially the leadership, high standing in society, sociopolitical connections, and wealth of those from elite families, would have been essential in this dynamic.

Conclusions

From our examination of the Livia cult and the monument to her in the Philippi forum; the veneration of Faustina the Younger; the role of women in traditional cults at Philippi and the surrounding area; the evidence from Paul's letter to the Philippians, Acts, Polycarp's epistle, and various apocryphal writings; evidence from the early Byzantine era; and

---

150. "Mariolatry," *Oxford Dictionary of the Christian Church*, 874.

modern demographic work, we can see that women played important roles in religious groups at both participant and leadership levels from the time of Paul onward. Women from elite, wealthy families, like their peers throughout the empire, used their wealth in service to their communities through the building of monuments, structures, statues, and worship spaces to garner favor with other elite families in the community, to act as patrons, and to demonstrate the carrying out of the duties inherent in their stations in life. Through voluntary associations, even nonelite women could participate and serve as leaders and patrons in groups that offered them and their families certain benefits.

In the first century, women at Philippi and the surrounding area—priestesses named on the Livia monument, donors in the Dionysos/LLH cult, Artemis worshipers on Thasos, Euodia, Syntyche, and Lydia—were fulfilling religious roles in the service of their communities and their voluntary associations similar to those that had existed for at least several centuries. These would have been many of the "people beside Paul." As Christianity took hold and grew during the second century, not only through worship of Jesus but also through the growing veneration of his mother, emperor/empress cult also grew. The cultural conversation and/or competition between Christianity and emperor/empress cult, along with the continuing devotion to pagan deities such as Artemis/Diana, Isis, and Dionysos/LLH, gave women ongoing opportunities to participate in religious activities that served their families and communities and also offered them solidarity with others, the assurance of a proper funeral, and in some cases hope in a life after death, a reunification with their deity, and participation in a heavenly banquet.

We can further conjecture that, in an atmosphere of imperial oppression, consistent poverty and want, and sporadic persecution of Christians, some women and men used their association and cultic memberships and influence to protest against or attempt to undermine the injustices around them. While women, even freeborn citizens or slaves who gained their freedom and accumulated wealth, were not able to participate in the political system like upper-strata men, they still exercised what influence they could have within the important religious context to fulfill their duties and serve their communities. We can hope to find more evidence of women's involvement at Philippi and the surrounding area as archaeological, literary, sociological, and hermeneutical knowledge expands.

The Economic Situation
of the Philippian Christians

Peter Oakes

In contrast to other places, the [Christian] community is probably composed not of the proletariat but mainly of members of the middle class,
so there are no gross social differences, and the suspicion of favoring
those with property and disadvantaging those without cannot arise if
Paul accepts some gifts. The veterans settled in Philippi are not slaves but
free people, who mainly own their land.... A church that is financially so
well placed can give Paul material support.[1]

Texts give us access not only to their author's message but also, with varying degrees of clarity, to historical evidence on a wide range of subjects:
evidence of linguistic usage at the time of the text; evidence of cultural
reference points and their significance; evidence of social structures, practices, and norms; and evidence of events and people. In the case of Philippians, we learn some significant points about the community of people to
whom Paul is writing. Understanding these people is important in itself,
as the present volume argues. It also helps our understanding of what the
letter means. Seriously inaccurate descriptions of the Philippian Christian

---

1. "Im Gegensatz zu andern Orten setzt sich diese Gemeinde warscheinlich nicht
aus Proletariat, sondern größtenteils aus Angehörigen des Mittelstandes zusammen,
so daß es keine krassen sozialen Unterschiede gibt und der Verdacht auf Bevorzu-
gung und Benachteiligung von Besitzenden und Besitzlosen nicht entstehen kann,
wenn Paulus irgendwelche Gaben annimt. Die in Philippi angesiedelten Veteranen
sind keine Sklaven, sondern freie Menschen, die meistenteils Grundbesitz als Eigen-
tum haben.... Eine Gemeinde, die finanziell so gut gestellt ist, kann Paulus materiell
unterstützen." My translation of Gerhard Friedrich, "Der Brief an die Philipper," *Die
kleineren Briefe des Apostels Paulus*, ed. H. W. Beyer et al., 9th ed., NTD 8 (Göttingen:
Vandenhoeck & Ruprecht, 1962), 92–93.

community, such as the one above, from Gerhard Friedrich's major 1962 commentary on the letter, distort the reading of the text. For instance, should the military metaphors in Philippians (e.g., 2:25) be read as a friendly accommodation to the cultural world of veteran soldiers hearing the letter, or are the hearers a group for whom military language might carry quite different connotations?

Community descriptions have many dimensions. Friedrich's description explicitly picks up on social class and on slave/free and military/non-military characteristics. These also imply dimensions of gender and of ethnicity (Roman/non-Roman). His particular interest is economic. This links to a prominent issue in the letter, that of the Philippians' gift to Paul (Phil 4:10–20). I will argue below that it also links to the topic of suffering in the letter. More broadly, any study of history from below must give very serious attention to economic matters. The very invisibility of most people in most historic textual evidence stems largely from their lack of access to resources: their economic exclusion. Moreover, for most people, the economic struggle looms very large indeed in their experience of life. The economic dimension is a key element of community description.

Gregory Bloomquist, writing in *Interpretation*, takes me to task for over-emphasizing economic suffering in my understanding of suffering among the Philippian Christians in *Philippians: From People to Letter*. He argues that I overlook the horrors of even a short stay in a Roman prison and of possible attacks such as the malicious burning of a Christian's field. As an example of such suffering, he cites the struggles over water supplies in Marcel Pagnol's *Manon des sources*.[2] Bloomquist's first point is well made. The horror of even a night in a Roman prison could haunt a person for a long time (see the vivid evidence presented by Angela Standhartinger in her chapter of this volume). However, his other points suggest that he and I are operating with different definitions of the word "economic." Burning of fields or the denial of water supply would be exactly the kinds of activities that I would see as economic attacks, causing economic suffering. A typical hypothetical example that I use in my book is of a baker being denied access to communal oven space.[3]

---

2. L. Gregory Bloomquist, "Subverted by Joy: Suffering and Joy in Paul's Letter to the Philippians," *Int* 61 (2007): 270–83, here 278 n. 34. Marcel Pagnol, *Manon des sources: L'Eau des collines* (Paris: Editions Flammarion, 1995).

3. Peter S. Oakes, *Philippians: From People to Letter*, SNTSMS 110 (Cambridge: Cambridge University Press, 2001), 89–91.

There are many possible definitions of "economics." The one that I am currently using is a fairly broad one: "the study of the allocation of scarce resources." Although this definition springs from modern economic theory,[4] it seems appropriate for any period. "Scarce resources" include money, labor, slaves, fields, and even water when its supply is under someone's control. Economics covers patterns of allocation of such resources, processes of allocation, and the identity or experiences of people either doing the allocating or receiving the allocations. However, a key thing to remember when applying a modern economic definition to an ancient setting is that ancient economies were what Karl Polanyi calls "embedded economies." Economic decisions in such economies were heavily dependent on power relationships. Resources were not primarily allocated by market forces.[5]

This chapter will present arguments for an alternative to Friedrich's economically optimistic evaluation of the situation of the Philippian Christians. It will also point to a couple of factors that suggest strategies that were available to the community in the face of economic difficulties. The starting points for most arguments will be texts from Philippians, with further evidence from Acts 16 and 2 Cor 8:1–4. Economic questions will be considered in relation to factors such as ethnicity, gender, work, suffering, and group structure.

"At Philippi": Philippians 1:1: The Socioeconomic Structure of the Town

One obvious starting point for understanding the community of the letter's recipients is the specifying of the place to which it was sent. Friedrich's description of the community rests on a view of the nature of the

---

4. Especially Lionel Robbins's *Essay on the Nature and Significance of Economic Science* (London: Macmillan, 1932). However, current textbook definitions tend to emphasise *choice*, e.g., Michael Parkin, *Economics*, 7th ed. (Boston: Addison Wesley, 2005), 2. For discussion of possible definitions and their implications see Peter S. Oakes, "Methodological Issues in Using Economic Evidence in Interpretation of Early Christian Texts," in *Engaging Economics: New Testament Scenarios and Early Christian Reception* (ed. Bruce W. Longenecker and Kelly D. Liebengood; Grand Rapids: Eerdmans, 2009), 9–34, esp. 11–12. See also Oakes, "Economic Approaches: Scarce Resources and Interpretive Opportunities," in *Studying Paul's Letters: Contemporary Perspectives and Methods*, ed. Joseph A. Marchal (Minneapolis: Fortress, 2012), 72–91, 77.

5. Karl Polanyi, et al., *Trade and Market in the Early Empires* (Chicago: Henry Regnery, 1971), 250.

population of the town as a whole.[6] At one level, his view appears to contain an error so broad as to be comic: his description collapses the century between the colonization of Philippi and the time of Paul's writing, giving the impression that the veterans who arrived in 42 and 30 BCE are still sitting there in the 50's or early 60's CE, having just taken off their armor and now waiting to hear what Paul says. Once we begin thinking more realistically about the time gap, we also become aware that there are a host of further issues in terms of what the society as a whole would have looked like, given that it was not simply a group of recently demobilized soldiers.

Philippi was a modest-sized Hellenistic town with an economic base in mining, agriculture, and, from the second century BCE, its location on the trade route of the Via Egnatia. In 42 BCE it was the site of the final battle of the Roman civil war following Julius Caesar's assassination. It then became part of a particularly brutal process of colonization. Of all Rome's colonizations, those of 42 BCE were the most controversial for Roman writers. Antony and Octavian donated to their veterans land from eighteen wealthy cities in Italy, causing outrage and local rebellion.[7] Philippi, the forward base of their defeated opponents, was suddenly added to this list after the battle outside its western walls. Here, there were not even the legal, moral, and political constraints that were overridden in Italy. The victors could take whatever they wanted. Unlike Italy, there was no one to document the dispossession of Greek farmers at Philippi. Whether they had owned the land or whether they had farmed it as tenants, the scarce resource of the fertile plain around Philippi would usually have been heavily farmed. The attractive fertility was, in fact, undoubtedly the Greek town's downfall. The issues at stake for the local region in the battle of Philippi are made dramatically clear by the report that Brutus, based at Philippi, had promised to his soldiers that, if they were victorious, they could sack Thessalonica (Plutarch, *Brut.* 46.1), which was a key supply base for, and supporter of, Antony and Octavian. In the event, the reverse took place. Antony and Octavian won the battle, declared Thessalonica a "free city," and colonized Philippi.

---

6. This is also true of many similar descriptions of the recipients, e.g., Kenneth L. Barker, ed., *The NIV Study Bible*, UK ed. (London: Hodder and Stoughton, 1987), 1767.

7. See, e.g., Appian, *Bell. civ.* 5.12.

What would this Roman colonization of the Greek town of Philippi have done to the socioeconomic structure of the town? Most New Testament scholars have imagined the population of Philippi to have been mainly Roman. One factor has been that Luke highlights the Romanness of the town (Acts 16:12, 20), and Paul alludes to Roman institutions (Phil 1:13; 4:15 [using a Latin loanword]; 4:22). Another has been the assumption that a town that is a Roman colony consists mainly of Romans. A third factor has been that most of the known inscriptions from first- and second-century CE Philippi are in Latin. This point is the most weighty and brings us to economic issues. The prevalence of Latin inscriptions reflects the relative status and wealth of Romans and non-Romans. If we remove the elite inscriptions from the reckoning, there are relatively few left—there is not a plethora of inscriptions from nonelite Romans. The Roman elite at Philippi kept tight control of power and wealth. Greeks show up at the economic margins. The temple inscriptions in the forum are in Latin, but the builders' marks on the joints of the columns are Greek.[8] In fact, as the scholar with probably the most thorough understanding of the Philippian inscriptions, Peter Pilhofer argues, the town would probably have had a majority of non-Romans.[9]

Turning to the issue of ownership: at colonization, the Romans would have taken almost all the good farming land in easy reach of the city. Although the "centuriation" patterns of colonial land allocation at Philippi have not survived, for comparison those around Corinth are very comprehensive.[10] Land ownership was spread (according to rank) among several thousand veteran soldiers. However, the discovery of quite a number of inscriptions of stewards of estates around Philippi is clear evidence of concentration of land-holding over the decades following the initial colonial distribution of the land among the veterans. Most strikingly, one landowner's steward has inscriptions on estates 38 kilometers apart.[11] Although

8. Paul Collart, *Philippes, Ville de Macédoine: depuis ses origines jusqu'à la fin de l'époque romaine*, Travaux et Mémoires 5 (Paris: École Française d'Athènes, 1937), 305.

9. Peter Pilhofer, *Philippi I: Die erste christliche Gemeinde Europas*, WUNT 87 (Tübingen: Mohr Siebeck, 1995), 92.

10. David G. Romano, "Urban and Rural Planning in Roman Corinth," in *Urban Religion in Roman Corinth: Interdisciplinary Approaches*, ed. Daniel Schowalter and Steven J. Friesen, HTS 53 (Cambridge: Harvard University Press, 2005), 25–59 (43–53).

11. Collart, *Philippes*, 289; Oakes, *Philippians*, 33.

some of these estates were likely built up by the colonial elite acquiring land beyond the area of the original distribution, there was probably also a strong process of the elite taking over land from the peasant colonists and their descendants. The absence of Greeks among the epigraphic remains of the elite implies that the elite at Philippi was now solidly Roman. In the first century CE, a few percent of the population, Roman elite families owned almost all the land, other property, and most slaves. Ownership of remaining land was mainly in the hands of those descendants of colonists whose families had not lost possession to the elite.

In terms of tenancy, the implication of the above is that most Romans and almost all Greeks who used land or urban property rented it from the Roman elite. At colonization, all the Romans were, in principle, farmers. Even after a century, probably a substantial majority of farmers living in or near the town were Roman, albeit mainly now as tenants rather than owners. The other tenants in the town either provided goods and services for those bringing in income from the land (and for each other) or were engaged in external trade.

Since at colonization, all the Romans were, in principle, farmers, the nonfarming free population, who sought income as craftworkers, traders, prostitutes, beggars, et cetera, would, at that point, be almost entirely Greek, that is, Macedonians, Greek-speaking immigrants such as Lydia, or Greek-speaking groups with affiliations to the culture of Thrace to the northeast of Philippi. During the following century, some Romans will have become nonfarmers, because they lost their land. Freed slaves, who were Roman citizens, will also have become part of the nonfarming population. The majority of nonfarmers will still have been non-Roman, but there will eventually have been a significant minority of Roman nonfarmers. In addition to household heads (usually male), who would be primary beneficiaries of income, the population included women, children, and various other types of dependent. All these would, in general, have had less access to resources than household heads would. In addition to the free population, there was a substantial number of both agricultural and urban slaves.

Although, as Lukas Bormann argues, there were still sufficient veteran soldiers settling at Philippi in the first century CE for them to be a significant factor in the town's governance and sense of identity[12] (epigraphic

---

12. Lukas Bormann, *Philippi: Stadt und Christengemeinde zur Zeit des Paulus,* NovTSup 78 (Leiden: Brill, 1995), 28.

evidence supports this), these were members of the small elite group in the town. Less well off first century veterans tended to settle close to their place of military service, where land was cheap and they might well already have families, rather than buy land in a relatively expensive, long-settled location such as Philippi. It is extremely unlikely that there were sufficient veterans in Philippi at the time of Paul's letter for them to have formed a substantial proportion of the recipients of the letter.[13]

Where within the socioeconomic structure that we have depicted would we find the Philippian Christians? A number of points in Philippians and elsewhere give us indications.

A Greek Letter to Predominantly Greek Recipients in Philippi

There is nothing unusual about Philippians being written in Greek. This was the case with all of the earliest Christian texts. There is not even anything unusual about a group of people at Philippi being able to understand Greek. Despite it being a Roman colony, the town's location meant that everyone would surely have been able to speak Greek. However, for a group in Philippi to be such that letters addressed to the group were in Greek gives us economically significant evidence about them.

The inscriptions carved into the hillside near the path to the theatre that list members of the association of the *cultores* of Sylvanus are written in Latin. The use of Latin at Philippi extends beyond official civic inscriptions in the forum to reach groups whose members included some of the elite, as well as other people of a range of statuses.[14] The Christian association at Philippi was not part of the town's Latin culture. It existed outside the locus of power, and because this was an embedded economy, this meant that the Christian group was also outside the main locus of economic success.

The impression of Greekness produced by the language in which the letter is written is reinforced by the names in the letter. Three of the named Philippians are Greek—Euodia, Syntyche, and Epaphroditus—and only one is Roman—Clement. Although it is unsafe to extrapolate far from a short list of people, the set of names acts as a useful confirmation of a general model of the Philippian Christian group as predominantly Greek.

---

13. For fuller discussion see Oakes, *Philippians*, 24–29, 50–54.

14. Peter Pilhofer, *Philippi II: Katalog der Inschriften von Philippi*. WUNT 119 (Tübingen: Mohr Siebeck, 2000), 163–66.

Conversely, it is quite strong evidence against a model of the Christian group as predominantly Roman. If the model of the Christian community is, say, two thirds non-Roman and one third Roman,[15] the probability of a random group of four members including at least three Greeks is more than 50/50. For the reverse model, with two thirds Romans and one third non-Romans, the probability would be less than one in eight. More broadly, having argued, above, that Romans were probably in a minority in the town, it becomes apparent that, in a reasonable model of the Christian community, where we would expect Romans to be underrepresented, we would certainly expect Romans to be in the minority.[16]

The experience of being a Greek in a Roman colony varied widely from place to place. In Asia Minor, "Romanization" of such places generally faded fairly rapidly.[17] In Corinth, the very layout of the forum, in which even the Roman buildings abandoned the colonial grid layout to follow earlier Greek orientations,[18] suggests ambiguity in the colonization there. A practical indicator was that, as Anthony Spawforth shows, five Greeks held the chief Roman magistracy in the first century.[19] Nothing like that seems to have happened at Philippi. Although the Romans could not do away with the Greek walls and theatre, they stamped the town center with an uncompromisingly Roman form. The colonial elite held power firmly.

As well as being excluded from most land ownership around the town, Greeks were excluded from citizenship.[20] Their main route of access to Roman citizenship (short of going away to serve in the army) would have

---

15. See the suggested figures in Oakes, *Philippians*, 61.

16. See ibid., 14–70.

17. Barbara Levick, *Roman Colonies in Southern Asia Minor* (Oxford: Clarendon, 1967), 161–62.

18. Romano, "Urban and Rural Planning," 30–41.

19. A. J. S. Spawforth, "Roman Corinth: The Formation of a Colonial Elite," in *Roman Onomastics in the Greek East: Social and Political Aspects*, ed. A. D. Rizakis, Meltēmata 21 (Athens: Research Center for Greek and Roman Antiquity; Paris: de Boccard, 1996), 167–82 (169); discussed in James Walters, "Civic Identity in Roman Corinth and Its Impact on Early Christians," in Friesen and Schowalter, *Urban Religion in Roman Corinth*, 397–417 (408).

20. For the unlikelihood of a grant of citizenship to a substantial number of Greeks at the time of colonization, see Adrian N. Sherwin-White, *The Roman Citizenship*, 2nd ed. (Oxford: Clarendon, 1973), 352; Peter A. Brunt, *Italian Manpower: 225 BC–AD 14* (Oxford: Oxford University Press, 1987), 253.

been for the elite only, via holding of magistracies,[21] but, as we have noted, the Greek elite disappeared after the colonization. Lack of citizenship had economic consequences. It meant liability to some taxes from which Romans were exempt. It also prevented access to various legal procedures.[22] This would have made it very difficult to resist expropriation of property.

For a nonelite Roman who owned property, the main route to avoid economic oppression by someone from the elite would generally have been to appeal to an elite patron for help. Such a patron could have helped in various ways in regard to legal matters. Patrons were also structurally important in various economic areas. Greeks would generally be excluded from Roman patronage and would thus be excluded both from the various resources controlled by patrons and from the possibility of a patron's brokerage with higher members of the elite.

Roman Craftworkers and the Like: 1 Thessalonians 4:11

The common scholarly view of the socioeconomic location of early Christians sees them as typically being craftworking families, traders, and so on. This is exemplified by the note about "working with your hands" in 1 Thess 4:11. This Thessalonian economic picture is actually particularly relevant for thinking about the Philippian Christians, because one effect of 2 Cor 8:1–4 is to lump together, economically, the Macedonian Christians. Paul gives the impression that the situation of poverty and suffering is the same across the various assemblies in the province. It would be beyond the scope of this paper to attempt a general discussion of the economic situation of first-century craftworkers. However, it is interesting to reflect on what it would mean, in Philippi, for Roman members of the church to be craftworkers and the like.

Although most Philippian Christians were probably not Roman, I suspect that Pilhofer's overstates this in describing Romans as *eine verschwindende Minderheit*, a vanishingly small minority.[23] A significant minority seem likely to have been Roman. Clement (Phil 4:3) is one out of four named recipients. My model of the Christian assembly at Philippi had

---

21. Peter Garnsey, *Social Status and Legal Privilege in the Roman Empire* (Oxford: Clarendon, 1970), 266.
22. Garnsey, *Social Status*, 262.
23. Pilhofer, *Philippi I*, 244.

about a third of the members being Roman.[24] There was possibly a higher proportion of Roman citizens there than in any other Pauline assembly.

In socioeconomic terms, who would these Romans have been? There are no signs of members of the colonial elite. There might have been some members of families of commuting peasant farmers: descendants of the original veteran colonist families still living in town and travelling out to their fields. However, the social groups more accessible to Paul and his followers, where his message is most likely to have made ground, are those engaged in town-based work, that is, craftworking families and people with similar occupations.

If our Roman Philippian Christians are members of craftworking families, this puts them mainly into either of two socioeconomic groups. First, they could be dispossessed peasant colonist families. As Joseph Marchal highlights, this process would have given many of the peasant colonist families a rather negative view of their colony (a colony that many of the settlers would also not have wanted to come to in the first place).[25] If a peasant family (i.e., a family dependent on farming a very small area of land) lost ownership of their land (often through foreclosure on a debt),[26] they might become tenants of the new owner. Much estate land was let out, rather than being farmed by slaves.[27] Alternatively, they might switch to a town-based occupation such as craftwork, possibly supplemented by casual farm work as hired help at peak seasons. These Roman, ex-peasant craftworkers would, in general, be on the same economic level as Greek craftworkers. However, the Romans would have the advantage of citizenship—although this was of limited economic significance for people without property. They would also have tended to have patronage links with better-off Romans. Ironically, a member of the elite who had lent them money, foreclosed on the debt, and taken their land was their most likely patron. Such patronage would have given client craftworkers some

---

24. Oakes, *Philippians*, 61.

25. Joseph A. Marchal, *Hierarchy, Unity, and Imitation: A Feminist Rhetorical Analysis of Power Dynamics in Paul's Letter to the Philippians*, Academia Biblica 24 (Atlanta: Society of Biblical Literature, 2006), 104–6.

26. Douglas E. Oakman, "The Countryside in Luke-Acts," in *The Social World of Luke-Acts*, ed. Jerome H. Neyrey (Peabody, MA: Hendrickson, 1991), 151–79 (157–58).

27. Philippe Leveau, *Caesarea de Maurétanie: Une Ville Romaine et ses Campagnes*, Collection de l'école française de Rome 70 (Rome: École Fr., 1984), 475.

economically tangible advantages: maybe, for example, in providing ways into networks of customers.

The second major group of Roman craftworkers would have been freed slaves and their descendants. Craig de Vos puts particular emphasis on this group in his socioeconomic analysis of the Philippian Christians. He argues that the Greek names in Philippians suggest that the Christians were largely freed slaves and hence Roman citizens—a radical difference from my own analysis.[28] It seems to me that de Vos mixes up the social significance of a Greek name in Rome with the social significance of a Greek name in Greece. As Pertti Huttunen shows, a study of epitaphs in Rome reveals that many people with Greek names were freed slaves.[29] A similar survey carried out in Greece, although it would pick up some slaves with Greek *cognomina*, would mainly reveal merely that most people with Greek names were Greek. More specifically, a difficulty with de Vos's view of Philippi is that his strongly Roman social structure would really need to have had, right from the beginning of the colony, the great majority of craftworking roles in the town filled by freed slaves. Since Philippi was not a general Roman colony like Corinth, many of whose initial colonists were freed slaves, but a veteran colony, all of whose initial colonists were veteran soldiers, this does not seem possible. At the beginning of the colony, most craftworking roles must have been filled by Greeks. Greeks will then have continued to fill most such roles.

Freed slaves automatically had patronal links with their former owner. This could be an economic drain on the freed slave's resources because of demands for continued unpaid, or poorly paid, service. Freed slaves were also often in financially precarious situations, because many either would have had to use most of their money (their *peculium*, the money earned from tips and customarily viewed as theirs, despite legally belonging to their owner) to buy their freedom or would have been freed only because they were now too infirm to be of economic benefit to their owners. On the other hand, the patronal links of freed slaves were often of benefit to them, especially as craftworking freed slaves. For instance, they would often have

28. Craig S. de Vos, *Church and Community Conflicts: The Relationships of the Thessalonian, Corinthian, and Philippian Christians with Their Wider Civic Communities*, SBLDS 168 (Atlanta: Scholars Press, 1999), 252–60.

29. Pertti Huttunen, *The Social Strata in the Imperial City of Rome: A Quantitative Study of the Social Representation in the Epitaphs published in the Corpus Inscriptionum Latinarum Volumen VI* (Oulu: University of Oulu, 1974).

been simply continuing to work in a business set up for them by their owner when they were slaves (although, in that case, they would also no doubt have been still giving part of the profit to their former owner). Some freed slaves were wealthy. There are examples of sarcophagi of such people at Philippi. However, freed slaves were excluded from political power, and, in most cases, they had little economic power.

Founded on a Women's Prayer Meeting: Acts 16:13–15

Whatever scenario one adopts for the composition of Acts, particular historical weight should probably be put on accounts of founding members of communities. Such memories are particularly likely to be preserved and to find their way into narratives. The story relating to Lydia and the gathering for prayer by the river is particularly interesting, because it goes against elements of the more typical patterns in Acts. In any case, at the time of Philippians, there are at least two Christian women, Euodia and Syntyche, who are prominent enough to be specially addressed in the letter. If, as these points suggest, the early Christian group at Philippi was predominantly female, this would only be in line with the general impression of the composition of Christian groups then and indeed in other periods.

If we take it that most of the Philippian Christians were women, what are the effects on our economic picture of the community? One effect is that, whatever the average social status of the Christians, they would not have access to the level of economic resources that we might normally associate with that status. Most economic resources were held by men. Wives, daughters, and sisters might share something of the status level of the male head of the household, but they would not have full access to the economic resources that typically went with that status. To take an example: if the daughter of a member of the decuriate, the town council, was a Christian, we would say that there was a member of the town's elite social group in the Christian assembly. However, the daughter would bring into the Christian group hardly any of the economic resources that her father had. An elite Christian woman did not represent the same economic resource to the group as an elite Christian man. There were exceptions to this rule, but it was generally true and not only for the elite but at all levels of society, even those where a family worked together as a unit.

A second economic effect of a predominance of women would be economic precariousness. All first-century life was precarious. A woman's economic life was particularly so, because she was generally dependent on a man. The risk of some economic resources being cut off from the Christian group was heightened by the financial dependence of women on men, especially where the man was not himself part of the group. In many cases, the sharpest form of this danger was divorce. Lilian Portefaix notes the economic consequences of this and the closing down of one possible resource in such situations by Christian intolerance of prostitution.[30]

Episkopoi and *Diakonoi*: Philippians 1:1

The fact that the Christian group has some designated officers makes it sound like an association of some kind. Pilhofer notes the comparison between the titles of Christian officers and those of the prominent local cult association of the *Heros Auloneites*.[31] Richard Ascough has also drawn similarities between the Christian groups in Macedonia and associations, especially craft-related ones.[32] It is not clear what the economic consequences of this comparison might be. Associations tended not to be economic mutual support groups, except in arranging payment for burial. Associations typically had a wealthy patron who paid for some communal meals. However, as de Vos argues, it is rather unlikely that the Philippian Christian group had such a patron.[33]

One implication of Paul's reference to several officers is that the Philippian Christian assembly was not very small. Such a level of organization would make little sense in a group of less than about twenty. The group is probably fifty upwards, in other words, some way above being just a few families—the larger the group, the wider the range of possible strategies for economic survival. On the other hand, larger groups are likely to be less homogeneous. Socioeconomic diversity and consequently tension are more possible.

---

30. Lilian Portefaix, *Sisters Rejoice: Paul's Letter to the Philippians and Luke-Acts as Received by First Century Philippian Women*, ConBNT 20 (Stockholm: Almqvist & Wiksell, 1988), 181–82.

31. Pilhofer, *Philippi I*, 140.

32. Richard S. Ascough, *Paul's Macedonian Associations: The Social Context of Philippians and 1 Thessalonians*, WUNT 2/161 (Tübingen: Mohr Siebeck, 2003).

33. de Vos, *Church and Community Conflicts*, 259.

Financial Support from Philippi: Philippians 4:10–20

The most specific piece of economic evidence in Philippians is Paul's expression of appreciation at the Philippian Christians having sent him a gift that, given its portability and relevance to a prisoner, must have been money (Phil 4:18). Moreover, he backs up his compliments by recalling their previous generosity when he was in Thessalonica (Phil 4:15). It is no wonder that scholars of Philippians tend to see the Christians as fairly well off, contrary to 2 Cor 8:1–4.

However, the argument from the Philippians' support of Paul to their supposedly comfortable financial position is far from compelling. The limited size of the probable sums of money involved in Philippian support of Paul is made particularly clear by 1 Thess 2:9. In a mission when he was receiving repeated financial support from Philippi ("also in Thessalonica you supplied my needs more than once," Phil 4:15), he could describe himself to the Thessalonians as having been "working night and day so as not to be some burden on you." Irrespective of the way in which the rhetoric of the two letters might be working, 1 Thess 2:9 and Phil 4:15 provide strong evidence that Paul was both receiving money from the Philippians and still doing craftwork in order to provide basic sustenance. This suggests that the group of people in Philippi are providing less that the living requirements of one or two craftworkers. This is not an amount of money that gives any indication of substantial economic resources among the Philippian Christians. They could be very poor and yet manage, as a group, to gather together a sum of a *sestertius* or two per day to send to Paul. It might well involve some financial sacrifice, but it does not require a significant average wealth among the group. To make the point cross-culturally: there are many churches of the very poor that manage to provide for at least the part-time financial support of a pastor.

Friedrich supports his view of the Philippian Christians with an implicit moral point: Paul could reasonably be willing to accept their financial support, because the community was *finanziell so gut gestellt* ("financially so well placed").[34] However, Paul does not seem to think about support in the way most of us would. As he says to the Corinthians, "I robbed other assemblies by receiving support from them so as to serve you" (2 Cor 11:8). The Corinthians were willing to support him, but, instead, he

---

34. Friedrich, "Der Brief an die Philipper," 93.

accepted money from assemblies in Macedonia (2 Cor 11:9) who were financially so badly placed that accepting their money was tantamount to robbery. It would be beyond the scope of this paper to explore Paul's surprising financial motivations. However, the historical point is that his decisions on accepting money for his support seem to have had no correlation with the level of financial resources in the supporting community.

Deep Poverty in Macedonia: 2 Corinthians 8:1–4

As part of Paul's attempt to persuade the Corinthians to participate in the collection for Jerusalem, he draws a comparison:

> I want you to know, brothers and sisters, the grace of God that has been given to the assemblies of Macedonia, that, during a severe testing in suffering, the overflow of their joy and their deep poverty have overflowed in the richness of their generosity. I testify that, according to their ability—even beyond their ability—they begged of us, with much earnestness, the favor and the sharing in the service for the holy ones. (2 Cor 8:1–4)

If Philippians was written in Ephesus, 2 Corinthians is from close to the same date. If Philippians is from Rome, it postdates 2 Corinthians by about seven years. In either case, the letters are close enough in time for this text to be relevant to our study. Paul refers to the Roman province of Macedonia. From his letters we know of Christian groups in Philippi and Thessalonica. Acts agrees with this and would add Beroea to the west of Thessalonica. Paul's assertions in these verses almost certainly include Philippi. This is especially likely because two of the points described, that the Macedonians are suffering and that they are giving, are attested of the Philippians elsewhere.

The phrase "deep poverty" is, in two senses, a relative term. First, it must imply that the Macedonian Christians have fewer economic resources than the Corinthians. This is essential to the rhetorical thrust of the passage. Second, it must imply that Paul sees the Macedonian Christians as being considerably poorer than was typical of first-century life as Paul had experienced it. Since the average first-century life was one of economic struggle, the Macedonian Christians' struggle must have been fairly extreme.

Wayne Meeks wisely cautions against getting too carried away by 2 Cor 8:1–4 as historical evidence. As he points out, in the very next chapter, Paul, astonishingly, admits to having also worked his rhetorical

strategy in reverse—having urged on the Macedonians' giving by telling them about the generosity of the Achaians (2 Cor 9:1–5).[35] However, the particular rhetorical elements about poverty and suffering in
8:1–4 seem very unlikely to have been used by Paul both ways. Paul gives
many indicators that he sees some Corinthians as not being poor (most
directly, Rom 16:2, 23). Moreover, he not only makes reference to Macedonian suffering and poverty but does so with very marked emphasis:
suffering "with great testing," poverty that is of "depth." We will have to
bring in other evidence to assess the extent and nature of the Philippian Christians' poverty that is attested in 2 Cor 8:1–4. However, this text
undoubtedly needs to be taken seriously—more seriously than scholars
have tended to do so far.

Suffering for the Sake of Christ: Philippians 1:29, et cetera

Bloomquist is right to highlight the theme of suffering in Philippians.[36]
Suffering runs right through the letter: the sufferings of Paul, of Christ, of
Epaphroditus, of the Philippians. Moreover, the cases of suffering are tied
together: Paul's with that of the Philippians (1:30; 2:17–18), Paul's with that
of Christ (3:10), Christ's with that of the Philippians (2:5, 8), even that of
Epaphroditus is brought into the general pattern by the rhetoric about him
risking his life on account of the work of Christ (2:30).

I would argue that, in general, the most prominent form of long-
term suffering because of a belief or practice tends to be economic. This
is especially so in Roman society where long-term imprisonment was not
normally used as a sanction.[37] Even though particular incidents such as
a beating would be highly traumatic, long-term problems would relate
mainly to economic issues. In the case of a beating, the key long-term issue
would surely be whether economically significant maiming took place? In
the marginal economic circumstances that characterized first-century life,
economic impairment was usually the most pressing danger.

---

35. Wayne A. Meeks, *The First Urban Christians: The Social World of the Apostle
Paul* (New Haven: Yale University Press, 1983), 65–66.

36. L. Gregory Bloomquist, *The Function of Suffering in Philippians*, JSNTSup 78
(Sheffield: JSOT Press, 1993), chs. 7–10.

37. Walter Eder, "Prison Sentence," *Brill's New Pauly*, ed. Hubert Cancik and
Helmuth Schneider, http://www.encquran.brill.nl/entries/brill-s-new-pauly/prison-
sentence-e420370.

The embedded nature of the ancient economy increases the likelihood of economic suffering for what was viewed as deviant practice, such as Christians' failure to continue honoring the Greco-Roman gods. Economic activity depended more on relationships and power than on the market. Portefaix's highlighting of the economic consequences of divorce is one example. Another would be the dangers facing a freed slave if he or she was found to be engaging in activities that their patron viewed as shameful. One way or another, everyone was dependent on economically vital relationships.

As with the poverty of the Philippian Christians, scholars are often rather reluctant to accept the historical evidence of suffering among the group. Even if they do accept it, they rarely explore the question of what that meant in practice. What could it involve? Execution or murder is unlikely to have taken place. They would have marked the letter more specifically. Long-term imprisonment, to make the parallel with Paul in 1:30 true in the most literal way, is unlikely, because it was not normal Roman punitive practice. On the other hand, Paul could have heard reports of, say, verbal abuse, damage to property, loss of trade, beatings by ordinary people or by order of magistrates, divorce, or disownment by families and patrons. Some of these are directly economic. All were likely to have economic consequences, bringing dishonor that endangered economically vital relationships. In the long term, after the abusive slogans have been painted over, after the bruises have healed, the most frequent deterioration of the Christian's daily life—their most common form of suffering—must surely have been in the exacerbation of the endemic precariousness of first-century economic existence.

Called to Mutual Support: Philippians 2:4

A sign that economic suffering was likely to be a factor in Philippi lies in the inextricable intertwining of themes of suffering and unity in Paul's letter. This is most obvious in the structure of Phil 1:27–2:4. The call to stand firm (Phil 1:27) is immediately linked to unity. After the reference to their suffering (Phil 1:29–30), Paul launches into impassioned rhetoric about unity, culminating with a call to look to each others' interests (Phil 2:1–4). This call to stand united under suffering seems to be Paul's most urgent concern in the letter.[38]

---

38. Theories such as that of Bruce Winter (*Seek the Welfare of the City: Christians*

A call to look to each other's interests in a time of suffering is clearly a natural and vital exhortation. In a time of threat to a group, group solidarity is an essential quality. However, it must be more than a quality. It must be a practice. What sort of practice would this mean for the Philippians? Take a step back and imagine what it means today for a poor church congregation living under an oppressive dictatorship. It could mean writing to the regional governor asking for the release of a congregation member in prison—although that might be counterproductive. It might well mean visiting the prisoner—although that would be dangerous. However, what it would certainly mean is taking meals to the prisoner's family who may have lost a key breadwinner or in other ways offering hospitality and economic support. Whatever forms of mutual support Paul expected of the Philippians, the list would surely include mutual economic support— in fact, that this would be the most common element of the practice of mutual support under suffering.

A motif in Paul's rhetoric on unity suggests a refinement to our picture of the economic situation of the Philippian Christians. The motif is of praise of loss of status. This is most clear in Paul's use of the story of Christ as a reinforcement to his call to unity. Paul makes the point three times. Christ avoids some aspect of high status in relation to equality with God (Phil 2:6). Christ lowers his status (Phil 2:7). He then humbles himself (Phil 2:8). All this gains God's approval (Phil 2:9). More subtly, Paul's account of himself also involves renunciation of status (Phil 3:7–8). More directly, part of the climax of Paul's call to unity is encouragement to humility and a converse call to avoid "empty glory" (Phil 2:3). Otto Merk sees this as a call to change one's attitude to social status.[39] This would undoubtedly be part of what was involved. However, Paul's insistence on the point suggests that it has a practical consequence related to his call for unity. The motif seems likely to indicate that there is some diversity of status among the Philippian Christians, even within their overall framework of general poverty. Praise of loss of status seems likely to be rhetoric implying a call for willingness to lose status. Since those with slightly higher status would tend

---

as Benefactors and Citizens, First-Century Christians in the Graeco-Roman World [Carlisle: Paternoster, 1994], 99), who sees the letter's rhetoric on unity as centering on the disagreement between Euodia and Syntyche, seem unlikely to give enough weight to the intertwining of the rhetoric on unity with the rhetoric on suffering.

39. Otto Merk, Handeln aus Glauben: Die Motivierung der Paulinischen Ethik, Marburger Th St 5 (Marburg: Elwert, 1968), 177–78.

to have more economic resources, such a call would be a valuable move in rhetoric aimed at promoting practical mutual solidarity in a group that was undergoing economic suffering.

Conclusions

The various New Testament texts that we have considered have led to a set of inferences about the economic situation of the people in Philippi who formed the Christian assembly at the period when Paul wrote to them. To what overall profile do these inferences point?

Despite complications due to Paul's rhetorical use of economic signals in 2 Cor 8:1–4, it is probable that the economic profile of the Philippian and Thessalonian Christians was below average for Paul's experience of first-century society and below that of the Corinthian Christians. This conclusion holds despite Phil 4:10–20 indicating that Philippians had sent money to Paul. The sums involved were probably very limited, especially while Paul continued to do craftwork himself.

The Greek language and names, in a letter to a group living in a colony under particularly firm Roman political and social control, places the recipients in a group that would tend to have less access to economic resources. In a Roman colonial setting, being Greek would also suggest that the group were predominantly not farmers, that is, it would place them mainly among people such as craftworkers and small traders. This fits the Greek Philippian Christians in with the social pattern often seen as typical of early Christians, as exemplified by 1 Thess 4:11. Assuming that Roman Philippian Christians such as Clement were also craftworkers or small traders, the colonial context would make them likely to be either members of dispossessed peasant colonist families or freed slaves.

Philippians, Acts 16, and, again, evidence of general social patterns in early Christianity suggest that the majority of assembly members would have been women. This is a further indicator of diminished access to the town's economic resources. On the other hand, the evidence of association-like internal organization (Phil 1:1) implies that the group was of a fair size (well over, say, twenty). Even among the poor this would give the group access to a total potential pot of money—to use, for instance, in times of crisis—which would seem high from the viewpoint of individual poor members.

The pervasive evidence of continuing suffering in Philippians implies economic difficulty. The main argument for this is the general one that the main long-term group-level consequences of suffering for following distinctive beliefs and practices tend to be economic. However, the argument for this being the case among the Philippians is strengthened by Paul's emphasis on mutual support (Phil 2:4) and on willingness to lose status (Phil 2:3, 6–8).

Overall the economic situation of the Philippian Christians appears to have been particularly difficult, even by first-century standards. The common, rather positive view of the Philippians' economic circumstances seems in need of revision.

COLLABORATION OF "SAMOTHRAKIASTS" AND CHRISTIANS IN PHILIPPI

Eduard Verhoef

Within the frame of the overarching theme of this study, I will try to describe the position of the young church among the other religions or cults in Philippi and especially its relation to the cult of Euephenes in the fourth and fifth century CE. I will argue that this relation is based on earlier good contacts.[1]

There were many religions and cults in the Roman Empire at the beginning of the Common Era (see the description of several cults in this volume in the chapter by Valerie Abrahamsen). Christians lived next to adherents of Diana, worshipers of the Egyptian goddess Isis, and so forth.[2] Until the forties of the fourth century, the Christians were a minority group. The number of Christians in the Roman Empire is usually estimated at 10 percent of the population for the year 300, that is, about six million people.[3] At this time, Christians were not yet allowed to practice their cult very openly. But the situation changed in the year 313 when Constantine the Great permitted Christians to erect their own churches. Around the year 350, it is estimated, more than 50 percent of the population of the Roman Empire were Christians.[4] In 380,

---

1. I would like to thank J. W. van Arenthals and G. M. Knepper for their feedback on this text.

2. Ekaterini Tsalampouni, *Makedonia in the New Testament Period* [Greek], Bibliotheca Biblica 23 (Thessaloniki: Pournaras, 2002), 21–33; Eduard Verhoef, *Philippi: How Christianity Began in Europe; The Epistle to the Philippians and the Excavations in Philippi* (London: Bloomsbury, 2013), 10–13.

3. Rodney Stark, *The Rise of Christianity: A Sociologist Reconsiders History* (Princeton: Princeton University Press, 1996), 7.

4. Ibid.

the Christian cult was made the official religion of the Roman Empire, and shortly afterwards other religions were declared illegal. From this time onwards, Christians often destroyed temples and shrines of other cults. The destruction of several temples in Ephesos is connected with the dominance of Christianity.[5] In Kipia, in the territory of Philippi, the sanctuary of the Heros Aulonitis was destroyed, possibly by Christians.[6] But in the first half of the fourth century, such violent acts were not yet possible. In these decades, Christians reacted differently to other cults.

Sometimes churches were built on grounds that had been used for temples. In such cases there is a "continuity of religious use."[7] Sometimes older rituals were continued by Christians, and in several cases examples can be given of cities where elements of local cults were integrated into the Christian religion. This phenomenon can be illustrated by examples in both Thessalonica and Philippi.[8] In Thessalonica the veneration of Demetrios by Christians took shape with the help of elements of the cult of Kabeiros,[9] and in Philippi it was the Kabeiric cult of Euephenes that influenced the developing Christianity.

In this essay I will investigate whether more can be said with regard to the role of the adherents of the cult of Euephenes in Philippi in relation to the growing Christian movement. What reason did they have to give permission to the Christians to build a church on their holy ground, and what reason did the Christians, for their part, have to build their first church in Philippi precisely in the *temenos*, the precinct of a heroon (a shrine for a hero)?

5. See Stefan Karwiese, "The Church of Mary and the Temple of Hadrian Olympios," in *Ephesos: Metropolis of Asia*, ed. Helmut Koester (Valley Forge, PA: Trinity Press International, 1995), 311–19 (313–15).

6. Chaido Koukouli-Chrysanthaki, "Κήπια—Αχροβούνι," *Archaiologikon deltion* 40 (1985): 263–66 (266).

7. Edward Norman, *The House of God: Church Architecture, Style, and History* (London: Thames & Hudson, 1990), 24.

8. See Eduard Verhoef, "Christians Reacted Differently to Non-Christian Cults," *HTS Teologiese Studies* 67 (2011): 265–71; and Verhoef, "Syncretism in the Church of Philippi," *HTS Teologiese Studies* 64 (2008): 697–714.

9. Katerina Tzanavari, "The Worship of Gods and Heroes in Thessaloniki," in *Roman Thessaloniki*, ed. D. V. Grammenos (Thessaloniki: Archaeological Museum, 2003), 177–262 (230).

It must be stated here that the tomb of Euephenes was a very special tomb.[10] It was located within the city walls, which points to a peculiar status of the tomb. The only sarcophagus was that of Euephenes, in a grave in the center of the burial chamber next to some niches for cinerary urns. Aristoteles Mentzos argues that this burial chamber was originally located outside the city walls and that it was just an ordinary tomb.[11] I do not agree. The trajectory of the Hellenistic walls is well known.[12] It is extremely improbable that the location of this tomb would have been outside the city walls, in which case the walls themselves would have necessarily followed a very irregular trajectory. Remnants of the Hellenistic city have been found even below the forum.[13] Accordingly, the location of the later forum was within the original city walls, and this must therefore be true for the nearby tomb of Euephenes as well.[14]

The Christian Cult Next to the Cult of Euephenes in Philippi: Situation Sketch

In the beginning of the fourth century, the Philippian Christians were allowed to build their first church, the Basilica of Paul, in the *temenos*, the courtyard around the shrine of Euephenes.[15] Euephenes, the son of Exekestos, was *mystes* of the Kabeiric cult of Samothrace. He was buried in a burial chamber in the center of the city, and a shrine was built for him above this burial chamber.

This Basilica of Paul was built circa 320 CE. We do not know of any magistrate pressure on the adherents of the cult of Euephenes to give up a part of their holy ground. The Christian church and the shrine of Euephenes shared one wall; the northern wall of the Basilica was the southern wall of the shrine. The southern wall of the Basilica was the

---

10. See Verhoef, "Syncretism in the Church," 698–69.

11. Aristoteles Mentzos, "Questions of the Topography of Christian Philippi" [Greek], *Egnatia* 9 (2005): 101–49 (117).

12. Michel Sève, "De la naissance à la mort d'une ville: Philippes en Macédoine; IVᵉ siècle av. J.-C.-VIIᵉ siècle ap. J.-C.," *Histoire Urbaine* 1 (2000): 187–204 (191–92).

13. See also Michel Sève and Patrick Weber, "Le côté nord du forum de Philippes," *BCH* 110 (1986): 531–81 (533); Tsalampouni, *Makedonia in New Testament Period*, 27; and Verhoef, "Syncretism in the Church," 698.

14. Michel Sève, *Guide du forum de Philippes*, Sites et Monuments 18 (Athènes: École Française, 2012), 12.

15. See Verhoef, "Syncretism in the Church," 702–3.

former southern wall of the *temenos* around the shrine of Euephenes. In the northwest part of this church, an inscription was made in the mosaic floor: Christ, help your servant Priscus with all his family.[16] The direction of this inscription made it legible only from the north side, that is, for people entering the church from the heroon. Charalambos Bakirtzis concluded that "the pagan and Christian sanctuaries were functioning simultaneously side by side."[17] The numerous shards of earthenware found in and on top of the burial chamber date from late Hellenistic and Roman times, while Roman building stones might point to a restoration in the first or second century of the Common Era.[18] Coins found around the shrine stem from late Roman and Byzantine times.[19] They show that people met there and brought their gifts to the shrine. At the beginning of the fifth century a new church, an octagon, was built, as well as several additional rooms. These rooms were located around the heroon in such a way that the heroon of Euephenes was left intact.[20] Apparently, even then the heroon was held in high esteem by the Christians in Philippi. Pelekanidis used the word "anomaly" with regard to the way the subsequent Christian churches and annexes were built there.[21] Pulling down the shrine and the heroon would have made a more regular building plan possible.

All these data suggest that the cult around the shrine of Euephenes did not stop when the first church was built and that there was no interlude

---

16. Peter Pilhofer, *Philippi II. Katalog der Inschriften von Philippi*, WUNT 119 (Tübingen: Mohr Siebeck, 2009), 393–94, no. 328.

17. Charalambos Bakirtzis, "Paul and Philippi: The Archaeological Evidence," in *Philippi at the Time of Paul and after His Death*, ed. Bakirtzis and Helmut Koester (Harrisburg, PA: Trinity Press International, 1998), 37–48 (43); see also Leonard E. Boyle, with respect to the San Clemente in Rome: "side by side with this church … there still continued to exist the Mithraic religion" (*A Short Guide to St. Clement's Rome* [Rome: Collegio San Clemente, 1989], 9).

18. G. G. Gounaris, *The Bathhouse and the Northern Outhouses of the Octagon at Philippi* [Greek], Bibliotheke tes en Athenais Archaiologikes Hetaireias 112 (Athens: Athenais Archaiologike Hetaireia, 1990), 56.

19. Gounaris, *The Bathhouse*, 57; Gounaris and E. Gounari, *Philippoi: Archaiologikos hodēgos* (Thessaloniki: University Studio Press, 2004), 77.

20. For these different building stages, see Verhoef, "Syncretism in the Church," 701–4, 712–14.

21. S. M. Pelekanidis, "ΑΝΑΣΚΑΦΑΙ ΟΚΤΑΓΩΝΟΥ ΦΙΛΙΠΠΩΝ," *Praktika tes en Athinais Archaiologikes Hetaireias* 15 (1960): 76–94 (88).

in the religious use of this site. These phenomena are rather striking. It must have been possible for the Christians to distance themselves from the heroon if they had wished to do so. A nice example of such an attitude is the way the Jewish synagogue in Sardis was located next door to an imperial cult hall, but there "the entranceway from the synagogue into that sanctuary was blocked off."[22] The Christians in Philippi allowed or maybe even preferred free access from and to the heroon of Euephenes. So, there must have been good relations between the adherents of the two cults. It is clear that such friendly relations and the frequent contacts must have led to syncretistic tendencies.[23]

It should be said here that syncretism is not necessarily a negative phenomenon. It can lead to very positive results. Συγκρητισμός (syncretism) originally meant a union of Cretan communities intended to reach a common goal.[24] Plutarch (Mor. 490b) said that in spite of their internal differences of opinion the Cretans collaborated when there was a common enemy: συνίσταντο, καὶ τοῦτ᾽ ἦν ὁ καλούμενος ὑπ᾽ αὐτῶν συγκρητισμός ("they joined forces, and this was what they called 'syncretism' "). Interpreted in this sense, syncretism is stronger than any accidental intercultural influence; it means joining with other people for whatever reason and looking for what connects people. It has a positive meaning and as such it can be significant for the development of any religious movement. Adherents of every cult will reckon with the way of thinking of the people they are living with. No religion can flourish within a vacuum, and every preacher will in one way or another connect to the range of ideas of his audience. A preacher will sometimes accept ideas of his audience as far as he can fit them in with his own convictions; in other cases he will reject them (see Acts 17:22–28). Christianity probably won more adherents by respecting old local cults and by adopting some of their elements than by isolating themselves from other religions.[25] We will see that adherents of the

---

22. Philip A. Harland, *Associations, Synagogues, and Congregations: Claiming a Place in Ancient Mediterranean Society* (Minneapolis: Fortress, 2003), 203.

23. Verhoef, "Syncretism in the Church," 707.

24. This noun has nothing to do with the verb κεράννυμι ("to mix"). See Eduard Schwyzer and Albert Debrunner, *Syntax und syntaktische Stilistik*, vol. 2 of *Griechische Grammatik*, 5th ed., Handbuch der Altertumswissenschaft 2.1.2 (Munich: Beck, 1988), 12: "Gemeingefühl der Kreter."

25. See Helmut Koester, who argued that Christianity "hat sich … stärker als andere religiöse Bewegungen seiner Zeit auf die verschiedensten kulturellen und geistigen Strömungen einstellen können und dabei sehr viel fremdes Gut aufgenommen

Samothracian mysteries as well were inclined to collaboration with other cults in order to reach their goals.

The Adherents of the Cult of Euephenes,
Mystes in the Kabeiric Cult of Samothrace

Who were the adherents of the cult of Euephenes, the initiate of the Kabeiric mystery cult of Samothrace? Can we form an idea of this group? We know just a few names of Philippian people who were initiated in the cult of Samothrace. Euephenes himself, the son of Exekestos, must of course be mentioned here. An unpublished inscription states that he was an initiate in the Kabeiric mystery cult of Samothrace.[26] There is an unpublished inscription from the end of the third or the beginning of the second century BCE that mentions four initiates from Philippi.[27] An inscription from the second or the first century BCE mentions a Philippian who was an initiate in the Kabeiric cult.[28] The first letter is lacking but -ιλιππευς is clearly legible (not -ιλππευς, as Nora A. Dimitrova wrote in her book). The place where the Philippian's name was written is damaged, and his name is illegible. Another inscription mentions next to initiates from Thasos a certain Marcus Antonius Optatus from Philippi.[29] This inscription is dated at the end of the second or the beginning of the third century CE. It shows that in this time people from Philippi were still interested in the Kabeiric cult. In spite of the small number of Philippian initiates that are known to us from the inscriptions, the central place of the shrine within the city shows that this cult was rather important and that there must have been many more adherents.

So we know of the shrine of Euephenes, an initiate of the Kabeiric cult at Samothrace, we know of just a few other initiates, and we know that people gathered there. These people lived in the period from the third

---

ehe es als synkretistische Religion den Anspruch durchsetzen konnte, Weltreligion zu sein" (*Einführung in das Neue Testament* [Berlin: de Gruyter, 1980], 172).

26. Pilhofer, *Philippi*, 393.

27. Susan Guettel Cole, *Theoi Megaloi: The Cult of the Great Gods at Samothrace*, EPRO 96 (Leiden: Brill, 1984), 25, 148.

28. Nora M. Dimitrova, *Theoroi and Initiates in Samothrace: The Epigraphical Evidence*, Hesperia Supplement 37 (Athens: American School of Classical Studies, 2008), 103–4.

29. Dimitrova, *Theoroi and Initiates in Samothrace*, 121–22; Pilhofer, *Philippi*, 883–85, no. 704a.

century BCE through the second century CE and maybe still in the third century. It is clear that these worshipers formed a community in one way or another, maybe called a θίασος (a religious guild) or a κοινόν (an association). In any case these people, initiated into the Kabeiric cult of Samothrace, must have had some sort of organization.

The Romans built a large bathhouse immediately north of the heroon at the end of the first century BCE.[30] They left the heroon intact. As the Christians built the Basilica of Paul within the precinct of the heroon, the shrine itself was left unaffected as well. This data and the inscription that mentions Marcus Antonius Optatus suggest that there was still some sort of cult on this site in the first Roman centuries. In itself, this is not very surprising. Several Hellenistic cults survived in the Roman period in other cities as well. In Thessalonica, the cult of Kabeiros had many adherents, and it even became more important during the first centuries CE. The cult of Artemis endured in Ephesos, and the cult of Aphrodite attracted many people in Corinth. And more examples can be given of Hellenistic cults during the Roman rule.

Other Adherents of the Samothracian Cult

Inscriptions found elsewhere may suggest what a cult related to Samothrace looked like. Susan Cole gathered ten inscriptions in which Σαμοθραικιασταί (Samothrakiasts) or τὸ κοινὸν τῶν Σαμοθραικιαστᾶν ("the association of Samothrakiasts") are mentioned. These inscriptions come from Lesbos and from the island of Rhodes and its surroundings.[31] As far as dating is possible, they are dated in the second and the first centuries BCE and in the first century CE. The term συμμύσται ("coinitiates") in one inscription implies that these Σαμοθραικιασταί were initiates.[32]

These inscriptions tell us that the "Samothrakiasts" held regular meetings[33] and that they honored people in particular cases. An inscription from Methymna, on the northwest coast of Lesbos, says that the Samothrakiasts sometimes held a procession to τὸ ἱερόν ("the holy place").[34] This

---

30. Gounaris and Gounari, *Philippoi*, 86.

31. Cole, *Theoi Megaloi*, 151, 156–58, 160–61, 163–64, 167.

32. Ibid., 158.

33. See, for example, Cole, *Theoi Megaloi*, 151, καθ᾽ ἑκάστην σύνοδον ("in every meeting").

34. Cole, *Theoi Megaloi*, 151.

ἱερόν cannot be localized exactly, but presumably it was in the neighbor-hood of the port of Methymna.[35] In some of these inscriptions, it says that the Samothrakiasts collaborated towards a common goal with τὸ κοινὸν τῶν Λημνιαστᾶν, τὸ κοινὸν τῶν Ἀφροδισιαστᾶν ("the association of Lemniasts, the association of Aphrodisiasts"). Sometimes they contrib-uted towards the expenses for a statue or for honoring a person with a golden wreath because of his virtuousness. This seems to suggest that these Samothrakiasts entered into relations with other religious groups rather easily. One inscription from Rhodes mentions a κοινὸν Σαμοθραικιαστᾶν Ἀφροδισιαστᾶν ("an association of Samothrakiasts, Aphrodisiasts").[36] The lack of a conjunction between the two names is striking. According to Cole, this seems to mean that the Samothrakiasts "worshipped Aphro-dite together with the Samothracian gods."[37] This is possible, but not at all certain. The next inscription mentioned by Cole comes from Rhodes as well, and it says that the Samothrakiasts honored a certain Moschion and that this Moschion was honored by two other groups, the Aphrodisiasts and the Panathenaists.[38] It is clear that in this inscription the Samothra-kiasts are distinguished from the Aphrodisiasts.[39] According to Cole, this Moschion "probably had belonged to all three of these associations."[40] An inscription, found rather close to Rhodes, mentions a certain Athenodo-tos, the son of Metrodoros, as the chairman of the Samothrakiasts *and* of the Orgeones *and* of the Mystai.[41] This inscription shows once again that there were several connecting threads between the Samothrakiasts and other religious groups.

Karl Lehmann carried out excavations on Samothrace for many years. Besides detailed analyses of several parts of the excavated area, he wrote a guide to the museum and the site. In this guide, he concluded that "at least from the Hellenistic time on, groups of initiates organized themselves into religious clubs as Samothrakiasts and had their own

---

35. Hans-Günter Buchholz, *Methymna: Archäologische Beiträge zur Topographie und Geschichte von Nordlesbos* (Mainz: von Zabern, 1975), 49.

36. Cole, *Theoi Megaloi*, 157.

37. Ibid., 85.

38. Ibid., 157–58.

39. For these names, see Franz Poland, *Geschichte des griechischen Vereinswesens* (Leipzig: Teubner, 1909), 56–70.

40. Cole, *Theoi Megaloi*, 85.

41. Edmond Pottier and Amédée Hauvette-Besnault, "Inscriptions d' Érythrées et de Téos," *BCH* 4 (1880): 153–82 (164–67).

congregational centres in numerous cities."[42] The groups of Samothrakiasts from Lesbos and from Rhodes are examples of the "religious clubs" mentioned by Lehmann.

I consider it very probable that the adherents of the cult of Euephenes in Philippi, the initiate of the Kabeiric cult of Samothrace, acted in a similar way as the Samothrakiasts from Lesbos and Rhodes. They met around a ἱερόν at the place where the Kabeiric initiate Euephenes was buried. It is important to note that this Euephenes was buried *intra muros*. This must mean that he was considered to have a very special status, because burial within the city walls was forbidden apart from exceptional cases. Maybe these adherents of the cult of Euephenes were even organized like the "religious clubs" of Samothrakiasts elsewhere. They may have had similar goals as the Samothrakiasts on Lesbos and on Rhodes, that is, stimulating virtuousness by honoring virtuous people, meeting regularly, and holding an occasional procession. It is interesting to see that two inscriptions from Philippi say that the adherents of Serapis honored people as well because of their good deeds.[43]

Some Striking Elements of the Samothracian Cult

Some important elements of the Samothracian mystery cult should be mentioned here that remind us of aspects of the Christian religion. Initiates were expected to confess their sins before they were allowed to the higher degree of ἐποπτεία.[44] Not everybody was happy with this prerequisite. The reluctance to confess one's sins is clearly demonstrated when the Spartan general Antalcidas said to the priest that the gods knew about his sins, and the Spartan commander Lysander stated that he would tell his sins to the gods alone.[45] According to Diodorus Siculus, it is said that people who took part in the Kabeiric mysteries lived more piously and more justly and better in everything, γίνεσθαι δέ φασι καὶ εὐσεβεστέρους

---

42. Karl Lehmann, *Samothrace: A Guide to the Excavations and the Museum* (Thessaloniki: Akamatis, 1998), 37.

43. Pilhofer, *Philippi*, 366–37, no. 307; 372–34, no. 311.

44. Karl Lehmann, "The *Epopteia* and the Function of the Hieron," in *The Hieron*, vol. 3.2 of *Samothrace*, ed. Phyllis Williams Lehmann (Princeton: Princeton University Press, 1969), 3–50 (15, 19); Lehmann, *Samothrace*, 81.

45. Naphtali Lewis, *Samothrace 1: The Ancient Literary Sources* (London: Routledge & Kegan Paul, 1959), 111–12.

καὶ δικαιοτέρους καὶ κατὰ πᾶν βελτίονας.[46] It is clear that ethical requirements played a role in this cult, which also involved purification[47] and a symbolic baptism in blood.[48] And, like in Christianity, everybody could participate in the Kabeiric cult of Samothrace, men and women, slaves and free people alike.[49]

It is worth mentioning here that, according to Clemens Alexandrinus and Firmicus Maternus, it was a murdered Kabeiros who was venerated in Thessalonica and who was supposed to save the city and its citizens from disasters even after his death.[50] But this amazing detail was not mentioned with regard to Lesbos, Rhodes, or Philippi. Nevertheless, several other points, mentioned above, show similarities with elements of the Christian tradition.

Mystery Cults and Christianity

Heikki Räisänen argued with respect to the mystery cults in general: "In most cases, the God has to undergo suffering, but this leads to victory in the end."[51] The history of religions school may have been too enthusiastic when they derived Christian sacraments from mystery religions, "but undoubtedly mystery language was adopted" in Christianity, and there were "many points of resemblance."[52] Or, as A. J. M. Wedderburn argued more cautiously: "Jewish Christians, including Paul, may have unwittingly taken over ... ideas and language that were shared by the mysteries and

---

46. C. H. Oldfather, *Diodorus of Sicily III* (Cambridge: Harvard University Press, 1970), 234.

47. Lewis, *Samothrace*, 111, no. 239; see Bengt Hemberg, *Die Kabiren* (Upssala: Almquist & Wiksell, 1950), 109–10.

48. See Lehmann "*Epopteia* and the Function of the Hieron," 23–26, 42–45; Lehmann, *Samothrace*, 45; see also Rex Witt, "The Kabeiroi in Ancient Macedonia," in *ΘΕΣΣΑΛΟΝΙΚΗ ΦΙΛΙΠΠΟΥ ΒΑΣΙΛΙΣΣΑΝ* [Studies on Ancient Thessalonica], ed. Polyxeni Adam-Veleni (Thessaloniki: Archaeological Museum, 1985), 964–77 (968–69).

49. Lehmann, *Samothrace*, 37.

50. Charles Edson, "Cults of Thessalonica," in Adam-Veleni, *ΘΕΣΣΑΛΟΝΙΚΗ ΦΙΛΙΠΠΟΥ ΒΑΣΙΛΙΣΣΑΝ*, 886–940 (921, 933–36).

51. Heikki Räisänen, *The Rise of Christian Beliefs: The Thought World of Early Christians* (Minneapolis: Fortress, 2010), 43; see Walter Burkert, *Ancient Mystery Cults* (Cambridge: Harvard University Press, 1987), 74–76.

52. Räisänen, *Rise of Christian Beliefs*, 46.

pagan religion," and "Gentile Christians, perhaps encouraged by these similarities, may have then interpreted the Christian faith in terms of their own religious traditions."[53] Such similarities paved the way for collaboration between Christians and adherents of other religious cults.[54] I consider the result of such a collaboration to be a form of syncretism, and, as said above, such syncretism is unavoidable and can be judged positively. No religion can take shape without syncretism. All people can do is fit new information into the framework of what is already known to them.[55] Examples of this phenomenon can be found in Philippi: a sarcophagus with the sculpture of the Thracian horseman was made for a priest of Isis,[56] and Asklepios and Serapis were related to each other according to an inscription discovered in the city center.[57] New religions always adopted local forms, and they sometimes collaborated with other cults. It is clear that Christians did the same. In Philippi they adopted words and forms from other cults, and they apparently collaborated with the adherents of the cult of Euephenes on some points. Of course, there were also many differences between Christianity and this cult. The devotion to Jesus Christ and to the apostle Paul, for example, distinguished the Christians from all other religious groups.

Religious Associations

Richard Ascough published a book in which he concluded that religious associations "make the best analogue" for the Christian community in Philippi.[58] Philip Harland stated that Paul "found the workshop or guild

---

53. A. J. M. Wedderburn, *Baptism and Resurrection: Studies in Pauline Theology against Its Graeco-Roman Background*, WUNT 44 (Tübingen: Mohr Siebeck, 1987), 163; see also Hans-Josef Klauck, *The Religious Context of Early Christianity: A Guide to Graeco-Roman Religions* (Minneapolis: Fortress, 2003), 152.

54. See Rodney Stark, *Discovering God: The Origins of the Great Religions and the Evolution of Belief* (New York: HarperOne, 2007), 199–202, 289–92.

55. As André Droogers argues, "religions rarely start from scratch, but are often a sequel to previous ritual forms and beliefs, incuding large parts of their social and cultural frameworks" ("Towards the Concerned Study of Religion: Exploring the Double Power-Play Disparity," *Religion* 40 [2010]: 227–38 [230]).

56. Pilhofer, *Philippi*, 533–34, no. 455a.

57. Ibid., 372–34, no. 311.

58. Richard S. Ascough, *Paul's Macedonian Associations: The Social Context of Philippians and 1 Thessalonians*, WUNT 2/161 (Tübingen: Mohr Siebeck, 2003), 161.

hall a key setting for his missionary activity."[59] He argued that such "networks could apparently form the primary basis of some nascent Christian groups."[60] We can easily imagine that the Christian community in Philippi was modeled on the basis of examples that were known. Even the titles ἐπίσκοπος ("overseer") and διάκονος ("deacon") (see Phil 1:1) were adopted from other associations.[61] The Christian association was just one among many. Next to differences, there were many analogies between them, and some associations even had similar goals. Against this background, it is understandable that sometimes these associations approached other groups in order to reach a common goal.

The Christian Church in the Temenos of Euephenes

Can we say more about the reasons for collaboration between the group around the heroon of Euephenes and the Christians? The group of adherents of the cult around the heroon of Euephenes was presumably smaller than the groups of Samothrakiasts on Lesbos and on Rhodes, but they had their own holy ground and their own heroon. Moreover, it was in the center of the city. A reason for some form of collaboration with the Christians could be that they felt a certain affinity with them. We know that the associations of Samothrakiasts on Lesbos and on Rhodes were inclined to collaborate with other religious groups.

Another reason for collaboration could be the depletion of funds after the internal difficulties of the third century CE (see in this volume the essay by Peter Oakes on the economic situation of the Christians in Philippi in the first century). The group around Euephenes may have needed the money and was probably therefore willing to allow a different religious group to use their ground. It is well known that the Roman Empire was struck by economic crises and inflation in the third century due to enduring and violent wars.[62] We know of emperors who travelled with their legions along the Via Egnatia, passing through Philippi. For example, Severus Alexander was there in 231 on his way to the Persians,

---

59. Harland, *Associations, Synagogues, and Congregations*, 261.

60. Ibid., 268.

61. Ascough, *Paul's Macedonian Associations*, 80–83, 161.

62. Carl Roebuck, *The World of Ancient Times* (New York: Scribner, 1966), 693–64; Georges Depeyrot, "Crise économique, formation des prix, et politique monétaire au troisème siecle après J.-C.," *Histoire & Mesure* 3 (1988): 235–47 (237).

and Carus in 283, again for a military campaign against the Persians.[63] An inscription was made in Philippi on the occasion of this campaign.[64] Another inscription was made after Constantine the Great had defeated Licinius. On his way for this campaign, Constantine had passed Philippi.[65] In the meantime, it had become evident that the Goths formed a real threat to this part of the Roman Empire, but it became more and more difficult for the Romans to maintain enough legions for the battles at the frontiers because of the high costs associated with such campaigns.[66] Inflation increased, and taxes were raised. The local authorities could no longer give financial support to local and state cults, and wealthy people saw their income decrease. Some cults were dependent on the generous gifts of these wealthy people.[67] W. H. C. Frend argued that the Mithraea, for example, were kept up with the money of rich worshipers. But in the middle of the third century "the supply was drying up as the crisis of the empire deepened."[68] Maybe the construction of the San Clemente on the Mithraic ground in Rome[69] is due to the fact that the adherents of Mithras could not afford to keep his shrine in good repair and tried to generate money by allowing Christians to build a basilica there.

Above, I mentioned the synagogue in Sardis. This synagogue was built in the late third century in the South Hall of the bath-gymnasium complex. As in Philippi, the question could be asked: why were the Jews allowed to build their synagogue there? Marianne Palmer Bonz argued with respect to Sardis: "its public and quasi-public corporations ... would

---

63. Paul Collart, *Philippes: Ville de Macédoine depuis ses origins jusqu'à la fin de l'époque romaine*, Travaux et Mémoires V (Paris: École Française d'Athènes, 1937), 518.

64. Pilhofer, *Philippi*, 262–63, no. 205; Cédric Brélaz, *Corpus des inscriptions grecques et latines de Philippes*, vol. 2: *La colonie romaine*, part 1, *La vie publique de la colonie*, Études épigraphiques 6 (Athènes: École française d' Athènes, 2014), 126–28, no. 27

65. See Pilhofer, *Philippi*, 300–301, no. 235; Brélaz, *Corpus des inscriptions*, 129–31, no. 29.

66. See Paul Lemerle, *Philippes et la Macédoine orientale à l'époque chrétienne et byzantine*, Bibiothèque des écoles Françaises d'Athènes et de Rome 158 (Paris: de Boccard, 1945), 107.

67. Marianne Palmer Bonz, "Differing Approaches to Religious Benefaction: The Late Third-Century Acquisition of the Sardis Synagogue," *HTR* 86 (1993): 139–54 (148).

68. W. H. C. Frend, *The Rise of Christianity* (Philadelphia: Fortress, 1984), 278.

69. See Boyle, "Short Guide," 9.

have suffered severe economic distress in the latter half of the third century.... It may have been necessary to turn over the South Hall to a private religious association in exchange for some measure of financial relief."[70] Apparently the Jews had the funds for financing the construction of a synagogue there. Presumably, they were less dependent on a few wealthy people or on the authorities. On the contrary, they could afford it because of the numerous small contributions from many adherents (see Philo, *Spec.* 1.76–78).

Circumstances were different in Philippi, and the events that interest us are dated some decades later. Nevertheless, there are similarities. Inscriptions indicate that in the first and second century CE public buildings and temples were often financed by the authorities or by a wealthy person in Philippi.[71] Such a situation is rather vulnerable to an economic crisis. On the other hand, the adherents of the cult of Silvanus show that they were not dependent on one person or only a few sponsors, but they collected money from quite a few members.[72] Accordingly they must have been less dependent on a single person or on the local authorities for their fundraising. Be this as it may, financial arguments will have played a role when the Christians were permitted to build their first basilica next to the heroon. This Basilica of Paul was built at the beginning of the fourth century. It is very well possible that the adherents of the old local cult could no longer afford to keep the heroon in good repair. In any case, it is certain that the authorities did not bring any pressure to bear on the Philippians for allowing the Christians to build a church there in the first decades of the fourth century. In the second century, the veneration of Artemis and the cult of Isis (see the chapter by Valerie Abrahamsen in this volume) had been banned to the Akropolis, but the cult around the tomb of Euephenes endured. At the time, it must have been a rather strong local cult. It had its roots in Samothrace, and related groups can be found in several places, such as Lesbos and Rhodes. But in the fourth century, they probably sought contact with another religious group.

---

70. Bonz, "Differing Approaches," 148.

71. See Pilhofer, *Philippi*, 249–51, 254–57, 271–72, 279–80, 283–87, respectively nos. 198, 201, 213, 221, and 226; Brélaz, *Corpus des inscriptions*, 110–12, 107–9, 266–69, 160–62, 276–80, respectively nos. 18, 16, 119, 49, 126.

72. See Pilhofer, *Philippi*, 205–10, no. 164.

The Christians were often pointed to as the people who had caused the mid-third century catastrophes,[73] and this hostility was not yet over. Only in 311 did Galerius call off the persecution of Christians. About one decade later, the Christians started to build their first church in Philippi. They were less dependent on support from the local authorities, just like the Jewish communities. They financed their activities with many modest gifts from their adherents and were accordingly less vulnerable to economic problems. Apparently, the Christians enjoyed building their first church in the city center close to the forum. It must have been a great opportunity to erect their first church there. It is clear that they must have considered the *temenos* of Euephenes's shrine appropriate for their church. Maybe they themselves found affinities as well with the cult of Euephenes. Beat Brenk argues: "Wie es scheint fand man in dem hellenistischen Heroon einen Anknüpfungspunkt, denn man hat dort die Memoria des Apostels Paulus angesiedelt" ("it looks as if people found a lead in the Hellenistic heroon, for they accommodated the *memoria* of Paul there").[74] An additional advantage was the nearness of running water in the public baths. Unlike the Jews in Sardis, they did not block up the entrance to the heroon. On the contrary, this entrance seems to have been used frequently. Maybe some persons joined both religious associations. All these facts make it probable that the collaboration between both communities was founded on earlier good relations. It is less probable that the Christians were initially opposed to the cult of Euephenes and afterward adopted its buildings and some of its rituals. It must have been a long growing process in which the people who joined the new Christian association took along some elements of their former cult, in some cases presumably that of Euephenes. The change over to another religious association was probably not a big step. There were several religious associations in Philippi. Some people had connections with two or three religious associations, which means that they were not mutually exclusive, and the Philippians were well known with the range of ideas of these associations. Many ideas were

---

73. Géza Alföldy, "The Crisis of the Third Century as Seen by Contemporaries," *GRBS* 15 (1974): 89–111 (102, 105, and 106).

74. Beat Brenk, *Die Christianisierung der spätromischen Welt*, Spätantike-Frühes Christentum–Byzanz B: Studien und Perspektiven 10 (Wiesbaden: Reichert, 2003), 8; but see Carola Jäggi, "Archäologische Zeugnisse für die Anfänge der Paulus-Verehrung," in *Biographie und Persönlichkeit des Paulus*, ed. Eve-Marie Becker and Peter Pilhofer, WUNT 187 (Tübingen: Mohr Siebeck, 2005), 306–22 (307).

rather generally accepted, as we have seen. The idea that all people were equal was proclaimed both in the Kabeiric cult and in Christianity. Therefore, it was not very difficult for the Philippians to become a member of another association. The adherents of the cult of Euephenes will not have abandoned all their rituals or ideas at the moment they joined another association, and, as I argued above, these two religious associations shared several ideas. This fact must have made collaboration much easier.

Conclusion

It is evident that adherents of both cults had an interest in collaboration. I cannot prove which reasons led to this collaboration, but I have shown what happened elsewhere. Problems with fundraising may have played a role; people who adhered to the Kabeiric cult of Euephenes may have been inclined to look for connections with other religious groups, as the Samothrakiasts were elsewhere. We do not know for sure, but such reasons seem plausible. With regard to the Christians, they must have found it a great idea to build their first church in the prestigious city center, and probably they were attracted by some elements of the Kabeiric cult as well. In any case, there were no insurmountable obstacles for them to build their first church in Philippi in the precinct of the Hellenistic heroon.

Response: Broadening the Socioeconomic and Religious Context at Philippi

Richard S. Ascough

The foregoing essays by Valerie Abrahamsen, Peter Oakes, and Eduard Verhoef raise important issues for a project that takes seriously a history from below that does not privilege elite writings and considers carefully the cultural situation at Philippi. All three of the essays focus to some degree on the socioeconomic and religious context of the early Christ-adherents. Although a full excavation of the site of ancient Philippi is far from complete, the authors use the extant material remains at the site and, by analogy, from elsewhere to construct the social situation of the Philippian Christ-adherents in the first few centuries. In the following response to these chapters, I will highlight some trends that I see among the three contributions.

There is considerable overlap in the depiction of the Philippian Christ-adherents in the three essays, and the differences might be explained by reference to the particular time period in which each author situates the investigation. Oakes highlights the situation in the first century, arguing that the Philippian adherents' economic status was subaverage and that they had limited access to resources. Already marginalized by their status as craftworkers and small traders, the predominance of women in the group would further separate them from their having any social or political power. Likewise, their use of Greek suggests that they were not among the higher status, Latin speaking elites of Philippi. In fact, Oakes suggests they were suffering at the hands of their peers due to their aberrant beliefs and practices, presumably having drawn attention to themselves by having their members—perhaps fifty or more according to Oakes—not participate in regular civic activities. Although some physical persecution might result, the net impact would be economic, affecting their livelihood and lifestyle, which is likely at the root of their suffering and the cause of their need to be mutually supportive.

In general I agree with Oakes's location of the Philippian Christ-adherents among the subelite Greeks of the city, although I would advocate for a smaller size group than he suggests, perhaps in the neighborhood of twenty or so. There are other associations that carry a number of titled officials for which the membership is around twenty, so his suggestion that the mention of *episkopoi* and *diakonoi* (Phil 1:1) indicates a larger group does not follow. I also want to push back somewhat on his argument that their suffering reflects a form of religious persecution, although he is likely correct that, if anything, it did not include murder and oppression but was more on the scale of harassment. Yet within Paul's rhetorical flourish in the first chapter, the text serves more to highlight his own troubles than that of the Philippians themselves, and when in the second chapter he invokes the hymn of Christ as exemplar, the emphasis is on Christ's taking on humble status rather than his suffering. This would certainly resonate among those whom Oakes describes as economically disadvantaged as the audience of the letter.

I would want to nuance Oakes's choice to define "economics" as "the study of the allocation of scarce resources." Although he calls this a "broad" definition, it seems to me to be too narrow in its employment of "scarce" resources. Why the qualifier "scarce"? A commodity that is readily available is not "scarce" in the sense of "hard to obtain." What makes it part of the economic system is the control of its distribution, as Oakes rightly recognizes in his example of water. For the most part, air is not a controllable commodity, and thus there is not a market in place; water is, however, controllable and thus regulated by those with the means to control it, be it individuals or governments. It is that very control that makes it possible for a commodity to become scarce and thus more valuable on the open market. I would suggest that perhaps a more rhetorically compelling definition of economics for a project tackling history from below is to forefront the aspect of control by those in positions of power. Again, as Oakes rightly notes, "economies [a]re heavily dependent upon power relationships." "Control" rather than "scarcity" highlights this—"economics" is the *control* and allocation of resources.

With this in mind, we can raise the issue of control with respect to Paul's rhetoric around the collection for Jerusalem and the contribution of the Philippians to his own work, both being examples of economic issues. Paul's language reflects both scarcity and abundance. He evokes scarcity through language of "extreme poverty" (2 Cor 8:2), Jesus's poverty (2 Cor 8:9), relief for others (2 Cor 8:13), "working night and day" (1 Thess 2:9), and claims of robbery of one group by another (2 Cor 11:8). In contrast, abundance is evoked in the language of abundant joy (2 Cor 8:2), overflowing rich generosity (2 Cor 8:2), "you might become rich" (2 Cor 8:9), and having "more than enough" (Phil 4:18). I am not as convinced as Oakes is that such rhetoric is more reflective of the situation on the ground in Philippi than Paul's rhetoric is elsewhere. This does not detract from Oakes's more solid demographic evidence from Philippi itself. I would, however, urge caution in using Paul's own language, as he is the one in control of the information that is being used in the raising of funds. Paul's rhetoric creates perceptions of scarcity and abundance in his attempt to raise funds for what will, ultimately, provide him (not his audiences) with status, and perhaps autonomy, among the leaders of Christ-adherents in Jerusalem.

Verhoef takes us forward into the early fourth century to examine the circumstances under which the Christ-adherents at Philippi would be allowed to build a large meeting place, the Basilica of Paul, in the courtyard of the shrine of Euephenes. In contrast to the picture forged by Oakes and, to some degree, Abrahamsen, Verhoef notes that Christ-adherents are financially stable and indeed somewhat well off. So much so, they are able to invest in real estate within the city itself. Verhoef likens the cult of Euephenes in Philippi to other "Samothrakiasts" who had regular meetings, honored people, held processions, and met in or at a "holy place." More strikingly, members of both genders and of varying status (slave, free, and freed) had ethical and purity requirements and underwent rituals around such. In this regard, they are much like the Christ-adherents in their demographics and organization. Verhoef notes that the economic challenges faced by the Euephenes association may well have led them to seek out partners with whom to share their resources, particularly their meeting location. That they would find affinity with the Christians is not surprising given the similarities noted above, but is striking in that it assumes the Christians are, at this point in time, financially able to enter into such a relationship. That is, they have income that can be disposed of in renting a meeting hall rather than meeting in someone's house. Eventually they could take over the site completely, presumably at considerable cost, since property in the center of the town was not likely to be inexpensive. In so doing, they must of necessity have friendly and stable relations with civic authorities and the elites of Philippi, otherwise their attempts to build in this location would surely be blocked. In the early fourth century, however, this shift is not surprising.

Verhoef rightly notes that similarities between new religious movements and local forms of religious group language and organization are unavoidable if the new religious movement is to take root in the local community. Whether deliberately or unwittingly, Paul and others have adopted and adapted such things. Although Verhoef rightly calls this a "form of syncretism," there is a stigma to the word "syncretism" that, for biblical scholars, too often evokes images of "pollution" or "corruption," particularly among those who would want to keep "Christianity" pure and free from the taint of its surroundings.[1] Such a position is, of course, nonsense, as no new religious movement can develop in a vacuum.[2] Verhoef recognizes this by rightly noting that "syncretism is not necessarily a negative phenomenon" as it indicates a deliberate (rather than accidental) choice to connect to other people or movements. He notes such connections in the arena of ideas, but I would add to this the aspect of social networking as a form of "syncretism," to which his data from the Samothrakiasts points. All of this is important for the writing of history from below in order to shift the predilection among many scholars in whose eyes Christianity must remain "pure" from so-called "pagan" influences.

How do we move from the fairly dire economic situation of the first-century Philippian Christ-adherents described by Oakes to the financially (and socially) better off adherents of the early fourth century described by Verhoef? Abrahamsen provides a bridge of sorts, as her essay begins with the first century but moves into the second and third centuries. Like Oakes, Abrahamsen sees among the Philippian Christ-adherents a largely female membership in which women provide leadership by drawing upon the strong, positive role models of the surrounding culture. In contrast to Oakes, however, she does think that the Christ-adherents have a benefactor, citing Lydia as one such example of a wealthy, subelite patron of the group. Among the many opportunities modeled for the Philippian women by elite and subelite women of the empire such as Livia, Eumachia, and Faustina were the construction of cult buildings and the filling of public

---

1. See Jonathan Z. Smith, *Drudgery Divine: On the Comparison of Early Christianities and the Religions of Late Antiquity*, CSJH (Chicago: University of Chicago Press, 1990).

2. Rodney Stark, *Discovering God: The Origins of the Great Religions and the Evolution of Belief* (New York: HarperOne, 2007), 290.

leadership roles within the associated groups. Certainly by the second century, we see in Christian writings such as the Infancy Gospel of James and the Acts of Paul and Thecla evidence of a growing veneration of women for roles they played in the life of Jesus and beyond. So strong was the impetus that male leaders felt threatened enough that they made attempts to reign in such movements, as was the case with Polycarp.

Moving beyond even the time frame of Verhoef, Abrahamsen points to inscriptions from the fifth or sixth centuries in which two female deacons and a canoness are memorialized within a Christian basilica. Although she notes it only in passing, one of the deacons, Agatha, was buried with her husband, also a group leader (treasurer), whose occupation was that of linen weaver. Perhaps a coincidence, but it is striking that he is not only involved in a small trade (as Oakes suggests for Christ-adherents in a much earlier time) but is employed in the wider garment industry (as was Lydia, according to Acts 16). A scenario in which we conjecture that women were the prime operators in moving the Christ-adherents from marginalized status in the first century to become prominent in the town center in the early fourth century is consistent with the pattern of women's leadership and civic benefaction traced by Abrahamsen.

Particularly striking in Abrahamsen's essay are the inscriptions acknowledging Liber, Libera, and Herakles to which Abrahamsen rightly points as examples of women's leadership in associations. Abrahamsen notes that the women named in these inscriptions "seem to have been able to act in ways similar to women from traditionally elite families" in terms of distributing their financial resources. She goes on to note the several links between the trio of deities and women, but I think the implications for understanding the context within which the Christ-adherents are located can be further developed.

Take, for example, the inscription indicative of an association of women, which reads, "Dedicated to Liber and Libera and Hercules. The *thiasus* of distinguished Maenads brought in water at their own cost."[3] This inscription was found in a small building, probably a house, underneath the baths south of Basilika B and can probably be dated to the late first

---

3. Peter Pilhofer, *Philippi II: Katalog der Inschriften von Philippi*, WUNT 119 (Tübingen: Mohr Siebeck, 2000), no. 340/L589; John S. Kloppenborg, and Richard S. Ascough, *Achaia, Central Greece, Macedonia, Thrace*, vol. 1 of *Greco-Roman Associations: Texts, Translations, and Commentary*, BZNW 181 (Berlin: de Gruyter, 2011), no. 71.

or early second century CE.[4] Although the inscription is in Latin, it uses a Latinized form of the Greek word θίασος (as do four other inscriptions from Philippi and its surroundings[5]). In addition, the term *maenadum* is more Greek than Latin and suggests that this association has modeled itself on literary antecedents from Greek tragedy such as Euripides's *The Bacchae*.[6] This would then caution us against making to make too much a distinction between a "Latin" culture at Philippi and the "Greekness" of others in the town, as does Oakes in his essay.[7]

Devotion to Dionysos is clear, as Abrahamsen notes, in the use of *thiasus* and *maenad*, the latter also being indicative of a largely (if not exclusively) female group. This group can be distinguished from another association of Dionysos in the town, either an all male or mixed Dionysos *thiasus* with whom Bithus[8] and the slave Lucius[9] are affiliated. The maenad inscription suggests a female association that has the economic means to pay for an aqueduct at Philippi. Since this and related inscriptions were found in the building under the baths, it is also possible that the smaller house served as a sanctuary for Dionysos.[10] Although groups of women involved in ritual frenzy in worshiping Dionysos initially took place outside town limits, this group eventually was integrated back into the town and became the locus of women's social and religious activity, even contributing to the town through their benefaction.

Abrahamsen has made a good case for the acceptance of women in positions of leadership in a number of elite and nonelite associations, including the Christian groups, although admittedly benefaction is not

---

4. Anne-Françoise Jaccottet, *Choisir Dionysos: Les associations dionysiaques ou la face cachée du dionysisme* (Zurich: Akanthus, 2003), 2:61.

5. Pilhofer, *Philippi II*, nos. 095/L346, 524/L103, 525/L104, and 529/L106.

6. Jaccottet, *Choisir Dionysos* 2:61.

7. On the bicultural nature of Philippi, see Charles Edson, "Double Communities in Roman Macedonia," in *Essays in Memory of Basil Laourdas*, ed. C. Edson et al (Thessalonica: Laourda, 1975), 97–102. Of twenty-one identifiable association inscriptions from Philippi and environs, eleven are Latin and ten are Greek. Within the town itself, eight are Latin and eight are Greek. More problematic is the dating of these inscriptions, which tend to be from the late first century or later or are of uncertain date, making their utility for understanding the earliest forms of the Christ-group somewhat problematic.

8. Pilhofer, *Philippi II*, no. 524/L103.

9. Ibid., no. 525/L104.

10. Jaccotte, *Choisir Dionysos* 2, 61.

likely to alleviate general poverty, since money donated was expended on group activities. To my mind, this economic poverty is a good explanation for "suffering" without necessitating any formal or informal persecutions. Yet, like Oakes, Abrahamsen thinks there is conflict between the Christ-adherents and civic authorities and/or residents when she conjectures "an atmosphere of imperial oppression, consistent poverty and want, and *sporadic persecution of Christians*" (my emphasis). She continues that association and cultic memberships were used to "protest against or attempt to undermine the injustices around them." On the contrary, associations provided a social outlet and an opportunity for replicating civic structures, but this was done in such a way as to demonstrate alliance with civic authorities rather than protest against them.[11] It is precisely when they were perceived to be "protesting" that the associations were made subject to the Roman laws that restricted their activities, laws that were always present but infrequently enacted.

There is not strong evidence, either inside the letters of Paul or in any external attestation, for claims of wide spread persecution of Christ-adherents in the first decades of the movement at Philippi. Paul's rhetoric of "suffering" could just as easily (and given the evidence Oakes gives of their economic status, more probably) reference their general economic woes. It is not necessarily the case that their adherence to the Christ cult would terminate the majority of their social and economic ties, at least no more than would be the case with their having joined a group of Dionysos devotees, or Isis devotees, or even the *thiasus* of distinguished maenads. It is only when we assume that "Christian" groups were sectarian groups (as argued by Ernst Troelsch, H. Richard Niebuhr, Max Weber, and others so long ago) that we see a correlation between their religious convictions and their social marginalization. When Paul's words are read through this lens, then I will grant that it sounds lot like religious persecution was the order of the day. But this notion of sectarian status (grounded, I suspect, in later pietistic concerns for the purity of Christian origins) strikes me as an oft-repeated assertion that as yet has not been fully demonstrated; thus, I would suggest that, rather than presume that Christ-adherents were singled out for their aberrant beliefs and practices, their economic situation is sufficient explanation for their suffering.

---

11. Kloppenborg and Ascough, *Greco-Roman Associations*, 5–6.

Finally, I want to add an observation on method. We need to face the fact that much of what we do in constructing a history from below will necessarily be speculative. I was struck how often in all three essays (and, I might add, in my own work) qualifiers such as "possibly," "might be," "may," and "conceivable that" occur. When dealing with nonelite groups, particularly the nonliterate, all of our conclusions must remain tentative. Given that the level of preservation of Philippi is not great and that archaeological excavation is not yet as extensive as it might be, we must remain humble in drawing our conclusions. This does not mean, however, that we simply default to older paradigms that privilege the writings of the minority elite, for conclusions drawn from this material should be equally humble and tentative (although often is not presented as such). Older assumptions are not the "real" or "true" picture until proven otherwise, although too often this is the presentation. Although the Philippian "church" remains in the minds of many scholars (and preachers) to be one in which economically stable benefactors of Paul give joyfully of their abundance in the face of religious persecution, often led by their male leaders (with grudging acknowledgement of possible female companions alongside), this picture is, to my mind, less convincing than the alternatives presented by Oakes, Verhoef, and Abrahamsen.

LETTER FROM PRISON AS HIDDEN TRANSCRIPT: WHAT IT TELLS US ABOUT THE PEOPLE AT PHILIPPI

Angela Standhartinger

In recent years, reconstructions of the Christ-community in Philippi have been much improved by research focusing on the letter's local and socio-historical context.[1] With the help of archaeological, numismatic, and epigraphic data and studies on the political, cultural, and social impact of Roman imperialism to the provinces of Roman east, we have learned a lot about the local environments of the *Colonia Iulia Augusta Philippensis*. But not at least because archaeological and historical data remain ambiguous and open to different interpretations, it still remains difficult to identify those everyday Philippians to whom Paul wrote and their specific social-cultural contexts in this particular Macedonian city.

---

1. Valerie A. Abrahamsen, *Women and Worship at Philippi: Diana/Artemis and Other Cults in the Early Christian Era* (Portland, ME: Astarte Shell, 1995); Lukas Bormann, *Philippi: Stadt und Christengemeinde zur Zeit des Paulus*, NovTSup 78 (Leiden: Brill, 1995); Peter Pilhofer, *Philippi I: Die erste christliche Gemeinde Europas*, WUNT 87 (Tübingen: Mohr Siebeck, 1995); Charalambos Bakirtzis and Helmut Koester, ed., *Philippi at the Time of Paul and after His Death* (Harrisburg, PA: Trinity Press International, 1998); Craig Steven de Vos, *Church and Community Conflicts: The Relationships of the Thessalonian, Corinthian, and Philippian Churches with Their Wider Civic Communities*, SBLDS 168 (Atlanta: Scholars Press, 1999); Peter Oakes, *Philippians: From People to Letter*, SNTSMS 110 (Cambridge: Cambridge University Press, 2001); Richard S. Ascough, *Paul's Macedonian Associations: The Social Context of Philippians and 1 Thessalonians*, WUNT 2/161 (Tübingen: Mohr Siebeck, 2003); Joseph A. Marchal, *The Politics of Heaven: Women, Gender, and Empire in the Study of Paul*, Paul in Critical Contexts (Minneapolis: Fortress, 2008); and Eduard Verhoef, *Philippi: How Christianity Began in Europe; The Epistle to the Philippians and the Excavations in Philippi* (London: Bloomsbury, 2013).

One social context of Paul's letter to the Philippians has been up to now mostly overlooked: the context in which the letter originated. There is one hard fact named in the letter, the fact that Paul wrote to the community in Philippi while he stayed in a Roman prison (Phil 1:7, 14). In order to bring Philippians down to earth into its concrete context, I will focus on this particular fact. What does imprisonment in Roman antiquity mean in practice to prisoners? How could a prisoner manage to write a letter? What can we know from Philippians about Paul's actual prison conditions and his ability to communicate with those outside? Why is Paul so zealous to write the Philippians at all? Finally, how might those people beside Paul have read and understood the letter, being aware of the context of its origins? In the following, I try to find some answers to these questions.

Paul in Captivity: Image and Realty

It has long been known that Paul was imprisoned many times and for long periods. Prison is the place most often chosen as the location where the pseudo-Pauline letters were supposed to have been written (see, e.g., Col 4:2–3, 10–15, 18; Eph 3:1–2; 4:1; 2 Tim 1:8, 12, 16; 2:15–18; 4:6–18; 1 Clem 5.6–7; Ignatius, *Eph.* 11.2–2.2; Polycarp, *Phil.* 9.2–3; 3 Cor 4:34–36). But prison, according to this thesis, has only advanced the effectiveness of the apostle, for the "chains" have become signs of divine legitimation and evidence of his apostolic authority.

However, until well into modernity the picture drawn in the Acts of the Apostles has been the primary shaping factor in the history of Paul's influence.[2] Acts both places Paul's imprisonments at the center of attention and at the same time systematically minimizes their effect on the apostle.[3]

---

2. Imprisonment is a major, if not the essential, focus of Acts's portrayal of Paul. "The space devoted to Paul in custody, Acts 21:33–28:31, is longer than that describing his missionary work (chaps. 13–19)" (Richard I. Pervo, *Acts: A Commentary*, Hermeneia [Minneapolis: Fortress, 2009], 556). Because Paul was already in prison in Philippi (Acts 16:23–40), had to face attempts at his arrest in Thessalonica (Acts 17:5–9), was on trial in Corinth (Acts 18:12–17), and in the background of a public investigation in Ephesus (Acts 19:23–40, where, however, Paul is almost invisible and is mentioned only in 19:30), and given the prophecies of his arrest at Jerusalem and his transfer to Rome (Acts 20:22; 21:10–14), the theme is even more dominant than this would suggest. The Acts of Paul narrates imprisonment in Iconium (3:17 [Acts of Thecla]; see also 2 Tim 3:11), Ephesus (9), Philippi (10), and Rome (14).

3. Pervo, *Acts*, 553–57.

It is for but a few hours that Paul is exposed to the darkness, filth, and close confinement of an ordinary prison (Acts 16:23–30; 22:25–29).[4] When torture occurs, it is immediately canceled and those responsible apologize profusely (Acts 16:23, 37–40; 22:24–29). Everyone from the prison keepers to the judges accord Paul great respect (Acts 16:36–39; 22:27–29; 23:23–35; 24:23; 27:1–3, 43; 28:16, 30–31). Arrest and hearing before judges become opportunities for mission (Acts 16:30–33; 26:28; 28:30–31).[5] It is precisely in and through his imprisonment that Paul demonstrates his superior morality and divine giftedness.[6]

The image drawn in Acts is, however, historically implausible. Even if Paul had Roman citizenship—which in my opinion is improbable[7]—he

---

4. The place of imprisonment in Jerusalem is not called a "prison" (φυλακή; δεσμωτήριον; εἱρκτή) but παρεμβολή (barracks): Acts 21:34, 37; 22:24; 23:10, 16, 32; see also Exod 29:14; Rev 20:19, etc. In Caesarea Paul stays in the *praetorium*, that is, within the palace of the Roman governor (23:35), where his custody is lightened immediately (ἄνεσις, Acts 24:23). Therefore Paul's conditions are much better than those of the Judean prince Agrippa in Rome during most of his imprisonment (see Josephus, *Ant.* 18.192–234). The manner of Agrippa's custody changed only in the very last days, after confirmation of the death of Tiberius, to that of Paul in Acts (*Ant.* 18.235). When Paul is transported to Rome, the fact that he is a prisoner seems almost forgotten (it is mentioned only in 27:1–3, 43). Julius, the centurion in charge of Paul, is so impressed by his prisoner that he treats him humanely and allows visits and attentions from friends (27:3; also, 24:23). In the ship Paul is free to amble about the deck, while ordinary prisoners would have been secured below in shackles (3 Macc. 4:7–19). At the end of the trip, Paul can even stay with his friends in Puteoli and welcome delegates from other communities (28:14–55; see also 28:17, 23). As Pervo observes (*Acts*, 671): "The primary fact is that Paul is not a prisoner in Acts 28:1–15.… Nothing in the first half of the final chapter indicates this status, and nearly everything denies it." In Rome "Paul was allowed to live by himself" (28:16) and to teach about the Lord Jesus Christ "with all boldness and without hindrance" (28:31).

5. See also Paul's speeches to the crowd in the temple (22:1–21) and his similar defense before Festus, Agrippa, and Bernice in 26:1–32.

6. For example, Paul stays put when the prison doors are opened (Acts 16:2–34; see also Lucian, *Tox.* 33) and takes care of the sailors and other prisoners in the ship (Acts 27:21–43).

7. In the first century, Roman citizenship was quite rare in the provinces, especially among Jews. Even municipal elites who were heavily involved in the imperial cult did not usually have it. Freedpersons in Rome and veterans received, if anything, Italian but not Roman citizenship. Acts uses citizenship as a narrative device in order to protect Paul from the customary torture (Acts 16:38; 22:20) and to place him on the same footing as the officials. See Wolfgang Stegemann, "War der Apostel Paulus ein

was still a more or less ordinary provincial citizen with a manual occupation (1 Thess 2:9; also Acts 18:2–3). The form of free house arrest, *libera custodia*, implied by Acts was a privilege of the Roman senatorial class and the very highest ranking provincial elites.[8] Paul's case is scarcely comparable to that of the Jewish prince Agrippa or of Locusta, Nero's medical adviser.[9] Moreover, the story Acts tells about the imprisoned apostle is not compatible with the information in Paul's own letters. Here Paul speaks instead of torture, hunger, nakedness, anxiety, and distress in his numerous experiences of imprisonment (1 Thess 2:2; 1 Cor 4:9–13; 2 Cor 6:4–5; 11:23–27; 12:10).

The picture in Acts has nonetheless influenced the interpretation of Philippians.[10] Attempts are made to use it to fill gaps in detail that Philippians leaves open. After all, Paul says in Philippians that he is in prison, but not where, how, and why. There is indication of a judicial process, but the accusation and the course of the proceedings are hidden behind formulations that are hard to interpret: ἐν τῇ ἀπολογίᾳ καὶ βεβαιώσει τοῦ εὐαγγελίου ("in the defense and confirmation of the gospel," 1:7); προκοπὴν τοῦ εὐαγγελίου ("progress for the gospel," 1:12); τοὺς δεσμούς μου φανεροὺς ἐν Χριστῷ γενέσθαι ἐν ὅλῳ τῷ πραιτωρίῳ καὶ τοῖς λοιποῖς πᾶσιν ("my bonds has become visible in Christ in the whole *praetorium* and to all the rest," 1:13). Assistance is sought by proposing that the imprisonment is in Ephe-

---

römischer Bürger," *ZNW* 78 (1987): 200–29; Karl Leo Noethlichs, "Der Jude Paulus: Ein Tarser oder Römer?" in *Rom und das himmlische Jerusalem: Die frühen Christen zwischen Anpassung und Ablehnung*, ed. Raban von Haehling (Darmstadt: Wissenschaftliche Buchgesellschaft, 2000), 53–84; Pervo, *Acts*, 554–56; Peter Pilhofer, "Einer der 5984072? Zum römischen Bürgerrecht des Paulus," *Neues aus der Welt der frühen Christen*, BWANT 195 (Stuttgart: Kohlhammer, 2011), 63–75. Differently, Heike Omerzu, *Der Prozess des Paulus: Eine exegetische und rechtshistorische Untersuchung der Apostelgeschichte*, BZNW 115 (Berlin: de Gruyter, 2002), 19–51.

8. Jens-Uwe Krause, *Gefängnisse im Römischen Reich*, Heidelberger althistorische Beiträge und epigraphische Studien 23 (Stuttgart: Steiner, 1996), 183–88.

9. See Josephus, *Ant.* 18.192–236; only after some time and because a member of the Tiberian family intervened for him did Agrippa's conditions change. Then he was given in charge "of a humane centurion" and was allowed to take a daily bath and "to have assistance from his friends" (*Ant.* 18.203; also, Acts 27:1–3). The *libera custodia* at home (Acts 28:16–31) is conceded to Agrippa only in the very last days of his custody (*Ant.* 18.235). For Locusta, a female member of the Roman nobility, see Tacitus, *Ann.* 13.15.

10. An extensive harmonization is provided by H. W. Tajra, *The Martyrdom of St. Paul*, WUNT 2/67 (Tübingen: Mohr Siebeck, 1994), 58–72.

sus, Caesarea, or Rome, supposing that Paul has been arrested because of the riot of the silversmiths or "the Jews" in Ephesus or in Jerusalem.[11] But after two years of confinement in Caesarea (Acts 24:27) or Rome (28:30), there was sympathy for Paul not only among the soldiers and centurions who watched over him, but even among governors, because they recognized that he was not a criminal (see also 2 Tim 2:9). The revelation of his citizenship (Acts 22:25) or the sympathy of Felix, Festus, Agrippa, and their wives (Acts 24:24–27; 25:1–26, 32) allowed him to hope that there would be a change in the trial process.[12] The greetings from "the emperor's household" (Phil 4:22) are thought to come from Paul's guards or from those in the *praetorium* he had been able to convert.[13] Even though Paul speaks of "chains," he has (nearly) complete freedom of movement.[14]

Of course, the exegetes do detect a number of conflicts in the content. Thus especially those who (with Acts) propose Rome as the place of origin date the composition to the year 62 or later, "since Luke's picture of the first two years in Rome (Acts 28:16, 30–31) seems to envision a somewhat less severe and perilous situation than Paul faces at the time of writing."[15] Others, who prefer Ephesus as the place of composition, emphasize the

---

11. Nikolaus Walter et al., *Die Briefe an die Philipper: Thessalonicher und an Philemon*, NTD 8.2 (Göttingen: Vandenhoeck & Ruprecht, 1998), 38–39, argues with Acts 19:26–40. Wilhelm Michaelis, *Der Brief des Paulus an die Philipper*, THKNT 11 (Leipzig: Deichert, 1935), employs Acts 17:5–9; 18:12–17. Both locate Paul's imprisonment in Ephesus. Gerald F. Hawthorne and Ralph P. Martin, *Philippians Revised*, rev. Ralph P. Martin, WBC 43 (Nashville: Nelson, 2004), 44, who locate Paul's imprisonment in Caesarea, postulate the situation of Acts 21–26.

12. See Jean-François Colange, *The Epistle of Saint Paul to the Philippians*, trans. A. W. Heathcote (London: Epworth, 1979), 9; Hawthorne and Martin, *Philippians*, 44.

13. See Acts 23:24, 26; 27:2–3, 43; 28:16, 30; Hawthorne and Martin, *Philippians*, 114; Gordon Fee, *Paul's Letter to the Philippians*, NICNT (Grand Rapids: Eerdmans, 1995), 114; Ulrich B. Müller, *Der Brief des Paulus an die Philipper*, 2nd ed., THKNT 11.1 (Leipzig: Evangelische Verlagsanstalt, 2003), 212. Also, Walter, *Brief an die Philipper*, 39.

14. Müller, *Brief des Paulus an die Philipper*, 52; Markus Bockmuehl, *The Epistle to the Philippians*, BNTC (Peabody, MA: Hendrickson, 1998), 64: with 2 Tim 2:9 (sic) Fee, *Paul's Letter*, argues that Paul was "literally chained to his guard."

15. Bockmuehl, *Epistle to the Philippians*, 32; see Peter O'Brien, *The Epistle to the Philippians*, NIGTC (Grand Rapids, Eerdmans, 1991), 26; Fee, *Paul's Letter*, 34–37; see Richard J. Cassidy, *Paul in Chains: Roman Imprisonment and the Letters of St. Paul* (New York: Crossroad, 2001). For Cassidy, Philippians is a rethinking of Rom 13:1-7 after two years' imprisonment in Rome.

"paucity of information" and explain it by saying that Paul wanted to divert attention from himself to the gospel.[16] Interpreters admire the "apostolic matter-of-factness" (Karl Barth) with which Paul passes over his own situation.[17] An interpretation very popular in post-World War I Germany presented the traumatized prisoners of war with the example of the imprisoned apostle, who instead of "giving vent to his bitterness" breathed "the powerful sigh of his pastoral love" toward the community.[18] In similar fashion, Wilhelm Michaelis and, after World War II, Gerhard Friedrich argued against the background of ancient papyrus letters written in captivity. Differently from these letters, Paul writes nothing about hunger, suffering, the conditions of his prison, and certainly not about liberation, but instead, with the aid of his trust in God, he shows himself superior to the situation of captivity.[19] This observation is also shared by newer approaches and is now traced to Paul's political stance, which called for distancing oneself from the world of Roman society.[20]

However, to this point very few have investigated whether and to what extent the living conditions of the 99 percent of the inhabitants of the Roman empire who were not members of the senatorial or equestrian classes and were born outside the royal palaces of Rome's allies are reflected in Philippians.[21] Still less frequently are the specific structures of communication for those in Roman custody studied; that is, few ask

---

16. Joachim Gnilka, *Der Philipperbrief*, HTKNT 10.3 (Freiburg: Herder, 1968), 55.

17. See John Reumann, *Philippians: A New Translation with Introduction and Commentary*, AB 33B (New Haven: Yale University Press, 2008), 191–97; Karl Barth, *Erklärung des Philipperbriefs*, 6th ed. (Zollikon: Evangelischer Verlag, 1947), 27.

18. Otto Schmitz, *Aus der Welt eines Gefangenen: Der Philipperbrief* (Giessen: Brunnen Verlag, 1988), 10. This popular commentary saw six new editions between 1922 and 1934.

19. Wilhelm Michaelis, "Die Gefangenschaftsbriefe des Paulus und antike Gefangenenbriefe," *NKZ* 36 (1925): 586–95. With the same source material but incorporating additional reports on the experience of German war prisoners, Gerhard Friedrich, "Der Brief eines Gefangenen," *Montatsschrift für Pastoraltheologie* 44 (1955): 270–80. See also Müller, *Brief des Paulus an die Philipper,* 52–53.

20. Robin Scroggs, "Paul the Prisoner: Political Asceticism in the Letter to the Philippians," in *Asceticism and the New Testament*, ed. Leif E. Vaage and Vincent L. Wimbush (New York: Routledge, 1999), 187–207; Cassidy, *Paul,* 163–209.

21. But see Craig S. Wansink, *Chained in Christ: The Experience and Rhetoric of Paul's Imprisonments*, JSNTSup 130 (Sheffield: Sheffield Academic, 1996), 27–95; Cassidy, *Paul,* 36–54. For Paul's custody in Acts see Brian Rapske, *The Book of Acts and*

the question how and what one could write while imprisoned. I will here support the thesis that the situation of composition in a Roman prison demanded a degree of ambiguity in speaking and writing that has made difficulty for interpreters of Philippians from then until now, for a letter written in prison must reckon with being read by more than the immediate addressees, namely, by the prison guards, police personnel, and judges.[22] Thus a letter from prison is always also an "open interaction between the subordinates and those who dominate," or, as the political scientist James Scott has called it, a "public transcript."[23] The question that then arises, however, is whether, behind the public transcript that is the letter to the Philippians, we may also discover a hidden transcript, a discourse "that takes place 'offstage,' beyond direct observation by power holders."[24]

In what follows I will first seek to clarify what Paul is conveying in Philippians, using other sources on the living conditions in ancient prisons. In a second step, likewise against the background of ancient parallels, I will describe the dangers of written communication from prison, as well as strategies for limiting the danger. Finally, I want to ask how the community in Philippi might have read the letter beyond what is obviously conveyed by it. Are there signals pointing beyond what is openly said to hidden content lying behind it? And if so, how can they be decoded?

Paul in Roman Custody (Grand Rapids: Eerdmans, 1994). On ancient prison conditions in general, see Krause, *Gefängnisse*.

22. But see recently Hans Dieter Betz, *Der Apostel Paulus in Rom*, Julius-Wellhausen-Vorlesung 4 (Berlin: de Gruyter, 2013), 25, 29. Betz located Paul's imprisonment with Acts in Rome in the late days of Nero and attributes the later death to the collapse of Roman law systems under Nero, asserted by Tacitus, *Ann.* 15.71. But Tacitus's image of Nero's reign might not be objective enough to draw such a conclusion. Tacitus's task, after all, was to present history in a way that his patron Trajan would appear as the only true reformer and best Caesar ever. In his 2015 commentary, *Studies in Paul's Letter to the Philippians*, WUNT 343 (Tübingen: Mohr Siebeck, 2015), Betz reads the letter as a *praemeditatio mortis,* a philosophical reflection on one's own death (see Plato, *Phaed.* 80e–81a; Cicero, *Tusc.* 3.29–32; and Seneca's letters, especially *Ep.* 54.2 and 107.3–4). As will become obvious in the following, I place Paul and his addressees in a lower stratum of ancient society.

23. James C. Scott, *Domination and the Arts of Resistance: Hidden Transcripts* (New Haven: Yale University Press, 1990), 2.

24. Ibid., 4.

Inside a Roman Prison

Besides the mainly late ancient law collections that touch on various procedural questions, we have at our disposal some indications for the living conditions in the prisons of the early imperial period in Stoic authors, novelistic narratives,[25] and Christian martyrdom narratives, as well as information from Roman historians and biographers and surviving papyrus documents containing petitions from prisoners. Each source has its own rhetorical intent. Christian martyrdom stories, ancient novels, and papyrus letters are intended to arouse sympathy by describing the conditions of imprisonment, either in order to achieve some amelioration or to underscore the great strength of their heroes in suffering. Stoic philosophers could demonstrate their inner freedom in dismal situations, historians the lawless, unjust, and hideous regimes of bad emperors. Rhetorical effects achieved by exaggeration cannot be excluded.[26] But references to the living conditions common in ancient prisons are also found in popular handbooks for the interpretation of dreams or astrology. This shows that the danger of being thrown into prison, remaining there for a long time, or dying from the conditions of captivity certainly existed for ordinary residents of the Roman empire.[27]

When Paul, in the prescript to Philippians, does not call himself "apostle," but speaks of himself and Timothy as "slaves of Christ" (Phil 1:1), we can read this as a description of the situation, for "slave of Christ" not only includes a dutiful relationship toward the community or God (2 Cor 4:5; Rom 1:1), but also connotes lack of freedom, distress, fear, and persecution (2 Cor 4:7–12), as well as human contempt (Gal 1:12). The self-description "slave" matches the life experiences of prisoners and not only in antiquity.

Paul expresses all the more gratitude to the community in Philippi that they have him in their hearts, "both in my bonds (ἐν τοῖς δεσμοῖς) and in the defense and confirmation of the gospel" (1:7). For most prisoners, however, fetters were a physical reality; that is, prisoners frequently had their feet placed in the stocks, and sometimes wore fetters on their necks and

---

25. See Philostratus, *Vit. Apoll.* 4.7–8, or the novella on the friendship between the Cynic philosopher Demetrius and his unlucky imprisoned friend Antiphilus in Lucian, *Tox.* 27–34.

26. See Wansink, *Chained in Christ*, 19–22.

27. Krause, *Gefängnisse*, 1–7.

hands as well.[28] Thus in the friendship novella in Lucian's dialogue *Toxaris*, we read of Antiphilus, who has had the misfortune to be imprisoned:

> Consequently, he sickened at length and was ill, as might be expected in view of the fact that he slept on the ground and at night could not even stretch out his legs, which were confined in the stocks. By day, to be sure, the collar was sufficient, together which manacles upon one hand; but for the night he had to be fully secured by his bonds. Moreover, the stench of the room and its stifling air (since many were confined in the same place, cramped for room, and scarcely able to draw breath). (Lucian, *Tox.* 29 [LCL, Harmon])[29]

While some parts of this description may have been chosen for rhetorical effect, binding and chains are frequent omens in Artemidorus's handbook for the interpretation of dreams. "If you think you have put on stilts, this means the fetters of criminals, since stilts are, as we know, made fast to the feet and alter one's free stride" (*Onir.* 3.15). Likewise, dreaming of the number ρ (100) is a bad omen, since "criminals are put in chains, and *pedai* (foot-fetters) makes 100."[30] In any case, it is striking that Paul writes only in Philippians that he *lies* (χεῖμαι, 1:16) in prison "for the defense of the gospel."[31]

Prisons were described as dark, humid, and hot, frequently overfilled and extremely filthy.[32] In Artemidorus's dream book, a dream in which

---

28. Ibid., 283–86; Wansink, *Chained in Christ*, 46–49.

29. The Jewish prince Agrippa was also chained, at least initially; see also Josephus, *Ant.* 18.195.

30. Astrologers and missionaries of non-Roman religions were generally in danger in the early empire (see, e.g., Cassius Dio, *His. Rom* 57.3–5). But chains could also be used as an argument in missionary competitions: see Juvenal, *Sat.* 6.559–561: "For nowadays no astrologer has credit unless he has been imprisoned in some distant camp, with chains clanking on either arm; none believe in his powers unless he has been condemned and all but put to death." (LCL, G. G. Ramsey).

31. Friedrich Büchsel, "χεῖμαι," *TDNT* 3:654, contra Walter Bauer, *Griechisch-Deutsches Wörterbuch* (Berlin: de Gruyter, 1988), 868; also Danker, *Greek-English Lexicon*, 537.

32. Cicero charges Verres that he had not allowed visits when he sent a member of the Roman aristocracy to prison (*Verr.* 2.5.8 [§21]). For the bad sanitary conditions in prison, see Lucian, *Tox.* 30; Seneca, *Ep.* 77.18. A bath was a special privilege (Josephus, *Ant.* 18.203), as was being "allowed to go to a better part of the prison to refresh" oneself (Mart. Perp. 3.6). See also Krause, *Gefängnisse*, 286–88.

one was kept in Hades meant prison (2.55), as did a dream of many lice (3.7). The martyr Perpetua writes in her diary: "I was terrified, as I had never before been in such a dark hole. What a difficult time it was! With the crowd the heat was stifling, then there were the many informers of the soldiers" (Mart. Perpt. 3.5 [Musurillo]).[33] Hunger was common.[34] This is bitterly complained of in letters from prisoners. Thus the flute player Petakos writes to Zenon: "Before you depart, please do not leave me behind in prison, for I lack the most essential things. I adjure you by the health of the father and siblings and the good of Apollonius. Farewell" (*PSI* 4.416, third century BCE).[35]

---

33. Herbert A. Musurillo, *The Acts of the Christian Martyrs* (Oxford: Clarendon Press, 1972), 109. Latin: *delator*, Greek: συκοφάντης: a "common informer, voluntary denouncer" (LSJ 1671). In a rhetorical exercise a son, guilty of matricide, who pleads to be sent to a public prison, imagines the situation there: "I can visualize the state prison, constructed of huge stone blocks, receiving through the narrow chinks just a faint semblance of light. Culprits cast into this prison look forward to the execution cell, and whenever the creaking of the iron-bound door stirs those helpless, sprawled out people, they are terrified, and by viewing someone else's punishment they learn of their own soon to come. Whiplashes crack, food is delivered in the foul hands of the executioner to those who then refuse it. The hard-hearted doorkeeper sits by, a man whose eyes would remain dry even when his mother weeps. Filth roughens their bodies, chains grip their hands tightly" (Calpurnius Flaccus, *Declamations* 4; trans. Lewis A. Sussman).

34. Krause, *Gefängnisse*, 279–308; Wansink, *Chained in Christ*, 63–66. Athenaeus, *Deipn.* 4.161c, describes prison fare as bread and water.

35. Πέτακος ὁ αὐλητής. πρὸ τοῦ σε ἀποδημῆσαι, ἵνα μή με καταλίπη[ι]ς ἐν τῶι δεσμωτηρίωι· οὐ γὰρ ἔχω τὰ ἀναγκαῖα· ἐναρῶμαί σοι τὴν ὑγίειαν τοῦ πατρὸς καὶ τῶν ἀδελφῶν καὶ τὴν Ἀπολλωνίου σωτηρίαν. εὐτύχει. Similar letters, e.g.: P.Petr. 3.36 verso (218 BCE): "To the Epimeletan Nicanor. I have often written to you, for I am utterly overcome in prison, I am dying of hunger.... Therefore I pray you, let me not perish of hunger in prison, but write to the jailer about it or send me to him ... that I may find rescue." See P.Petr. 3.36 recto (third century BCE); P.Yale 42 (229 BCE); White, *Ancient Letters*, 54–55 (no. 28); P.Oxy. LVI 3870 (sixth/seventh century CE); P.Cair. Masp. I 67020 (sixth century CE) or the ostracon O.Mon.Epih.117 (sixth century CE): "we were at pains and wrote to you and you have forgotten us in the captivity where we are, while they hung us up backward and took our breath out (of our bodies), and you did not visit us. For we gave our life for you; look you have forgotten us. Don't trust the men, lest they kill us. For as the Lord lives, if you don't reach us today with the money, there will be no life left in us. Send the rations for us to the jailer and give loaves and ... give it to Pesenthios and Panoute, from ... her and Thekla. Pay the wage of ... who shall bring this potsherd to you" (Roger S. Bagnall and Raffaella Cribiore,

It is clear in Phil 1:7 that Paul is awaiting trial. He alludes to the legal proceeding with the juridical term ἀπολογία (defense speech) and the naming of a judicial location (*praetorium*). The Latin loanword πραιτώιον (*praetorium*) designated the tent of a general in the Roman army or a palace, especially that of a governor in the provinces.[36] Thus the reference is not to the prison, but to the place of judgment.[37] In the provinces, only the governor had the authority to conduct judicial proceedings and issue judgments.[38] For this purpose, he traveled to the various points of assembly within his province. During his absence, judicial proceedings were in abeyance, which often led to long periods of imprisonment. Besides the numerous contacts and journeys between the community and Paul that must have taken place during the time when Philippians was being written and the travel plans (Phil 2:24; see also Phlm 24), incompatible with Rom 15:28–29, the place of judgment being called *praetorium* speaks in favor of the composition of Philippians in an eastern province.[39] The agreement with the horrible danger of death (τηλικοῦντος θάνατος) seen in retrospect in 2 Cor 1:8–10 and the sentence of death (τὸ ἀπόκριμα τοῦ θανάτου) already received in the province of Asia, together with the fears in Phil 1:20–23;

Women's Letters from Ancient Egypt 300 BC–AD 800 [Ann Arbor: University of Michigan Press, 2006], 246).

36. See Suetonius, *Aug.* 24 (general's tent); Epictetus, *Diatr.* 3.22.47; *Martyrdom of Perpetua* 3.7 (palace); for the governor's palace: Mark 15:16; Matt 27:27 (Jesus is tortured there); John 18:28, 33; 19:9 (Pilate's headquarters); Acts 23:35 (Herod's palace, taken over by the governors Festus and Felix). For more instances of *praetorium* as a governor's palace in other provinces see Cicero, *Verr.* 2.4.65; 2.5.92; *BGU* 1.288.14; P.Oxy. III, 471.115 (*Acta Maximi*), etc.

37. There is no evidence that a *praetorium* was ever an official prison. When Paul is in custody in Herod's palace in Acts 23:35, this is meant as a very special honor; see Rapske, *The Book of Acts*, 156–58.

38. Krause, *Gefängnisse*, 64–65.

39. Those who favor Rome as the place where Philippians was written mainly follow the argumentation of J. B. Lightfoot, *Saint Paul's Epistle to the Philippians* (New York: Macmillan, 1888), 99–105, who argues that because ἐν ὅλῳ τῷ πραιτωρίῳ (in the whole Praetorium) is parallel to τοῖς λοιποῖς πᾶσιν (to all the rest) Paul does not mean a place but a group of people, the Praetorian Guard as the emperor's elite troops and bodyguards. They speculate that the soldiers in charge of Paul in Acts 27:1–3, 43; 28:16 are members of the Praetorian Guard (see O'Brien, *Epistle*, 92–94; Fee, *Paul's Letter*, 113–14; Betz, *Studies*, 136 n. 13). But there is no evidence for this speculation besides that the Praetorian Guard might be called *praetorium* (Pliny the Elder, *Nat.* 25.6.17; Tacitus, *Hist.* 1.20.3; 2.11.3; Suetonius, *Nero* 9).

2:17–18 suggests composition during an imprisonment in Ephesus.[40] The amnesty practiced when a new emperor succeeded to office, particularly for his predecessor's political prisoners, would also explain the utterly surprising release of the group of apostles, described in 2 Cor 1:8–10 as God's deed and a miracle.[41] Paul and his fellow prisoners would then have been released, altogether surprisingly and in spite of a death sentence already pronounced, at the end of 54 or beginning of 55 because of the ascent of Nero to the throne.

The death sentence referred to in 2 Cor 1:8–10 means that the judicial process had not resulted at all favorably for Paul and his coworkers.[42] Scholars have discussed *seditio* or *crimen maiestatis* as possible charges, against the background of Acts.[43] However, in Acts, Paul and his companions are frequently charged with instigating riots, but everywhere the accusation turns back immediately on the accusers themselves (see Acts 16:20–21;

---

40. See Reumann, *Philippians*, 13–14; Heike Omerzu, "Spurensuche: Apostelgeschichte und Paulusbriefe als Zeugnis einer ephesischen Gefangenschaft des Paulus," in *Die Apostelgeschichte im Kontext antiker und frühchristlicher Historiographie*, ed. Jörg Frei, Clare K. Rothschild, and Jens Schröter, BZNW 162 (Berlin: de Gruyter, 2009), 295–326.

41. On amnesties after the death of the former emperor, see Krause, *Gefängnisse*, 218–22. See also Cassius Dio, *His. Rom.* 59.6.2: "He [Caligula] freed those who were in prison, among them Quintus Pomponius, who for seven whole years after his consulship had been kept in jail and maltreated. He did away with the complaints for *maiestas*"; Cassius Dio, *Hist. Rom.* 61.4.2: "Of the persons in prison—and a very large number were thus confined—he liberated those who had been put there for *maiestas* and similar charges, but punished those who were guilty of actual wrongdoing. For he investigated all the cases very carefully, in order that those who had committed crimes should not be released along with those who had been falsely accused, nor the latter, on the other hand, perish along with the former." Also, Suetonius, *Claud.* 15.4. Cassius Dio, *Hist. Rom.* 78.3.3 reports a speech of Antoninus Pius in the Senate in Rome: "Listen to an important announcement from me: that the whole world may rejoice, let all the exiles who have been condemned, on whatever charge or in whatever manner, be restored." Sometimes Roman governors released prisoners simply out of arbitrary benevolence; see Krause, *Gefängnisse*, 213–18.

42. Paul in 2 Cor 1:8–11 speaks of a group ("we"). It is hard to say whether Timothy, cosender and coslave in Phil 1:1, is inside or outside the prison.

43. See Omerzu, *Prozess des Paulus*, passim. That there were not more charges under the *lex maiestatis* between 41 and 60 CE (compare Scroggs, "Paul the Prisoner," with Richard Baumann, *Crime and Punishment in Ancient Rome* [London: Routledge, 1996], 62–83) might be true for Rome and Roman aristocrats, but our evidence is not good enough to draw any conclusions for the provinces.

17:5–9; 19:23, 40; 21:27–40; 24:5, etc.).[44] One of the few other accusations was that "they are all acting contrary to the decrees of the emperor, saying that there is another king named Jesus" (Acts 17:7). This, as an attempted coup, would be equally dangerous, but it is just as impossible to confirm, either in Acts or in Paul.[45] Paul himself speaks to the contrary in Philippians of "the defense and confirmation of the gospel" (1:7, 16). However, the key word βεβαίωσις (confirmation), which unlike ἀπολογία (apology) is not part of legal language, is difficult to interpret.[46] Nevertheless, most exegetes join Adolf Deissmann in thinking that ἀπολογία refers to the refutation of the accusations and βεβαίωσις to "the presentation of positive proofs of the truth."[47] But βεβαίωσις, which belongs in the contexts of philosophy, oaths, and the language of business, means the solidifying or confirmation of promises, statements, or knowledge previously uttered.[48]

---

44. See Omerzu, *Prozess des Paulus*, 124–41, 188–218, 252–58, 424–39; Pervo, *Acts*, 406–7, 420–21, 454–55, 498–502, 596–97. Fomenting a riot would be a dangerous accusation, as Acts 19:40 says. See Christian Gizewski, "Maiestas," *Brill's New Pauly*, ed. Hubert Cancik and Helmuth Schneider, http://brillonline.nl/entries/brill-s-new-pauly/maiestas-e718120: "The death penalty or the heaviest other punishments were exacted for the *crimen maiestatis* directed 'against the Roman people and its safety' (*adversus populum Romanum vel securitatem eius*), which could be committed by Romans or subjected provincials, by the planned killing of a magistrate, by armed revolt or preparation for the same, by the liberation of prisoners or hostages, by the occupation of public and sacred buildings or by co-operation with an enemy power (*hostis*)" (Codex justinianus 48.4.1.1). See also Wilfried Nippel, *Public Order in Ancient Rome*, Key Themes in Ancient History (Cambridge: Cambridge University Press, 1995), 47–57, 106–22.

45. The closest parallel is Luke 23:2, but here again it is a false accusation. It may have been an actual charge against some Christians; see Justin, *1 Apol.* 11.

46. See also Acts 22:1; 25:16; 2 Tim 4:16; Luke 12:11; 21:14, etc.

47. Adolf Deissmann, *Bibelstudien* (Marburg: Elwert, 1895), 103–4. The defense before the court will be both an *evictio* and a *convictio* of the gospel. (Also, Deissmann, *Bible Studies: Contributions, Chiefly from Papyri and Inscriptions, to the History of the Language, the Literature, and the Religion of Hellenistic Judaism and Primitive Christianity*, trans. Alexander Grieve [Edinburgh: T&T Clark, 1901].) Lightfoot, *Saint Paul's Epistle*, 85: "As ἀπολογία implies the negative or defensive side of the Apostle's preaching, the preparatory process of removing obstacles and prejudice, so βεβαίωσις the positive or aggressive side, the direct advancement and establishment of the gospel." See also Reumann, *Philippians*, 118.

48. E.g., Heb 6:16; Rom 15:8; Epictetus, *Diatr.* 2.18.32; Philo, *Abr.* 273; *Jos.* 165; *Spec.* 2.13; *Legat.* 153–162. In contract law, βεβαίωσις means "the seller's confirmation of a sale" or a guarantee: Friedrich Preisigke, *Wörterbuch der griechischen Papy-*

That is, in using βεβαίωσις Paul underscores that he is not deviating from the gospel, that in fact his situation is strengthening and confirming it.

But what does "gospel" mean in this context? For Paul, gospel is "*terminus technicus* for the orally proclaimed message of the suffering, death, and resurrection of Christ as an eschatological event."[49] As a *nomen actionis*, εὐαγγέλιον describes not only the content of the message (e.g., 1 Thess 1:9–10; 1 Cor 15:3–5), but also the act of conveying the message (Phil 4:3; see 2 Cor 2:12; 1 Thess 1:5). The two meanings cannot be separated (Rom 1:1, 16; 1 Cor 4:15; 9:14, 18). And it is by no means only Paul and his coworkers who proclaim the gospel, but also and especially the communities (Phil 4:3; 2 Cor 8:18; 1 Thess 3:2). Indeed, in Phil 1, it is *only* others who "speak the word" (1:14) and proclaim Christ (1:15, 17–18).

Paul reports that, despite his imprisonment in that place, Christ is being proclaimed (1:14–18). This seems to be quite a risky business (τολμάω) that only a few dare to attempt (v. 14). There are also those who οἰόμενοι θλῖψιν ἐγείρειν τοῖς δεσμοῖς μου (v. 17). The phrase is usually translated "intending to increase my suffering in my imprisonment" (NRSV).[50] But the first "my" is not in the text. One might also translate, "they think that the sorrow is a result of my chains." Then those who proclaim Christ because of envy and rivalry (v. 15) would not be subjective enemies, but objectively concerned. Perhaps Paul can also rejoice even when Christ is proclaimed only "for show" (προφάσει, v. 18).

Paul hopes for himself, instead, that whether in life or in death "Christ will be exalted … in [his] body" (Phil 1:20). As in 1 Cor 4:9–13 or 2 Cor 4:8–12, for him (still) physical existence is the medium of proclamation, not in sovereign superiority to the external situation, but in distress, persecution, and oppression (2 Cor 4:8–9), in hunger, thirst, nakedness, and

---

rusurkunden (Wiesbaden: Harrassowitz, 1925), 1:263; Heinrich Schlier, "βεβαίος," *TDNT* 1:600–603. There is no forensic usage of the word apart from Phil 1:7.

49. Helmut Koester, "Evangelium," *RGG*⁴ 2:1736. See also Georg Friedrich, "εὐαγγέλιον κτλ," *TDNT* 2:707–37.

50. Those who translate without "my" interpret freely: Lohmeyer, *Die Briefe an die Philipper, an die Kolosser und Philemon*, KEK 9, 13th ed. (Göttingen: Vandenhoeck & Ruprecht, 1964), 36: "während, meine Fesseln zu verunglimpfen" ("intending to disparage my chains"); Gnilka, *Philipperbrief*, 59: "weil sie meinen, Trübsal auf meine Fesseln zu legen" ("because they mean to lay my afflictions on my chains"); Hawthorne and Martin, *Philippians* 38: "moved by selfish ambitions"; Reumann, *Philippians,* 166: "because they suppose thereby to stir up trouble for my imprisonment."

beatings, as the dregs of all things to other people (1 Cor 4:11–13), and above all in imprisonment and before the governor's court.

When Paul speaks of the "confirmation" (βεβαίωσις, 1:7), progress (προκοπή, 1:12), or defense (ἀπολογία, 1:7, 16) of the gospel, he is thinking not so much of missionary preaching as of sheer existence and survival in prison. This is itself an expression of the gospel. As suggested already in 1 Cor 4:9–13 and then explicitly in Phil 3:10 and 2 Cor 1:8–10, Paul identifies his suffering in prison with the content of the message, the suffering and death of Christ. This may also explain the information Paul conveys to the community that is so difficult to understand, namely, that his "chains in Christ" have become known to the whole *praetorium* and to everyone else as well (1:13). In any case, Paul everywhere else speaks of imprisonment, blows, and torture in the same breath and makes them, provocatively, a sign of his service as apostle of Christ.[51]

In ancient legal custom, torture was part of a court proceeding;[52] there was no way of gathering evidence, so an attempt was made to force a confession. Accusation, imprisonment, and torture were practically synonymous and were frequently listed together.[53] For Tertullian, therefore, the practice of torture was part of the exercise of office as well as the soldier's calling.[54] Torture repeatedly resulted in false self-accusations.[55] But its primary purpose was the discovery of coconspirators and accomplices. Consequently, torture was practiced even after sentencing.[56] Many sought to protect themselves against betrayal and handing over their friends

---

51. See 2 Cor 6:5: ἐν πληγαῖς, ἐν φυλακαῖς, ἐν ἀκαταστασίαις, ἐν κόποις, ἐν ἀγρυπνίαις, ἐν νηστείαις ("in beatings, in imprisonments, in mob violence, in sufferings, in deprivations of sleep, in fastings"); 2 Cor 11:23: ἐν φυλακαῖς περισσοτέρως, ἐν πληγαῖς ὑπερβαλλόντως, ἐν θανάτοις πολλάκις ("far more imprisonments, with countless floggings, and often near death").

52. Krause, *Gefängnisse*, 291–95; Wansink, *Chained in Christ*, 50–55. Even in Acts a beating follows Paul's arrests (Acts 16:23; 22:25). His claim of citizenship serves to rescue him from torture in Acts 22:25.

53. E.g., Artemidorus, *Oneir.* 1.77; 2.14; 3.59; Suetonius, *Claud.* 34.1; Epictetus, *Diatr.* 2.2.8–26; Seneca, *Ep.* 9.5–6; Pliny the Younger, *Ep.* 10.96.8.

54. Tertullian, *Idol.* 17.3; *Cor.* 11.1.

55. Suetonius, *Dom.* 8.4; Philostratus, *Apoll.* 5.24.

56. Tacitus, *Ann.* 15.56–69; Cassius Dio, *Hist. Rom.* 56.16.3–4; Lucian, *Tox.* 28; Ammianus Marcellinus, *Roman History* 12.7–17. See also Mark 15:16–20; Matt 27:27–31; John 19:2–3.

and associates by committing suicide.[57] For others, torture resulted in death.[58] At the same time, prisoners in antiquity depended on helpers and supporters.[59] Matthew's Gospel and the Letter to the Hebrews both urge such support, and Christians' care for prisoners was familiar to ancient writers as early as the second century.[60] Prisoners frequently were dependent on their families or friends for food.[61] Efforts were also made to support them at their trials or at least to ameliorate their prison situation.[62] It was the usual thing to bribe the guards to obtain access to the prisoners.[63] Of course, visitors and supporters were in danger of being imprisoned themselves, as coconspirators and collaborators.[64]

---

57. Tacitus, *Ann.* 4.45; 15.57 (the example of a heroic woman).

58. Krause, *Gefängnisse*, 295–99; Diodorus Siculus writes that Eunus, the leader of a slave rebellion in Sicily in the second century CE, was so severely tortured in prison that "his flesh disintegrated into a mass of lice" (34/35.2.23). See Ammianus Marcellinus, *Roman History* 12.13; Eusebius, *Hist. eccl.* 5.1.27.

59. Krause, *Gefängnisse*, 288–91; Wansink, *Chained in Christ*, 78–84.

60. In the last judgment scene in Matt 25:36, 39, 43, visiting those in prison is one of the good works the king will remember, and Hebrews encourages: "Remember those who are in prison, as though you were in prison with them; those who are being tortured, as though you yourselves were being tortured" (13:3). Lucian, *Peregr.* 12–13, refers to this Christian behavior in his satire on the Cynic philosopher Peregrinus Proteus (see below).

61. Krause, *Gefängnisse*, 280–83. Tertullian, *Mart.*, criticizes lavish banquets provided in prison for those awaiting martyrdom.

62. See Martyrdom of Perpetua 3.6; Lucian, *Peregr.* 12–13: "Then at length Proteus was apprehended for this and thrown into prison, which itself gave him no little reputation as an asset for his future career and the charlatanism and notoriety-seeking that he was enamoured of. Well, when he had been imprisoned, the Christians, regarding the incident as a calamity, left nothing undone in the effort to rescue him. Then, as this was impossible, every other form of attention was shown him, not in any casual way but with assiduity, and from the very break of day aged widows and orphan children could be seen waiting near the prison, while their officials even slept inside with him after bribing the guards. Then elaborate meals were brought in, and sacred books of theirs were read aloud, and excellent Peregrinus—for he still went by that name—was called by them 'the new Socrates.' Indeed, people came even from the cities in Asia, sent by the Christians at their common expense, to succour and defend and encourage the hero" (Harmon, LCL).

63. See Lucian, *Tox.* 30; Acts of Paul and Thecla 18.

64. Philostratus, *Vit. Apoll.* 4.46, writes that in prison the philosopher Musonius refused to converse openly with Apollonius "in order that both their lives might not be endangered." Later, when Apollonius is about to be imprisoned, he advises his student Damis: "I do not wish that you should be a sharer of my fate through being detected

The community in Philippi supported Paul from a distance, for one thing through a sum of money that approached or even exceeded the Philippians' capacity.[65] On the other hand, they also sent Epaphroditus as their "apostle" and agent (λειτουργός) to support Paul in his imprisonment (4:18–19; 2:30). Paul calls him, respectfully, "brother," "coworker," and "fellow soldier" (συστρατιώτης, Phil 2:25).[66] It is possible that he was arrested when he delivered the money. One indication of this could be Phlm 23, if Epaphras is a short form of Epaphroditus.[67] In any case, while he was with Paul, he has fallen deathly ill (Phil 2:27, 30). Paul parallels the fate of Epaphroditus with the biography of Christ. Alluding to verse 8 in the hymn, γενόμενος ὑπήκοος μέχρι θανάτου ("became obedient to the point of death"), he says of Epaphroditus in Phil 2:30 that he is μέχρι θανάτου ἤγγισεν ("came close to death") for the work of Christ. Thus Epaphroditus has not tried to escape risk in his service as agent.[68] The news of his severe illness causes anxiety and concern both to the community in Philippi and

---

by your dress, which will betray you and lead to your arrest" (7.15). See also Eusebius, *Mart. Pol.* 3.4; Cassius Dio, *Hist. Rom.* 58.3.7; Brian Rapske, "The Importance of Helpers to the Imprisoned Paul in the Book of Acts," *TynBul* 42 (1991): 3–30.

65. The communities in Macedonia were especially poor (2 Cor 8:2) and under severe pressure and persecuted (see 1 Thess 2:1–2; Phil 2:28). What Epaphroditus brings with him is more than Paul expected, and it seems he is concerned that the Philippians are now in need (Phil 4:18–19).

66. For a different reconstruction of Epaphroditus and his service to Paul, see the following chapter, by Marchal, in this volume.

67. In Phlm 23, Epaphras is called fellow prisoner (συναιχμάλωτος). Greetings are sent also from Mark, Aristarchus (from Thessalonica in Macedonia, Acts 20:4; 27:2), Demas, and Luke. It is not clear if they are in prison with Paul or not. Romans 16:7 shows that Paul sometimes met other sisters and brothers in Christ in prison. Colossians 4:10–14 interprets the list of names from Philemon as fellow prisoners; 2 Tim 4:10–11 expands the legend. Here Demas, "in love with this present world," has deserted, and only Luke is with Paul. Mark seems to be away, but "Paul" asks that he come back.

68. There is only one known parallel for παραβολευσάμενος (Phil 2:29). In an inscription for Olbia (*IosPE* I 21) on the Black Sea, one can read: "It was testified everywhere on earth, that for the sake of friendship in legal strife (by taking cases) up to the Emperors" (ἀλλὰ καὶ [μέχρι] περάτων γῆς μαρτυρήθη τοὺς ὑπὲρ φιλίας κινδύνους μέχρι Σεβαστῶν συμμαχίᾳ παραβολευσάμενος); see Reumann, *Philippians*, 432; Adolf Deissmann, *Licht vom Osten* (Tübingen: Mohr Siebeck, 1923), 69. The expression παραβάλλεσθαι ψυχήν ("to gamble with one's life") appears first in Homer (*Il.* 9.322) and then often of people who serve their communities (e.g., 2 Macc 14:38; Diodorus Siculus, *Bibl. hist.* 30.9.2; Cassius Dio, *Hist. Rom.* 1.5.13).

to Paul (2:26–27), and Paul now wants to send Epaphroditus back so that their and his concern will be somewhat reduced.[69] Whether that is an actual possibility for Timothy as long as Paul is imprisoned (Phil 2:19–24), we again do not know. However, it was possible for Paul to compose and send letters.[70]

Writing in Prison

Paul is not the only person to write letters in prison. Papyrus archives contain a number of letters of petition in which prisoners complain of illegal treatment, beg for favor or bread, or seek witnesses.[71] In literature also there is mention of writings composed in prison. Socrates is supposed to have composed songs of praise to Apollo when he was in prison.[72] Others wrote verses or comedies, their wills, or letters.[73] But writing in prison was dangerous. "Sextius Paconianus was strangled in prison for verses which he had there indicted against the sovereigns" (Tacitus, *Ann.* 6.39 [Moore]). Sometimes even allusions in writings were sufficient to bring about an arrest.[74]

What was said or written in prison could be used against the author. Fellow prisoners could hope to lighten their punishments by betraying their cellmates or accusing them, truthfully or falsely.[75] In addition, spies were sent into prisons to sound out the prisoners.[76] In other ways as well,

---

69. The word ἀδημονέω (2:26) means "to be sorely troubled or dismayed, be in anguish" (LSJ 21). Sending Epaphroditus back will decrease their sorrow only in part (ἀλυπότερος, 2:28).

70. In Phlm 22, Paul is obviously more optimistic.

71. Plea to be released from prison: P.Polit.Jud. 2; *SB* I 4301; PSI VII, 807; asking for a witness: P.Yale 34. See also the papyri mentioned in note 35.

72. Plato, *Phaedr.* 60D; Diogenes Laertius, *Lives* 2.42; Epictetus, *Diatr.* 2.6.26–27; unspecified writing: Epictetus, *Diatr.* 2.1.32.

73. See Aulus Gellius, *Noct. att.* 3.3.15: "So too we are told of Naevius that he wrote two plays in prison, the *Soothsayer* and the *Leon*, when by reason of his constant abuse and insults aimed at the leading men of the city, after the manner of the Greek poets, he had been imprisoned at Rome by the triumvirs." See Tacitus, *Ann.* 6.38; Philostratus, *Vit. Apoll.* 4.46 (see below).

74. See Suetonius, *Tib.* 61: "A poet was charged with having slandered Agamemnon in a tragedy, and a writer of history of having called Brutus and Cassius the last of the Romans."

75. Krause, *Gefängnisse*, 299–301.

76. See Martyrdom of Perpetua 3.5 (above); Philostratus, *Vit. Apoll.* 4.42; 7.27.36; Achilles Tatius, *Leuc. Clit.* 7.3; John Chrysostom, *Juv.* 2–3.

the Caesars were not the first to collect information about the population and its political attitudes.[77] Thus it was a popular saying in antiquity that "a monarch has many eyes and ears."[78] In Rome the systematic construction of a system of "internal security" began with Augustus at the latest.[79] In the provinces, this was the responsibility of the governor, and he could make use of military personnel for the purpose.[80] According to Tertullian, *ben-*

---

77. In doing so they followed Aristotle's political theory: "The tyrant must see to it that none of the things his subjects say or do escape his notice; rather, he must have spies [κατασκοπός], like the women called 'tablebearer' (προσαγωγεύς / προσαγωγίς / ποταγωγίς) at Syracuse and the spies [ὠτακοθστής] that Hieron used to send whenever there was any gathering or conference, for when men fear such as these they speak less freely and if they do speak freely they are less likely to escape notice" (Aristotle, *Pol.* 1313b.11–16). Plutarch writes that the Persian Darius II Nothus (fifth century BCE) was the inventor of spies (Plutarch, *Curios.* 522f–523a). See also Clearchos from Soloi in Athenaeus, *Deipn.* 255f–256b; Frank Santi Russell, *Information Gathering in Classical Greece* (Ann Arbor: University of Michigan Press, 1999), 103–21; Jakob Seiber, "Der Geheimdienst Alexanders des Grossen (336–325 v. Chr.)," in *Geheimdienste in der Weltgeschichte*, ed. Wolfgang Krieger (Cologne: Anaconda, 2007), 21–33. On the Roman secret service, see Rose Mary Sheldon, *Intelligence Activities in Ancient Rome* (London: Frank Cass, 2005); Otto Hirschfeld, "Die Sicherheitspolizei im römischen Kaiserreich," in *Kleine Schriften* (Berlin: Weidmannsche Buchhandlung, 1913), 577–623.

78. Lucian, *Ind.* 23; see Xenophon, *Cyr.* 8.2.11–12: "Many 'eyes' and many 'ears' were ascribed to the king"; Philostratus, *Vit. Apoll.* 4.43: "Tigellinus ... used all the eyes with which the government sees, to watch Apollonius, whether he was talking or holding his tongue, or sitting down or walking about, and to mark what he ate, and in whose houses, and whether he offered sacrifice or not."

79. See Rose Mary Sheldon, *Intelligence Activities in Ancient Rome*, 150–63. In his speech to Augustus, Maecenas shapes the matter thus: "And inasmuch as it is necessary, for these and other reasons, that there should be persons who are to keep eyes and ears open to anything which affects your imperial position, in order that you may not be unaware of any situation that requires measures of precaution or correction, you should have such agents, but remember that you should not believe absolutely everything they say, but should carefully investigate their reports" (Cassius Dio, *Hist. Rom.* 52.37.2).

80. See Norman J. E. Austin and N. Boris Rankov, *Exploratio: Military and Political Intelligence in the Roman World from the Second Punic War to the Battle of Adrianople* (London: Routledge, 1995), 142–69. In the early empire, it was mainly soldiers called *frumentarii* who acted as imperial messengers, couriers, informers, policemen, and spies. Later a civil intelligence service was built up, employing *curiosi* (from *curiosus*, "prudent," "eager to learn") and *argentes in rebus*. Sheldon, *Intelligence Activities in Ancient Rome*, 250–74.

eficiarii and *curiosi* in Rome maintained lists of suspected persons, including Christians, and he accuses bishops of attempting to shield themselves and their fellow believers by the use of bribes.[81]

Epictetus therefore warns against letting one's tongue run too freely:

> A soldier, dressed like a civilian, sits down by your side and begins to speak ill of Caesar, and then you too, just as though you had received from him some guarantee of good faith in the fact that he began the abuse, tell likewise everything you think and the next thing is—you are led off to prison in chains. (Epictetus, *Diatr.* 4.13.5)

Written reports and letters thus represented a potential danger, especially if one were already under suspicion. A later legend even tells of Alexander the Great

> that once, when he wished to sound the feelings of the soldiers, he told any who had written letters to their people in Macedonia to hand them to the messengers whom he himself was sending, who would faithfully deliver them.... In this way Alexander got hold of the letters of those who had written favorably and of those who complained." (Q. Curius Rufus, *History of Alexander* 7.2.36 [Rolfe, LCL])

By having the letters read, he obtained a clear picture of the loyalty of his soldiers and separated the unreliable into a single unit to which he gave the most dangerous missions.

Since letters were in danger of being read even by persecutors, attempts were made to conceal their content.[82] Antiquity already possessed an appa-

---

81. Tertullian, *Fug.* 13.5–6: "I know not whether it is matter for grief or shame when among hucksters, and pickpockets, and bath-thieves, and gamesters, and pimps, Christians too are included as taxpayers in the lists of free soldiers and spies."

82. In Cicero's correspondence we sometimes hear of intercepted letters (e.g., *Fam.* 12.12.1; *Att.* 5.3.2; *Ep. Brut.* 2.5; also Cassius Dio, *Hist. Rom.* 57.23; Plutarch, *Dion* 14). Cicero was acutely aware of the risks of communication through letters: "I shall not often write and tell you what I think about politics in general, since a letter of that sort has its dangers" (*propter periculum eius modi litterarum* [*Fam.* 13.68.2 (Cary, LCL)]). Later in life he wrote: "So henceforward I won't write to you what I am going to do, only what I have actually done. Every spy [κωρυκαῖος] in the country seems to have an ear cocked to catch what I say" (*Att.* 10.18.1 [Bailey, LCL]). On the problems of privacy and secrecy of letters in antiquity, see Wolfgang Riepl, *Das Nachrichtenwe-*

ratus of secret writing and cryptography.[83] Techniques of concealment also included content that was as opaque as possible,[84] the use of pseudonyms, riddling speech, or writing in another language.[85] Thus Cicero, under political pressure, writes to his trusted friend Atticus:

> But I write this in haste and I am really afraid of saying too much. In future letters I shall either put everything down in plain terms, if I get hold of a thoroughly trustworthy messenger, or else, if I write obscurely, you will none the less understand. In such letters I shall call myself Laelius and you Furius. The rest shall be in veiled language (ἐν αἰνιγμοῖς). (Cicero, *Att.* 2.19.5 [Bailey, LCL])[86]

---

sen des Altertums mit besonderer Rücksicht auf die Römer (Leipzig: Teubner, 1913), 279–322.

83. Even in antiquity there existed a great many ways of encoding information to keep it secret. Caesar is said to have used a secret form of writing in which each letter of the alphabet is replaced by the third coming after it, i.e., an A is replaced by a D (Suetonius, *Iul.* 56.6; Gell. *NA* 17.9.1–5). Augustus used a simpler code in which B stands for A, C for B, etc., but double A for X (Suetonius, *Aug.* 88). The Greek specialist on warfare Aeneas Tacticus provides most detailed extant account of methods of sending secret messages in *How to Survive under Siege*, 31–35 (fourth century BCE). Other lists of cryptographic methods are found in Aulus Gellius, *Noct. att.* 17.9; see also Anne Kolb, "Cryptography," *Brill's New Pauly*, ed. Hubert Cancik and Helmuth Schneider, http://referenceworks.brillonline.com/entries/brill-s-new-pauly/cryptography-e623760.

84. The father of Philolas, the conspirator against Alexander, is said to have written in a letter to his son: "First, look out for yourselves, then for yours; for thus we shall accomplish what we have planned" (Q. Curius Rufus, *History of Alexander* 6.9.14 [Rolfe, LCL]). Nevertheless, Alexander discovered the hidden message.

85. Disguise was even an esoteric technique in the Platonic school. In (Pseudo)-Plato's *Second Epistle* 312d, Plato writes: "Now I must expound it [the doctrine concerning the nature of 'the First'] in a riddling way (δι' αἰνιγμῶν) in order that, should the tablet come to any harm 'in fold of ocean or of earth,' he that readeth may not understand" (Bury, LCL); see Plutarch, *Dion* 21.1.4.

86. Also, *Att.* 2.20.3: "Of the political situation I shall say little. I am terrified by now for fear the very paper may betray us. So henceforward, if I have occasion to write to you at any length, I shall obscure my meaning with code terms (ἀλληγορίαις)." Other examples of pseudonyms and code words: *Att.* 18.8; 2.13.1; 2.3.1; 2.9.1; *Fam.* 6.2.3; 11.13.1. Passages in Greek: *Att.* 6.4.3; 6.5.1–2, 4; 6.6.1; 6.9.2; 6.7.1; 9.4.2; 14.14.2; etc. See also John Nicholson, "The Delivery and Confidentiality of Cicero's Letters," *CJ* 90 (1994): 33–63.

According to Philostratus, Apollonius obscured his statements in a letter
to the philosopher Musonius, who had been thrown into prison by Nero,
with allusions to legend and mythology:

> Apollonius to Musonius the philosopher, greeting. I would fain come
> unto you, to share your conversation and lodgings, in the hope of being
> some use to you; unless indeed you are disinclined to believe that Hera-
> cles once released Theseus from hell; write what you would like me to do.
> Farewell. (Philostratus, *Vit. Apoll.* 4.46)[87]

A letter from a Roman public prison, written by a prisoner who was in the
midst of a probably political, but in any case life-threatening legal procedure, was always risky. The risk extended not only to the sender and his
or her immediate associates—that is, Paul, Timothy, and Epaphroditus—
but to the addressees as well. Governors were always trying to uncover
accomplices by means that certainly included torture in order to assess the
extent of the danger.[88] Consequently we should not be surprised if in Philippians some things are said only obliquely and in concealed form.[89] The
unnamed "loyal companion" (4:3) is one example; another are the greetings from "those of the emperor's household" (οἱ ἐκ τῆς Καίσαρος οἰκίας;

---

87. Another enigmatic letter full of allusions to myth and legend comes from
the historian Ammianus Marcellinus (fourth century CE): "Now that the envoys of
the Greeks have been sent far away and perhaps are to be killed, that aged king, not
content with Hellespontus, will bridge the Granicus and the Rhyndacus and come to
invade Asia with many nations. He is naturally passionate and very cruel, and he has
as an instigator and a better, the successor of the former Roman emperor Hadrian;
unless Greece takes heed, it is all over with her and her dirge chanted" (*Roman History*
18.6.18). The meaning of the letter is, as Ammianus writes, "that the king of the Persians had crossed the rivers Anzaba and Tigris, and, urged on by Antoninus, aspired
to the rule of the entire Orient" (10.6.19 [Rolfe, LCL]).

88. Pliny the Younger, *Ep.* 96.8: "After receiving this account, I judged it so much
the more necessary to endeavor to extort the real truth, by putting two female slaves
to the torture, who were said to officiate in their religious rites."

89. Dieter Georgi, *Theocracy in Paul's Praxis and Theology* (Minneapolis: Fortress,
1991), 72: "Paul's correspondence with the Philippians during this imprisonment does
not contain such unambiguous political and social allusions. But the very observation
demonstrates the political nature of Pauline theology in general. Because he is in the
hands of the Romans and therefore in immediate political danger, he has to be careful
and change his tone. It is also characteristic, however, that he does not completely sup-
press the political and societal dimension in these letters written during his imprisonment, but rather disguises it."

4:22), which is more likely a code word for "fellow prisoners" than—as the vast majority of scholars since the end of the nineteenth century claim—a *terminus technicus* for slaves, freedmen, and freedwomen of the household of Caesar.[90] There is simply no evidence for the latter meaning in the pre-Constantine era.

---

90. Since Lightfoot, *Saint Paul's*, 171–78, οἱ ἐκ τῆς Καίσαρος οἰκίας have been identified as imperial slaves. Contrary to Ferdinand Christian Baur, *Paulus, der Apostel Jesu Christi* (Leipzig: Fues, 1867), 65–67, who used Phil 4:22 as an argument against the genuineness of Philippians, because he saw in it an anachronistic reference to the Clement legend (see Phil 4:3; *Clementine Homilies*), Lightfoot formulated the thesis that "the 'domus' or 'familia Caesaris' (represented by the Greek οἰκία Καίσαρος) includes the whole of the imperial household, the meanest slaves as well as the most powerful courtiers" (171; see also Theodor Zahn, *Einleitung in das Neue Testament*, [Leipzig: Deichert, 1906], 1:391 n. 1 [§31]). In this way Lightfoot could resolve the problem of Phil 4:22 without the anachronistic idea of the conversion of members of the imperial family in the first century. But there were two slippery aspects to the thesis that were later forgotten. (1) *Familia Caesaris* is an artificial modern expression. Thus P. R. C. Weaver, *Familia Caesaris: A Social Study of the Emperor's Freedmen and Slaves* (Cambridge: Cambridge University Press, 1972), 299, concludes: "'Familia Caesaris', in the general collective sense in which it is used throughout this study, does not occur in the ancient sources. Where the phrase does occur without further determination in the inscriptions and literary texts, the reference is to a particular 'familia' or branch of the administration, and has a purely local significance." An example is the waterline workers in Rome mentioned by Frontinus, *De aquaeductu urbis Romae* 116, which included two groups, one public and one belonging to Caesar (*Familiae sunt duae, altera publica, altera Caesaris*). The emperor's freedmen and women were called *liberti Augusti* (see also the inscription from Philippi in Peter Pilhofer, *Philippi II: Katalog der Inschriften von Philippi*, WUNT 119 [Tübingen: Mohr Siebeck, 2000], 288–90, no. 282/L370), and slaves were "*Caesaris servus*" (Weaver, *Familia Caesaris*, 300). (2) Lightfoot's formula "represented by the Greek οἰκία Καίσαρος" conceals the fact that at least in the first century there is no example of the use of οἱ ἐκ τῆς Καίσαρος οἰκίας for "imperial slaves and freedpersons," and the only instances in the second century are in Christian literature. When Greek-speaking authors used οἰκία Καίσαρος, they meant either the imperial dwelling (Plutarch, *Caes.* 63.9; *Cic.* 28.2; 47.6) or the imperial family (Philo, *Flacc.* 35). The owner of Callixtus of Rome mentioned by Hippolytus, Carpophorus "from the emperor's house," a wealthy banker, might be a slave or freedman on the basis of his Greek name; however, he is probably not a Christian, but instead a "faithful man" (*Haer.* 9.12; see the other ἄνδρες πιστοί in Hippolytus, *Haer.* 9.17.2; 6.16.1). It is questionable whether the "cupbearer" and his friends mentioned in Mart. Paul 14.1 as being from the imperial house can serve as an attestation for the expression, since this work is literarily dependent on Philippians and Acts. The earliest interpreters of the passage consistently understand the emperor's house

But Philippians uses code words primarily at the level of content. We have already identified the keyword "gospel" as such above. Although there would certainly be something to be said about "that what affecting me" (τὰ κατ᾽ ἐμέ 1:12; also 2:23), Paul communicates his situation in terms of the concept of gospel in such a way that he can hope that the real news remains a closed book to uninitiated readers. The tension between communication ("but I want you to know") and concealment ("progress of the gospel," "chains revealed in Christ") allows the censors and persecutors to hear nothing but religious nonsense or "an insane and measureless superstition" (Pliny the Younger, *Ep.* 96.8). But for initiates, silence itself causes the empty spaces to speak; it all presupposes the experiences named in 1 Cor 4:9–13; 2 Cor 6:4–10; 11:23b–33; and elsewhere, but not here formulated. The community can, therefore, with the aid of the codes of the theology of the cross that was known and shared among them, understand chains as an expression of the gospel, of God's solidarity with the suffering of those held bound, manifested also in God's messengers (Phil 2:8; 2 Cor 2:14, and elsewhere).[91]

But what is it that is so important that Paul simply must convey it to the community in Philippi, despite the danger posed by writing in prison?

Receiving Letters from Prison

Why is Paul so zealous to write the Philippians at all? There is not one answer to this question, but at least three. What we know as the canonical

---

as the imperial palace (John Chrysostom, *Hom. Phil.* 16.4 [PG 62:294: βασιλικῇ οἰκία]; John of Damascus, *Commentarii in epistulas Paulis* [PG 95, 881: οἶκος βασιλικός]) and find great consolation in the fact that Paul teaches "how even some royal persons have accepted the divine gospel and led away alive into life some of the household companions of the godless emperor" (Theodoret, *Interpretatio in XIV epistulas sancti Paulis* [PG 82:589]). Thus because οἱ ἐκ τῆς Καίσαρος οἰκίας are not simply to be identified with the Latin *familia Caesaris* as a group of imperial slaves and freedpersons, the formula could obliquely refer to those who are living in a house belonging to Caesar, thus, for example, Paul's fellow prisoners.

91. Commentators customarily fill this lacuna with the aid of Acts: "Paul has taken the initiative during his legal process in Ephesus of revealing his Roman citizenship to the authorities" (Reumann, *Philippians*, 192; see O'Brien, *Epistle*, 92, and elsewhere). "Paul wants them [the Philippians] not to be anxious about him, because his circumstances, rather than being a hindrance to the gospel ... have in fact led to its advance. To advance the gospel has been his lifelong passion" (Fee, *Paul's Letter*, 111; also Bockmuehl, *Epistle*, 74; Müller, *Brief des Paulus an die Philipper*, 52, and elsewhere).

Philippians is a collection of three letters sent by Paul over a certain amount of time, only edited by the Philippians later, in the second century when they started to disseminate what Paul had written to them.[92] The Philippians took the short recognition and receipt of their gift, now Phil 4:10–20, brought by Epaphroditus to Paul as letter A and placed it at the end of their letter as "a nice memorial" to themselves.[93] They placed the farewell letter, which Paul sent to them at the moment when he finally "despaired of life itself" (2 Cor 1:8), in chapter 3:2–21 (letter C). They framed those two, the earlier letter A and the later letters C with the so-called letter of joy (Phil 1:1–3:1; 4:1–7, 20–23), or letter B.

One answer to the question why Paul took the risk of writing from prison might be found in the history of his relationship to the people in Philippi. He came to Philippi shortly after his split from Antioch (Gal 2:11–14; Acts 15:36–40) and his former friends around Barnabas (Phil 4:15). The Philippians became not only proselytes but also Paul's new mission partners (4:14; 1:5, 7).[94] It is likely that Paul continued to organize

---

92. On canonical Philippians as a collection of three letter fragments see, among others: Angela Standhartinger, "'Join in Imitating Me' (Philippians 3.17): Towards an Interpretation of Philippians 3," NTS 54 (2008): 417–35. As Polycarp shows in his own letter to the Philippians (Polycarp, Phil. 13.1), the community actively pursued the dissemination of Paul's letter: "Both you and Ignatius have written me that if anyone is travelling to Syria, he should take your letter [literary letters: γράμματα] along also. This I will do, if I get a good opportunity, either myself or the one whom I will send as representative, on your behalf as well as ours" (trans. J. B. Lightfoot and J. R. Harmer, The Apostolic Fathers [Grand Rapids: Baker Books, 1889]).

93. See Günther Bornkamm, "Der Philipperbrief als paulinische Briefsammlung," in Geschichte und Glaube (München: Kaiser, 1971), 2:195–205 (203): "mit der Briefsammlung (wird) der von Paulus ausgezeichneten Gemeinde zu Philippi ein schönes Denkmal gesetzt."

94. Scholars discuss this partnership between Paul and the Philippians in different social models of the Roman world: as a consensual societas: see J. Paul Sampley, Pauline Partnership in Christ: Christian Community and Commitment in Light of Roman Law (Philadelphia: Fortress, 1980); in the social framework of friendship: Gerald W. Peterman, Paul's Gift from Philippi: Conventions of Gift Exchange and Christian Giving, SNTSMS 92 (Cambridge: Cambridge University Press, 1997); the Roman patronage system: Bormann, Philippi, 161–205; Peter Lampe, "Paul, Patrons, and Clients," in Paul in the Greco-Roman World: A Handbook, ed. Paul Sampley (Harrisburg, PA: Trinity Press International, 2003), 488–523; Steve Walton, "Paul, Patronage and Pay: What Do We Know about the Apostle's Financial Support?" in Paul as Missionary: Identity, Activity, Theology, and Practice, ed. Trevor J. Burke and Brian S. Rosner (London: T & T Clark, 2001), 220–33; or most recently "broker": David Briones,

his mission activities in ways similar to Antioch. According to our information from Acts, the community, with the help of the Spirit (Acts 13:3; also Phil 1:19), elected Paul, Silvanus (a person with a Latin name), and Timothy and commissioned them to travel to neighboring cities (Thessaloniki) and provinces (Achaia, Athens, and Corinth) to spread the gospel (Acts 13:2–14:28). At least we know that the Philippians financed those three twice in Thessaloniki (Phil 4:16) and later also in Corinth (2 Cor 11:8–9).[95] Further, it is remarkable that the only person called apostle in Philippians is not Paul but Epaphroditus, the delegate of the Philippians (Phil 2:25: ὑμῶν ἀπόστολος). Second Corinthians 8:23 names even more apostles (ἀπόστολοι ἐκκλησιῶν) who were commissioned by them to collect to money for Jerusalem.

Perhaps Paul's long stay in Corinth and later Ephesus brought their close relationship to a crisis. The beginning of the short receipt in Phil 4:10–20 sounds a bit ironic: "I rejoice in the Lord greatly that now at last your thoughts for me bloomed into fruition." Paul admits that they temporarily lacked opportunity (ἠκαιρεῖσθε δέ), but we also do not hear much from Philippi for some time.[96] It was only after Paul and Timothy (with Titus and Silvanus? see 2 Cor 1:19) were relieved from the almost deathly danger "in the province of Asia" (2 Cor 1:8–10) that they immediately traveled to Macedonia again (2 Cor 2:12–13; 7:5). From that moment forward, Philippi and the other Macedonian communities seemed to be enthusiastic supporters of the collection for the poor sisters and brothers in Jerusalem. They not only were the first to be prepared (2 Cor 8:1–4), but also plan to travel as its delegates (2 Cor 9:4, 8:23).[97]

"Paul's Intentional 'Thankless Thanks' in Philippians 4.10–20," *JSNT* 34 (2011): 47–60. Beyond many helpful insights, each of these models more or less rely upon elite ethics, whose application seems to me a bit problematic for this not-so-well-off, Greek speaking community in a Roman context. Further, what has become most obvious in the application of the Roman patronage systems to Philippians is that our text blends the strong hierarchies of the system. Both parties, Paul *and* the Philippians, are described as patrons and as clients.

95. Thereby, the community seems to have been rather poor (see 2 Cor 8:1–4). Although they send money twice (Phil 4:16), the money was not enough to match Paul's need (2 Thess 2:9). See also the chapter by Oakes in this volume.

96. Paul plans to travel through Macedonia in 1 Cor 16:5; 2 Cor 1:16, but at least changed the plans of 2 Cor 1:16.

97. The journey to bring the money to Jerusalem starts in Philippi according to Acts 20:4–6. See also Rom 15:26.

So when the Philippians sent their apostle Epaphroditus with their gift (4:18), Paul definitely owed them a response. It seems to have been hard for him to accept the amount of money, which he suspects has caused the community to be in want (Phil 4:18–19; see 2 Cor 8:2). But with an ironic reference to Stoic self-contentment (4:10–13), he admits how much he depends on them. [98] In contrast to a self-sufficient (αὐτάρκης) Stoic sage, he is desperately in need of friends and partners in his θλῖψις, his pressure, oppression, and affliction.[99] Therefore, he emphasizes his gratitude for the gift, but even more for contacting him. He delegates the thanks to God by presenting the gift from the Philippian people as an offering (Phil 4:18) that will find its way back to fill up their needs (Phil 4:19). At the same time, he interprets this engagement of the Philippians as a resumption of their shared efforts that will directly fill their account (4:17). But what one lacks in this short note, however, is any information about Paul's current situation, the reason and circumstances of his θλῖψις, and what happened to the projects he was assigned by the community.

In the letter of joy (Phil 1:1–3:1; 4:1–7), Paul seems to be much more eager to "let them know" (1:12) what is going on with him in prison and court but, as I argued above, not in an open manner. How might the Philippians have read and interpreted this letter?

Reading a Letter from Prison

The letter of joy must have been written later than the receipt of Phil 4:10–20. Meanwhile, Epaphroditus became desperately ill and recovered again while staying with Paul (2:25–30), and the message of this illness has reached already Philippi (2:26). One can also deduce from the letter that they raised some more questions. What is going on with Paul, and what

---

98. The whole passage sounds very similar to what could be said for example by Epictetus: "Lift up your neck at last like a man escaped from bondage, be bold and look towards God and say, 'Use me henceforward for whatever Thou wilt; I am of one mind with Thee; I am Thine; I crave exemption from nothing that seems good in Thy sight; where Thou wilt, lead me; in what raiment Thou wild, clothe me. Wouldst Thou have me to hold office, or remain in private life, to remain here or go into exile; to be poor or be rich? I will defend all these Thy acts before men; I will show what the true nature of each thing is'" (*Diatr.* 2.16.41–42 [Oldfather, LCL]).

99. See Michaelis, "Gefangenschaftsbriefe," 590, on Phil 4:11–12: "we read between the lines that he would probably have had to experience a prisoner's hunger."

is his case? What happened to our shared efforts? And will he return to Philippi again?

To the last question, Paul answered with a yes and a no at the same time. On the one hand, he emphasizes his deep longing to meet those in Philippi again (1:8, 24–26; 2:24), and he recommends Timothy whom the community already knows well as somebody who distinguished himself in the same manner as Paul in his service for the gospel (2:22).[100] He might become Paul's substitute and replacement in the meantime or if things get worse for Paul (2:19–23). On the other hand, he admits the possibility that he might not get this chance (1:20-24; 2:17–18). In suggesting this "no," Paul drew on religious imagery: "to be with Christ" (1:23); "being poured out as a libation" (2:17); and a remarkable reiteration of the terms joy and rejoice (2:17–18). Both terms are repeated constantly in the whole letter (1:4, 18–19, 25, 2:2, 28–29, 3:1; 4:1, 4) thus indicating more than its basic tone.

In the following, I aim to demonstrate the thesis that Paul tries to answer the communities' questions by using a religious language as a disguising code. For that I try to reconstruct how the people in Philippi might have decoded that language and interpreted the letter by detecting the hidden messages that could only be communicated beneath the surface of the text.

Sending Epaphroditus the Philippians looked after Paul, visited him (ἐπισκέπτεσται, see Matt 25:43), and thus became both guardians (ἐπίσκοποι) and servants (διάκονοι; Phil 1:1, see service [λειτουργία]; 2:30) for Paul and Timothy. Therefore, the so-called letter of joy (Phil 1:1–3:1; 4:1–7) is imbued with expressions of gratitude for the solidarity and sympathy of the community in Paul's imprisonment.

The deep sympathy is especially expressed in the *prooimium* or thanksgiving prayer at the beginning (1:3–11). But not all references here are particularly clear. We can translate verse 3 in two different ways: "I thank my God whenever I think of you" or "I thank my God for all your remembering [me]." The same phenomenon appears also in verse 7, where again we cannot decide whether Paul intends to say "because you hold me in your heart" or "because I hold you in my heart." The opening

---

100. Phil 2:22: ὡς πατρὶ τέκνον σὺν ἐμοὶ ἐδούλευσεν εἰς τὸ εὐαγγέλιον ("that he served with me to the gospel like a child to his father"). Note that the father in this sentence is the gospel, not Paul. Paul and Timothy are siblings and coslaves in their service for the gospel.

thanksgiving passage blurs subjects and objects, makes Paul and the Philippians commutable, and thereby connects both parties utterly.

This communion is especially expressed in prayer (v. 4). The prayer of petition (δέησις) is central to the letter of joy.[101] It is effective for and in fact is *the* way to the apostle's rescue (1:19).[102] Alluding to his situation, which he experienced as hopeless (see also 1:21–23), Paul uses a quotation from Job 13:16 in verse 19, the figure of the suffering just one. In chapter 13 of that book, Job, against the advice of his friends, challenges God to a debate over justice. With Job, Paul feels himself abandoned in his prison by many people (1:15–18). But this congregation stands by his side and can, so Paul hopes and expects, effect his rescue through their prayers, with the help of the Holy Spirit (1:19–20). The account of prayer in Phil 1:3–11 is thus by no means banal or simply due to the letter genre. Prayer is the effective tie not only between people separated by distance (see also 2 Cor 1:11; 9:14), but also between human beings and God (Phil 4:6; 2 Cor 9:14). Prayer is therefore also described as a place of joy (μετὰ χαρᾶς τὴν δέησιν ποιούμενος, 1:4).

Joy is a gift of the Holy Spirit (Phil 1:19; 1 Thess 1:6; Gal 5:22).[103] In the Jewish biblical tradition, it is God's gift.[104] Philo can even say: "Rejoicing is most closely associated with God alone" (Philo, *Abr.* 202 [Colson, LCL]). Joy thus has a transcendent dimension. It is part of the heavenly world. It is expressed in worship and festival.[105] The letter of joy also links rejoicing to

---

101. Of the seven times Paul uses the word δέησις, four are found in the letter of joy (Phil 1:4, 19; 4:6).

102. Some months later, Paul wrote retrospectively of his imprisonment and the prospect of continuing shared ministry: "as you also join in helping us by your prayers, so that many will give thanks on our behalf for the blessing granted us through the prayers of many" (2 Cor 1:11). What Paul asks for is prayer that will make it possible for many to give thanks to God for the grace given to Paul and his fellow prisoners, which delivered them from certain death (2 Cor 1:9–10).

103. See Hans Conzelmann, "χαίρω κτλ," *TDNT* 9:359–72.

104. Philo, *Legat.* 3.219; *Abr.* 203–205; *Spec.* 2.53–55; and elsewhere.

105. Realized eschatology is likewise expressed in the contemporary cult of the emperor; see Philo, *Legat.* 15–20, or the inscription from Assos in Troas (37 CE): "Since the leadership of Gaius Caesar Germanicus Augustus, hoped for through the prayer of all people, is proclaimed to all, the cosmos has experienced unlimited joy. Every city and every people has hastened to behold the god as though the sweetest age were now presented to all people" (*SIG* 2.795–99). *Caesar est causa laetitiae populi urbesque* (Seneca, *Clem.* 1.2).

cultic language (2:16–18). Joy has an ecclesiological dimension; it happens "in the Lord" (3:1; 4:4). The existence of the congregation as a community is thus already a manifestation of divine activity in the world and so of joy. But joy also characterizes the eschatological situation (Rom 14:17). It will be fulfilled at the judgment, when the community will receive an abundance of fame "for … progress and joy in faith" (1:25–26) and thus magnify not only itself, but also Christ, Paul, and the glory and praise of God (1:11; 2:11). In a countermovement the community is the apostle's credential. Its existence and cooperation in the gospel (1:5) are the basis and precondition for his glory (2:16; 4:1), and probably for that reason they are his joy (4:1; 1 Thess 2:9). This means that for Paul joy, to be really joy, requires community and mutuality above all (Phil 1:19, 25; 2:2, 17–18, 28–29; also Rom 12:15).[106] In the community between the imprisoned Paul and the congregation in Philippi, eschatological joy becomes reality. It enables Paul and his fellow prisoners to hope for continued life (1:24; 2:19–24). It is the tangible presence of God.

What completes Paul's joy (2:2) is the unanimity within the community. Here the description in Phil 2:1–4 adopts a political ideal of the surrounding world: *concordia* or ὁμόνοια was regarded in the imperial period as the crucial basis for inner peace and fortunate circumstances.[107] But here the unanimity is not some kind of (hierarchically) structured order; it is grounded "in Christ" (2:1, 5). Joy is "Christ's work" (2:30), described in the hymn. In that the Philippians "in humility (τῇ ταπεινοφροσύνῃ) regard others as better than yourselves" (2:3), they are imitators of the one who, by "humbling himself" (ἐταπείνωσεν ἑαυτόν, 2:8), was wholly human even

---

106. After being released from prison, Paul wrote in 2 Cor 1:13–14: "and I hope that you will know completely, as you also knew us in part, that we are your boast, just as you are ours on the day of the Lord Jesus."

107. H. Alan Shapiro and Tonio Hölscher, "Homonoia/Concordia," *LIMC* 5 (1990): 479–98 (493). See Bruce Winter, *Seek the Welfare of the City: Christians as Benefactors and Citizens*, First-Century Christians in the Greco-Roman World 1 (Carlisle: Paternoster, 1994), 82–86; Angela Standhartinger, "Die paulinische Theologie im Spannungsfeld römisch-imperialer Machtpolitik: Eine neue Perspektive auf Paulus, kritisch geprüft anhand des Philipperbriefs," in *Religion, Politik und Gewalt*, ed. Friedrich Schweitzer, Europäischen Kongresses für Theologie 12 (Gütersloh: Gütersloher Verlagshaus, 2005), 364–82; and Standhartinger, "Eintracht in Philippi: Zugleich ein Beitrag zur Funktion von Phil 2,6–11 im Kontext," in *Paulus—Werk und Wirkung: Festschrift für Andreas Lindemann zum 70. Geburtstag*, ed. Paul-Gerhard Klumbies and David DuToit (Tübingen: Mohr Siebeck, 2013), 149–75.

unto death. Because he made himself in solidarity especially with suffering humanity in his death on the cross, he was exalted by God and in fact identified with God's very self (2:9–11). Hence the community also is not working solely for its own salvation (2:12). Because God is at work not only in Christ (2:9–11) but also in the community (2:13), it is likewise empowered to be a light for the world (2:15; see also 4:5).

Therefore, Paul remembers their common spirit with joy (2:2). They are in fact participants (1:5, 7) and fellow strugglers (1:27; 4:3) in the gospel for which he lies in chains, the gospel that is revealed by those chains.[108] Paul is certain that the one who has begun a good work in them will complete it "by the day of Jesus Christ" (1:6). The only mention of judgment in the letter of joy is in the expression found only here, ἡμέρα Χριστοῦ (1:5, 11; 2:16).[109] This formulation emphasizes the presence of Christ.[110] In anticipation of Phil 2:15 and the hymn (2:6–11), Paul wishes that the community may be "pure" and "blameless" on that day and filled with "the harvest of righteousness that comes through Jesus Christ," which increases glory and thereby God's very self by singing God's praise together with all creation (1:11; see also 2:11). The way there is love, which here in Phil 1:9 overturns every ancient doctrine of knowledge by moving not from perception to knowledge, but by overflowing simultaneously "with knowledge and full insight."[111] Paul's thesis is that with the aid of this love-filled perception the community can test "what is best" and "on what all depends."[112]

---

108. The κοινωνία will last forever. This means that the Philippians share also in suffering. Only in Philippians is it said: "he has granted you the privilege not only of believing in Christ, but of suffering for him as well" (1:29). The Philippians share with Paul in the same struggle.

109. Also, ἄχρι ἡμέρας Χριστοῦ Ἰησοῦ (1:5) and εἰς ἡμέραν Χριστοῦ (1:8; 2:16; see also 2 Cor 1:8).

110. Although the day of the Lord will come (1 Thess 5:2, 4), the Thessalonians are already "children of light and children of the day" (1 Thess 5:5).

111. Αἴσθησις is perception and experience obtained through the senses. This is the sole appearance of αἴσθησις in the New Testament. Philosophers debated whether sense perception could in fact lead to knowledge. Middle Platonic philosophy denied it (Philo, *Cher.* 41.52; *Migr.* 5; Gerhard Delling, "αἴσθησις," *TDNT* 1:187–88). For Stoics, however, perception of human neediness was still the starting point for the philosophical path to knowledge. See Epictetus, *Diatr.* 2.11.1: "The beginning of philosophy with those who take it up as they should, and enter in, as it were, by the gate, is a consciousness (συναίσθησις) of a man's own weakness and impotence with reference to the things of real consequence in life."

112. Τὸ διάφερων means literally "what distinguishes." Some interpreters infer

With his letter from prison, Paul gives thanks for the community and solidarity of the congregation and above all for its existence. The existence of the community is not merely a pledge that Paul did not "run in vain or labor in vain" (2:16; 1:27). The existence of the community is important for Paul's very survival, especially in prison. It gives him consolation, is a sign of God's love, mercy, and graciousness (1:7; 2:1). Thus the space of joyousness is revealed between Paul and the community, helping him and them to resist the physical and psychic experiences of imprisonment (1:15–18, 23; 2:27–28) as well as the possible death and loss of the apostle (1:18–26; 2:17–18; 3:1; 4:4). The joy shared by Paul and the community is for both parties an expression of the presence of God and their eschatological existence. Joy and effective prayer require the exchange expressed in the letter. Perhaps this is the reason why Paul and the community exposed themselves to the risk of a letter from a Roman prison.

Conclusion: Philippians as Hidden Transcript

I hope I have shown that Phil 1:1–3:1 and 4:1–7 (20–23) reflect the reality of ancient imprisonment, with shackling, hunger, torture, and mortally threatening conditions, as well as the dangers of arbitrary court proceedings. This appears not only in the little that Paul conveys about his imprisonment and court experiences (Phil 1:7, 12–13; 2:25–30), but also in the whole structure of the communication. The danger that the letter of a (political) prisoner could be read by his accusers, jailers, judges, or despairing fellow prisoners and used against him was high. The danger of jeopardizing the recipients as well was no less. The letter of joy thus shows itself on the surface to be a public transcript, an "open interaction between the subordinates and those who dominate."[113]

I hope, however, that I have also shown that the letter contains a second level of communication. Its message is, in any case, concealed in

---

here a technical philosophical term as a contrast to the Stoic τὰ διάφορα (what is morally indifferent) and translate "that on which all depends." Where τὰ διαφέρωντα appears in philosophical contexts it means "what is at stake, interests" (see Plutarch, *Mor.* 43E; 73A). Τὰ διαφέρωντα can, finally, also describe what is weighty, significant, essential, the essential part (τὸ διάφερων μέρος) in a legal decision (P.Oxy. 1204.11), someone outstanding in favor toward people (I.Priene 247.4). In Rom 2:18 the determining measure is the law.

113. Scott, *Domination and the Arts of Resistance*, 2.

blanks, allusions, and religious codes such as gospel, prayer, joy, future judgment, none of which is further explained in Philippians.[114] Concepts from the surrounding world are transformed by subtle shifts (Phil 2:1–5). References remain open (Phil 1:3, 7, and frequently); at crucial points the verb is missing (see Phil 1:11; 2:5); semantic breaks are created (Phil 1:7, 9) or the discourse already begun suddenly and without transition shifts to religious metaphors (Phil 2:15–18). Thus Paul seems in fact to have succeeded in keeping the community largely hidden from persecutors and spies.

There is some evidence that the people beside Paul in Philippi read the letter beyond what is obviously conveyed by it. They identified themselves with Paul's case in such a way that after his release they engage enthusiastically for the collection for Jerusalem. They stayed in solidarity with Paul even beyond his later death. As Polycarp of Smyrna shows in his *Letter[s] to the Philippians* (Polycarp, *Phil.* 13.1), the community actively pursued the dissemination of Paul's letter a century later.[115] It is therefore likely that they also edited our now-canonical Philippians into its final form.[116] Polycarp—the first known reader of this letter (or letters; see Polycarp, *Phil* 13.1)—reports that those Philippians of the second century remembered Paul as their martyred friend (Polycarp, *Phil* 1.2–3; 9.1–2). This long-lasting loyalty might be another proof that the people beside Paul at Philippi had been able to decode the message beyond what was openly conveyed. By this they helped to resist those political Roman forces that brought him into jail.

The techniques of "disguise" and "euphemism" thus reveal Philippians as also a "hidden transcript."[117] Hence the primary goal of the letter is maintenance of the discourse between the community and the apostle.

---

114. See also the Pauline concepts of χάρις (1:7) or δικαιοσύνη (1:11).

115. See the quotation of Polycarp, *Phil.* 13.1 in n. 92 above.

116. See Standhartinger, "Join in Imitating Me."

117. Eric Heen, "Phil 2:6–11 and Resistance to Local Timocratic Rule: *Isa theō* and the Cult of the Emperor in the East," in *Paul and the Roman Imperial Order*, ed. Richard A. Horsley (Harrisburg, PA: Trinity Press International, 2004), 125–53, was the first to argue that the hymn in Phil 2:6–11 is a hidden transcript, designed to present an alternative view of reality against the dominant one of Caesar and the local elites in the Roman East. For Heen, the phrase τὸ εἶναι ἴσα θεῷ (2:6) should be understood against the public transcript of the emperor, who was also said to be "equal to God." The hymn, therefore, is a protest against the abuse of patronal power and effects a symbolic reversal of power relations.

Theologically, this meant for both parties an experience of joy, community, and mutual care through prayer, communion in the Spirit, demonstration of the gospel, eschatological hope, affection, love, consolation, et cetera. Politically and structurally, it means above all the ability to communicate "beyond direct observation by powerholders." Scott has therefore pointed to the "importance of mutuality" for the "hidden transcript":

> The hidden transcript does require a public—even if that public necessarily excludes the dominant. None of the practices and discourses of resistance can exist without tacit or acknowledged coordination and communication within the subordinate group. For that to occur, the subordinate group must carve out for itself social spaces insulated from control and surveillance from above.... The hidden transcript has no reality as pure thought; it exists only to the extent it is practiced, articulated, enacted and disseminated within these offstage social sites.[118]

The existence of the community in Philippi, its praxis of the gospel, and its solidarity and loyalty to Paul, who is proclaiming in his body the self-emptying of God, even beyond his later death, shows that this hidden transcript did in fact ground a political praxis of resistance.

---

118. Scott, *Domination and the Arts of Resistance*, 118–19. See Richard A. Horsley, "Introduction," in *Hidden Transcripts and the Art of Resistance*, ed. Richard A. Horsley, SemeiaSt 48 (Atlanta: Society of Biblical Literature, 2004), 1–26 (10).

Slaves as Wo/men and Unmen: Reflecting upon Euodia, Syntyche, and Epaphroditus in Philippi

Joseph A. Marchal

Paul names several people beside himself in his letter to the Philippians. These include Timothy (Phil 1:1; 2:19–24), Epaphroditus (Phil 2:25–30; 4:10–20), Euodia, Syntyche, and Clement (Phil 4:2–3). Who are these people? They certainly could be some of those "people beside Paul" on which this collection seeks to reflect. But three of these seem especially important rhetorically in the letter. The exhortation to Euodia and Syntyche displays a major concern and even the climax of the letter,[1] as it turns more explicitly to address them to "think the same thing" as Paul.[2] These verses are a key moment where Paul blends unity arguments with hierarchical claims to model status. Epaphroditus functions as one such model

---

1. See, for instance, Cynthia Briggs Kittredge, *Community and Authority: The Rhetoric of Obedience in the Pauline Tradition*, HTS 45 (Harrisburg, PA: Trinity Press International, 1998); and Joseph A. Marchal, *Hierarchy, Unity, and Imitation: A Feminist Rhetorical Analysis of Power Dynamics in Paul's Letter to the Philippians*, Academia Biblica 24 (Atlanta: Society of Biblical Literature, 2006). See also David Garland, "The Composition and Unity of Philippians: Some Neglected Literary Factors," *NovT* 27 (1985): 141–73; and Carolyn Osiek, *Philippians, Philemon*, ANTC (Nashville: Abingdon, 2000), 109–15.

2. See the analyses in Kittredge, *Community and Authority*, 91–94, 105–10; and Marchal, *Hierarchy, Unity and Imitation*, 147–52 and 189–90. (See also the earlier suggestion in Mary Rose D'Angelo, "Women Partners in the New Testament," *JFSR* 6 (1990): 65–86, esp. 75–76.) Kittredge argues that the recurrence of the *phronein* language in these verses "strongly suggests that it is the point to which the letter has been leading" and that "Euodia and Syntyche should be considered central to the rhetorical problem" (Kittredge, *Community and Authority*, 92 and 93). Marchal elaborates that these verses fit into the overarching frame of the letter, highlighting both this mindset (*phronein*) and the stress on sameness (*to auto*, 4:2) (Marchal, *Hierarchy, Unity, and Imitation*, 148).

that supports Paul's rhetorical plan in the letter (Phil 2:25–30).[3] However, he appears in more than one section since he seems to be connected to whatever "gift" was provided by the Philippian assembly community for Paul (Phil 4:10–20). Unlike Timothy and Paul, then, these three figures provide compelling opportunities to learn more about some of the people from the Philippian *ekklēsia*.

It becomes important, then, to try to situate Euodia, Syntyche, and Epaphroditus in the social conditions of Philippi and, in doing so, to discern the forms of social stratification in the wider context and in the developing assembly community. As has been often discussed in Philippians scholarship, Philippi is the famous site of a key battle in Rome's civil wars and became a *colonia* of the Roman Empire in the century previous to the creation of the letter.[4] These historical and political factors—the military and the imperial—are intertwined with another institution central to the Romans: slavery. This empire was a slave-based economy and society, and the major sources for slaves in the empire were military ventures and trade. Given this *colonia*'s aforementioned military history and its location on the Roman Via Egnatia, there were certainly slaves at Philippi and thus quite likely in the assembly community that received Paul's letter.[5]

---

3. On Epaphroditus's rhetorical role in the letter, see Kittredge, *Community and Authority*, 87–88, 95–96; and Marchal, *Hierarchy, Unity, and Imitation*, 139–41, 171–73, 186–87. For an examination of Epaphroditus in light of conventions of commendation, see Efraín Agosto, *Servant Leadership: Jesus and Paul* (St. Louis: Chalice, 2005), 140–44.

4. See, for example, Edgar M. Krentz, "Military Language and Metaphors in Philippians," in *Origins and Method: Towards a New Understanding of Judaism and Christianity; Essays in Honour of John. C. Hurd*, ed. Bradley H. McLean, JSNTSup 86 (Sheffield: Sheffield Academic, 1993), 105–27; Timothy C. Geoffrion, *The Rhetorical Purpose and the Political and Military Character of Philippians: A Call to Stand Firm* (Lewiston, NY: Mellen, 1993); Krentz, "Paul, Games, and the Military," in *Paul in the Greco-Roman World: A Handbook*, ed. J. Paul Sampley (Harrisburg, PA: Trinity Press International, 2003), 344–83. For a summary and assessment of this background, Paul's rhetoric, and the scholarly examination thereof, see Joseph A. Marchal, "Military Images in Philippians 1–2: A Feminist Rhetorical Analysis of Scholarship, Philippians, and Current Contexts," in *Her Master's Tools? Feminist and Postcolonial Engagements of Historical-Critical Discourse*, ed. Caroline Vander Stichele and Todd Penner, GPBS 9 (Atlanta: Society of Biblical Literature, 2005), 265–86; and *Hierarchy, Unity, and Imitation*, 29–34, 50–72.

5. For a brief treatment of this imperial and material history, see Chaido Koukouli-Chrysantaki, "Colonia Iulia Augusta Philippensis," in *Philippi at the Time of Paul*

Indeed, recent social historical work on the *colonia* and the *ekklēsia* at Philippi describe slave and *liberti* ("freed," or better: manumitted) populations in both. Peter Oakes, for example, approximates that slaves made up 15–30 percent of the "town" and 12–25 percent of the "church."[6] Craig de Vos tends to stress the importance of manumitted slaves in the assembly, highlighting that most of the figures in the letter (and in Acts 16) have Greek names, which in turn "probably suggests the church was largely comprised of *liberti*."[7] Though de Vos tends to be less numerically precise than Oakes in his modeling of the community, he generally acknowledges that there were some slaves in the assembly, pointing mostly to Phil 4:22's "public slaves, that is, members of the *familia Caesaris* at Philippi."[8] Richard Ascough places the Philippian *ekklēsia* in the context of other religious voluntary associations, whose membership were typically composed of the poor, slaves, and freed slaves.[9] Ascough notes the same reference to the *familia Caesaris* when he argues how unlikely it was that any in the *ekklēsia* community would have been from the elite ranks in the *colonia*.[10] Oakes attempts to account for freed figures, but he also stresses that the difference between enslaved and manumitted may not always be as significant as some more modern readers have been inclined to see it: "freed slaves generally became clients of their former owners and often contin-

---

and after His Death, ed. Charalambos Bakirtzis and Helmut Koester (Harrisburg, PA: Trinity Press International, 1998), 5–35.

6. See, for example, figure 10 in Peter Oakes, *Philippians: From People to Letter*, SNTSMS 110 (Cambridge: Cambridge University Press, 2001), 17 and his discussion on 48–50 and 60–62.

7. Craig Steven de Vos, *Church and Community Conflicts: The Relationships of the Thessalonian, Corinthian, and Philippian Churches with Their Wider Civic Communities*, SBLDS 168 (Atlanta: Scholars Press, 1999), 254; see also 258.

8. Ibid., 260; see also 260–61, 286–87; and Oakes, *Philippians*, 66.

9. See Richard S. Ascough, *Paul's Macedonian Associations: The Social Context of Philippians and 1 Thessalonians*, WUNT 2/161 (Tübingen: Mohr Siebeck, 2003), 51–54. See also John S. Kloppenborg, "Collegia and *Thiasoi*: Issues in Function, Taxonomy, and Membership," in *Voluntary Associations in the Graeco-Roman World*, ed. John S. Kloppenborg and Stephen G. Wilson (New York: Routledge, 1996), 16–30 (23).

10. See Ascough, *Paul's Macedonian Associations*, 127–28. For further background on the slaves and freed slaves in the imperial family, see P. R. C. Weaver, *Familia Caesaris: A Social Study of the Emperor's Freedmen and Slaves* (Cambridge: Cambridge University Press, 1972).

ued to perform the same services for them as before."[11] (Indeed, I will revisit at least one way in which the obligations of freed slaves continue in the analysis to follow.)

All three of these improve upon and specify recent efforts to think about the relative status of members of these assembly communities by considering the impact of slavery and manumission in Philippi.[12] Where Oakes brings greater precision to a broad picture of the *colonia* and *ekklēsia*, de Vos and Ascough aim to consider the named figures in the letter at greater length. Oakes asserts that "we cannot build a great deal upon the individuals in the letter but they are worth noting, and do fit with our model.… I have not managed to make headway on the likely social status of bearers of these names, although *Syntyche* sounds like various slave names."[13] Nevertheless, Euodia, Syntyche, and Epaphroditus all have Greek names, which serve as potential indices of their status and ethnicity.[14] De Vos maintains that both of the female figures were likely *liberta* with relatively low status, highlighting two known inscriptional occurrences of freed slaves named Euodia.[15] Ascough agrees that the few names encountered in the letter, including Euodia and Syntyche, reflect

---

11. Oakes, *Philippians*, 92. For more on manumission, see J. Albert Harrill, *The Manumission of Slaves in Early Christianity*, HUT 32 (Tübingen: Mohr Siebeck, 1995).

12. For one valuable debate about the applicability of poverty scales, for instance, see Steven J. Friesen, "Poverty in Pauline Studies: Beyond the So-Called New Consensus," *JSNT* 26 (2004): 323–61, and the responses by Peter Oakes, "Constructing Poverty Scales for Graeco-Roman Society: A Response to Steven Friesen's 'Poverty in Pauline Studies,'" *JSNT* 26 (2004): 367–71; and John Barclay, "Poverty in Pauline Studies: A Response to Steven Friesen," *JSNT* 26 (2004): 363–36. While Friesen considers in great detail several named figures in Romans and 1 Corinthians, for instance, he does not consider the specifically named figures in Philippians, making only broad observations about the communities in Macedonia (both Thessalonica and Philippi). See Friesen, "Poverty in Pauline Studies," 348–58. One of Oakes's critiques of Friesen's work was his use of figures from a premodern city such as Florence that was not a slave city (unlike the cities of the Roman Empire). See Oakes, "Constructing Poverty Scales for Graeco-Roman Society," 367 (see also 370–71).

13. Oakes, *Philippians*, 64.

14. For further reflections on the potential historical roles of these two women in Philippi as a colonial "contact zone," see Marchal, *The Politics of Heaven: Women, Gender, and Empire in the Study of Paul*, Paul in Critical Contexts (Minneapolis: Fortress, 2008), 91–109, 166–76.

15. See de Vos, *Church and Community Conflicts*, 252–56. The Euodia references are in *NewDocs* 4:178–79; *IG* 5.2.277; and *CJ* 1.391. The third reference describes a

the members' lower status.[16] Drawing upon different references than de Vos, however, Ascough finds one instance for each of these as slave names still while noting that "it is difficult to judge their exact status."[17] Names with positive connotations of success or luck (as Euodia and Syntyche do) can also reflect the Roman predisposal to mock their social inferiors with names such as "Lucky."[18] At the least, names such as Syntyche's can reveal an instrumental view of other humans: "either her parents or her owners wished the best *for themselves* in naming her."[19] Again, de Vos is confident that Epaphroditus's name reflects his potential *libertus* status: "although it was not a particularly common name, those so named were commonly of servile origin."[20] Ascough arrives at a similar conclusion about Epaphroditus's status but, again, on a different basis than de Vos. Indeed, Ascough remarks upon the commonness of this name, "particularly among those in the lower ranks of society, namely slaves or freedmen."[21]

All of these studies indicate the likelihood (though not a "proof") that these named figures were slaves or freed slaves. Unfortunately, the nature of the ancient materials will never insure certitude about the precise location, condition, or status of any of those who are not among the few imperial elite in the first century. Most particularly, there is a fundamental problem of sources whenever one is seeking either to understand ancient slavery *or* to construct a history from below. (Pursuing a history from below about enslaved or manumitted members of the Philippian *ekklēsia* seems all the

---

Euodia married to a man of Judean descent, who would have likely been of lower status as well. See de Vos, *Church and Community Conflicts*, 256.

16. See Ascough, *Paul's Macedonian Associations*, 124–25.

17. Ascough, *Paul's Macedonian Associations*, 125. Here Ascough is referring to L. C. Reilly, *Slaves in Ancient Greece: Slaves from Greek Manumission Inscriptions* (Chicago: Ares, 1978), 49, 115.

18. See, for instance, Clarice J. Martin, "The Eyes Have It: Slaves in the Communities of Christ-Believers," in *Christian Origins*, vol. 1 of *A People's History of Christianity*, ed. Richard A. Horsley (Minneapolis: Fortress, 2005), 221–39 (228); as well as Ascough, *Paul's Macedonian Associations*, 125.

19. Ascough, *Paul's Macedonian Associations*, 125, emphasis added.

20. De Vos, *Church and Community Conflicts*, 256. Here he notes the indices of *ILS* and *SIGLM*.

21. Ascough, *Paul's Macedonian Associations*, 124. G. H. R. Horsley describes Epaphroditus as "exceedingly common" and identified it as "the thirteenth most frequently attested Greek personal name" at Rome (most of them coming out of the first century CE). See *NewDocs* 4:21–22. See also Reilly, *Slaves in Ancient Greece*, 40–41; and *NewDocs* 5:112.

more difficult, then!) This is evident, for example, throughout the various entries of the first volume of *A People's History of Christianity*, on *Christian Origins*, where the "problem of sources" must often be addressed explicitly before proceeding.[22] J. Albert Harrill reflects similarly on the obstacles to studying ancient slaves: "Primary evidence is rare, and the little that does survive emanates virtually exclusively from ancient slaveholders and does not express the views of the slaves themselves."[23] Clarice Martin reflects upon how this difficulty is only compounded further by the tendencies of both the Pauline letters and Pauline interpreters: "The dim, ad hoc flashes of the lives of slaves in the assemblies of Christ remain shrouded in the concealed world of shadows on offer in standard scholarly reconstructions."[24] Almost always, then, there will only be indirect references to those people lower in the various intertwined hierarchical institutions (or kyriarchies; see more below) of the first century. There is a reason, after all, that the aphorism tells us history is written by the winners. Thus, while I will not aim here to prove that Euodia, Syntyche, or Epaphroditus were (freed) slaves, I also cannot ignore the possibility that one or more of them might just represent one of those "dim, ad hoc flashes," flashes that then call for greater consideration.

Wo/men and Unmen

In what follows, then, I attempt to pursue further considerations of what those lives of Philippian (freed) slaves in the assembly community *might* have looked like. In doing so, this study can move from the degrees of imprecision, vagueness, and uncertainty that will, by necessity, surround these exact figures toward the places scholars *can* know much more about ancient slavery. In an attempt to fill in these gaps, one can turn to the voluminous scholarship on slavery in the Roman Empire.[25] Even as most of the

---

22. See, for instance, the introduction by Richard A. Horsley, "Unearthing a People's History," in Horsley, *Christian Origins*, 1–20, especially 14–16. See also the opening sections of Carolyn Osiek, "Family Matters," in Horsley, *Christian Origins*, 201–20; and Martin, "Eyes Have It."

23. J. Albert Harrill, "Paul and Slavery," in Sampley, *Paul in the Greco-Roman World*, 575–607 (575). See also Harrill, *Slaves in the New Testament: Literary, Social, and Moral Dimensions* (Minneapolis: Fortress, 2006).

24. Martin, "Eyes Have It," 224.

25. See, to start, Keith Hopkins, *Conquerors and Slaves*, Sociological Studies in Roman History 1 (Cambridge: Cambridge University Press, 1978); Moses I. Finley,

remains continuously come from the perspective of the slaveholder, the ubiquity of slaves throughout Rome and its colonies provides key insights for constructing aspects of slaves' and freed slaves' lives. Because recent sociohistorical scholarship suggests the distinct possibility that there were (freed) slaves in the Philippian *colonia* and *ekklēsia* and that even some of the figures named in the letter could be among them, this gives scholars interested in "people beside Paul" the occasion to pursue different kinds of questions.

First, the presence of slaves and freed slaves, some of whom were female, challenges scholars to ask: are these "the people" for whom we are looking? If so, then one must also consider whether and how much women and/or slaves "count" as people. If one proceeds only on the basis of the ancient sources (and most of the history of biblical and classical interpretation), then the answer to these sorts of questions would likely be "no." As classical scholars Sandra Joshel and Sheila Murnaghan stress, femaleness and slavery were similarly differentiated concepts and locations in Greco-Roman contexts:

> Women and slaves were similarly distinguished from free men by their social subordination and their imagined otherness. Both were excluded from full participation in political life; both occupied an ambiguous position in the patrilocal family as indispensible outsiders; and both were viewed as morally deficient and potentially dangerous.[26]

Martin similarly reflects upon the impossible importance of studying those who are not seen as meeting the threshold of the "normal" person: "To focus on slaves in a history book may appear as a contradiction in

---

Ancient Slavery and Modern Ideology (New York: Viking Press, 1980); Orlando Patterson, *Slavery and Social Death: A Comparative Study* (Cambridge: Harvard University Press, 1982); Keith Bradley, *Slavery and Society at Rome*, Key Themes in Ancient History (Cambridge: Cambridge University Press, 1994); Peter Garnsey, *Ideas of Slavery from Aristotle to Augustine* (Cambridge: Cambridge University Press, 1996); and Page duBois, *Slaves and Other Objects* (Chicago: University of Chicago Press, 2003). For the study of slavery and Paul's letters, begin with the works of Harrill (variously cited above); Allen Dwight Callahan, Richard A. Horsley, and Abraham Smith, eds., *Slavery in Text and Interpretation*, Semeia 83–84 (Atlanta: Society of Biblical Literature, 1998); and Jennifer A. Glancy, *Slavery in Early Christianity* (Minneapolis: Fortress, 2006).

26. Sandra R. Joshel and Sheila Murnaghan, eds., *Women and Slaves in Greco-Roman Culture: Differential Equations* (London: Routledge, 1998), 1–21, esp. 3.

terms. History presumably focuses on human beings."[27] Grappling with what counts as a "human," or who are among the "people," reminds that such categories are socially and politically constructed terms, often along the lines of gender, race, ethnicity, sexuality, and economic and colonial placement. As Elisabeth Schüssler Fiorenza has noted, "feminists have learned that words such as 'human' or 'worker' or 'civil society' are gender-typed and often are not meant to include the rights and interests of wo/men."[28] Historically, whole groups of humans have been classified as inhuman, thus enabling further dehumanizing structures and practices. Such practices are, at least ostensibly, what a "people's history" project seeks to counter. If such projects seek not to reinscribe such dominating and dehumanizing dynamics but, rather, to move somehow against or outside of them, they must learn from feminist, antiracist, postcolonial, and queer approaches to history.

In what follows, then, I aim to make one specific contribution to this pursuit by drawing upon feminist and occasionally queer (or at least gender-critical) resources.[29] Doing so better facilitates the answering of the questions before me when I encounter the potential (freed) slaves Euodia, Syntyche, and Epaphroditus. In seeking to outline what their lives could have looked like and what place they had in the *colonia* and the *ekklēsia* at Philippi, these approaches should allow more specified constructions of these "people," beyond the recurrently idealized (and whitewashed) peasant subjects or downtrodden workers in other people's history projects.[30] It is not that class, or better, status, drops out of the following analysis. Instead, I aim to underscore how the status of the enslaved and manumitted is always also gendered in specific ways. Because the impact

---

27. Martin, "Eyes Have It," 221.

28. Elisabeth Schüssler Fiorenza, *Wisdom Ways: Introducing Feminist Biblical Interpretation* (Maryknoll, NY: Orbis, 2001), 56. This historical practice of treating women and other subordinated groups as not fully human is one of the reasons Schüssler Fiorenza prefers the cheeky definition of feminism as "the radical notion that women are people." See Schüssler Fiorenza, *Wisdom Ways*, 55–57. For more on this spelling of wo/men (with a / between the o and m), see the discussion to follow.

29. For one attempt to develop a feminist, postcolonial approach to this kind of history from below project in and through the study of Paul's letters, see Marchal, *Politics of Heaven*, especially 24–36 and 139–44.

30. This study, then, aims to move differently from certain Marxist-influenced projects, and their limited reflections on the importance of gender and sexuality, for instance. See also the discussion in Marchal, *Politics of Heaven*, 27–34 and 140–43.

of slave institutions and practices was so variegated and, in turn, conditioned every aspect of the enslaved or manumitted's life, it will be my strategy to select one aspect that works rather effectively as a register and gauge for their gender *and* status (or, rather, their gendered status). The (freed) slave's place is quite notably refracted through those acts, attitudes, and bodily comportments that moderns have tended to call sexuality.[31] Indeed, the sexual practices, but more often, uses of slaves constitute one area in which the study of slavery is currently expanding.[32] This is certain to provide new, challenging, and even disturbing possibilities for understanding those potential (freed) slaves in the Philippian assembly community, while indicating their specifically gendered status in the Roman imperial context.

If Euodia, Syntyche, and/or Epaphroditus are (freed) slaves, then this provides that rare opportunity, one of those aforementioned "dim, ad hoc

---

31. For some more recent reflections on the problem of the history of "sexuality" as it pertains to the ancient Greek and Roman contexts, see David M. Halperin, *How to Do the History of Homosexuality* (Chicago: University of Chicago Press, 2002), and then as it relates to the study of biblical (and Pauline) texts, see Marchal, "'Making History' Queerly: Touches across Time through a Biblical Behind," *BibInt* 19 (2011): 373–95. Halperin, among others, is responsible for the notion that those in the first century might somehow be "before sexuality." See, for instance, Halperin, John J. Winkler, and Froma I. Zeitlin, eds., *Before Sexuality: The Construction of Erotic Experience in the Ancient Greek World* (Princeton: Princeton University Press, 1990); and Halperin, *One Hundred Years of Homosexuality: And Other Essays on Greek Love* (New York: Routledge, 1990).

32. See the early essay by Sheila Briggs, "Paul on Bondage and Freedom in Imperial Roman Society," in *Paul and Politics: Ekklesia, Israel, Imperium, Interpretation; Essays in Honor of Krister Stendahl*, ed. Richard A. Horsley (Harrisburg, PA: Trinity Press International, 2000), 110–23; and then Glancy, *Slavery in Early Christianity*; Briggs, "Slavery and Gender," in *On the Cutting Edge: The Study of Women in Biblical Worlds; Essays in Honor of Elisabeth Schüssler Fiorenza*, ed. Jane Schaberg, Alice Bach, and Esther Fuchs (New York: Continuum, 2003), 171–92; Carolyn Osiek, "Female Slaves, *Porneia*, and the Limits of Obedience," in *Early Christian Families in Context: An Interdisciplinary Dialogue*, ed. David L. Balch and Carolyn Osiek (Grand Rapids: Eerdmans, 2003), 255–74; Margaret Y. MacDonald, "Slavery, Sexuality, and House Churches: A Reassessment of Colossians 3.18–4.1 in Light of New Research on the Roman Family," *NTS* 53 (2007): 94–113; Bernadette J. Brooten with Jacqueline L. Hazelton, eds., *Beyond Slavery: Overcoming Its Religious and Sexual Legacies*, Black Religion, Womanist Thought, Social Justice (New York: Palgrave Macmillan, 2010); and now Joseph A. Marchal, "The Usefulness of an Onesimus: The Sexual Use of Slaves and Paul's Letter to Philemon," *JBL* 130 (2011): 373–95.

flashes," to reflect upon not only those people besides Paul, but also those who were lower in various intersecting hierarchies of the Roman empire. Because such flashes are so meager and so few, this problem of sources underscores and then impresses upon me that this is a chance, if but a momentary one, for a feminist interpreter to pursue in the midst of a history from below project.[33] After all, as Joshel and Murnaghan remind, "The few texts authored by women and slaves that do survive are in highly conventional forms, such as epitaphs on tombstones, in which the dominant language of the culture tends to obscure individual testimony."[34] This persistent problem of sources, in fact, demonstrates why it is so important to attempt to understand something more about Epaphroditus, Euodia, and Syntyche, even when there are only some traces of them embedded within the rhetoric of this letter and even when one might approach them with the help of such epitaphs, funerary reliefs, or scraps of papyrus (as I will do below).

This also demonstrates why it is important and useful to proceed with the help of various feminist contributions, particularly considering how long feminist biblical scholars have had to deal with enforced silences and obscurities in historical and rhetorical analyses. This has particularly been the case when feminist work has grappled with Paul's letters, as Schüssler Fiorenza, Antoinette Clark Wire, and Cynthia Briggs Kittredge have done.[35] If scholars attempting to promote a people's kind of history

---

33. On the scarcities and silences of sources about (freed) slaves, especially in terms of any "direct" sources or references, see again Harrill, "Paul and Slavery," 575 and 585–56; Martin, "Eyes Have It," 221-28; and Joshel and Murnaghan, "Introduction," 19–21. On the difficulties and abilities of a larger and more contemporary set of slave narratives and speakers still to communicate across the boundaries of enslaving and enslaved figures, see Vincent L. Wimbush, "Interpreters—Enslaving/Enslaved/Runagate," *JBL* 130 (2011): 5–24 (15–17).

34. Joshel and Murnaghan, "Introduction," 19. See also Joshel, *Work, Identity, and Legal Status at Rome: A Study of the Occupational Inscriptions*, Oklahoma Studies in Classical Culture 11 (Norman: University of Oklahoma Press, 1992).

35. See Elisabeth Schüssler Fiorenza, *But She Said: Feminist Practices of Biblical Interpretation* (Boston: Beacon, 1992); Schüssler Fiorenza, *Rhetoric and Ethic: The Politics of Biblical Studies* (Minneapolis: Fortress, 1999); and Schüssler Fiorenza, *Wisdom Ways*; Antoinette Clark Wire, *The Corinthian Women Prophets: A Reconstruction through Paul's Rhetoric* (Minneapolis: Fortress, 1990); Kittredge, *Community and Authority*; and Kittredge, "Rethinking Authorship in the Letters of Paul: Elisabeth Schüssler Fiorenza's Model of Pauline Theology," in *Walk in the Ways of Wisdom: Essays in Honor of Elisabeth Schüssler Fiorenza*, ed. Shelly Matthews, Cynthia Briggs

are genuine in their call for interdisciplinary approaches geared to dealing with just such problems, then they would be best advised to learn from feminist forms of historiography that have dealt with the slight evidence of life in Corinth, Thessalonika, or Philippi provided by Paul's letters.[36] For a "people's history" to live up to its name, it must be able to deal with the dearth of direct sources by adapting more creative strategies to do work unlike many previous, traditional kinds of historical projects. Feminist interpreters like Schüssler Fiorenza and Wire have demonstrated that, if one intends to learn about those on the other side of a rhetorical exchange (such as Euodia, Syntyche, or Epaphroditus), then one must learn to "read against the grain" of Paul's prescriptive arguments.[37] This may not "prove" their particular status or location in the Philippian assembly, but it does factor for the dominating and dehumanizing dynamics present in Pauline epistles and interpretation and, in turn, allows for alternative constructions of historical perspectives in the audience (like those of women, slaves, the people, and/or those below). In this way feminist approaches will help me as I try to move from the rhetoric of Philippians to the wider context that is about, if not always from those "below," and then back again to the rhetoric of the letter, all in order to access alternative forms of historical perspective.

In order to "catch" how such figures from below might be operating in the communities to which Paul wrote, then, it is also wise to adapt concepts that help the contemporary reader to understand the specific ways in which people like the enslaved and manumitted were placed in terms of gendered status. Here, the insights of both feminist and queer biblical interpreters provide unique opportunities through terms like "wo/men" and "unmen," in particular.

The first of these terms, wo/men (which also appeared above), is a product of Schüssler Fiorenza's particular penchant for creatively insightful

---

Kittredge, and Melanie Johnson-DeBaufre (Harrisburg, PA: Trinity Press International, 2003), 318–33.

36. See, for instance, Horsley, "Unearthing a People's History," 5; and Warren Carter, "Matthew's People," in Horsley, *Christian Origins*, 138–61 (140); both are adapting Peter Burke, "Overture: The New History; Its Past and Future," in *New Perspectives on Historical Writing*, ed. Peter Burke, 2nd ed. (University Park: Pennsylvania State University, 1992), 1–23 (3).

37. See Schüssler Fiorenza, *Rhetoric and Ethic*, 105–48, 175–94 (also *Wisdom Ways*, 183–86); and Wire, *Corinthian Women Prophets*, 1–11.

terminological twists. Schüssler Fiorenza added the slash symbol partway through the word women (and also woman) in order to challenge monolithic or essentializing definitions and highlight that there are differences within and between women.[38] Such a spelling also suggests (both cheekily and quite seriously) that wo/men can be used as a replacement for supposedly generic language like mankind or perhaps even people: "'Wo/man' denotes not one simple reality, and 'wo/men' is often equivalent to 'people.'"[39] Thus, this term complicates the picture of how gender is constructed and how wo/men are situated in their contexts. Furthermore, it underscores how gendered terms are also used to define and describe non-elite or subaltern males "as wo/men."[40]

The more that one reflects upon Schüssler Fiorenza's use of wo/men, the more it both describes and critically qualifies how the "people" in "people's history" has tried to function. With its attention to the differences within and between group members (wo/men), it stresses how women are among these peasants (they are not separate categories or groups) and that the majority of the world's poor are women.[41] Thinking critically about how this word operates also reminds that the deployment of the term "woman" also naturalized a range of dynamics in the ancient world besides gender difference: "Strictly speaking, slave wo/men and alien resident wo/men were not considered to be wo/men."[42] Thus, wo/men encourages, even requires, greater reflection on who is addressed by terms of human belonging and insistently shows how specificities matter for situating people (or rather, wo/men) in social structures and settings. The terms of womanliness or femininity have been applied to both females

---

38. Schüssler Fiorenza first began using this spelling of wo/man and wo/men in *Jesus: Miriam's Child, Sophia's Prophet; Critical Issues in Feminist Christology* (New York: Continuum, 1994). For initial definitions and elaborations on "wo/men," see Schüssler Fiorenza, *Rhetoric and Ethic*, ix; and *Wisdom Ways*, 57–59, 107–9, and 216.

39. Schüssler Fiorenza, *Rhetoric and Ethic*, ix. Women (and others historically classified as "like women") have often had to "think twice" about whether they are included in supposedly universal statements such as "all men are created equal." Now Schüssler Fiorenza advocates that male readers will need to reflect when wo/men is being used in an inclusively generic sense or in a more specific way (excluding at least some males). See Schüssler Fiorenza, *Wisdom Ways*, 57–58.

40. See Schüssler Fiorenza, *Wisdom Ways*, 58 and 216.

41. Ibid., 59.

42. Ibid., 108. See also Elizabeth Spelman, *Inessential Woman: Problems of Exclusion in Feminist Thought* (Boston: Beacon, 1988).

and nonelite males, any others who might have been historically classified as somehow "like women." As a result, wo/men can be equivalent to
the kind of nonelite "people" sought in (much of) people's history, since
it operates as a replacement of sorts for phrases like "women and other
unpersons."[43] Such nonpersons likely included the enslaved and manumitted in the ancient world, even as they also functioned as limit cases for the
elite, imperial, and mostly male sources in the ancient world.[44]

So, "wo/men" might be one good way to describe such figures and
discern something about their gendered status, but more than occasionally so would "unmen." Jonathan Walters introduces this helpful label for a
series of people, because most of our Greek and Roman sources insist that
not all adult males would have been seen as "real men" (viri) in the ancient
world.[45] Walters, for instance, highlights that "youths, slaves, eunuchs, and
sexually passive males were something else."[46] This something else was
more than a bit "like women," as Michel Foucault highlights about the
typical and mostly nonproblematic objects for elite males' pleasure with
the sloganistic triad "women, boys, slaves."[47] Viri is not a term that can be
applied to all males (as one *might* think of "men" now), but they exclude
nonelite working groups, slaves, or any conquered or disreputable person.
Gender, ethnic, and economic categories intertwine in this system, as
Marilyn Skinner notes: "an impoverished, freed, or slave individual of
non-Italian, and especially Greek or eastern Mediterranean, background
will inevitably be feminized as well."[48]

---

43. See, for instance, Schüssler Fiorenza, *But She Said*, 37.

44. For further reflections on the limits, overlaps, ambiguities, and exclusions
performed by various uses of (and between) women and slaves, see Joshel and Mur-
nagahn, "Introduction."

45. See Jonathan Walters, " 'No More Than a Boy': The Shifting Construction of
Masculinity from Ancient Greece to the Middle Ages," *Gender and History* 5 (1991):
20–33. Later, see Walters, "Invading the Roman Body: Manliness and Impenetrability
in Roman Thought," in *Roman Sexualities*, ed. Judith P. Hallett and Marilyn B. Skinner
(Princeton: Princeton University Press, 1997), 29–43.

46. Walters, "No More Than a Boy," 30.

47. Michel Foucault, *The Use of Pleasure*, vol. 2 of *The History of Sexuality*, trans.
Robert Hurley (New York: Vintage, 1990), 47.

48. Marilyn B. Skinner, "Introduction: *Quod multo fit aliter in Graeci...*," in Hallett and Skinner, *Roman Sexualities*, 3–25 (20); also, Amy Richlin, "Pliny's Brasserie,"
in Hallett and Skinner, *Roman Sexualities*, 197–220.

This differentiation from classical studies between "men" and "unmen," then, connects in many points not only with Schüssler Fiorenza's wo/men, but also with her analytic concept of kyriarchy. As a replacement for patriarchy and its more simplified, dualistic analysis of power in gendered terms, kyriarchy highlights how multiple and mutually influential structures of domination and subordination function together in pyramidal relations determined not only by sexism, but also by racism, classism, ethnocentrism, heterosexism, colonialism, nationalism, and militarism (among others).[49] Kyriarchy is a system where only certain kinds of males are "men"—elite, educated, freeborn, propertied, imperial, and typically from particular racial/ethnic groups—who rule all who might be wo/men—females but also nonelite, uneducated, enslaved, subaltern, and/or often racially or ethnically dominated groups of males. This sort of analysis explains how elite groups in the ancient context could and would differentiate between "real" men and unmen, as Walters and others have highlighted. Compare, for instance, the description of this ancient social-sexual protocol by Stephen Moore with the definition of kyriarchy offered by Schüssler Fiorenza:

> Moore: A rather more complex picture emerges. In the centre of the circle or at the apex of the pyramid, were adult free males, supremely, though not exclusively, those of high social standing (rulers, magistrates, heads of elite households, patrons, etc.), while around them, or below them, were others who, each in their own way, were conceived as *unmen*, or at least as *not fully men* (women, youths, slaves, "effeminate" males, eunuchs, "barbarians," etc.).[50]

> Schüssler Fiorenza: [Kyriarchy] seeks to redefine the analytic category of patriarchy in terms of multiplicative intersecting structures of domina-

---

49. Schüssler Fiorenza coined this term based on the Greek word for lord or master, *kyrios*, a title that would have also been used for a husband, father, slaveowner, and/or an imperial authority. For an introductory definition to this neologism, see Schüssler Fiorenza, *Wisdom Ways*, 1, 118–24, 211; and *Rhetoric and Ethic*, ix. See also Schüssler Fiorenza, *Bread Not Stone: The Challenge of Biblical Interpretation*, 10th anniversary ed. (Boston: Beacon, 1995), 211 n. 6; and *But She Said*, 8, 117.

50. Stephen D. Moore, "Que(e)rying Paul: Preliminary Questions," in *Auguries: The Jubilee Volume of the Sheffield Department of Biblical Studies*, ed. David J. A. Clines and Stephen D. Moore, JSOTSup 269 (Sheffield: Sheffield Academic Press, 1998), 249–74 (261). Here Moore alludes to and summarizes points from Walters, "No More Than a Boy," esp. 31.

tion. Kyriarchy is a socio-political system of domination in which elite educated propertied men hold over wo/men and other men. Kyriarchy is best theorized as a complex pyramidal system of intersecting multiplicative social structures of superordination and subordination, or ruling and oppression.[51]

The "rather more complex picture" Moore presents en route to queerly interrogating Paul's letters echoes, but does not specifically refer to, Schüssler Fiorenza's kyriarchy (perhaps even to his work's own detriment). Yet, this social-sexual protocol reflects precisely the kinds of pyramidal relations of power that Schüssler Fiorenza dubs kyriarchy. Walters similarly maps this protocol: "At the apex are the small class of *viri*, true men, adult Roman citizens in good standing, the impenetrable penetrators."[52] As one travels down this pyramid, those with lower social status have less and less protection and are more and more appropriate to use for (sexual) penetration, marking them as feminized, as nonmen.[53] Thus, similar to how Schüssler Fiorenza conceived of wo/men, this kyriarchical system categorizes "the penetrated as 'unman,' using 'woman' to exemplify the unman."[54] Women (and) (freed) slaves (both male *and* female [freed] slaves) are stratified and signified similarly, if not always interchangeably.[55] This demonstrates how status is gendered and can be especially gauged by the contemporary category sexuality. Erotic contact is not just some "private" matter, nor is it a thing that people do with one part of their bodies. Rather, it is a reflection of the way embodied entities ("people") are placed in relation to each other, as an expression of their social status.[56] This standing is exemplified and stratified by a range of interwoven

---

51. Schüssler Fiorenza, *Wisdom Ways*, 211.

52. Walters, "Invading the Roman Body," 41.

53. On "nonmen," see also Craig A. Williams, *Roman Homosexuality: Ideologies of Masculinity in Classical Antiquity* (New York: Oxford University Press, 1999), 160–81.

54. Walters, "Invading the Roman Body," 33. See also, Skinner, "Introduction," 14.

55. Again, similar treatment in ancient protocols for elite imperial, free males does not necessarily indicate "solidarities" between various groups appropriate for penetrative use. See, for instance, the various contributions of Murnaghan and Joshel, *Women and Slaves in Greco-Roman Culture.*

56. There are moments in which Moore's initial presentation of this work from classical scholars virtually reduces the system to a class hierarchy. See, for instance, Moore, "Que(e)rying Paul," 267. As the discussion above indicates, though, the system involves much more (pun not intended). For further elaboration upon this hierarchical point of view as it relates to queer modes of biblical interpretation, see Moore,

factors, including gender, sexuality, status, ethnicity, age, economics, and imperial location.

Attending to such conceptualizations, then, can further illuminate those "dim, ad hoc flashes of the lives of slaves in the assemblies of Christ," as well as identify how Paul's own arguments specifically fit into this interlocking system of overlapping and mutually influential dynamics. Who are the people in a people's history kind of project? It now seems that one very good answer would be the kinds of wo/men and unmen discerned and described by feminist, gender-critical, and queer approaches. If Euodia, Syntyche, and Epaphroditus were enslaved or manumitted members of an *ekklēsia* in this Roman *colonia*, then, they would likely be these kinds of wo/men and unmen, subject to a range of interlocking sociopolitical forces and structures.

The Use of Slaves and Freed Slaves

It becomes vital, then, to inquire further into some of the conditions for these wo/men and unmen. Since the numbers of wo/men and unmen would be massive in the Roman empire, it is helpful to focus upon the institution of slavery. Nevertheless, slavery touched every element of living in the ancient world, so one cannot hope to offer a comprehensive overview of such social conditions in a brief span of time and space either. This is why I have aimed to focus specifically on one aspect—sexuality— as a register that reflects gender and status, or better, gendered status, in the imperial context of the Philippian *colonia* and *ekklēsia*.[57] This involves recalling not only that Philippi is a *colonia*, but also that it is part of the Roman Empire's slave-based economy. If there were any (freed) slaves in the *colonia* and *ekklēsia* at Philippi, they were likely affected by the positions held and practices maintained by those higher in the *vir*-ile kyriarchies of the empire.

For instance, attitudes about slave (and other socially subordinate) bodies are conditioned by elite imperial male (or kyriarchal) concerns

---

God's Beauty Parlor: And Other Queer Spaces in and around the Bible, Contraversions: Jews and Other Differences (Stanford, CA: Stanford University Press, 2001), 133–72 and especially 135–46.

57. Other works in this volume might exemplify how an analysis could attend to other parts of these multiple and overlapping factors for the "people beside Paul" in Philippi.

about the proper use of pleasure, χρῆσις ἀφροδισίων. In keeping with the protocol briefly surveyed above, the correct forms of χρῆσις (or *chrēsis*) relate to and communicate one's status both generally—in a context where there is an "isomorphism between sexual relations and social relations"— and thus, specifically—where women, slaves, the conquered, and other males of lower status and age (wo/men and/or unmen) were the proper objects for use.[58] Craig Williams attests that this attitude toward the use of slaves was so ubiquitous and unexceptional that a "comprehensive catalogue of Roman texts that refer to men's sexual use of their male and female slaves would be massive," since "it was simply taken for granted that this kind of freedom (or rather, dominion) was one of the many perquisites of being a Roman slave owner."[59] This terminology of use (χρῆσις and χράομαι) recurs across the centuries, as the sexual use of slaves persistently reflects both Greek and Roman views of gendered status, economically and erotically.[60] In discussing the relevance of this asymmetrically gendered sexual protocol for the interpretation of another of Paul's letters (Romans), Bernadette Brooten stresses that "Greek authors from the classical period through late antiquity use both the noun *chrēsis* and the verb *chraomai* ('to use') in a sexual sense. A man 'uses' or 'makes use of' a woman or a boy."[61]

These "uses" for the slave subordinate in status reflect the blithely utilitarian disposition of the elite imperial male protocol of penetration. Horace, for example, recommends a utilitarian attitude to fulfilling one's desires for food, drink, and, of course, sex:

> Now really, when your throat is parched with thirst, you don't ask for golden goblets, do you? When you're hungry, you don't turn your nose up at everything but peacock and turbot, do you? When your crotch is throbbing and there is a slave-girl or home-grown slave-boy ready at

---

58. Foucault, *Use of Pleasure*, 215.

59. Williams, *Roman Homosexuality*, 31.

60. See Herodas, *Mimes* 5.6; 6.29 (also 6.55, 78); Pseudo-Lucian, *Erōtes* 10, 25, 27; Athenaueus, *Deipn.* 604 D, 604E; Xenophon of Ephesus, *Eph.* 1.13.6; Epictetus, *Ench.* 33.8; Plutarch, *Mor.* 140B; 288A; 750D–E; see also Horace, *Sat.* 1.2.114–119; Seneca, *Controversiae*, 4.10; Martial, *Epigrams* 1.84; and Petronius, *Satyricon* 75.11.

61. Bernadette J. Brooten, *Love between Women: Early Christian Responses to Female Homoeroticism*, The Chicago Series on Sexuality, History, and Society (Chicago: University of Chicago Press, 1996), 245. Here Brooten also cites (as this article might) the standard dictionary entries for χρῆσις and χράομαι in LSJ and BAGD.

hand, whom you could jump right away, you don't prefer to burst with your hard-on, do you? I certainly don't. I like sex that is easy and obtainable. (Horace, *Sat.* 1.2.114–119)[62]

The sentiment reflected in the text, though satiric, is also indicative of an attitude about the appropriate, fulfilling, and perhaps safest outlet for satisfying urges and needs: slaves function interchangeably with each other (across gender) and with other "basics" to keep the elite imperial male sated and out of trouble. Even among philosophers advocating moderation, such as Epictetus and Plutarch, the terminologies of use and the management of food, drink, and slaves in the household recur.[63] The sexual use of slaves and other subordinate bodies is not only permitted, but it could also be the means of maintaining the elite imperial male's status as virtuous in the management of one's wider household (and often, by extension, the empire).[64] Indeed, Pauline interpreters like David E. Frederickson comment on passages like these to stress "the pervasive interpretation of sexual activity as use."[65]

The trouble avoided by the elite male slaveowner in Horace and these philosophers becomes a repetitive source of trouble, however, for the protagonists of ancient Greek novels from Chariton, Longus, Achilles Tatius, and Xenophon of Ephesus. In these, male and female masters dispose with enslaved heroes (who show themselves to be truly noble, because they are nobly born) as they please, arranging for sexual exchanges or seeking their own fulfillment with both female and male slaves.[66] In one such episode within the story of Anthia and Habrocomes, the star-crossed lovers beg

---

62. The translation can be found in Williams, *Roman Homosexuality*, 32. (Compare, for example, the more sanitizing translations in the LCL edition of Horace.)

63. For example, Epictetus prefaces his advice on χρῆσις by instructing: "In things that pertain to the body take only as much as your bare need requires, I mean such things as food, drink, clothing, shelter, and household slaves; but cut down everything which is for outward show or luxury" (*Ench.* 33.7). See also Epictetus, *Ench.* 41, where he worries over excessive time spent on bodily matters such as exercise, eating, drinking, defecating, and sex.

64. See Plutarch, *Mor.* 140B; 288A; 750D–E.

65. David E. Frederickson, "Natural and Unnatural Use in Romans 1:24–27: Paul and the Philosophic Critique of Eros," in *Homosexuality, Science, and the "Plain Sense" of Scripture*, ed. David Balch (Grand Rapids: Eerdmans, 2000), 197–222.

66. See, for example, Achilles Tatius, *Leuc. Clit.* 5.17; Chariton, *Chaer.* 2.6; Longus, *Daphn.* 4.11–19; and Xenophon of Ephesus, *Eph.* 1.16; 2.9; 5.7.

their pirate marauder (and soon to be owner) to stop the killing, but "take the cargo, master, and take us as slaves" (*Eph.* 1.13.6). Their pleading to be taken as slaves is paralleled to and analogized with the taking of "the cargo," τὰ χρήματα, goods, property, or chattel to be used.[67]

From this kind of perspective, the treatment of social subordinates like slaves does not "count" as ethically or socially significant, showing in turn the lesser significance of slaves in general. This view toward sexual use, in particular, is manifest in the casual glibness of the jokes that follow upon Haterius's explanation in Seneca:

> He said, while defending a freedman who was charged with being his patron's lover: "Losing one's virtue is a crime in the freeborn, a necessity in a slave, a duty for the freedman." The idea became a handle for jokes, like "you aren't doing your duty by me" and "he gets in a lot of duty for him." As a result the unchaste and obscene got called "dutiful" for some while afterwards. (*Controversiae* 4.10)

The sequence described by Seneca illustrates the elite Roman predisposal to joke about others' sexual vulnerability: *officiosi* becoming a demeaning pun for "doing one's duty" sexually.[68]

In these sources, then, the joke is perhaps even more "on" the slave *and* the freed slave. Indeed, Haterius's words in Seneca reflects the ongoing vulnerability of even the freed slave, the figure presumed to be dutiful in continuing to submit to a sexual use by the master.[69] This expectation of ongoing service demonstrates how the relative frequency of manumission should not be mistaken for the emancipation of slaves from within a flawed, but mostly altruistic institution.[70] As Keith Hopkins has detailed,

---

67. One can find in the biblical corpus a similar lumping of goods with slave bodies to be used and exchanged in Roman imperial commerce (Rev 18:11–13).

68. For a fuller grasp of the often ugly, if colorful, sexual humor of the Romans, see Amy Richlin, *The Garden of Priapus: Sexuality and Aggression in Roman Humor*, rev. ed. (New Haven: Yale University Press, 1992). Paul Veyne notes: "A much repeated way of teasing a slave is to remind him of what his master expects of him, i.e., to get down on all fours." See Paul Veyne, "Homosexuality in Ancient Rome," in *Western Sexuality: Practice and Precept in Past and Present Times*, ed. Philippe Ariès and Andre Béjin (Oxford: Oxford University Press, 1985), 26–35 (29).

69. For this ongoing "duty of deference," see also Moore, "Que(e)rying Paul," 266; and Walter, "No More than a Boy," 29.

70. Finley's work aims to counteract such claims for an exceptional, compassionate, and/or altruistic form of slavery in antiquity (see Finley, *Ancient Slavery*). In Pau-

manumission functions "not as a solvent of the slave system, but as a major reinforcement."[71] Manumission is not a softening, but a tightening strategy for keeping slaves under control. Though there is typically little to no interest in the perspective of social subordinates like slaves and freed slaves in these sources, dutiful compliance certainly makes it easier to manage the kyriarchical dominion over slaves, as reflected in the acquiescent words of freed slave characters like Petronius's Trimalchio or in Arrian's accounts of the freed slave philosopher Epictetus.

Even as slaves had no legal or cultural right to refuse commands, masters frequently chose suasion as much as force in order to more effectively exercise control. The incentive and promise of manumission and the various stories and sayings that justify the social order described thus far would be just two examples of their attempt to rule through persuasion. In the scheme to get the enslaved hero Habrocomes for his pirate master's sexual use in Xenophon of Ephesus's *Ephesiaca*, Habrocomes is advised to show affection (ἀγαπᾶν, 1.16.3) to his new master. Yet, as part of the same attempt at suasion, he is told to obey (ὑποχούειν, 1.16.5) his master when he is commanded. Later in the novel, when the other half of the star-crossed couple Anthia is sold into prostitution, a similar strategy is applied with the pimp "alternately asking her to cheer up and making threats" (5.7.3). Hopkins reminds that "as in other slave societies, the tie between master and slave could be warm; this warmth did not necessarily lessen exploitation; though it may have softened the slave's feelings about it."[72] The language of affection and positive feeling toward the slave or between master and slave are not mitigations of this kyriarchical system, but expressions of its inner workings.

Cultivating this feeling of connection to the master is a savvy strategy for running the hierarchical household and empire in antiquity, especially because slaves are bodies that have been removed from various forms of connection. Orlando Patterson's classical formulation of the constituent elements of slavery stresses slaves' permanent natal alienation, their sym-

---

line studies, see Briggs, "Paul on Bondage," especially 111–14, 120–21. For an argument on the difference between manumission and emancipation, see Allen Dwight Callahan, "Paul, *Ekklēsia*, and Emancipation in Corinth: A Coda on Liberation Theology," in Horsley, *Paul and Politics*, 216–23.

71. Hopkins, *Conquerors and Slaves*, 118.

72. Ibid., 154.

bolic and social removal from the bonds of their ancestral kinship.[73] Slaves are dissociated from their ethnicity, kinship, culture, and locale, so that they might be integrated into a different family (the master's) and incorporated into a particular role in a kyriarchically stratified household structure. Slaves simultaneously "had no family" and were deeply embedded in a *familia* and *domus* to be managed by the *paterfamilias*.[74]

Not only, then, should one consider an expanded version of family in examining Roman imperial era slavery, but one must also grapple with an expanded ambit of relations for whom the slave is available to be used, sexually or otherwise. As Moses I. Finley stresses, this kyriarchical system involved "the direct sexual exploitation of slaves by their masters and the latter's family and friends."[75] The friends and family members of slaveowners did not need to go to brothels (where the clientele for those enslaved bodies were lower in status themselves) since their slaves could serve as "private prostitutes" for them.[76] Providing this service to friends and family, though, can be a matter to be carefully negotiated between friends becoming patron and client. On this matter, Horace gives a warning: "Let no maid or boy within your worshipful friend's marble threshold inflame your heart, lest the owner of the pretty boy or dear girl make you happy with a present so trifling or torment you if disobliging" (*Ep.* 1.18.72–75). Horace indicates that one has to be deliberately prudent when developing a friendship with, and accepting gifts from, a powerful man. If one

---

73. See Patterson, *Slavery and Social Death*; also Finley, *Ancient Slavery and Modern Ideology*, 75.

74. On slavery within conceptions of "family," see Beryl Rawson, ed., *The Family in Ancient Rome: New Perspectives* (Ithaca, NY: Cornell University Press, 1986); Carolyn L. Osiek and David L. Balch, *Families in the New Testament World: Households and House Churches*, The Family, Religion, and Culture (Louisville: Westminster John Knox, 1997); and Osiek and Balch, eds., *Early Christian Families in Context: An Interdisciplinary Dialogue*, Religion, Marriage, and Family (Grand Rapids: Eerdmans, 2003).

75. Finley, *Ancient Slavery*, 96.

76. On this status differentiation in terms of the sexual use of slaves and prostitutes, see Bettina Eva Stumpp, *Prostitution in der römischen Antike* (Berlin: Akademie, 1998), 26. For further context about the Roman legal and economic conditions for prostitution, see Thomas A. J. McGinn, *Prostitution, Sexuality, and the Law in Ancient Rome* (New York: Oxford University Press, 1988); and *The Economy of Prostitution in the Roman World: A Study of Social History and the Brothel* (Ann Arbor: University of Michigan Press, 2004).

owes the new friend (too much), the minimal gain in political advantage could be outweighed by the loss of self-determination or control in new obligations. The advice, of course, assumes that free men are giving slaves for these purposes, even as it advises care.[77] It stresses once more that this sexual use of male or female slave is mostly trivial; the significance of the exchange is not in the treatment of the slave, but in the relationship with the master and the friend.

Thus, by briefly focusing on one dynamic, sexuality, within this slave-based economy, while setting it broadly in a number of intersecting and mutually influential dynamics (like gender, status, ethnicity, and empire), this study has pried a small, but insightful opening into the complex inner workings of the ancient kyriarchical system in which Paul and the Philippians lived and argued.

Euodia, Syntyche, and Epaphroditus as Wo/men and Unmen

A Papyrus and a Portrait

This chapter began with reflections upon three particular figures named in Paul's letter to the Philippians, figures who likely were enslaved or manumitted. Thus, their lives would have also been conditioned by the dynamics and practices described thus far. One can expand the potential picture of someone named Epaphroditus, for example, through more careful consideration of the imperially gendered and sexualized system of slavery. For instance, Jennifer Glancy's study highlights a papyrus from Oxyrhynchus about an enslaved Epaphroditus: "Apion and Epimas proclaim to their best-loved Epaphroditus that if you allow us to bugger you it will go well for you, and we will not thrash you any longer."[78] In one sentence, then, one has a combination peculiar to contemporary interpreters

---

77. Williams highlights Porphyrio's claim that this warning of Horace to Lollius is referring to Virgil's acceptance of the beautiful *puer* Alexander from Pollio (described in Seutonius, *Virgil* 9). See Williams, *Roman Homosexuality*, 275, nn. 106 and 110; Horace, *Epist.* 1.18.75. The passage in Seutonius once more displays how the term "boy" (*puer, pais*) is used for male slaves, as one cannot give just any "boy," but slave "boys" can be given.

78. See Glancy, *Slavery in Early Christianity*, 53; translating and discussing P.Oxy. 42.3070. This papyrus is further discussed in Dominic Montserrat, *Sex and Society in Greco-Roman Egypt* (New York: Kegan Paul, 1996), 136–38.

unaccustomed to the ancient use of slaves: affectionate language of love, an attempt at "persuasion" (or coercion) and the exchange of penetration for (other forms of) physical violence. This enslaved Epaphroditus is not an isolated exception, as another Oxyrhynchus papyrus records the third sale of a young slave boy bearing the same name.[79] Indeed, even the freed-man philosopher Epictetus (whose disposition toward use was discussed above) was himself freed by a prominent imperial freedman-turned-owner Epaphroditus. Thus, in just three instances of the name Epaphroditus, one has reflected a microcosm of some of the significant dynamics in ancient slavery: the commodification of bodies, the coercion and sexual use, and the hierarchical tutelage of even the enslaved, so that one might aspire to be both freed and possess one's own commodified and vulnerable bodies to use.[80]

Likewise, one can expand the picture for the paired female figures Euodia and Syntyche through further reflections on material remains. An under-utilized study by Mary Rose D'Angelo provides just such an opportunity to consider these two wo/men in light of a funerary relief of two freed slaves.[81] The relief fits within the genre of *libertini* portraits, depictions of freed slaves that function "as substitutes for ancestor por-traits by which freedmen and women celebrate the legitimacy of the new family created when they were freed."[82] As natally alienated and kinship-displaced people, such portraits demonstrate the kinds of commitment freed slaves could make, especially when they were manumitted together (*conlibertae*). What makes this particular funerary relief remarkable is not simply its depiction of two freedwomen, but that they were represented clasping each others' right hand in a sign of marriage (*dextrarum inuctio*) and that this depiction was then recut in a likely attempt to obscure at

---

79. See P.Oxy. 60.4068; Glancy, *Slavery in Early Christianity*, 87.

80. This "hierarchical tutelage," in fact, might just be how kyriarchical relations of power perpetuate themselves as the dynamics move downward in and through the pyramidal structure.

81. See D'Angelo, "Women Partners." See the illustration in "Women Partners," 66; from British Museum Sculpture 2276; Susan Walker and Andrew Burnett, *Augus-tus: Handlist of the Exhibition*, Occasional Paper 16 (London: British Museum Publi-cations, 1981), 43–47.

82. D'Angelo, "Women Partners," 68; see also Diana E. E. Kleiner, *Roman Group Portraits: The Funerary Reliefs of the Late Republic and Early Empire* (New York: Gar-land, 1977), 23–24.

least one of their genders.[83] Since scholars have generally presented the first-century *ekklēsia* communities (like the one at Philippi) as including a significant amount of freed slaves, D'Angelo briefly reflects upon what this funerary relief might reveal about those fleeting, if significant recognitions of pairs like Tryphaena and Tryphosa (Rom 16:12) or Euodia and Syntyche (Phil 4:2–3).[84]

Certainly, this study gives me a chance to reconsider the use of conventional modes by freed slaves, where dominant language (even of the visual variety) could have been adopted but adapted. Such material remains demonstrate that slaves and freed slaves likely worked to develop and then support alternative kinds of bonds; the script of the masters was not always (if you will pardon the term) slavishly followed. Such sculptures and papyri are not some kind of material record about these three particular figures—Epaphroditus, Euodia, and Syntyche—but they do indicate how a history from below must try to be creative with the limited resources available and pursue interdisciplinary lines of approach and argument. This is particularly the case if one aims to do more than replicate standard approaches or rely upon the perspective of Pauline epistles and interpretations. Such an understanding of these contexts and connections will be especially important to keep in mind as I return to an analysis of Paul's arguments in Philippians.

Euodia and Syntyche in the Letter

Indeed, reflecting upon the role of Euodia and Syntyche in this letter reveals the arc and disposition of the letter overall. The intensity with which Paul repeats and structures his letter's entire argument in terms of a "same mindset" (1:7; 2:1–5, 20; 3:15, 19) running up to this exhortation to Euodia and Syntyche (4:2–3) indicates that this passage's concern with their mindset (τὸ αὐτὸ φρονεῖν) is no mere aside. Paul wants them to "think the same thing" as he, but what exactly is this mindset of Paul's? The letter's unity rhetorics have often been highlighted to emphasize Paul's use of friendship terms and conventions. Indeed, most malestream scholarship focuses upon reconstructing a "friendly" Paul and a glowingly sweet version of this letter and, thus, Paul's relationship with the Philippians.

---

83. See the discussion in D'Angelo, "Women Partners," 65–72.
84. Ibid., 72–77 and 81–85.

However, as Kittredge has definitively shown, obedience rhetorics are also a central and unavoidable element to Paul's argumentative plan in the letter.[85] Where Kittredge and my own analyses differ are the degrees to which these rhetorical elements are intertwined. Kittredge presents the presence of both friendship and obedience language as a conceptual tension, contradiction, and discontinuity in the letter.[86] I posit, however, that these are only apparent tensions if one does not take into account the ancient settings where affectionate friendship and hierarchical obedience rhetorics were both compatible with each other and, in turn, combined to reinforce institutional arrangements like patronage, the military, and the empire in general.[87] Given the brief contextualization (above), one can also note how such blending of affection with obedience, warmth with hierarchies was a feature of the masters' perspective on and within ancient slavery. In short, one can see how Paul's argument is in greater continuity with this way of thinking and arguing: he is seeking unity through conformity to his way of thinking and the accompanying obedience, due to Paul (and, thus, his vision of the community). I will have the occasion to return to the difficulty and density of these friendly kinds of patronage arguments once Epaphroditus is reconsidered as well.

But, first, it is important to recognize how this conceptual blending occurs in the arguments immediately within and around the exhortation to Euodia and Syntyche. One could object, for instance, that Paul uses rather positive descriptions for these two wo/men and likely (freed) slaves. They "costruggled" with Paul and appear to be listed among the coworkers he mentions in Phil 4:3.[88] As a result, it appears that Paul is seeking for them to think the same thing as he on "friendly" terms. Of course, if this is a

---

85. See, for instance, the discussion in Kittredge, *Community and Authority*, 96–100, 108–10.

86. Ibid., 56, 98, and 110.

87. On such combinations and then an overview analyzing how they combine in the letter, see Marchal, *Hierarchy, Unity, and Imitation*, 64–70, 115–56.

88. For considerations of their roles beyond what will be discussed in this chapter, see Lillian Portefaix, *Sisters Rejoice: Paul's Letter to the Philippians and Luke-Acts as Received by First-Century Philippian Women*, ConBNT 20 (Stockholm: Almqvist & Wiksell, 1988), 135–54; Wendy Cotter, "Women's Authority Roles in Paul's Churches: Countercultural or Conventional?" *NovT* 36 (1994): 350–72; and Nils A. Dahl, "Euodia and Syntyche and Paul's Letter to the Philippians," in *The Social World of the First Christians: Essays in Honor of Wayne A. Meeks*, ed. L. Michael White and O. Larry Yarbrough (Minneapolis: Fortress, 1995), 3–15.

targeted or even climactic instance of these arguments for similar mindset, then it is apparent that (Paul at least thinks) he is not on such stable and similar grounds with Euodia and Syntyche. His argument is proceeding as if they do not agree with him.[89] This also accounts for why Paul turns to a third party, the "yoke-fellow," to help him to convince Euodia and Syntyche to adopt this proper mindset. The exceedingly positive ways in which Paul describes this figure, something like "my true comrade" (Phil 4:3), emphasizes a close, collaborative relationship between them: they are "well yoked." From this wording, it seems that Paul thinks the audience will also know who this true comrade of Paul's is. If someone is so clearly tied to (and somehow similar to) Paul that she or he need not be named, it only accentuates the likelihood that there are members of the community in his audience that are just as clearly *less* linked to and *less* like him. The passage appears to be aiming for conformity to a particular kind of unity, but it does so through arguments that differentiate.

The potential ambiguity of this passage continues even into the very last phrase: "whose names are in the book of life." This "book of life" appears in apocalyptic literature and reflects the dualistic idea that only *some* names will be written within it.[90] But to which names does the letter refer? It might be including Euodia and Syntyche, who are the referent for the first relative pronoun in the sentence, but it may only refer to the immediately preceding group: "the rest of my coworkers" (Phil 4:3). Yet, one of the major purposes of the letter has been to create and reinforce certain boundary lines for (Paul's version of) the assembly community, and Paul has already evoked images of destruction and apocalyptic fear (Phil 1:28; 2:12; 3:15, 19) for those who get on the wrong side of his arguments. This reference to the book, then, might be a veiled warning for

---

89. Wire, for example, has shown the flaw in assuming in advance that Paul proceeds from a place of agreement and acceptance of his authority in the audience. Indeed, Paul's letters seem to demonstrate a rather different picture than this. Once one acknowledges the letters as attempts at persuasion, then "on whatever points Paul's persuasion is insistent and intense, showing he is not merely confirming their agreement but struggling for their assent, one can assume some different and opposite point of view in Corinth from the one Paul is stating" (*Corinthian Women Prophets*, 9). Earlier Wire maintains that "those in clear disagreement with Paul should be the ones most accessible through his rhetoric" (*Corinthian Women Prophets*, 4).

90. In the apocalyptic literature, see Dan 12:1; 1 En. 47:3; Rev 3:5; 13:8; 17:8; 20:12, 15; 21:27; but see also Exod 32:32; Isa 4:3; Ezek 13:9; Ps 69:28; Luke 10:20; Heb 12:23.

those who do not adhere to Paul's version of communal unity: any disagreement would mean exclusion of one's name from the book. If figures like Euodia and Syntyche respond in obedient conformity to Paul's arguments here, then they would "fit" with his implication about the rest of the coworkers. Failure to do so would make them more like the various negative figures described in the letter (opponents, dogs, and enemies).[91]

Paul's brief exhortation argument, directed to Euodia and Syntyche, seems to alternate between quickly complimentary descriptions of these two wo/men as those who costruggled with Paul and a veiled threat if they do not follow the argument he has been developing throughout the letter.[92] The sentence immediately preceding this exhortation fits this broad tendency of alternation as well. Paul uses one of his favorite familial terms—ἀδελφοί—to address his audience as kin ("brothers" or, perhaps, "siblings"), but he also retains his hierarchical preeminence over them by presenting them as his στέφανός—his "crown" or military imperial laurel (4:1). Though Paul twice describes the audience as his "beloved" in order to enjoin them to stand firm, Kittredge reminds that previous forms of such affectionate address are part of Paul's calls for their obedience, with fear and trembling no less (in 2:12).[93] Though Paul might be inclined to mix friendship and obedience arguments, affection with fear and threats, such combinations and their resonances across the letter stress that the exhortation to Euodia and Syntyche is a targeted example of the kind of obedience and conformity Paul has been seeking throughout Philippians.

It appears, then, that there are several ways that Paul's arguments are more compatible with, than contrary to the practices and positions of ancient slaveholders. Recall, for instance, that Xenophon of Ephesus's *Ephesiaca* used precisely the same combination of language, exhorting the slave to show a classically "Christian" affect ἀγάπη ("love," 1.16.3) to his new master, even as he is ordered to obey (ὑποκουείν, 1.16.5).[94] It may not

---

91. On the antimodel argumentation in 1:15–17, 28; 2:15, 21; 3:2, 18–19, see Marchal, *Hierarchy, Unity, and Imitation*, 188–9.

92. This tensive situation might also indicate an additionally foreboding connotation to Paul's claim that the "Lord is near" (Phil 4:5).

93. Kittredge highlights: "Beginning with *hoste* and using the form of address *agapetoi*, this injunction resembles the verse that follows the Christ hymn and refers to the congregation as 'obeying' (2:12)" (*Community and Authority*, 92).

94. Recall also that pimps (typically owners of slaves used primarily as prostitutes) did the same thing, combining threats with appeals to positive emotion (in the same story, 5.7.3).

be entirely surprising, then, to link the indications of Paul's disagreement with Euodia and Syntyche and the possibility that these two wo/men were slaves or freed slaves. This difference in gendered status, in fact, could be a reason for their accompanying difference in perspective. Paul's use of fictive kinship forms for the community, like others in these developing communities, would stand out in new ways, then. If Euodia and Syntyche are trying to work out some alternate forms of commitment and kinship (as the *conlibertae* in the funerary relief likely did), these forms might have been marked by greater difference or departure from ancient kyriarchal norms than those that were tweaked but mostly repeated by Paul.

This raises additional questions about the one who was more closely yoked to Paul than Euodia and Syntyche (in 4:3) and, thus, less like these other two wo/men in the Philippian *ekklēsia*. Might, then, this "true comrade" represent a different perspective on such ways of arguing about and organizing the community? If Paul shows a casual continuity with elite imperial slaveowning attitudes, then, it is possible this third party is highlighted, because he displays a similar continuity, quite possibly because he himself comes from the slaveowning ranks. Indeed, when dealing with such small developing communities, it is even possible that Paul's comrade was Euodia and Synytche's master, whether in slavery or manumission. This could further illuminate why Paul has asked this third party to "take hold with these" (feminine plural, 4:3, implicitly Euodia and Synytche). Scholars typically presume a neutral-to-positive meaning of help or assistance (συλλαμβάνου) for this instruction, but if these two wo/men already owe obedience and other duties to him, the collaborative term can assume other connotations, including seizing, grasping, or apprehending.[95] Such a situation would reflect the elites' simultaneous dependence upon slaves (and freed slaves) and the coercion with which they exercised their dominion. In order to be able to rely upon such figures, to get the social inferior to act in conformity with kyriarchal demands and dispositions, real imperial men must give wo/men, slaves, and freed slaves a "course of supervised exploitation."[96] Might this be a more fitting scenario for Paul's request of his true comrade or even for the letter as a whole?

---

95. Indeed, one other possible use of this verb, involving conception (see LSJ), recalls one of the chilling uses of female slave bodies: as receptacles of use and producers of additional humanesque tools for use.

96. Joy Connolly, "Mastering Corruption: Constructions of Identity in Roman

This alternation of affection and obedience, like the combination of friendship with hierarchical argumentation, reflects the kyriarchical mindset on the gendered status of supposed social inferiors like slaves and freed slaves. As in other ancient texts, Paul's letter also displays the mixed place of slaves (and freed slaves) as the internal outsider of kinship. This demonstrates the importance of presenting a counterpoint to this perspective, as I aimed to do with the reflections on the funerary relief. Even when conventionally kyriarchal forms of representation are used, they could be adapted to different ends than someone like Paul has taken in this letter. This possibility, as well as the blending of love and obedience, draws my attention back to how Paul applies the Christ hymn and the potential alternative provided by the presence of the hymn itself. From Paul's perspective, the lesson of this hymn is obedience, given his immediately following instruction (ὑπηκούσατε, 2:12; echoing ὑπήκοος, 2:8). Yet, since the letter presumes a difference in perspective from Paul's (if not, why else write the letter?), it is probable that others in the *ekklēsia* community that used and even developed this hymn did so with and from this difference in perspective. Kittredge even argues that the hymn reflects the work of Euodia and Syntyche, among others, in the community at Philippi.[97] This hymn, then, could have been a resource for the development of alternative forms of community, kinship, and connection as further departures and distinctions from the kyriarchal perspectives of this slave-based empire.[98]

Epaphroditus in the Letter

This picture is further complicated when we consider the role of Epaphroditus in the letter, mostly within 2:25–30, but secondarily in 4:10–20. Epaphroditus is introduced as a supporting model to Paul's argument and as a support to Paul himself. The letter stacks several descriptions of this possible (freed) slave, emphasizing his relationship to Paul and then to

---

Oratory," in Joshel and Murnaghan, *Women and Slaves in Greco-Roman Culture*, 130–51 (138).

97. See Kittredge, "Rethinking the Authorship," especially 324–26.

98. The potential difference between how a slave and a slaveholder would read or perceive parts of this letter (like the Christ hymn) is raised by the reflections in Briggs, "Can An Enslaved God Liberate? Hermeneutical Reflections on Philippians 2:6–11," *Semeia* 47 (1989): 137–53, esp. 142. For a different set of reflections, see the chapter by Brawley in this volume.

the Philippian assembly community (and then to both): "my brother and coworker and cosoldier, and your messenger and server of my need/use [χρεία]" (2:25). Typically, scholars stress the financial element of the Greek term χρεία, "need" (particularly as it will relate, also, to 4:10–20), yet one might also note how χρεία shares its root with the terms χρῆσις and χράομαι discussed above.[99] Within the work of Epictetus, for example, χρεία functions similarly to depict the "use" of slaves (and others):

> For there is some use [χρεία] in an ass, but not as much as there is an ox; there is use also in a dog, but not as much as there is in a slave; there is use also in a slave, but not as much as there is in your fellow citizens. (Epictetus, *Diatr.* 2.23.24)[100]

Here Epictetus discusses in an ascending hierarchical chain the relative uses which one might find in various creatures, with slaves functioning in between animals and other humans/citizens. By describing Epaphroditus in this fashion, Paul's argument reflects the assumed utility of someone sent by the assembly to do a public duty or service (λειτουργία). Epaphroditus can be sent back and forth by Paul and other parties, functioning as an instrument to be used for their own purposes. Indeed, this is the occasion for the introduction of him into the plan of the letter: Paul's plan to send him back (likely with the letter) to the Philippians (emphasized twice, at the start of the section in 2:25 and again in 2:28). Paul's argument presumes that he, and others, can use and move this embodied entity as they see fit. If Epaphroditus were a slave or freed slave, the letter's disposition corresponds well with what one might expect from a colonized setting in Philippi. This "unman" is exchanged in an imperial context where (freed) slaves are put to a range of uses, including the embodied and erotic uses that are one common register of their gendered status.

---

99. See also, for example, the entry on χρεία in LSJ, where the term is both related to these roots or word "family" branches and described most broadly in terms of use and service (including intercourse). One should be careful, however, not to assume that the economic and the embodied elements of the ancient slave system are somehow separable; those who *own* slaves draw an economic benefit from disposing these "animate tools" in whatever fashion they saw fit (see, e.g., Aristotle, *Pol.* 1.1–7). Glancy highlights the use of "body" (σῶμα) to describe the slave as a human body, but also as property, a thing to be exchanged and used. See Glancy, *Slavery in Early Christianity*, 36–37.

100. On this passage, see also Glancy, *Slavery in Early Christianity*, 33.

Again, given the terms of affection used in the opening of the section, some might be inclined to object and insist on excluding the possibility of such direct physical use or the implicit degradation of Paul's repetition of such terminologies of use. But, as was highlighted in the preceding sections, about both ancient slaves and Euodia and Syntyche, this mixture of affectionate address and obedient use, closeness and subjection was characteristic of this slave-based economy and society. As Hopkins reminds: "this warmth did not necessarily lessen exploitation; though it may have softened the slave's feelings about it."[101] Indeed, this strategy for managing (freed) slaves may account for why Epaphroditus was, in turn, in distress and longing for at least some members of the Philippian community (2:26). Paul's description of Epaphroditus casts him in the role of the loyal and fearful (freed) slave, reflecting the kinds of natally alienated, semireassimilated, but still subordinate positions that was the slave's in this context, a "member" of a different kind of family, but still disposable for so many uses. If Epaphroditus's feelings have been "softened" in this fashion, he functions even more powerfully in the letter's argumentation as a model of willing obedience, going and doing what he is told.[102] If the appeal to Euodia and Syntyche is one of the major purposes of this letter, then, it is possible that Epaphroditus is so depicted as a counterimage to these two wo/men, those who are not "thinking the same thing" as Paul and not maintaining a disposition of willing obedience. In the version presented by the letter, Paul's Epaphroditus is more like Petronius's Trimalchio or Arrian's Epictetus, an accepting and acceptable kind of (freed) slave, who always does his or her duty.

Even if Epaphroditus was not a slave or freed slave, his rhetorical function in the letter is slave-like: obedient and secondary to the agenda of Paul. The situation of Epaphroditus is only raised in order to explicate Paul's own views and priorities.[103] Epaphroditus recovers, due to divine

---

101. Hopkins, *Conquerors and Slaves*, 154.

102. For two rather different views on the potentially commendable or supporting model role of Epaphroditus, see, for example, Agosto, *Servant Leadership*, 142–44; and Marchal, *Politics of Heaven*, 60–62, 73, 86. For the use of supporting models to strengthen Paul's rhetorical vision, in contrast to the perspective of Euodia and Syntyche, see Kittredge, *Community and Authority*, 96, 108; and Marchal, *Hierarchy, Unity, and Imitation*, 147–49, 186–87, 189–90.

103. See also the reason why Paul is sending Timothy (for Paul's own good spirits, εὐψυχῶ, 2:19) and how Paul asserts that he hopes to make his own trip soon too (2:24).

mercy on him, but more especially *on Paul*: the deity serves to preserve Epaphroditus in order to spare *Paul* any additional trouble (Phil 2:27). This fits with the overall pattern in this brief letter, since Paul used the first person singular adjective or pronoun more than fifty times in its four chapters.[104] Paul discusses his desire to send Epaphroditus to the Philippians, not to relieve Epaphroditus, but for the benefit of the assembly and of Paul. Epaphroditus is secondary and instrumental in such argumentation. The letter stresses that the matter of Epaphroditus is actually more "about" the relationship between Paul and the Philippian assembly members. From Paul's perspective this "unman" matters only so that "he might fulfill your [pl.] lack to my service" (Phil 2:30).

The potential historical situation for Epaphroditus could be further illuminated, then, by a comparison with the letter to Philemon, a letter which scholars simply take for granted as being "about" a slave or at least Paul's attitude about this slave. Indeed, it is not uncommon for interpreters of Philemon to connect Onesimus's role to that of Epaphroditus's in Philippians.[105] Both letters explicitly allude to Paul's imprisonment at the time of composition (Phil 1:7, 13–14, 17; Phlm 1, 9, 10, 13, 23), and both discuss sending figures back to the addressees, Epaphroditus in Phil 2:25, 28 and Onesimus in Phlm 12. Craig Wansink's work is especially helpful in connecting these two elements in both of the letters, situating them in terms of ancient imprisonment practices where a prisoner was dependent upon messengers and attendants for connection and even survival.[106]

For further reflections on the sheer number of first-person references in this section, see Marchal, *Hierarchy, Unity, and Imitation*, 138–41 and 186–87.

104. Brian J. Dodd, *Paul's Paradigmatic "I": Personal Example as Literary Strategy*, JSNTSup 177 (Sheffield: Sheffield Academic, 1999), 171. See also Robert T. Fortna, "Philippians: Paul's Most Egocentric Letter," in *The Conversation Continues: Festschrift for J. Louis Martyn*, ed. Robert T. Fortna and Beverly R. Gaventa (Nashville: Abingdon, 1990), 220–34.

105. See, for example, Craig S. Wansink, *Chained in Christ: The Experience and Rhetoric of Paul's Imprisonments*, JSNTSup 130 (Sheffield: Sheffield Academic Press, 1996), 175–99; Agosto, *Servant Leadership*, 114–19; as well as Harrill, "Paul and Slavery," 591–92; L. Michael White, "Paul and *Pater Familias*," in Sampley, *Paul in the Greco-Roman World*, 457–87, esp. 469, 484; and Peter Lampe, "Paul, Patrons, and Clients," in Sampley, *Paul in the Greco-Roman World*, 488–523, especially 501–2.

106. See especially Wansink, *Chained in Christ*, 27–95. Also Richard J. Cassidy, *Paul in Chains: Roman Imprisonment and the Letters of Paul* (New York: Crossroad, 2001). For further considerations, see the chapter by Standhartinger in this volume.

Whether they were sent with messages, business matters, or gifts (to those in or out of prison), slaves and freed slaves were often dispatched to deliver such items and themselves on behalf of their masters. This also fits with the general colonial setting where slaves would be the ones sent to engage in day-to-day trades and purchases.[107] This could also explain the recurrence of financial language about gifts, debts, and accounts in both letters (Phil 2:30; 3:7–8; 4:10–20; and Phlm 17–20).[108] Slaves themselves can be exchanged and used among "family and friends."[109] While slaves can be the result of debts as well, the use of another's slave can become, in turn, a source of further obligation to the one giving the slave (as Horace so warned in the discussion above).

When placed within the wider settings of ancient prisons and the other "prison letter" of Paul's, Paul's arguments about Epaphroditus can be viewed as Paul's careful negotiation of his own use of this likely (freed) slave sent by the Philippians. This explains why the conclusion of the small section about Epaphroditus seeks to characterize the relationship between Paul and the Philippians as one of obligation, not of Paul's obligation to them, but of theirs to Paul (2:30). In short, Paul is attempting to achieve a similar reversal in 2:25–30 and then 4:10–20 as he did with Onesimus's owner in Phlm 17–21. The contortedly careful argumentation of 4:10–20 (what is sometimes referred to as a "thankless thank you"[110]) could be an

---

107. See, for instance, the discussion in Ascough, *Paul's Macedonian Associations*, 121–22; and Wansink, *Chained in Christ*, 182–84.

108. On the significance of the marketplace language for reconstructions of the assembly community at Philippi, see Ascough, *Paul's Macedonian Associations*, 118–22. On the commercial language of 4:10–20 (including δόμα and καρπός in 4:17), see G. W. Peterman, *Paul's Gift from Philippi: Conventions of Gift-Exchange and Christian Giving*, SNTSMS 92 (Cambridge: Cambridge University Press, 1997). On such language and dynamics in Philemon, see Martin, "The Rhetorical Function of Commercial Language in Paul's Letter to Philemon (Verse 18)," in *Persuasive Artistry: Studies in New Testament Rhetoric in Honor of George A. Kennedy*, ed. Duane F. Watson, JSNTSup 50 (Sheffield: JSOT Press, 1992), 321–37; and Norman R. Petersen, *Rediscovering Paul: Philemon and the Sociology of Paul's Narrative World* (Philadelphia: Fortress, 1985), 90–102.

109. For further reflections on the uses to which a slave might be put, including among friends and family, as it relates to an analysis of Philemon, see Marchal, "Usefulness of an Onesimus."

110. On this "thankless thanks," see Marvin R. Vincent, *Critical and Exegetical Commentary on the Epistles to the Philippians and to Philemon*, ICC (Edinburgh: T&T Clark, 1897), 146.

indication that Paul is trying to find a way to accept the use of something(s) (possibly including someone) sent to him, without agreeing that this puts him in a situation of debt to the Philippian assembly members that sent them. Since Paul received the gifts brought to him by, or through, Epaphroditus (παρὰ Επαφροδίτου, 4:18), it is indeed possible that (at least) part of what was sent as aid or gift to Paul was the (freed) slave body of Epaphroditus (slaves are things to be used, τὰ χρήματα).[111] Paul acknowledges the receipt of more than one "thing" (the plural τὰ παρ' ὑμῶν, "the (things) from you (pl.)," in 4:18); and slaves are often included in lists of valuable things sent, given, traded, or exchanged. This background should help fill out the examination of the "financial" language in the letter, given that slaves are embodied items used economically. (Slavery is as much an economic relationship, as a gendered, erotic, or social one, and each of these elements are intertwined with each other.)

The difficulty owners had with relying upon slaves and freed slaves to do so many things for them, while still maintaining their own authority and the slaves' subordination, is a persistent issue in the Greco-Roman context.[112] Paul appears to be grappling with a similar difficulty, layered with concerns about potential patron-client dynamics, here. He seeks and has already used the benefit of the support from the slaveowners in the Philippian assembly, but he wants to avoid being subordinate to them now in a patron-client relationship. This is why he insists that, though he never *really* needed their aid (Phil 4:10–13), all of *their* needs or uses (πᾶσαν χρείαν ὑμῶν) will be fulfilled by "my God" (Phil 4:19), in exchange for providing useful things to Paul (Phil 4:15–18). Throughout this argument, Epaphroditus functions merely as the instrument, routed between Paul and the audience, whose arrival and return Paul must carefully negotiate. Paul must convince the Philippian assembly members that he is still the one in authority and control (not unlike how the "real man" must demonstrate his own place in the social-sexual protocol of gendered status already discussed). This would explain why Paul argues that he used, but did not need or rely upon either Epaphroditus or the assembly members who sent these "things."

---

111. See, for instance, Xenophon of Ephesus, *Eph.* 1.13.6. The Greek of this phrase requires that one provide a plural noun for the "things" received by Paul from the assembly addressees (τὰ παρ' ὑμῶν, "the [things] from you [pl.]," 4:18) from/through Epaphroditus.

112. See the discussion in Joshel and Murnaghan, "Introduction," 12–14.

Furthermore, as part of his argument about returning Epaphroditus, Paul shaped a claim for how the willingly obedient figure should be an example to the whole of the *ekklēsia* at Philippi. If one agreed and adhered to such argumentation, Paul is not only not the assembly's client, but they have also learned to respond obediently to him as the authority and they his social inferiors. They owe him; they should obey and conform to his way of thinking (see the similar reversal in Phlm 19–21). Such obedience would indicate that the audience has learned to "think the same thing" as Paul, unlike Euodia and Syntyche. As suggested earlier, Epaphroditus functions in the letter as a counterimage to Euodia and Syntyche. Such a counter would be even more powerful on Paul's part if the three figures had shared some degree of gendered status as slaves or freed slaves, as wo/men and unmen (as I suggested in the opening sections).

Conclusion

This letter's mixing of affection and obedience, as well as the availability of an unmanned or wo/manly body like Epaphroditus as an instrument to be sent back and forth, would slide comfortably in a context determined by an ancient imperial *ethos* of slavery that wove together gender, sexuality, and status. Paul even seemed to be concerned in ways that Horace thought an elite imperial free man should be about accepting too much help from a friend/patron via his (or her) slaves. Given its consonance with this imperially gendered slave system, this particular kyriarchy, Paul's perspective in Philippians certainly does not seem to be the kind of "people's" perspective sought in my study. Even if Paul himself was not the *pater familias* of a large estate of people and/as property, his arguments depict him in a similar fashion—as the head of an *ekklēsia* kind of kin group seeking his own authority and their obedience and conformity in return.

At the very least, though, Paul seemed to think that two of these community members are not thinking this way. If the letter's reference to Euodia and Syntyche is one of those aforementioned "dim, ad hoc flashes," then scholars would do well to pay closer attention to how slaves and freed slaves were conditioned, positioned, and potentially resisted the system of gendered status. Paul's disagreement with these two wo/men likely reflects that there were different historical perspectives on the *ekklēsia* community at Philippi, making it possible that Euodia, Syntyche, and other wo/men and unmen in the audience operated from different social and political perspectives than the one Paul offers here, mostly in continuity with kyriarchical systems. If Paul's picture of Epaphroditus was a counter to a vision of this alternative kinship community presented by wo/men, unmen, or people like Euodia and Syntyche, then it is a distinct possibility that these *ekklēsia* members operated in modes somehow counter to the Roman Empire's kind of kyriarchy in this *colonia*. These possibilities are just that—possible—though they are more than that—precious, even—given how silent most ancient sources, as well as most Pauline epistles and interpreters are about those who would have been living, organizing, and struggling from below.[113] Just as figures such as Euodia and Syntyche did not simply "think the same thing," interpreters must creatively and constructively improvise to write more than just the same kinds of history. Further attention to feminist, gender-critical, and even queer approaches in such projects should help illuminate other shadows cast over the various wo/men and unmen who populated and propelled these communities.

---

113. Joshel and Murnaghan are adeptly circumspect, though, in cautioning: "The nature of ancient evidence thus forces us to deal with a profound silence that lies behind all the noise generated by our sources. In attending to the silenced people of antiquity, we are always in danger of ourselves generating more noise, obscuring them further through our own projections" ("Introduction," 20). Joshel and Murnaghan connect this advisory to the work of Gayatri Chakravorty Spivak, particularly in "Can the Subaltern Speak?" in *Marxism and the Interpretation of Culture*, ed. Cary Nelson and Lawrence Grossberg (Urbana: University of Illinois Press, 1988), 271–313. For further reflections on Spivak for these sorts of projects, see Marchal, *Politics of Heaven*, 31–36, 142–44.

Response

Antoinette Clark Wire

Angela Standhartinger's and Joseph A. Marchal's essays can be seen as parallel studies in that they focus on a particular, radically disadvantaged group in the society of the time and place of Paul's Philippian letter, Standhartinger on the imprisoned and Marchal on the enslaved (although Marchal sets out to consider women as well as slaves, it is the enslaved or freed of both genders that get his attention). The parallel between the two chapters extends to the fact that each group is a victim of social structures and practices. They are *im*prisoned, *en*slaved, and should be described that way. What has been done to them restricts their humanity, body and soul, even sometimes to the point of death. The essays make an extended study of these radical social restrictions, showing us from wide sources that it was much worse than we had thought. Standhartinger does this about imprisonment by revealing how we have softened Paul's mention of his "bonds" by assuming from the accounts in Acts that he received near-senatorial privileges, ignoring the catalogues of terrors he gives in letters not subject to prison censorship. Marchal has intensified our shock at what happened under Greco-Roman slavery, showing how the enticement of manumission only reinforced the system and, even when realized, left the freed person under lifetime obligation. Finally, he focuses on the most intimate services required, which were themselves only masked by gestures of benevolence.

In these ways each essay makes a major contribution to our understanding of the radical restrictions within which so many people in the world of the Philippians letter had to live their lives. Yet I will respond, not to this big picture, but to the way each study draws from and applies these insights to the Philippian letter itself. I will take the chapters in turn, saying where I am quickly convinced and where I find my picture of the letter does not yet switch over to a new picture.

To take Marchal on slavery first, I find this argument very suggestive, giving me another angle on Philippi if its named participants are all of slave origin. Yet I balk at two points, first, that it can be taken as probable that Epaphroditus, Euodia, and Syntyche were enslaved or *liberti/ae*, and second, that sexual service is being implied in Paul's probable relation to them. On these names as indicating slave origins, Marchal cites de Vos, but it is not clear if he does more than show that these names are used for slaves in some cases, at least Epaphroditus and Euodia. Would there be any way to be more definitive on the proportion of uses of these names that indicate slave origins—drawing perhaps from the work of people building prosopographies from inscriptions and literature in Roman Greece and Macedonia? Even in doing this, I think of two cautions: the free poor, such as the farmer or street hawker, may be invisible in these sources, because they have no affiliation with elite families or money for grave markers. Also families of freed people might pass their names down to generations where the slave origins are no longer status-indicative. Lacking at present such statistical work, Marchal depends on the broader proposals concerning the percent of people in a city who are either enslaved or freed. He does point out the discrepancy between Oakes's proposal of about 25 percent enslaved and de Vos's view (based on Joshel) of 33 percent enslaved plus 35 percent *liberti/ae*, that is, 68 percent in all, at least among urban artisans, but then sides with de Vos. Is this solid enough evidence that we can read Philippians in terms of these three people being slaves and/or freed?

The crucial question is, of course, what Paul's own rhetoric reveals. Can we say that he treats them as enslaved or freed in the way he says "I urge Syntyche" or "I have sent him back"? Is he bending over backward to compensate when he calls Epaphroditus "brother, coworker, comrade in arms"?

As to the relevance of the sexual use of the enslaved to this Philippian letter, I find myself unpersuaded. Though Paul uses χράομαι or χρῆσις to mean sexual use in Rom 1:26 and possibly 1 Cor 7, he uses this root regularly in other senses, and it does not appear in Philippians at all—unless you include the more distant χρεία which Paul applies first to Epaphroditus and then to God, both of whom have met his need (2:25; 4:19). He does speak of Epaphroditus as their λειτουργός on his behalf. Frederick W. Danker in his revision of Walter Bauer's lexicon describes λειτουργία as "the usual designation for a service performed by an individual for the state or public cult…, in our literature almost always used with some sort of religious connotation," suggesting "an aura of high status for those who render" any type of service.[1] The difficulty of taking it as the sexual service of an enslaved or freed person is compounded by Paul's usage when he says that Epaphroditus "came near to death for the work of Christ, risking his life in order to substitute for your inability to carry out the λειτουργία you owe me" (2:30).

I point to this problem not to deny that sexual service was demanded from enslaved people and conceded to elite men by their families. I think of a wealthy Indian landlord in Berkeley who was recently caught importing rural village girls for this purpose with his family's knowledge. It is said that even Ghandi was given a girl raised in the family when he was old "to keep him warm at night." Granted that an enslaved person who washes and feeds someone may be the one most physically intimate with him or her. I mention this with the thought that a study of how prophets and apostles were fed by others and had their clothes and rooms and probably bodies washed by others might be a place to center a study of Paul in relation to other figures like Timothy and Epaphroditus, a study that could then move into questions of both possible slave status and/or possible sexual relations. I say this not to ignore the sexual use of enslaved people but to show it was the extreme case of a broad social divide, still very much with us, between those who serve and those who are served. This kind of study could be relevant for understanding Paul's practical relationships with the Christian communities, since he depicts that he himself serves them, even when in prison.

Speaking of prison, Standhartinger has given us quite an eyeful, earful, and noseful. I was reminded of the prisons in old China and, I hear, in much of Latin America today, where people's welfare depends on family or friends who bring the food and drink and clean the premises, in essence living with the prisoner—but with the ability to go out and procure necessities. Money from Philippi would be useless unless someone could get to the market, coming back with something for the guard as well. So Timothy need not be either "inside or outside the prison" as Standhartinger asks, but may be both, thanks to the Philippians's gift via Epaphroditus.

As to the need for a "hidden transcript" when writing to and from prison, that is intriguing. Standhartinger indicates that the phrase "those

---

1. Frederick William Danker, Walter Bauer, William F. Arndt, and F. Wilbur Gingrich, eds., *A Greek-English Lexicon of the New Testament and Other Early Christian Literature*, 3rd ed. (Chicago: University of Chicago Press, 2000), 591.

of Caesar's house" still has us in the dark, but might it not stir up the censors? The σύζυγος, I think, may be a woman on Paul's side of the argument—like Chloe in Corinth, not just because Clement and Origen think it refers to Paul's wife, but because Paul expects that she can appropriately get close to the women and persuade them. But why is she in disguise? Is she possibly the source of the funds or at least the collector and better left anonymous? When we were in Philippi recently, my first time to see it, we did find a Hotel of Lydia, which, I might say, did not speak for her affluence.

The larger question of whether Paul's theology is being expressed in a way that hides something from the outsiders is less clear to me. If so, what is he hiding? The fact that he gives no catalogue of his sufferings, no cry of anguish over his persecution as in 2 Cor 1:8–11, may reflect the specific function of those forms to boast his trials or to seek sympathy in Corinth. Here he may not want the Philippians to imagine the details—or he knows that Epaphroditus will provide them to an excess. But for what might the censors be looking? Standhartinger cites Erik Heen, who apparently sees Paul's claim that Jesus did not grasp after equality with God as an anti-imperial statement hidden in a hymn. But what is hidden in the extended claim to find joy in suffering? Paul does ask for their prayers that he says could bring about his rescue, yet that request is hardly disguised. He avoids speaking about divine punishment for his accusers or jailers when he looks forward to the day of Jesus Christ, but is their punishment a preoccupation that he has suppressed, or is it not his focus?

One thinks in this connection about the very different rhetoric of John of Patmos. How did that letter/apocalypse get delivered safely? Was he only ostracized, not imprisoned? Or did he make seven copies? Perhaps I am so programmed to read Paul's rhetoric as constrained strictly by persuasion of his addressees that I am not allowing myself to entertain another constraint, but Standhartinger has persuaded me that I must consider this possibility. Yet when she finds that this letter reads as an interaction between one who dominates and his subordinates, I tend to see that not as a disguise but as Paul's way of cultivating this relationship. But, I admit, to teach suffering as a necessary passage to glory does operate as a mode of resistance, as Adela Yarbro Collins has said of Revelation.[2] Per-

---

2. See, for instance, Adela Yarbro Collins, *The Combat Myth in the Book of Revelation* (Missoula, MT: Scholars Press, 1976), 231–34.

haps this strategy is so strange to the imperial context and so covered in positive theological claims here in Philippians that it would not be evident for what it is, and in this sense the letter would be a "hidden transcript."

From now on we will perforce read Philippians aware of the enslaved and of the imprisoned among our progenitors.

Out-Howling the Cynics:
Reconceptualizing the Concerns of Paul's Audience from His Polemics in Philippians 3

Mark D. Nanos

Recent efforts to revisit the interpretation of Philippians, including those from a people's history approach, retain the consensus interpretation for identifying the targets of Paul's oppositional polemic in these verses.[1] Even those that focus on the political (i.e., Roman imperial) as well as Greco-Roman polytheistic pagan[2] social context of the letter overall do not question the traditional view that Paul negatively values the continuation of Jewish identity and Judaism (or Christian Judaism) in his communities as well as in his own life. They suppose that the concern of the audience addressed in Philippi is *Judaism*, as if it is an alien element for a Pauline community, although this supposition primarily derives from the framework imposed on the letter (from prevailing constructions of Paul as well as of his communities as Christian in sharp contrast to Jewish/Judaism) rather than from the information derived from within it.[3]

---

1. Aspects of the argument of this chapter first appeared as Mark D. Nanos, "Paul's Polemic in Philippians 3 as Jewish-Subgroup Vilification of Local Non-Jewish Cultic and Philosophical Alternatives," *Journal for the Study of Paul and His Letters* 3 (2013): 47–92.

2. Admittedly anachronistic, the term is employed herein to refer to those who are neither Jewish nor Christ-followers, with no negative judgment intended.

3. See, e.g., Peter Oakes, *Philippians: From People to Letter*, SNTSMS 110 (Cambridge: Cambridge University Press, 2001), 105, 111–12, 117–18; Richard S. Ascough, *Paul's Macedonian Associations: The Social Context of Philippians and 1 Thessalonians*, WUNT 2/161 (Tübingen: Mohr Siebeck, 2003), 203–5; Erik M. Heen, "Phil 2:6–11 and Resistance to Local Timocratic Rule: *Isa theo* and the Cult of the Emperor in the East," in *Paul and the Roman Imperial Order*, ed. Richard A. Horsley (Harrisburg, PA: Trinity Press International, 2004), 125–53; Craig Steven de Vos, *Church and Com-*

These contextual decisions have been repeated with little discussion of the indirect nature of the evidence on which they depend or exploration of alternatives, although these decisions have an enormous impact on how the letter is interpreted as well as how one constructs Paul and Christian origins in general and how one discusses Paul's identity, teaching, and behavior relative to Judaism more specifically. Similarly, these decisions about the context influence the way that other Christ-following Jewish groups are conceptualized, including the other apostles and Paul's relationship to them. Most pertinent to this essay, these decisions impact constructions of the identity and concerns of Paul's audience, including what kinds of options they are understood to be exploring or at least what Paul (and his interpreter) supposes them to be exploring, which figure into explanations about what prompted him to write this letter and what he meant to communicate therein.

Anyone entering into research on Philippians, including someone focused on a people's history approach, is naturally influenced by such conclusions, beginning with the framing of the options to explore. However, since Paul nowhere explicitly identifies those he denounces as Jews, Christ-followers (or "Christians"), missionaries, outsiders, or opponents of Paul for that matter, is it not time to revisit the evidence, both for constructions of Paul as well as of his Philippian audience?

Reconceptualizing the Philippian Context

In my view, the evidence available from Paul's rhetoric should lead us to reconceptualize our hypotheses for identifying "the Philippians" addressed in this letter. The concerns of the Philippians and Paul can be interpreted within a Greco-Roman cultural and political-religious context apart from imagining that it revolves around Paul's resistance to people or matters identified with Jewishness. This rereading begins with the introduction of

---

munity Conflicts: The Relationships of the Thessalonian, Corinthian, and Philippian Churches with Their Wider Civic Communities, SBLDS 168 (Atlanta: Scholars Press, 1999), 263–75, challenges the prevailing views in a manner closest to the one proposed here. Also critical of the prevailing view in various ways and to various degrees, although often still conceptualizing Paul's opposition to be Jewish or Jewish Christian missionaries, see Karl Olav Sandnes, *Belly and Body in the Pauline Epistles*, SNTSMS 120 (Cambridge: Cambridge University Press, 2002). Some note that the conflict in Philippi was probably precipitated by the withdrawal of Christ-followers from traditional and imperial-related cults.

a simple but important hypothesis to explore: if Paul writes from within Judaism, not Christianity, from and to those who understand themselves (non-Jews as well as Jews) to practice Judaism within (sub)groups that are distinguished by their convictions about Jesus but are otherwise still members of larger Jewish communities (which are themselves minority communities and, in the case of Philippi, probably very small in number), then it is logical to explore very different connotations for Paul's language than the traditional approaches have taken into consideration.[4]

When Paul's polemics as well as the rest of his message are read from this perspective, his concerns can be understood to express *his Jewish sensibilities* and *his commitment to the practice of (Jesus-as-Messiah-based) Judaism within his communities—even by those non-Jews whom he insists remain non-Jews.*[5] Instead of warning against the practice of Judaism, as usually understood, Paul wants his audience to be fully acculturated into Judaism (i.e., into a Jewish cultural and social way of thinking and living) and thus into assessing the groups he decries as competitors

---

4. This proposition is explained and explored in Mark D. Nanos and Magnus Zetterholm, eds., *Paul within Judaism: Restoring the First-Century Context to the Apostle* (Minneapolis: Fortress, 2015).

5. See Mark D. Nanos, "Paul and Judaism: Why Not Paul's Judaism?" in *Paul Unbound: Other Perspectives on the Apostle*, ed. Mark D. Given (Peabody, MA: Hendrickson, 2010), 117–60. Reference herein is made to Jews and Jewish and Jewishness or Judaism, unless the geoethnic element of Judeaness is perceived to be specifically more salient (note: non-Jews could also be Judeans, just as today non-Jews can be Israelis). That there was a religious dimension to Judean/Jewish ethnicity properly named Judaism seems to me evident from relevant sources for discussing Paul's period. See Daniel R. Schwartz, " 'Judaean' or 'Jew'? How Should We Translate *Ioudaios* in Josephus?" in *Jewish Identity in the Greco-Roman*, ed. Jörg Frey, Daniel R. Schwartz, and Stephanei Gripentrog, Ancient Judaism and Early Christianity 71 (Leiden: Brill, 2007), 3–27; Schwartz, *Judeans and Jews: Four Faces of Dichotomy in Ancient Jewish History* (Toronto: University of Toronto Press, 2014); Margaret H. Williams, "The Meaning and Function of *Ioudaios* in Graeco-Roman Inscriptions," ZPE 116 (1997): 249–62; Shaye J. D. Cohen, *The Beginnings of Jewishness: Boundaries, Varieties, Uncertainties*, HCS 31 (Berkeley: University of California Press, 1999), 69–139; David Goodblatt, *Elements of Ancient Jewish Nationalism* (Cambridge: Cambridge University Press, 2006); Siân Jones and Sarah Pearce, eds., *Jewish Local Patriotism and Self-Identification in the Graeco-Roman Period*, JSPSup 31 (Sheffield: Sheffield Academic, 1998); Anders Runesson, "Inventing Christian Identity: Paul, Ignatius, and Theodosius I," in *Exploring Early Christian Identity*, ed. Bengt Holmberg, WUNT 226 (Tübingen: Mohr Siebeck, 2008), 59–92. Contra Steve Mason, "Jews, Judaeans, Judaizing, Judaism: Problems of Categorization in Ancient History," *JSJ* 38 (2007): 457–512.

whose influence upon them should be resisted. In other words, the idea of "Judaizers" as the opposition in Philippi is questionable (in addition to being grammatically inaccurate); rather, in a very different direction, Paul may seek to influence his audience to become completely "jewish-ish," albeit within the terms Paul develops around his Jewish subgroup's propositional claims about the significance of Jesus.[6]

In this alternative approach to Paul's interests and those of his audience, the issue revolves around how to live within Judaism, within Paul's new Jewish subgroups, where identity and concomitant behavior involved in living according to Jewish norms creates conflicts (especially for the members who remain non-Jews) with the cultural values and behavior of the larger (non-Jewish and non-jewishly oriented lifestyles of the) Greco-Roman population. For non-Jews, that includes new tensions with their families as well as friends, neighbors, and the civic leaders who populate the cultural context in which they live and move and the social world in which they are identified, carry on relationships, and access goods. These forces present challenges to the Jewish ideals Paul upholds for how non-Jews turning to God through Jesus as Christ should now think and live, including how they should remain faithful and suffer as required by the marginalized state this creates for them. To put this another way, a torah-centered communal way of life (i.e., one based on God's "instructions" for how to live rightly, which is the general meaning of *nomos* when used by Jews to translate from the Hebrew, rather than "law" per se) is by definition countercultural in terms of the dominant social values, politics, and practices of cult in Philippi. The addressees are learning an alternative *Jewish* way of life from Paul's teaching, from Scripture, from the subgroup members who are Jews (if there are any), and from the larger Jewish community (however large or small it is in Philippi, it would represent a minority group and culture, but one in which their own groups function as subgroups). From Paul's overall positive approach to them, it seems that they are not resisting Paul's influence toward a more Jewish way of life but rather are confused about what that means for them as non-Jews within the larger non-Jewish networks in which they live and also—assuming that there is a Jewish communal presence in Philippi—what it means within

---

6. Mark D. Nanos, "Paul's Non-Jews Do Not Become 'Jews,' But Do They Become 'Jewish'? Reading Romans 2:25–29 within Judaism, alongside Josephus," *Journal of the Jesus Movement in Its Jewish Setting* 1 (2014): 26–53; Paula Fredriksen, "Judaizing the Nations: The Ritual Demands of Paul's Gospel," *NTS* 56 (2010): 232–52.

the larger Jewish communities within whom they now seek to live according to Jewish norms as non-Jews participating in subgroups of Jews that
are themselves somewhat different from other Jewish subgroups.

If Paul practices and teaches the practices of Judaism to these assemblies as subgroups within the larger Jewish communities, this shifts the
focus from Paul opposing Jewish interests among his audiences to him
opposing continued non-Jewish ways of thinking and living that he considers no longer appropriate for followers of Jesus, including non-Jews,
whom he seeks to influence to living according to Jewish norms. At the
same time, he insists that they must remain non-Jews who do so. This
is based on his theological focus that faithfulness to the chronometrical
claim of the gospel that the end of the ages has begun within the midst of
the present age requires that non-Jews remain non-Jews just as it requires
that Jews remain Jews, thereby demonstrating in their assemblies the
propositional claim that the awaited time of *shalom* among all of humankind predicted by the prophets has dawned.[7]

This way of framing Paul and his probable concerns and those of
his audience in Philippi, as well as of those of whom Paul warns them to
beware, offers several new avenues for interpreters to explore by way of
the evidence provided by Paul's rhetoric. There is not space to develop the
alternatives in full here, so I will focus on the language of verses 2–3 and
verses 18–19, accompanied with sideward glances at other language in the
chapter and in the letter.[8]

My research leads me to believe that the most likely referents of Paul's
vilification are neither Jews nor Judaism, nor Christ-followers (nor from
so-called Jewish Christianity), nor outsiders to Philippi on a mission to
counter Paul's influence, although they are possibly opponents of Paul and
his influence upon these non-Jews. I think it probable that the influences
Paul addresses in Philippi arise from local Greco-Roman "idolatrous" cults
and/or philosophical groups and their various behavioral norms, which
are, from Paul's perspective, in conflict with the values that these non-Jews

---

7. Nanos, "Paul and the Jewish Tradition: The Ideology of the *Shema*," in *Celebrat-
ing Paul: Festschrift in Honor of Jerome Murphy-O'Connor, O.P., and Joseph A. Fitzmyer,
S.J.*, ed. Peter Spitaler, CBQMS 48 (Washington, DC: Catholic Biblical Association of
America, 2012), 62–80.

8. There is also not space to discuss the various partition theories for the letter or
letters, but it is relevant that the various positions depend upon how they read 3:2 as a
break from the concerns raised earlier in the letter.

should now subscribe to in their new identification within Jewish communal subgroups and within Judaism, even as they remain non-Jews. That is why Paul appeals to himself and others (including, most importantly, Jesus himself) whom he represents as models for them throughout chapter 3 and the rest of the letter—which he sets in contrast to the conflicting models they observe and encounter in their current circumstances from those who do not share Paul's views (3:2–9, 15–17; 3:20–4:2; also 1:9–11; 1:27–2:18; 4:8–9; *passim*).

There are a number of suggestive candidates to explore for identifying the influences and influencers he opposes for the Philippians, including cults associated with various goddesses and gods (images of some of these evil workers, some with dogs, are "cut into [*katatome*]" the rock wall of Philippi). I have discussed those options in some detail elsewhere;[9] herein I will restrict my discussion to the implications of reading Philippians based on the supposition that the exigencies, as Paul perceives them to be, are related to concerns of his audience arising from circumstances that have to do with Cynic elements. This approach to the possible dynamics on the ground in Philippi offers interesting new elements to consider for constructing the identity, circumstances, and concerns of these Philippians, as well as generates new implications for the study of Paul. But before a new approach can be undertaken in full, it is important to show why the prevailing views should be questioned, even if the alternatives explored thereafter may be different from the ones I suggest.

The Prevailing View of Those Paul Opposes

Paul sharply warns the Philippians in 3:2 to "beware of the dogs ... the evil workers ... the mutilation"; in verse 3 he offers a sharp contrast to "we who are the circumcision"; and in verses 18–19 he engages in vilification again by way of several similarly derogatory epithets. His rhetoric suggests specific referents would be immediately indicated for his audience, yet his polemical approach is too vague to provide clarity for the later reader. Nevertheless, the commentary tradition might lead one to suppose otherwise, as it upholds relatively consistent identifications for the context of Paul's vituperation: Paul is opposing "Jews" who are (usually) also "Christians"[10]

---

9. Nanos, "Paul's Polemic."

10. Although the label "Christian" is usually employed in discussions of Philippians, it is avoided hereafter for describing the probable historical addressees, because

(hence, Jewish Christians and "Judaizers"[11] are common descriptions); furthermore, they are "missionaries" who advocate circumcision and who have traveled to Philippi to do so in direct opposition to Paul and his mission (hence, "opponents" and "outsiders").[12] Their goal can almost always be summarized as being to influence Paul's addressees to undertake proselyte conversion and other elements of a Jewish way of life, behavior that Paul is understood to adamantly oppose as inappropriate if not entirely obsolete for those who believe in the gospel of Jesus Christ.[13] This para-

---

it is anachronistic and not helpful for trying to imagine the pre-Christianity setting of Paul's audiences, "Christ-followers" is adopted instead. Nevertheless, "Christian" is used sometimes herein to highlight the conceptual paradigms at work in the traditional interpretations being discussed, for which Christians and Christianity are what is indeed envisioned.

11. The term "Judaizers" is grammatically inaccurate to refer to those who seek to influence non-Jews toward Judaism, although that is its common usage for discussions of Paul's "opponents." Instead, the term should be used (if at all) to refer to those who undertake becoming Jews, i.e., proselytes who have "judaized." See Cohen, *Beginnings of Jewishness*, 175–97; and Nanos, *The Irony of Galatians: Paul's Letter in First-Century Context* (Minneapolis: Fortress, 2002), 115–19.

12. Although Paul's warning opposes the influence of some people or groups on those to whom he writes, the label "opponents" is avoided here unless it can be established from Paul's argument that he is being opposed.

13. In addition to the commentaries, specialized studies include John J. Gunther, *St. Paul's Opponents and Their Background: A Study of Apocalyptic and Jewish Sectarian Teachings*, NovTSup 35 (Leiden: Brill, 1973), 2, for a list of seventeen options that are usually discussed for identifying those Paul opposes in Phil 3, all (but one: gnostics) of which focus on Jews or Jewish Christians, even when some other options are explored in addition; and see variously Helmut Koester, "The Purpose of the Polemic of a Pauline Fragment," *NTS* 8 (1961–1962): 317–32; A. F. J. Klijn, "Paul's Opponents in Philippians iii," *NovT* 7 (1964): 278–84; Carl R. Holladay, "Paul's Opponents in Philippians 3," *ResQ* 12 (1969): 77–90; Robert Jewett, "Conflicting Movements in the Early Church as Reflected in Philippians," *NovT* 12 (1970): 362–90; Walter Schmithals, *Paul and the Gnostics*, trans. John E. Steely (Nashville: Abingdon, 1972), 65–122; E. Earle Ellis, "Paul and His Opponents: Trends in Research," in *Christianity, Judaism and Other Greco-Roman Cults: Studies for Morton Smith at Sixty*, ed. Jacob Neusner (Leiden: Brill, 1975), 264–98; Joseph B. Tyson, "Paul's Opponents at Philippi," *PRSt* 3 (1976): 82–95; David E. Garland, "The Composition and Unity of Philippians: Some Neglected Literary Factors," *NovT* 27 (1985): 141–73; Kenneth Grayston, "The Opponents in Philippians 3," *ExpTim* 97 (1986): 170–72; E. P. Sanders, "Paul on the Law, His Opponents, and the Jewish People in Philippians 3 and 2 Corinthians 11," in *Anti-Judaism in Early Christianity: Paul and the Gospels*, ed. Peter Richardson and David M. Granskou (Waterloo: Wil-

digm (with slight variations) has limited the interpretive options explored for constructing Paul's thought and behavior as well as that of his address-ees in Philippi to conflicting views of the role of Judaism (i.e., Jewish ways of life based upon torah-prescribed norms) and thus bears witness to a broad trajectory of Paulinism ("Gentile Christianity") read in opposition to Judaism throughout his letters.

That traditional case is predicated on the following interpretive decisions:[14] Paul's warning in verse 2 to beware of "the dogs" is taken to be a reversal of supposedly stereotypical Jewish slander of non-Jews as dogs, thus Paul's denunciation of Jews and their influence is from a per-spective calculated to appeal to his audiences' resentment toward Jewish ethnoreligious arrogance. The warning to beware of "the evil work-ers" ostensibly suggests Christ-following Jewish missionaries who have arrived or are anticipated to be on their way: Paul subverts their claim to bring *good* news or uphold the place of *good* works, combinations of faith and actions that interpreters have associated with gospel-based values for "Christian" *Jewish* groups in contrast to Paul's "Christian" universalist (read: *gentile*) faith-alone-based groups. The epithet "the mutilation" sup-posedly represents a negative reversal of the value of circumcision aimed at those who promote this rite, since Paul is understood to conflate the two in verse 3 in order to draw a supersessionistic "Christian" contrast: "we are the circumcision." Then Paul ostensibly denounces his (former) Jewish credentials in verses 3–9 as meaningless, amounting literally to "crap" or at least euphemistically to "rubbish" (NRSV), compared to his new identity in Christ (σκύβαλα, verse 8). Furthermore, in verses 18–19,

---

frid Laurier University Press, 1986), 75–90; L. Gregory Bloomquist, *The Function of Suffering in Philippians*, JSNTSup 78 (Sheffield: JSOT Press, 1993), 198–201; Jerry L. Sumney, *"Servants of Satan," "False Brothers" and Other Opponents of Paul*, JSNTSup 188 (Sheffield: Sheffield Academic, 1999), 160–87; B. J. Oropeza, *Jews, Gentiles, and the Opponents of Paul: The Pauline Letters*, Apostasy in the New Testament Commu-nities 2 (Eugene, OR: Cascade, 2011), 204–23. For good summaries in commentar-ies, see Peter Thomas O'Brien, *The Epistle to the Philippians*, NIGTC (Grand Rapids: Eerdmans, 1991), 26–35; John Reumann, *Philippians: A New Translation with Intro-duction and Commentary*, Anchor Yale Bible (New Haven: Yale University Press, 2008), 460–81.

14. The following details and conclusions are so widespread that there is little reason to refer the reader to any particular interpreter; they will be found, with little variation, in every commentary and specific discussion of the situation in Philippi, such as those listed above.

his specific invectives toward those accused of being "the enemies of the cross of Christ, whose end is destruction, whose god is the belly, who even glory in their shame, who are thinking earthly [thoughts]," are usually aligned with errors attributed to Judaism, including to Jews who have become Christ-followers but continue to practice and promote Judaism, which Paul is understood to oppose (unlike the case in v. 2, the commentary tradition does recognize several other possible referents for the invectives in vv. 18–19).[15]

These decisions are elements of a popular paradigm that often frames how the conflicts suggested by Paul's polemics have been interpreted since F. C. Baur: the Petrine/Jewish Christianity versus Pauline/Gentile Christianity trajectory. According to this construction of Christian origins, Paul's mission is understood to be experiencing a challenge from a countermissionary program under the leadership of James and Peter, and his letters reflect this more global dynamic. Thus Paul's polemics in Philippians are expected to be expressing resistance to intruders, *opponents* from *outside* of his communities who are Jewish Christ-followers (often they are proposed to be associated with the ostensible Galatian opponents).[16] In addition to the influence of this historical paradigm, it has become commonplace to uphold the idea that reading Paul in opposition to fellow Christ-followers is attractive, because it focuses on Paul's criticism of fellow "Christians," thus making it an expression of inter-Christian polemic rather than an attack on Jews or Judaism. Would that it were so.[17]

---

15. Gerald F. Hawthorne, *Philippians*, WBC 43 (Waco, TX: Word, 1983), 163. These include various kinds of antinomian Christ-followers, gnostic Christ-followers, as well as "pagans."

16. My challenge to the basis of such identifications is a central topic in *Irony of Galatians*, including why there is no evidence that Paul was being opposed or that the influencers have come from outside of Galatia; rather, the evidence suggest that Paul is opposing the influence of local groups and social identity norms.

17. Since it remains the practice of Judaism that Paul supposedly attacks, I do not find the benefits asserted as benign as proposed to be, nor the paradigm itself very convincing; see Mark D. Nanos, "How Inter-Christian Approaches to Paul's Rhetoric Can Perpetuate Negative Valuations of Jewishness—Although Proposing to Avoid that Outcome," *BibInt* 13 (2005): 255–69.

Paul's Polemical Warnings in Verse 2

"Beware[18] the Dogs"

In a recent publication, I explained many problems with the traditional view that Paul intended to signal Jews of any kind when referring to dogs in 3:2; I will repeat a only few salient points here.[19] The common refrain that Paul is engaged in reversing toward Jews a traditional Jewish invective aimed at non-Jews cannot be substantiated: there is no literary evidence from Paul's time or before (and virtually none afterwards) that Jews referred to non-Jews as dogs to express ethnic prejudice. There are a number of alternative referents to consider; some offer little clarity for the specific situation in Philippi, others are very suggestive—they all indicate the probability of non-Jews as the referents.

In a general sense, it is possible that Paul refers to dogs, often females ("bitches"), in the usual derogatory way that it was employed then and since, so that it holds no clues to the identity of the referents.[20] It is also possible that, for this referent as well as evil workers and mutilation, Paul is drawing on an intertextual echo from 1 Kgs 18:1–22:40 in order to evoke God's action by way of the flesh with which Paul contrasts his and his audience's behavior in verse 3. In this story, in contrast to Elijah (with whose experiences Paul explicitly compares himself in Rom 11:1–5), "evil

---

18. It is unclear whether βλέπετε here signifies "to beware of" (as in issuing a warning), "watch out for," or alternatively "to behold" (as in "to consider" or "reflect upon"). It is not of significance for this essay to decide; based on the negative characterizations posed in the epithets, it probably communicates that the referents are to be avoided. For opposite conclusions, see George D. Kilpatrick, "ΒΛΕΠΕΤΕ, Philippians 3.2," in *In Memorium Paul Kahle*, ed. Matthew Black and George Fohrer (Berlin: Alfred Töpelmann, 1968), 146–48; Jeffrey T. Reed, *A Discourse Analysis of Philippians: Method and Rhetoric in the Debate over Literary Integrity*, JSNTSup 136 (Sheffield: Sheffield Academic, 1997), 244–46.

19. Mark D. Nanos, "Paul's Reversal of Jews Calling Gentiles 'Dogs' (Philippians 3:2): 1600 Years of an Ideological Tale Wagging an Exegetical Dog?" *BibInt* 17 (2009): 448–82.

20. Grayston, "Opponents in Philippians 3," 171, similarly notes that Paul's usage here may be likened to the general statement today, "Look out for those rats." He also similarly argues that the insult is most logically focused on non-Jews. Alan H. Cadwallader, *Beyond the Word of a Woman: Recovering the Bodies of the Syrophoenician Women*, ATF Biblical Series 1 (Adelaide, Australia: ATF Press, 2008), for full discussion of gender issues raised by this epithet.

working false prophets" (1 Kgs 18:19–19:1) "mutilate themselves" in order to "persuade" the gods (1 Kgs 18:28, which uses a verbal form of the same word used by Paul), and the house of Ahab and Jezebel is condemned to be eaten by dogs (1 Kgs 21:22–29; see also 2 Kgs 9:33–37; 10:11, 17). One may wonder if Paul had been reflecting on this text when he composed his thoughts for this letter. If so, perhaps Paul introduces polemic here that has little to do with contemporary details about the identity of those he opposes in Philippi, his language reflecting his negative characterization of any influence or influencers who might be on the scene in terms that reflect scriptural polemics, often against idolatry and those who seek to invoke other gods to action.

The possible specific referents that are called to mind by the epithet "dogs" are very interesting. They include several deities, magic, prostitution, and several philosophical groups, especially the Cynics.

"Beware the Evil Workers"

The designation "evil workers" provides little basis from which to construct any specific identity.[21] Contrary to the traditional interpretations, there is no philological reason to understand workers to signify either travelers or missionaries, that they have arrived from outside of Philippi or are anticipated to do so, or that the referents are either Jewish or Christ-followers. Likewise, there is no signal that Paul is reversing the labeling of themselves as workers of good or proponents of the role of good works alongside of faith, as some suggest. For the most part, the identity signified by this phrase is filled out on the basis of decisions made about Paul's use of dogs and mutilation or from other factors. There is, however, one section of Acts (16:16–21) that is worth considering (regardless of how anachronistic appeal to Acts might be, which I am not seeking to dispute), since it involves Paul interacting with a slave woman who is accused of making money for her owners by engaging in divination, prophecy, or fortune telling (μαντευομένη), someone who would most certainly be seen as an *evil worker* by Paul.[22]

---

21. *Pace* Takaaki Haraguchi, "Das Unterhaltsrecht des frühchristlichen Verkündigers: Eine Untersuchung zur Bezeichnung ἐργάτης im Neuen Testament," *ZNW* 84 (1993): 178–95.

22. It is interesting to note that the Septuagint always refers to μαντεύομαι in pejorative terms connected with the practices of non-Israelites: those who speak falsely

The author of Acts describes this woman having the "spirit of python [πνεῦμα πύθωνα]"; that is, she was able to speak in an alternate voice; this is called "belly-talking."[23] It is possible that the woman represented the cult of Apollo (the special god for Augustus, who won the battle for him at Philippi!) or Cybele or was some other kind of "belly-talker" uttering strange voices.[24] Certainly her association with the belly is suggestive, since Paul will later polemicize against those whose "god is their belly" in Phil 3:19. When Paul exorcised the spirit from her, he and Silas were dragged before the magistrates in the marketplace and accused of engaging in *Jewish* activities that were unlawful according to *Roman* customs. This implies that the fortune-telling business operated within the confines of Roman policy, expressing civic cult that could be linked with honoring Caesar as lord, in contrast to the lord whom Paul promotes. The tension runs along a Jewish/non-Jewish institutional line, and the specific matter is whether this group's expression of Judaism conforms to the prevailing non-Jewish legal-cultural norms to which every Jewish group is expected to subscribe in the colony of Philippi.

The point is that independent of larger constructions of Paul's opponents, "evil workers" would not likely denote Jewish missionaries of any sort, but would probably be aimed at Greco-Roman religious or philosophical rivals who challenge the practices of Paul's addressees for not meeting community standards for Jewish practice. For Paul, it would not be hard to imagine that he would regard such activity to represent "enemies of the cross of Christ," to which he refers later in Phil 3:18; moreover, all of his language in chapter 3 could apply to such behavior from his perspective. The referents for this epithet must be decided on other evidence.

---

and evil workers whose influence should be resisted by the people of God: Deut 18:10 (note, a passage cited in Acts 3:22 and 7:37); 1 Sam 28:8; 2 Kgs 17:17; Mic 3:11; Jer 34:9; Ezek 12:24; 13:6, 23; 21:21, 23, 29; 22:28; see Todd Klutz, *The Exorcism Stories in Luke-Acts: A Sociostylistic Reading*, SNTSMS 129 (Cambridge: Cambridge University Press, 2004), 216, 225, and his larger discussion of this incident in Acts 16 (207–64).

23. David Edward Aune, *Prophecy in Early Christianity and the Ancient Mediterranean World* (Grand Rapids: Eerdmans, 1983), 40–41, 268–69.

24. Plutarch, *Def. orac.* 9.414E, calls these soothsayers ventriloquists (note: *engastrimythoi*, "belly-talkers") who uttered words beyond their control. See Menander, *Theophoroumenê* (act 2, scene 1), for similar possession by Cybele.

"Beware the Mutilation"

This is the warning most central to the traditional identification of Jews and specifically of Jews who supposedly promote proselyte conversion (circumcision). "The mutilated ones," or "mutilation [κατατομήν]," is interpreted to be an allusion to a stereotypical Greek and Roman derogatory description of Jewish circumcision, often as if Paul had written "the mutilators" instead. That interpretation is in keeping with the assumption that Paul opposes those promoting circumcision and that Paul was opposed to circumcision itself, maintaining that all such ritual or outward or simply torah-defined identity behavior was no longer appropriate for Christ-followers. The prior decision that Paul was reversing the negative epithet dogs, supposedly used by Jews toward non-Jews but now ostensibly reversed by Paul to describe Jews, leads interpreters to suppose that Paul is also playing the same game with mutilation, and vice versa. If such claims for Paul's use of dogs is without merit, one of the strengths of the traditional approach to mutilation as a continuation of that line of argument for Paul is suspect, at the very least. If it, too, is found to be unlikely, then this further undermines the traditional argument about the referents for dogs, since each of these two epithets has been approached as confirming the identification of Jews for the other one. I suggest that they instead work together to confirm the likely identification of the referents for all of the warnings aimed specifically toward *non-Jewish* influences that are to be avoided by Christ-followers, non-Jews as well as Jews.

Obviously, deciding that Paul opposed the circumcision of the sons of Jews who turned to Christ in addition to non-Jews completing the rite of proselyte conversion is of enormous significance for constructions of Paul and his communities. If mutilation is the way that Paul values circumcision, then the traditional conclusion that Paul no longer practices Judaism and opposes the continuation of Jewish identity and behavior for all Christ-followers gains significant support here. Grammatically, however, this epithet does not indicate opposition to those who promote mutilation; rather, it denotes those who are mutilated and is a comment upon those in that state. Moreover, the Hebrew Bible refers to mutilation in very different terms than circumcision. It makes plain the Jewish aversion to "mutilation" as practiced by the idolatrous nations (Lev 19:28; 21:5 [LXX uses the verbal form of the same Greek word for mutilation as Paul]; 1 Kgs 18:28; Hos 7:14). Yet interpreters of Paul fail to contemplate that this negative valuation of the practices of the non-Jewish world from the perspective of one still shaped by and practicing Judaism might be guiding Paul's view of the situation of the non-Jews he addresses.[25]

Interpreters maintain that "circumcision" is in view when Paul contrasts it with "mutilation" in part because of the influence of prevailing constructions that understand Paul to be against the practice of the torah; thus Paul's language in the following verses ostensibly conflates together rather than contrasts mutilation and circumcision: "for we are the circumcision, who serve God in/by spirit [or: who serve (enabled) by God's Spirit] and boast [revel/glory] in Christ Jesus and do not trust in [or: persuade by] flesh" (v. 3). This conflation is further supported by the way that Paul's dissociating argument about his own Jewish credentials in verses 4–9 is interpreted to indicate that he no longer values or practices the torah-oriented norms he details, which include his circumcision as an infant. Note, however, that in verse 3 Paul does not write of being "the *true* circumcision," "the *spiritual* circumcision," or "the circumcision *of the heart*," although interpreters proceed as if he had done so, and often translations explicitly add these qualifiers.[26] At least if he had dissociated circumcision in the way interpreters have, it might suggest that the comparison is with others who claim to be "the circumcision," against whom he makes a superior claim to that moniker. But Paul does not seem to be troubled that trust in the flesh would be conflated with circumcision, a God commanded cut made around the flesh. He does not write that "we are not the mutilation"

---

25. Heinrich August Wilhelm Meyer, *Critical and Exegetical Handbook to the Epistles to the Philippians and Colossians, and to Philemon,* trans. J. C. Moore and William P. Dickson, 6th ed., H. A. W. Meyer's Commentary on the New Testament (Peabody, MA: Hendrickson, 1983), 122, is adamantly opposed to the idea: "A description of *idolatry* with allusion to Lev 21.5, 1 Kgs 18.28, et al. ... is quite foreign to the context."

26. E.g., NASB: "for we are the 'true' circumcision," which is notably preceded by translating "mutilation" as "beware of the false circumcision"; J. B. Lightfoot, *St. Paul's Epistle to the Philippians: A Revised Text with Introduction, Notes and Dissertations,* 12th ed., 4 vols., J. B. Lightfoot's Commentary on the Epistles of St. Paul (Peabody, MA: Hendrickson, 1995), 144–45; Hawthorne, *Philippians,* 126; F. F. Bruce, *Philippians,* A Good News Commentary (San Francisco: Harper & Row, 1983), 80; Karl P. Donfried and I. Howard Marshall, *The Theology of the Shorter Pauline Letters,* New Testament Theology (Cambridge: Cambridge University Press, 1993), 152; Gordon D. Fee, *Paul's Letter to the Philippians,* NICNT (Grand Rapids: Eerdmans, 1995), 298–99; Markus Bockmuehl, *The Epistle to the Philippians,* BNTC (Peabody, MA: Hendrickson, 1998), 191; Stephen E. Fowl, *Philippians,* The Two Horizons New Testament Commentary (Grand Rapids: Eerdmans, 2005), 147–48.

either. And most notably, Paul did not write, "we are the Christians," "the Christ-followers," or even "the church"![27]

The traditional interpretation, moreover, fails to answer a number of questions, including the following: Why would he identify himself and his audience as "the circumcision" without qualifying the term if he meant to degrade this specifically Jewish rite as merely "mutilation" in the preceding statement? And when he does qualify it in the following explanation, why does he do so in positive terms, as representative of marking those who live unto the Lord as the circumcised ones? Moreover, in verse 5, why does he choose to include his own circumcision at eight days old in his catalog of honored identity alongside of righteousness according to the torah, perpetuating the historical Jewish perspective on this particular cut as something wholly different than mutilation, but also not as if he has changed its usage to signify something spiritual or broadly applied to all Christ-followers?

Paul claims that "we are the circumcision" (without the qualifiers that translators and commentators find necessary to add) when writing to a presumably largely, if not entirely, uncircumcised audience, which profoundly effects the interpretation of the name calling in verse 2. Paul appears to play on the similarities of sound in Greek between "mutilation" and "circumcision" (κατατομή/περιτομή); that is, he uses paronomasia, similar sound for effect, a point that is all the more significant to the degree that Paul's letters are understood to be designed for oral presentation. Although a play on sounds can be made in order to equate two different things, which is what the interpretive tradition requires here,[28] it can also emphasize just how different the two elements are. I submit that this pun communicates to the hearer that these two items, ending in roughly similar sounds and sharing reference in that syllable to cutting, should *not* be in any sense naively understood as *comparable*! They are as *different* as cutting *around* and cutting *into*, as *different* as making a covenant with Israel's God *or* with other gods, with serving by spirit *or* serving by flesh.

When the contrastive element is recognized, it suggests that Paul's polemic is not aimed at Jewish people or groups, Christ boasters or not. In the balance of verse 3, he does not differentiate in strictly Christ-oriented based terms; rather, glorying in Christ is one of three elements. The other

---

27. Contra Reumann, *Philippians*, 472–78.
28. Köster, "κατατομή," *TDNT* 8:109–11; Sumney, *"Servants of Satan,"* 166.

two are declarations that any Jewish group would be expected to make ("serving God in/by spirit" and "not trusting in [or: persuading by] flesh"). If we allow that other Jewish groups could also claim a messianic element if not also orientation, which the proper name "Christ" in our translations tends to obscure, then even this element need not suggest anything other than a particular Jewish group's emphasis on a specific messianic figure, Jesus. It is thus unlikely that Paul is setting out circumcision as a metonym for Christ-following identity in contrast to Jewish identity or in contrast to other Christ-following groups (who would also claim to glory in Christ Jesus), whether Jewish or not, or even other Jewish messianic groups.[29] Instead, he is claiming Jewish-group based identity and ways of living combined with the subgroup Jesus Christ-following based identity and ways of living in contrast to non-Jewish, non-Jesus Christ-following based identities and ways of living.

I propose that Paul does not reject circumcision identity for himself or his audience: he claims this rite to be "ours." He also does not claim to be "the nonmutilation" or "noncircumcision" group either, which should give pause to interpreters who believe Paul is using these terms synonymously. That is not to deny the aural pun between mutilation and circumcision in Greek, but to challenge the direction in which it has been interpreted. The pun is based on *contrasting*—not comparing—circumcision to mutilation as its mirror opposite. Paul's language here echoes the Maccabean slogan, "we are the circumcised" (1 Macc 1:15, 48, 60–61; 2:44–46; 2 Macc 6:10). In other words, circumcision functions as a metonym for the ethnoreligious identity of Judaism in contrast to all other ethnoreligious identities.[30]

Paul's slogan is based on internalizing circumcised identity as exceptional, as identifying a group that is set apart to God in a way that is to be both celebrated as superior to the practices of other nations and that carries within itself a responsibility to uphold those superior, spiritual values

---

29. Contra N. T. Wright, "Paul's Gospel and Caesar's Empire," in *Paul and Politics: Ekklesia, Israel, Imperium, Interpretation; Essays in Honor of Krister Stendahl*, ed. Richard A. Horsley (Harrisburg, PA: Trinity Press International, 2000), 160–83 (174–77). Although I disagree with this analysis, which is based on a decision for "mutilation" which I am challenging herein, the admission of "pagan" referents for the first two epithets is to be noted.

30. Nina Livesey, *Circumcision as a Malleable Symbol*, WUNT 2/295 (Tübingen: Mohr Siebeck, 2010), for a recent discussion of various ways of construing the meaning of circumcision by Paul and his contemporaries, although she does not come to the same conclusion I am suggesting for Paul's contrast here.

in the midst of them, which Paul enumerates in the balance of verse 3 and thereafter in verses 4–6. Paul is drawing a communal boundary around the addressees as members of the circumcised, that is, of Judaism, and thus different from the foreskinned in the ways that characterize Judaism as practiced by the subgroups of Christ-followers, whether they are circumcised (Jews) or foreskinned (non-Jews). That this metonymical identity excludes noncircumcised males in the community in literal terms is notable, but what has been apparently overlooked for interpreting its meaning here is *that it is no less problematic at the literal level for excluding any women in the community!* Yet interpreters do not thereby conclude from this text that there are no women in the community (the letter makes plain that there are) or that female identity and ways of life are replaced or eliminated or spiritualized by "Christianity," unlike the way that circumcision is interpreted here. Although we may find the metonymic choice of "circumcision" to signify "Judaism" insufficient due to its noninclusiveness, Paul appears to proceed as if this metonym communicates the inclusion of the males who are not circumcised as well as the females in these groups of Christ-followers, and he uses this language to communicate that this identity obliges them to identify themselves *within Judaism* (i.e., "Jewish ways of living," albeit as interpreted by a specific subgroup) in contrast to the "pagan" alternative non-Jewish ways of living available to them. "The circumcision" represents their group identity within Judaism, not their individual physical or spiritual state.

Reading Paul's denunciation of mutilation apart from signifying circumcision but rather in terms of non-Jewish groups and behavior from the majority culture opens several interesting pathways to explore. In the context of the city of Philippi, one might expect (from the point of view of a Jewish writer) that mutilation would be a term of reference to signify those castrated, such as the *galli* of the Cybele cult, or some other kind of mutilation associated with similar religious observances (see 1 Kgs 18:28, mentioned above).[31] Self-mutilation is widely associated with "pagan" groups and the way that they seek to provoke God to action (to persuade

---

31. Mary Beard, John A. North, and S. R. F. Price, *Religions of Rome*, 2 vols. (Cambridge: Cambridge University Press, 1998), 218–19. For more on the *galli*, including discussion of their self-mutilation by laceration during traveling blood-letting rituals, see Susan M. Elliott, *Cutting Too Close for Comfort: Paul's Letter to the Galatians in Its Anatolian Cultic Context*, JSNTSup 248 (London: T&T Clark, 2003), 158–229, esp. 189–93.

by or trust in flesh), including by those who employ magic. As will be discussed, a Jew such as Paul might also associate such behavior with Cynics.

Philippi and Philippians

Paul's letter was sent to a Romanized city, populated by many Romans, with special colony status, highly stratified according to Roman elites' standards (inescapable maintenance of status and distinctions), agriculturally oriented (and thus highly interdependent), and with Romanized Greek, Macedonian, Thracian, and other peoples.[32] Many gods were worshiped, and many cults are attested from the material remains. Roman religious practice was characterized by civic ideology, which incorporated the local gods and cults.[33] Inscriptions indicate that Romanized foreign cults such as the Egyptian gods and Cybele were linked to the practice of imperial cult.[34]

This milieu should, on its own merits, warrant an investigation of Philippians based on the supposition that Paul's negative references signal a call for resistance to the influence of "non-Jewish" or "pagan" factors on the addressees. When combined with my working hypothesis that Paul continued to practice Judaism and establish groups practicing Judaism (albeit having a significant proportion of non-Jews), this naturally suggests that his teaching challenges how they negotiate their new social identity within the larger non-Jewish world, in addition to how they do so within the larger (non-Jesus-oriented) Jewish community (however small it may be). Thus

---

32. Lukas Bormann, *Philippi: Stadt und Christengemeinde zur Zeit des Paulus*, NovTSup 78 (Leiden: Brill, 1995), 11–84; Peter Pilhofer, *Philippi I: Die erste christliche Gemeinde Europas*, WUNT 87 (Tübingen: Mohr Siebeck, 1995); Chaido Koukouli-Chrysantaki, "Colonia Iulia Augusta Philippensis," in *Philippi at the Time of Paul and after His Death*, ed. Charalambos Bakirtzis and Helmut Koester (Harrisburg, PA: Trinity Press International, 1998), 5–35; Charalambos Bakirtzis, "Paul and Philippi: The Archaeological Evidence," in Bakirtzis and Koester, *Philippi at the Time of Paul*, 37–48; de Vos, *Church and Community Conflicts*, 234–50; Oakes, *Philippians*, 1–76; Joseph H. Hellerman, *Reconstructing Honor in Roman Philippi: Carmen Christi as Cursus Pudorum*, SNTSMS 132 (New York: Cambridge University Press, 2005).

33. Beard, North, and Price, *Religions of Rome*, 167–363; John Scheid and Janet Lloyd, *An Introduction to Roman Religion* (Bloomington: Indiana University Press, 2003).

34. Bormann, *Philippi*, 54–60; Hawthorne, *Philippians*, xxxiv. On the Thracian, Greek, and other indigenous practices see especially Pilhofer, *Philippi I*, 49–113; Hellerman, *Reconstructing Honor*, 100–109.

I expect his letters to express Jewish sensibilities (including specifically Christ-based Jewish subgroup sensibilities) that he believed would shape his audiences' worldviews in directions new to them. Given this perspective, it seems to me that Paul is in this letter expressing a general revulsion toward the practices of some of the idolatrous cults and/or philosophical and other cultural norms that conspire to shape the thinking and behavior of his disciples in direct contrast to the (Christ oriented Jewish subgroup) values to which he wants them to now subscribe. If we begin to construct the audience by working backwards from the rhetorical clues within Paul's letter, these seem to suggest several interesting possibilities for what those he sought to influence in Philippi were being otherwise drawn toward to express their new-found commitment to being members of the gatherings of those who confessed allegiance to Jesus Christ.

Although there is little evidence of Jewish communities in Philippi at the time,[35] the absence of any Jews during Paul's period would be remarkable. The author of Acts 16:11–40 imagined that discussing a Jewish community there would be believable for his audience, even if this constitutes questionable evidence, since Paul wrote years earlier. In that report, there is communal opposition from crowds and magistrates in response to the particular kind of Jewish influence on their Romanized cult that the stranger Paul was perceived to represent.

Of particular interest for this enquiry, the account in Acts does seem to reflect some of the tensions that arise in Philippians. Paul's call to suffer for the message of good in Jesus Christ in Phil 1:27–30 and 2:12–18, following discussion of his own faithful persistence in the face of suffering imprisonment by Roman authorities (Phil 1:12–26)—albeit not in Philippi but from where he writes this letter—has led commentators to recognize that the threat to the addressees involves at least in part opposition to changes in their behavior that run afoul of their local "pagan" civic context. This is also supported by Paul's comments to the Thessalonians about his previous experience in Philippi (1 Thess 2:1–2). He explains that he suffered there, being insulted with insolence (with *hubris*). He feels that he was treated shamefully for behavior considered unbecoming according to Roman customs of religious expression, which pitted Paul's confession of

---

35. Ascough, *Paul's Macedonian Associations*, 191–212, traces the evidence. There are no material remains for our period and, besides the generalization in Philo, *Legat.* 281–282 (making reference to Macedonia among the many provinces of Rome with Jewish populations), no literary evidence except in Paul and Acts.

a Jewish figure (Christ/Messiah) against the idolatrous orientation of the Philippian cults toward many gods, including Caesar as lord and savior of humankind. These various accounts agree that Paul's proclamation of Jesus Christ as lord is opposed, because it does not conform to the city's expression of Roman cultural values.

If Paul was engaged in calling the Philippians, although non-Jews, away from compromising accommodation to their Roman social world, he would be seeking to persuade them to think and behave differently, to resist being shaped by the worldview that has fashioned their self- and group-identity since birth. That world was the one in which status and access to goods had been gained and could still be gained. It was thus in continued competition with their new marginalizing social reality as Christ-following non-Jews within this (newly emerging on the scene) Jewish coalition. If taken in this direction, the construction of those Paul opposes in Phil 3 need not be approached as if it is so different from the dynamics of the oppositional context suggested in chapter 1 of the letter, where "pagan" elements are often recognized.

Paul's Cynic-Like Argument

A number of Paul's epithets in verse 2 and verses 18–19 are commonly associated with denunciations of philosophical groups by their rivals. As Julian puts the case, philosophical groups would denounce the others as "sorcerers and sophists and conceited and quacks," (*Or.* 6.197 [Wright, LCL]). The satirist Timon denounced Epicurus as "the lowest *dog* among the physicists."[36] Although later than Paul, Lucian refers to the philosophers whom he is about to encounter as "beasts" who "act like *dogs* that bite and devour one another" (*Pisc.* 36; see *Vit. auct.* 10; also Gal 5:15).[37] In a similar way, Philo depicts the virtues of the Therapeutae in contrast to

> the banquets of others, for others, when they drink strong wine, as if they had been drinking not wine but some agitating and maddening kind of liquor, or even the most formidable thing which can be imagined for driving a man out of his natural reason, rage about and tear things to

---

36. Norman Wentworth DeWitt, *St. Paul and Epicurus* (Minneapolis: University of Minnesota Press, 1954), 24; Abraham J. Malherbe, *Paul and the Popular Philosophers* (Minneapolis: Fortress, 1989), 84.

37. Malherbe, *Paul and the Popular Philosophers*, 84.

pieces like so many ferocious dogs, and rise up and attack one another. (*Contempl.* 40)

In general terms that apply to some of the language in verses 18–19 as well, Philo states:

> When it [covetous desire] affects the parts about the belly it makes men gluttonous, insatiable, intemperate, debauched, admirers of a profligate life, delighting in drunkenness, and epicurism, slaves to strong wine, and fish, and meat, pursuers of feasts and tables, wallowing like greedy dogs; owing to all which things their lives are rendered miserable and accursed, and they are reduced to an existence more grievous than any death. (*Spec.* 4.91)

Cynics as Dogs

Beyond this general usage, the epithet "dogs" especially calls to mind the Cynics, among other religious-philosophical groups. The philosophical group known in English as Cynics is based on the Greek word for "dogs" (κύων; ὁ κυνικός).[38] They aspired to outdo all others in "doggish" behavior! Yet this option has been rarely noted and not pursued even then. It is more commonly noted that the language in verses 18–19 could express negative views of Cynics as well as Epicureans and other philosophical groups. These have probably not been developed for verse 2 because of the force of the traditional interpretation for controlling the options to explore here[39] and because mutilation is not usually associated with such groups,[40] although certainly a case can be made for Paul seeing such philosophers as

---

38. Philo, *Plant.* 151; Epictetus, *Diatr.* 3.22; Diogenes Laertius, *Lives* 6 (passim); Lucian, *Demon.* 21; Athenaeus, *Deipn.* 3.96–99; Clement, *Strom.* 8.12.4–7; Abraham J. Malherbe, ed., *The Cynic Epistles*, Resources for Biblical Study (Missoula, MT: Scholars Press, 1977), 99; Leif E. Vaage, "Like Dogs Barking: Cynic Parrêsia and Shameless Asceticism," *Semeia* 57 (1992): 25–39; Francis Gerald Downing, *Cynics, Paul, and the Pauline Churches* (London: Routledge, 1998), 35, 40.

39. Downing does not understand Paul to be referring to Cynics here, because he is convinced that this language is "so clearly directed against 'Judaisers'"; he understands Paul in Philippians to be moving away from earlier expressions of Cynicism, and he observes that if taken to refer to Cynics here, verses 2 and 19 "would have afforded a still clearer sign of a break with Cynics!" (*Cynics, Paul, and the Pauline Churches*, 35, 40, 272 n. 5).

40. Reumann, *Philippians*, 471–72.

evil workers. As will be discussed, it is also possible to propose Cynics for mutilation and many of the other invectives in verses 18–19.

During Paul's time, anyone warning to beware of the dogs, if not imagined to be taken to refer literally to the animal, might be expected to first of all suppose that the referent was the Cynics. They were a common presence in towns and cities during Paul's time, including in the public squares, where they lived and carried on their lives in squalor calculated to offend. Cynics were famously characterized as harassing those passing their way by "barking" insults at them for living according to the norms of "civilized" behavior. As a result of their lifestyle and tactics, Cynics were regularly accused of shamelessness. It was common for Cynics to be called "mad" (as in "mad dogs") because of their ascetic lifestyle (Pseudo-Socrates, *Ep.* 6.1; 9.3; Dio Chrysostom, *Disc.* 34.2–4; 45.1; 66.25; 77/78.41–42; Pseudo-Lucian, *Cynic Ep.* 5) and unconventional, vulgar behavior (Dio Chrysostom, *Disc.* 8.36; 9.8).[41] They sought to provoke the realization that civilization masks the way in which humans exploit each other under the cover of civility, in effect exemplifying the worst of behavior associated with the uncontrolled passion of dogs. By eschewing the trappings of society and behaving like dogs, the Cynics ostensibly avoided that hypocrisy and exemplified instead the philosophical ideals that should be the central purpose of human life (ironically, a lie exposed by their own dependence upon those who participated in society to gain the goods upon which Cynics relied, however meager, through begging).

The various epithets and invectives Paul employs in 3:2 and 18–19 can be aligned with his probable view of Cynics. "Evil workers" in the general sense of his estimation of their influence is not hard to imagine, although "mutilation" seems to present a challenge. We will consider both of these and then briefly survey the invectives arising in verses 18–19: "the enemies of the cross of Christ, whose end is destruction, whose god is the belly, who even glory in their shame, who are thinking earthly [thoughts]."

Cynics as the Mutilation and the Evil Workers

The Cynic option can also be explored in terms of the epithet mutilation, as surprising as that might seem.[42] There are both specific and general

---

41. Malherbe, *Paul and the Popular Philosophers*, 159–60.

42. Reumann, *Philippians*, 472, who is otherwise one of the few to consider Cynics the possible referent for "dogs," omits this option, because he finds the other

elements that can be construed as mutilation from the point of view of rivals, especially if the rival is shaped by and communicating based upon Jewish sensibilities. The accusation of mutilation might be another way of saying what is reported negatively of a virtuous Cynic according to Julian: "with his hair unkempt and his clothes in tatters on his chest and wearing a wretched cloak in severe winter weather: 'What evil genius can have plunged him into this sad state which makes not only him pitiable … neglecting everything and no better than a beggar!'" (*Or.* 6.198 [Wright, LCL]).

In a more graphic direction, Diogenes is reported to have endorsed cannibalism as a "natural," ideal way of eating in some cultures (*Lives* 6.73). In his polemic against Cynics, Philodemus (first century BCE) proclaims that Cynics usually "kill dying members of their family with their own hands and eat them."[43] In a Cynic Epistle addressed to "the so-called Greeks," the corpses of executed criminals (on the cross and on the rack) are derided for having no good use "except to eat as the flesh of sacrificial victims" (εἰ μὴ ὥσπερ ἱερείων σάρκας ἐσθίειν), a paraenetic harangue on the immorality of non-Cynics, who ignore what nature teaches (Diogenes, *Ep.* 28).[44] The Cynics turned the normally negative connotations of cannibalism into a positive icon of their movement's αὐτάρκεια ("self-sufficiency"), παρρησία ("bold speech"), and freedom from cultural conventions."[45] The

---

two warnings to be "specifically Jewish—one would not call wandering Cynic freeloaders 'workers,' and 'incision/circumcision.' "

43. Ragnar Höistad, *Cynic Hero and Cynic King: Studies in the Cynic Conception of Man* (Uppsala: Lund, 1948), 147–48.

44. Malherbe, *Cynic Epistles*, 121. This Cynic topos may inform Trimalchio's satire of cannibalism in Petronius, *Sat.* 141; see Albert Henrichs, *Die Phoinikika des Lollianos: Fragmente eines neuen griechischen Romans*, Papyrologische Texte und Abhandlungen 14 (Bonn: Habelt, 1972), 70 n. 78.

45. John L. Moles, "Cynic Cosmopolitanism," in *The Cynics: The Cynic Movement in Antiquity and Its Legacy*, ed. Robert Bracht Branham and Marie-Odile Goulet-Cazé (Berkeley: University of California Press, 1996), 112, 117; James Romm, "Dog Heads and Noble Savages: Cynicism before the Cynics?" in Branham and Goulet-Cazé, *Cynics*, 122–23; Derek Krueger, "The Bawdy and Society: The Shamelessness of Diogenes in Roman Imperial Culture," in Branham and Goulet-Cazé, *Cynics*, 226–27; Sarah Rappe, "Father of the Dogs? Tracking the Cynics in Plato's Euthydemus," *CP* 95 (2000): 291–93; Michel Onfray, *Cynismes: Portrait du philosophe en chien* (Paris: Bernard Grassett, 1990), 99–114; Höistad, *Cynic Hero and Cynic King*, 145–46. The Cynic ideal of ἀνθρωποφαγία entered Stoic traditions about the wise; see Richard Bett, *Sextus Empiricus, Against the Ethicists (Adversus Mathematicos*

relevance for defining those who might be regarded by Christ-followers as "enemies of the cross of Christ" involved in "mutilation" is intriguing.

In yet another direction, Diogenes was said to live in an urn in Athens within the *Metroön* (Mother's Building), which was the location of the cult of the Mother of the Gods, Cybele, with obvious associations to mutilation arising in that cult (see Diogenes Laertius, *Lives*, 6.23; *Ep.* 16).[46] Also, Cynics were accused of eating the food left at crossroads in the "Suppers of Hekate," an association that also arises in Talmudic literature, and thus, although depicting a later time, nevertheless reflects Jewish stereotypical notions about and polemic concerning Cynics. This brings up a specific "Jewish" context to consider in more detail.

Menahem Luz argues that third-century rabbis discuss Cynics when defining madmen in the Talmud, where they are called *kynukos,* versus the madman, who is called *kurdyakos* (y. Git. 7.1; y. Ter. 1.1; and b. Hag. 3b–4a).[47] The *kynukos* (i.e., the Dog/Cynic) is one who is characterized by four things: he "sleeps in the graveyard, burns incense to the demons, rends his clothing and destroys what people give him" (y. Git. 7.1 [Luz]). Consider that the "mad"—those suffering demon possession—were commonly depicted as mutilating their clothes and their bodies, including in the gospel accounts (Matt 8:28–34; Luke 8:27). Such an image and association could easily be applied to dismiss the tattered *tribon* (cloak) that Cynics wore with great pride (Diogenes Laertius, *Lives* 6.22; 7.87; Lucian, *Dial. mort* 1.332; Pseudo-Lucian, *Cynic* 1). The case can be considered all the stronger if we take into consideration Hekate's association with dogs in her persona and as her companions depicted in iconography, as well as in

---

XI) (Oxford: Clarendon, 1997), 32, 207–9, 265; and Paul A. Vander Waerdt, "Zeno's Republic and the Origins of Natural Law," in *The Socratic Movement*, ed. Vander Waerdt (Ithaca, NY: Cornell University Press, 1994), 300–301. See also F. Gerald Downing, *Cynics and Christian Origins* (Edinburgh: T&T Clark, 1992), 50, 173–74; and the response by Andrew McGowan, *Ascetic Eucharist: Food and Drink in Early Christian Ritual Meals* (Oxford: Clarendon, 1999), 73–75.

46. On the other hand, the Cynic Heraclitus of Ephesus criticized the castration of priests in the cult of the Mother Goddess, likening it to men enslaving men and impious behavior toward nature, wherein dogs do not castrate other dogs (Harold W. Attridge, *First-Century Cynicism in the Epistles of Heraclitus* [Missoula, MT: Scholars Press, 1976], 85).

47. M. Luz, "A Description of the Greek Cynic in the Jerusalem Talmud," *JSJ* 20 (1989): 49–60.

the puppy meat of which offerings to her consisted.[48] Then the rabbis were involved in punning on *kynukos* all the more, involving double entendre, as was Lucian when speaking of Cynics eating of the suppers of Hekate, that is, the dogs eating dog food (Lucian, *Vit. auct.* 9).

The rabbis drew a comparison between the madman who destroys what he receives and the Cynic who celebrated the dispossession of property. This was stereotypically referred to as defacing of currency (Diogenes Laertius, *Lives* 6.37, 87; Lucian, *Vit. auct.* 9). The defacing of currency by chisel stands for the mutilation of prevailing social convention by their development of frank speech and provocative lifestyle, as well as being a play on what "incision" of the coin signifies, namely, "mutilation": the Cynics celebrate κατατομή!

For our purpose, these associations might also help explain why Paul includes evil workers and the mutilated along with reference to the dogs: Paul's polemic builds upon stereotypical associations one might expect from the perspective of his Jewish sensibilities where such "pagan" groups are concerned.

Of course, the vague label of "evil workers" could be used for just about anyone or group whose influence Paul opposed. There are, nevertheless, specific associations with Cynics that can be drawn. Just as the belly-talking girl with the spirit of Pythos described in Philippi in Acts 16 can be associated with Apollo, so too the Cynics can be associated with Apollo, the Pythos, and the Delphic precept to "know thyself," which is a central theme in Julian's discussion of the Cynics (*Or.* 6.183–89; also Diogenes Laertius, *Lives* 6.21).

There are many parallels in Philippians with Cynic discourses, although only a few can be discussed here. It seems that Paul is engaged in challenging Cynics over who has the rightful claim to be upholding such ideals. In a sense, Paul may be seeking to out-Cynic the Cynics, to

---

48. Hecate was a ubiquitous goddess often accompanied by dogs, portrayed as a dog, and dogs (puppies) were sacrificed to her and prepared in cakes presented at her shrines. She was a goddess especially associated with passageways and crossroads, that is, with places of liminal danger. She was also involved in conducting the dead safely to Hades, or not doing so, and the goddess of magicians. Her cult is ancient, popular with Thracians as well as Greeks, and known as Trivia by the Romans (lit. "three ways"), for statues of her were erected where three roads met, and votive offerings were made for guidance and safety.

be claiming to have the right to be called the good worker and accuse the other of being the bad one.

Like Paul, the Cynics sought disciples (Epictetus, *Diatr.* 3.22.23–26),[49] or in their terms, like physicians, they sought to bring healing to those willing to listen by way of challenging the status quo that sickened the minds of the people, from which they needed to recover by seeing through the conventions to their true nature.[50] Like a surgeon, the Cynic must cut first with bold speech (παρρησία) before healing can begin (Diogenes Laertius, *Lives*, 6.69; Pseudo-Diogenes, *Ep.* 27–29), which parallels Paul's appeal to his bold speech (παρρησία) for the benefit of the Philippians and others whom he seeks to persuade (1:20). Diogenes claims that his dog-like style is undertaken on behalf of others: "Other dogs bite their enemies, but I my friends, to save them."[51] The true Cynic even practices the art of confronting others, understanding the ridicule of themselves that results to be for the ultimate benefit of their victim/accuser as well as for their own training in endurance (Diogenes Laertius, *Lives* 6.64), a feature that is interesting to compare with how Paul defines his own evaluation of the negative response that his activity, and that of his addressees, elicits. Diogenes is also the example of how to live well with nothing, including in suffering (Epictetus, *Diatr.* 3.22.45–61). Compare Paul telling the Philippians of his wrongful suffering being gain to him with that of his audience representing a privilege (Phil 1:27–30; see also 1:16–26; 4:10–14).[52] If those who argue that Philippians represents a Greco-Roman letter of friendship are correct,[53] then the parallels Paul draws between his service

---

49. John Moles, "'Honestius Quam Ambitiosius'? An Exploration of the Cynic's Attitude to Moral Corruption in His Fellow Men," *JHS* 103 (1983): 103–23 (112).

50. See Diogenes Laertius, *Lives* 6.4, 6; Dio Chrysostom, *Discourses* 8.5–7; 32.17; 33.6–8, 44; Ps.-Diogenes, *Ep.* 28; 29; Ps.-Socrates, *Ep.* 24; Epictetus, *Diatr.* 3.22.72–74; and see Plutarch, *How to Tell a Flatterer from a Friend* 59C–60B, 61D–62C, 73D–74DE; *Progress in Virtue* 80B–C; Malherbe, *Paul and the Popular Philosophers*, 131–35; Luis E. Navia, *Diogenes of Sinope: The Man in the Tub*, Contributions in Philosophy (Westport, CT: Greenwood, 1998), 136; on *typhos*, see 141.

51. Attributed to Diogenes by John Stobaeus, *Anthology* 3.13.44, among examples of παρρησία.

52. See also Stanley K. Stowers, "Friends and Enemies in the Politics of Heaven: Reading Theology in Philippians," in *Thessalonians, Philippians, Galatians, Philemon*, vol. 1 of *Pauline Theology*, ed. Jouette M. Bassler (Minneapolis: Fortress, 1991), 118.

53. L. Michael White, "Morality between Two Worlds: A Paradigm of Friendship in Philippians," in *Greeks, Romans, and Christians: Essays in Honor of Abraham J.*

to the addressees at enormous personal cost, like that of Christ toward them (emphasized in ch. 2), is delivered in a way arguably calculated to draw comparisons to the style of delivery that Cynics championed, albeit in person rather than in letter form.

The parallels between Paul's approach to the Philippians and Cynic discourses are intriguing, and several more fall into this general category around what kind of worker Paul is when compared to the Cynics, especially in his approach in chapter 3. Paul's emphasis on endurance, including appeal to the athletic imagery of training to succeed to make the case (vv. 12–16), parallels the common Cynic topos on discipline or practice in training (ἄσκησις), often made in similar athletic terms, in order to be able to persist in the face of constant resistance and discouragement from all other sources.[54] Paul's emphasis on self-denial in order to succeed (vv. 7–21; 4:5–13) is similar to the concerns of the Cynics to gain self-mastery (ἐγκρατὴς ἑαυτοῦ), the exercise of which will fly in the face of conventional measures of success.[55] Paul's use of harsh, abusive, and even crass street-language throughout chapter 3 (especially the use of "crap" in v. 8), in order to express prophetic critique of the cultural alternatives and any pressure to conform therewith, is similar to the kind of startlingly bold speech (παρρησία) characteristic of Cynics's howling.[56] Finally, in sharp contrast

Malherbe, ed. David L. Balch, Everett Ferguson, and Wayne A. Meeks (Minneapolis: Fortress, 1990), 201–15; Stowers, "Friends and Enemies," 105–21.

54. Diogenes Laertius, *Lives* 6.49, 70–71; Pseudo-Crates, *Ep.* 16, 20, 21, 33; Pseudo-Diogenes, *Ep.* 31; Epictetus, *Diatr.* 3.22.51–52; Robert Bracht Branham and Marie-Odile Goulet-Cazé, "Introduction," in Branham and Goulet-Cazé, *Cynics*, 26–27.

55. Diogenes Laertius, *Lives* 6.27–30, 45, represent examples of the critique, e.g., of the need for one to be better trained than a Spartan warrior, to be master of one's self more than of another man, to do more to uphold the laws than do the rulers themselves; see *Lives* 6.23, 31–34, 59; 7.172; Pseudo-Crates, *Ep.* 11, 12; Pseudo-Diogenes, *Ep.* 12; 14; Epictetus, *Diatr.* 3.22.51–52; Dio Chrysostom, *Or.* 6.8–9; Anthony A. Long, "The Socratic Tradition: Diogenes, Crates, and Hellenistic Ethics," in Branham and Goulet-Cazé, *Cynics*, 28–46. That self-mastery was also a Roman value and also espoused by the Stoics (Epictetus, *Diatr.* 3.12 [about Cynics]; 3:13.2; Seneca, *Ep.* 18.5–13; 108.15–16, 23) should not be overlooked; Griffin, "Cynicism and the Romans: Attraction and Repulsion," in Branham and Goulet-Cazé, *Cynics*, 201–2.

56. Perhaps there is a parallel concern in Paul's mention of receipt of funds from the Philippians in 4:10–19, wanting to make sure that they understood it was not required, and the implicit contradiction Cynics created with their eschewing of work for pay in order to remain free (the highest value: *Lives* 6.69–71; Lucian, *Demon.*

to Paul's claim that "our citizenship is in heaven" rather than in this world (Phil 3:19–20), Cynics claim to be "citizens of the world [κοσμοπολῖται]." That is, they claim not to be constrained by conformity to the conventions of the citizens of any particular city, but true only to their own self-judgment about what is virtuous in universal terms (Diogenes Laertius, *Lives* 6.63).[57] Cynics could be regarded as a positive example for their lack of concern for gaining honor according to the Roman cultural status norms, thus competing on similar grounds for the same kind of people as could have been found in the audience at Philippi. However, their immodest and immoral behavior would have also provided stark contrast and, thus, a quite negative example for an audience also influenced by Jewish communal standards.

Cynics and Later Invectives (3:18–19)

The invectives used later in the chapter are also fruitfully reconsidered in the light of the Cynics. It seems highly unlikely that Paul would refer so vaguely to these *"enemies of the cross of Christ,"* for example, if it were a denouncement of Christ-followers, because they still upheld Jewish values (as it is often maintained). Indeed, anyone challenging Paul and his groups for allegiance to Christ could be accused of being an enemy of the cross of Christ.[58] Paul's invective could be a response to anyone who held that those aligned with someone who was executed as a feared terrorist is an enemy of the empire.[59] There is no special indication of Cynics, but it is not hard to imagine that Cynics, who were also often maligned as enemies of the empire, could be in view, either because they sought to declaim the Christ-followers as more threatening than themselves to the interests of

---

21), yet at the same time begging. In other words, they are complicit in the nonfreedom of those from which they receive support, although their philosophy claims to uphold practicing it without harming the other (i.e., that they are friends of humankind [φιλανθρωπία]: Diogenes, *Ep.* 28.3; Heraclitus, *Ep.* 7.2; Dio Chrysostom, *Or.* 4.24; Epictetus, *Diatr.* 3.22.81; 3.24.64; Lucian, *Demon.* 11, 21; Julian, *Or.* 6.201; see also Moles, "Honestius Quam Ambitiosius," 112–16).

57. J. M. Rist, *Stoic Philosophy* (Cambridge: Cambridge University Press, 1969), 58–59.

58. See Sumney, *"Servants of Satan,"* 171.

59. Richard A. Horsley and Neil Asher Silberman, *The Message and the Kingdom: How Jesus and Paul Ignited a Revolution and Transformed the Ancient World* (New York: Grossett/Putnam, 1997), 202, suggest verses 18–19 refer to Nero.

the Philippians or, alternatively, that the Christ-followers were being compared to the Cynics as enemies of Rome and Paul was seeking to dissociate them from comparisons based on such ideals and norms (they had their own Christ-based Jewish associations, not those of the Cynics). We will discuss these options, among others.

The accusation that someone's or some group's "end is destruction" is also quite vague. In 1:28, Paul uses the same language about opponents of the addressees, or perhaps in a more general sense, of opponents of the message of Christ: "For them this is evidence of their destruction, but of your salvation. And this is God's doing." Here too, the story of Elijah and the prophets of Baal may be at work in Paul's choice of language. Nevertheless, Paul's phrase could easily be taken as ironic criticism of the ultimate ends of several philosophical groups. More specifically, though, Cynics were regarded as actively seeking self-destructive courses of behavior as part of their mission, which Paul may well have in mind when referring to those whose "end is destruction."[60] If the audience in Philippi showed no concern for gaining honor according to the Roman cultural status norms, then the Cynics could be regarded a positive example, particularly when they called for a return to natural living before civilization's so-called civilizing norms cloaked the legitimation of moral, political, and economic exploitation of the many by the few, for which they were sometimes severely punished in the Roman period.[61] Of course, if they were also attracted to or organized by Jewish communal standards (such as the kind listed in vv. 18–19), the Cynics's immodest and immoral behavior would be problematic.[62] Would Paul not have found Cynic agnosticism (Lucian, *Zeus Refutatus* 15; Tertullian, *Nat.* 2.2)[63] a sign of their ultimate end, that is, their destruction?

The polemical charge that someone's or some group's "god is the belly" is relatively common among philosophers. Among ancient moral philosophers, accusations of serving the belly for pleasure and to avoid

---

60. See Downing, *Cynics, Paul, and the Pauline Churches*, 143–50.

61. See Dio Cassius, *Hist. Rom.* 56, for insulting magistrates publicly, i.e., *parrēsia*; Seneca, *Ep.* 20; Branham and Goulet-Cazé, "Introduction," 12–18; Griffin, "Cynicism and the Romans," 190–204; Navia, *Diogenes of Sinope,* 146.

62. And according to the standards of some others who otherwise admire the Cynic tradition, such as Lucian in *Demonax, De morte Peregrini,* and *De fuga in persecutione*; Branham and Goulet-Cazé, "Introduction," 17.

63. Marie-Odile Goulet-Cazé, "Religion and the Early Cynics," in Branham and Goulet-Cazé, *Cynics,* 47–80.

responsibility to one's fellow citizens were often contrasted with the self-discipline required of athletes or soldiers, not unlike what we find in Paul's language in this chapter.[64] In general, the Cynics attacked the indulgence of human appetite as misguided. However, this critique was not one-dimensional, since dogs by nature are stereotypically maligned for overeating. Diogenes speaks against indulging appetites (Diogenes Laertius, *Lives* 6.60), but Cynics cleverly expressed preference for eating during *symposia* (suggesting the vice of gluttony) in order to seek to subvert the conventional attention to word games at the meals. Cynics thus sought to attack civilized *talk about* morality instead of undertaking to *practice* actual moral behavior—since those enjoying the symposia gained the wealth that made such civilized dinner entertainment possible through the immoral exploitation of the poor, at least from the perspective of Cynic guests. For this insulting behavior, the Cynics were maligned as dogs whose god is the belly (*Lives* 6.61, 270c–d; see also Athenaeus, *Deipn.* 3.96f–100b).

When Paul writes of those "who glory in their shame," this language can naturally refer to any behavior that is contrary to what Paul believes honorable behavior should be. The phrase can refer euphemistically to the Cynic's strategic public demonstration of animal-like behavior, including stereotypical provocative acts such as farting, defecating, masturbating, and the like, in order to expose that conventions of human social behavior are human constructions: the Cynic thus glories in his shame (Diogenes Laertius, *Lives* 6.69; Diogenes, *Ep.* 44). This language is close to that used by Lucian when specifically writing of a Cynic who practiced erections in public, euphemistically referring to the penis as the "shameful thing [αιδοιον]" (*Peregr.* 17). Hesychius included reference to the "the shameless one" in his lexicon entry for κυών: "the male member, and the barking animal, *and the shameless one*, and the star, and the sea animal."[65] Later lexicons continue to equate Cynics and shamelessness.[66]

---

64. Sandnes, *Belly and Body*, 35–60; Bloomquist, *Suffering in Philippians*, 131–33, 178–81, 197–201 (also 90).

65. Hesychius of Alexandria, *Lexicon*, ed. Kurt Latte (Copenhagen: Ejnar Munksgaard, 1953), 2:555, entry Kappa 1763; also H. Ulonska, "Gesetz und Beshneidung: Überlegungen zu einem paulinishcen Ablösungskonflict," in *Jesus Rede von Gott*, ed. D. Koch (Gütersloh: Gütersloher Verlag Mohn, 1989), 314–31 (327).

66. Frederic Sylburg, ed. *Etymologicum magnum* (Leipzig: Wiegel, 1816), col. 498: "Dog for the philosopher who does the same as dogs do." "Shameless ones" is also

Paul's criticism of those who "think earthily" or "terrestrially" could be aimed at the Cynic philosophical stance that upholds the function of language is to identify the objects of the physical world, not to play linguistic games, as is the case in the discourse of philosophy and science. Even ordinary speech acts are misguided, and reading and writing maligned: "nothing can be either defined or explained, except by pointing to the object."[67] This observation can be combined with the Cynic's general disdain for religious beliefs and practices, for concern with those things about which we cannot know.[68] The idea of living according to "nature" is at work here, that the processes of the physical world occur according to their nature, their essence, the logical laws that govern them, and not outside sources such as divine figures.[69] Cynics were not necessarily opposed to religion as much as to public expressions of religion, and different Cynics expressed different sensibilities, from opposition to the gods to belief in the gods but not in the human conventions for defining and worshiping, especially images and temples and ritual practices like sacrifices.[70]

From the perspective of common social conventions, including Jewish ones, Cynics can easily be associated with the derisive language Paul employs in verses 18–19, whose "god is their belly," who "glory in their shame," and who actively seek self-destructive courses of behavior as part of their mission: whose "end is destruction," as Paul might put the case.[71]

What Does Paul's "Cynical" Approach Suggest about the People He Addressed in Philippi?

It is not clear that Paul had in view Cynics or Cynic-related concerns in chapter 3 or throughout the letter, but we have surveyed several suggestive reasons to consider this a relevant way to interpret Paul's rhetoric and the possible ways that those Paul addressed are thinking, or at least considering how to think, about themselves as well as Paul. In addition to being sug-

---

offered as a definition here. See the *kuōn* entry of the Hellenistic Apollonius Sophista, *Lexicon Homericum*, ed. J. C. Molini (Paris: Molini, 1773), 2:510.

67. Navia, *Diogenese of Sinope*, 94.

68. Ibid., 113–14.

69. Ibid., 116.

70. See, for example, Heraclitus, *Ep.* 4.10–13, 17, 20–26; 5.14; 9.15–19; Lucian, *Demon.* 11; 27; 32; Dio Chrysostom, *Or.* 12; and Maximus of Tyre, *Or.* 2.

71. See Downing, *Cynics, Paul, and the Pauline Churches*, 143–50.

gested by elements within Philippians, it is also inferred by Paul's account of his experiences in Philippi when writing to the Thessalonians.

In 1 Thess 2:1–2, Paul indicates that he had suffered shameful treatment in Philippi before his arrival in Thessalonica. Abraham Malherbe compares Paul's language in 2:1–8 to intra-Cynic discourse in particular. For example, the Cynic Dio Chrysostom denounced certain Cynics who did not represent the Cynic ideals to which Dio subscribed in polemical terms similar to those reflected in Paul's denunciations. Paul's description of his willingness to suffer for speaking boldly in spite of the negative reaction of the crowd is similar to Dio's portrait of the true Cynic philosopher's bold struggle against social pressure (vv. 1–2). Also similarly, Paul claims to preach unlike the charlatans who deceive and lead their hearers into error (v. 3).[72] The way that Paul related these experiences in Philippi to the Thessalonians might suggest that he is building on the fact that the Thessalonians know him to have been mistaken for a Cynic when he was in Philippi (perhaps also by those who responded positively to his message?). If so, then there is good reason to suppose that, when Paul wrote to the Philippians, he sought to express himself in contrast to certain stereotypical Cynic qualities that could be easily polemicized or even to be exemplifying popular philosophical ideals to which he believes his audience subscribes.[73]

What might an identification of Cynics as the target of Paul's invectives and the overall way that he shapes his arguments in this letter suggest about the identity of the audience in Philippi and their concerns? Several options readily come to mind.

One option could be that Paul's addressees were being maligned by their non-Jewish families and neighbors as Cynics or Cynic-like for failing to uphold the norms of social life to which they had formerly subscribed as fellow non-Jews. Their family life had likely been characterized previously by the pursuit of honor and success on their non-Jewish society's prevailing terms. These non-Jews have entered into a new minority culture when they began to gather with Jewish subgroups, and that was the case all the more, because these Jesus Christ oriented subgroups were themselves in some ways upholding norms that ran counter to those of the larger Jewish communities. Declaring allegiance to a Jewish messianic figure was dan-

---

72. Malherbe, *Paul and the Popular Philosophers*, 35–48.

73. See also Gerd Theissen, *The Social Setting of Pauline Christianity: Essays on Corinth*, trans. John H. Schütz (Philadelphia: Fortress, 1982), 39.

gerous even for Jewish groups to uphold, and many would likely resist such assertions by their Jewish peers and all the more by non-Jews meeting among them, who would be expected to express these sentiments to other non-Jews, raising awareness and concern that there was something dangerous going on in their local Jewish communities (see Acts 16–21, passim). In response to the kinds of behavioral changes and declarations of new allegiances that non-Jewish followers of Jesus in Paul's groups were making, it would be natural for their families and neighbors to classify their newly adopted counter-cultural lifestyles as Cynic or at least Cynic-like.[74] They might even be considering themselves Cynics, or on their way to becoming Cynics, and thus looking to Cynics and their teaching and cultural norms for guidance in their new lives as followers of a messianic deviant according to Roman legal and cultural norms. In either of these directions, if the case, then this letter bears witness to Paul's response to a way of understanding their new identity. On the one hand, he regards many Cynic norms as inappropriate for them to internalize for themselves; on the other hand, he appeals to parallel countercultural norms modeled by Judaism in his own way of life and that of Jesus: it is to these that they should look for guidance. Being misunderstood is to be expected, including being misunderstood in the direction of being Cynics or Cynic-like: they must recognize the difference, that they are those who have instead joined a Jewish society and that they are called to constantly bear witness to that society's propositional claims as the basis for their thinking and way of life until justice is fully realized.

In a slightly different direction, Cynics might be attacking his addressees. Non-Jews pledging allegiance to a Jewish messianic figure crucified by the Romans may be perceived to be Cynic-like in many ways, whether mistakenly or because they are seeking to live like and identify themselves in Cynic terms. The Philippians's commitment to Christ and the norms of the Jewish groups to which they have become members could bring criticism upon them from Cynics or from those who appreciate Cynic values for having failed to exemplify Cynicism because of these conventions and beliefs, which are in some ways Jewish, but in other ways seem to be hard to square with the prevailing Jewish norms with which non-Jews are familiar. If so, then Paul would be seeking to warn them to avoid being disturbed

---

74. This is a central idea for how Paul would have been perceived among non-Jews for Downing, *Cynics, Paul, and the Pauline Churches*, although, interestingly, not with respect to Philippians.

for failing to live up to Cynic standards, while encouraging them to stand fast in the face of opposition that misunderstands who they are and what they represent, even if it rightly recognizes that they hold to values that are countercultural in some ways that parallel Cynic norms.

It is within the scope of either of these options that Paul's Christ-following non-Jews may be looking to Cynics as role models in view of the alienation they were suffering since becoming followers of this Jewish subgroup loyal to Jesus Christ. Cynics had a kind of loose affiliation rather than a formal one with initiation rites, and Cynic was a rather loosely used term, along the lines of defining a "hippy" in more recent years. It was not unusual for Cynics to consider others claiming this identity or adopting certain behavior to be imposters by their own standards. In this scenario, the non-Jews beginning to follow Jesus in Philippi were attracted to Cynics as role models, but at the same time they were experiencing rejection to their aspirations for status on such terms not only from their families and neighbors among whom they had formerly sought success according to prevailing norms, but even from Cynics for failing to conform adequately to the ideals by which they should be able to rightly consider themselves Cynics!

If his addressees thought of Paul as a Cynic, then it is likely that they thought that becoming Cynics or Cynic-like was an ideal to be pursued. It may well be how they perceived Jesus; thus it was the way that they sought to become like Jesus as well as Paul.[75] If they did not think of Paul as a Cynic, yet their families and neighbors did, that might also be suggestive. Paul would seek to provoke them to (re)consider whether they have misunderstood Paul, or Cynics, or both.

It is intriguing to wonder whether this was indeed the option that his addressees were exploring if not also adopting in order to make sense

---

75. It appears that the Philippian audience is approached by Paul from the assumption that they are in general favorably disposed toward Paul and his work, based on his confident and overall generous and positive approach to them, praise of them, and their participation in his collection project apparently in a more supportive and generous way than some of Paul's other assemblies responded to this request of them. Although Paul's rhetorical approach could be calculated to gain their trust more than a witness to it, his argument appeals to suffering some kind of distress by which he seeks to identify them with himself in their pursuit of similar goals. From this shared set of values, at least what he and they (from his rhetorical point of view) suppose to be shared, he seeks to set out more accurately (from his vantage point) how they ought to proceed, including some things and people that they ought to avoid.

of the implications of the message of Christ as they interpreted it after Paul departed. The one to whom they claimed loyalty was executed by the Romans as a threat to society, not unlike the Cynics considered themselves and were considered by many to be, which may have suggested a positive affiliation to pursue. His message led them into a marginalized identity and threatened their access to honor and goods: how were they to negotiate living "in the present age," although claiming to be living according to the chronometrical proposition that "the end of the ages had dawned," which was to be exemplified in their communal and personal lives? Had they become aware of their group as a subgroup of Jewish communal ways of living that was itself countercultural, not only in terms of the Roman city in which they lived and into which they had been enculturated, but also in terms of the larger Jewish community and its other, various (rival?) subgroups in Philippi or elsewhere throughout the empire? In such a place, without Paul to guide them into his own particular Jewish Christ-based subgroup's way of interpreting the options for how they should now live, did they suppose that the Cynic culture offered them the best alternative to explore to make sense of their new identity, for how to be non-Jews in a new, unconventional Jewish subgroup?

If so, then Paul's presentation of his message to them in very Cynic-like terms may have been constructed with the expectation that they would recognize that, in spite of its similarities to Cynic values and the marginalization they suffered, their new identity was also very different from that of the Cynics—or should be. In this direction, it may be that Paul wants them to "consider" as in "reflect on" the Cynics (and or other groups), which as noted earlier, is the way that some have argued that the repetition of βλέπετε in Phil 3:2 should be interpreted, rather than "beware" of or "watch out" for them. Paul may be, as it were, seeking to out-howl the Cynics, as well as perhaps to demonstrate the failure of any criticism of his addressees based upon comparisons to Cynics. For Paul argues that they are to value identity and life-style norms in Christ above the status and access to goods that might be available to them through compliance with the majority cultural values, including the Jewish majority cultural values, but also with any countercultural groups and values that may seem to provide available models or to be attractive options. Although Cynics may vie for the right to be the *top dog* among themselves, Paul denies that this should be so for himself (Phil 3:4–14, even if his argumentative strategy betrays his dependence upon being able to make just that claim!) or anyone else who shares his loyalty to Christ; even Christ himself did not do so (Phil 2:5–8)!

If Cynics were in view, Paul would presumably want to clarify the differences between his addressees as members of the Jewish community ("we are the circumcision") and Cynics or other similar representatives of "non-Jewish" cultural values (the "dogs," "evil workers," "mutilation," etc., of vv. 2, 18–19). If so, then Paul dissociates them from Cynics in polemical style, making plain the ethos of Christ-followers within this Jewish subgroup (they are those who worship God by spirit, boast in Jesus Christ, and do not seek honor-ranking in normal social terms [or perhaps, who do not seek to persuade by παρρησία according to the flesh]; vv. 3–21). All such ranking, however desirable, as birth and fidelity obviously remain for Paul himself in order to make his point—a valuation that he apparently believes his audience shares with him to expect it to carry the rhetorical weight his argument depends upon—is mere "crap" *if* it would threaten to come between him and his standing in Christ above *all other honors*.[76] Paul calls his audience to share this comparative point of view toward any "pagan" rank and privilege that might lead to discrimination among themselves.

In short, in terms of understanding the people in Philippi to whom Paul wrote, they seem to be suffering an identity crisis that involves social pressure to which Paul can liken his own suffering. They need to sort out what it means to remain non-Jews who pledge allegiance to a Jewish figure based upon the teaching of a Jewish figure who passed through their city establishing new Jewish subgroups, but he (Paul) is no longer among them to offer daily guidance when the complications of this new commitment arise in their lives. They are thus looking for models and affiliations that offer guidance and relief. Paul's response suggests that he regards their intentions as good, but some of the options that they are tempted to explore, whether out of interest or as a result of pressure, to be inappropriate for them. His Cynic-like approach to them suggests that some of these options involve Cynic or Cynic-like influences, which he seeks to exploit in order to turn them toward different conclusions than they might otherwise derive for themselves. Paul calls them to explore their new identity instead within Judaism as followers of the way of life of Jesus,

---

76. Similarly, see William S. Campbell, " 'I Rate All Things as Loss': Paul's Puzzling Accounting System; Judaism as Loss or the Re-evaluation of All Things in Christ?" in Spitaler, *Celebrating Paul*, 39–61.

which was also exemplified by Paul. He is a marginalized Jew, just as they find themselves to be marginalized non-Jews, but their new, shared affiliation is within Judaism nevertheless and not within their respective local civic contexts. In due time, their faithfulness to that affiliation will result in success that will be made plain for all to see.

Conclusion

Although recent interpreters of Philippians observe that a tension between honoring Christ versus honoring Caesar appears to be a major concern of this letter—for example, in Phil 1:27-30 (that their suffering is like Paul's, who is in prison for anti-imperial activity); Phil 2:5-15 (the elevation of Jesus to lord of all rather than Caesar's claim to that role); and Phil 3:20 (their citizenship in the colony of heaven rather than Philippi)— they have not focused on a clash of values with "pagan" culture in Phil 3:2-19, because they continue to draw on the traditional interpretation of these verses, wherein Paul's opposition is supposedly from Jewish or Jewish Christian missionaries.[77] In view of the many options discussed, however, it is unlikely that Paul's argument and the specific phrases he employed in Phil 3 suggest that he was opposing Jews or problems arising from rivalry with Jews (Christ-following ones, or not) or Jewish ways of life (Judaism). Quite to the contrary, Paul appears to oppose local "pagan" influences and influencers and to promote Jewish values and ways of life. In the face of competing non-Jewish "pagan" communal alternatives on offer in Philippi with which his (primarily if not exclusively) non-Jewish addressees are tempted to identify (seek status and goods), Paul seeks to persuade them to instead identify with Paul's Jewish norms because they are followers of Christ.

---

77. There is a growing consensus on the imperial context of Paul's rhetoric in certain texts: see, e.g., R. R. Brewer, "The Meaning of πολιτεύεσθε in Phil 1:27," *JBL* 73 (1954): 76–83; E. C. Miller, "Πολιτεύεσθε in Phil. 1.27: Some Philological and Thematic Observations," *JSNT* 15 (1982): 86–96; David Seeley, "The Background of the Philippians Hymn (2:6–11)," *Journal of Higher Criticism* 1 (1994): 49–72; Gordon D. Fee, *Philippians*, IVP New Testament Commentary Series 11 (Downers Grove, IL: InterVarsity Press, 1999), 29–33; Bockmuehl, *Philippians*, 234–45; Oakes, *Philippians*, 129–74; Wright, "Paul's Gospel," esp. 173–81; de Vos, *Church and Community Conflicts*, 263–75.

I thus suggest that Paul's appeal to his own Jewish identity and behavioral credentials in 3:4–6 was not presented to oppose alternative Jewish groups or individuals appealing to their superior Jewish identity and behavioral credentials, but to qualify his authority to instruct them to adopt a path that will not resolve their marginalization on any other community's, subgroup community's, or even countercultural community's terms. He did not want to give the impression that they were to compete for honor or rank on Jewish or non-Jewish terms or that he did so either, thus he qualified the advantages of his own ranking—although at the same time implicitly (i.e., rhetorically) appealing to his advantaged identity in order to make his point.[78] In other words, interpreters miss the rhetorical force of his point when suggesting that Paul here denounces his "past" identity as a Jew who practiced Judaism: his argument is predicated upon his audience knowing him to be a Jew who "still" practices Judaism in exemplary fashion. Thus he wants to communicate that he does not let the social advantage that normally accompanies that Jewish identity come before his shared identity with them "in Christ"; neither should they seek social advantage among themselves by the various "pagan" communal terms available to them. The qualification is based upon a comparative identity he shares with them, that of knowing or seeking to know and be known by God in Christ—"everything" else pales *in comparison*.

For Paul's addressees, the "pagan" identity and behavioral alternatives were not brand new. They had guided their self and group identity until they became followers of Christ, and they still appear to offer desirable advantages. It is not easy for them to abandon the status and access to goods that affiliation with these "pagan" groups can offer, especially when they cannot claim access to status and goods as if they had become Jews, since unlike Paul, they have been and remain non-Jews. But Paul has brought them into Judaism, with the result that they are confused and seeking relief from the consequences that have developed from their ambiguous new identity in Christ-following Jewish (sub)groups. Even though Paul could easily seek honor in Jewish community terms, as the addressees are tempted to

---

78. Joseph A. Marchal, *The Politics of Heaven: Women, Gender, and Empire in the Study of Paul*, Paul in Critical Contexts (Minneapolis: Fortress, 2008), discusses many factors to consider for undertaking a people's history approach to Philippians, including a sustained analysis of Paul's reinscription of various cultural values he ostensibly opposes in the actions of others, a dynamic that interpreters often fail to recognize in their advancement of Paul as role model.

seek to be able to do in "pagan" community terms, he calls them to resist that temptation (even if we witness him doing just that to make this point). Together they must suffer communal disapproval for their identification with the marginalized community of believers in Jesus Christ, whom they believe to be the true "lord" of all.

Paul's call to suffering for faithfulness to the example of Christ (and of Paul himself) echoes Elijah's pointed language, which, as noted earlier, seems to be a salient passage for Paul when he composed Philippians, especially chapter 3. Paul's approach bespeaks a conflict between the Christ-following Judaism into which these non-Jews have now been, or should be, enculturated, and the alternatives outside of this Judaism to which they may be attracted or by which they may be threatened: "How long will you keep hopping between two opinions? If the Lord is God, follow Him; and if Baal, follow him!" (1 Kgs 18:21, JPS).

If chapter 3 is interpreted around a conflict between Jewish and "pagan" values and groups, perhaps Cynics (or various cults and other possibilities in some combination), especially over the terms of conflicting imperial allegiances (citizenship), then this language can be integrated into the overall focus of the letter. That appears to revolve around the choice that Paul calls his audience in Philippi to make between the "pagan" cultural alternatives that remain attractive or otherwise constrain the options available to themselves if they wish to avoid suffering and the Jewish cultural values that their commitment to Jesus as Christ should compel them, from Paul's point of view, to undertake instead.

This alternative at least raises the prospect of considering new ways to understand how these conflicting cultural norms might be shaping the lives of the audience and the choices they are making before the arrival of Paul's letter, as well as how they might react to it. I hope that sufficient questions have been raised to encourage interpreters to reconsider perpetuating the prevailing paradigm when sketching out the options to consider for Paul's communication goals, as well as the identity and concerns of Paul's audience.

An Alternative Community and an
Oral Encomium: Traces of the People in Philippi

Robert L. Brawley

Unmistakably the recipients of Philippians told their own stories and took initiatives to make major shifts in identity and behavior related to their narratives. Joining a new group with a foreign orientation was the product of a narrative that began with deficiencies, closely related to their social and economic situation, and belonging to the assembly played a major role in surmounting them. But their initiatives are hidden under the initiatives of another—Paul. They are subjects of his discourse rather than spokespersons of their own. Is it possible for them to speak for themselves?

Because the perspectives in Philippians are Paul's, reading his epistle against the grain is a necessity.[1] Thus, when Paul argues polemically (e.g. Phil 1:15; 3:2, 18–19) or offers models of behavior (Phil 2:19–30; 3:17) or urges conformity to one orientation (Phil 2:1–5; 4:2) or constructs alienating identities of others, reading against Paul's privileged voice amplifies voices in the assembly. Reading against the grain unveils dimensions of power and subordination, highlights and values difference, and reveals where Paul distorts by silence and silencing others (Phil 1:15; 3:18–19). What gaps indicate how Paul failed to mention people who were obviously active in the assembly?[2] For instance, Epaphroditus was the assembly's apostle to Paul

---

1. E.g., Elisabeth Schüssler Fiorenza, *Rhetoric and Ethic: The Politics of Biblical Studies* (Minneapolis: Fortress, 1999), 138–42; Elizabeth Castelli, *Imitating Paul: A Discourse in Power*, Literary Currents in Biblical Interpretation (Louisville: Westminster John Knox, 1991); Cynthia Briggs Kittredge, *Community and Authority: The Rhetoric of Obedience in the Pauline Tradition*, HTS 45 (Harrisburg, PA: Trinity Press International, 1998); and Joseph A. Marchal, *The Politics of Heaven: Women, Gender, and Empire in the Study of Paul*, Paul in Critical Contexts (Minneapolis: Fortress, 2008).

2. "Rather than understand the text as an adequate reflection of the reality about

(Phil 2:25). Others had to have been active behind the scenes. But Paul is silent about who spearheaded the project.

For three reasons, however, very little reading against the grain appears in what follows. First, reading against the grain builds images of the recipients by unearthing opposition and difference from Paul. Its eye is set on conflict, which is not to be denied, but characterization by opposition still means measuring one by the other.[3] A thesis of this essay is that beyond internal tensions, the assembly creatively developed its own alternative community in a context where they were socially and politically marginalized. Second and closely related, both Paul and the Philippians were vanquished victims of the empire.[4] Together they contended against dominant imperial systems. Third, traces of the people, their initiatives and actions, and something of their voices and stories, are available in Paul's discourse by reading carefully with the grain.[5] These traces come to light by discerning common ground that Paul shares with the Philippians and by noticing where Paul gives information about them and their actions. For example, interchanges around the sending of Epaphroditus and his illness (Phil 2:25–30; 4:18) mean that both Paul and the Philippians knew stories of struggles some of which the Philippians had to have narrated simply because they are the ones who informed Paul.

This chapter takes six steps: (1) locating the members of the Philippian assembly in local hierarchical systems of the Roman Empire; (2) determining how their identity and roles emerge from the ways Paul addressed them; (3) inquiring into how their stories of struggles and beneficence, which are reflected in Paul's discourse, contribute to their identity, and how telling their own story was itself one of their initiatives; (4) ascertaining how their perspectives and values appear where they shared Paul's views; (5) retrieving imprints of their initiatives and actions in Paul's account; and (6) envisioning how they likely appropriated Paul's

---

which it speaks, we must search for clues and allusions that indicate the reality about which the text is silent" (Elisabeth Schüssler Fiorenza, *In Memory of Her: A Feminist Reconstruction of Christian Origins* [New York: Crossroad, 1983], 41).

3. Opposition defines each pole by the other (James C. Scott, *Domination and the Arts of Resistance* [New Haven: Yale University Press, 1990], 10–19).

4. Brigitte Kahl, *Galatians Re-imagined: Reading with the Eyes of the Vanquished*, Paul in Critical Contexts (Minneapolis: Fortress, 2010).

5. Ann Laura Stoler, *Along the Archival Grain: Epistemic Anxieties and Colonial Common Sense* (Princeton: Princeton University Press, 2009), 50. This is closely related to Schüssler Fiorenza's call to search for clues and allusions (n. 2 above).

letter in repeated oral performances of it. This essay makes no pretense of painting a complete picture. It attempts rather to contribute some brush strokes to a portrait of the assembly under the presupposition that multiple approaches in distinct investigations are complementary.[6] Complementarity is a desideratum, because reading against the grain runs the risk of emphasizing tensions at the expense of mutuality whereas reading with the grain runs the risk of emphasizing mutuality at the expense of tensions.

Locating the Members of the Assembly in Imperial Systems

The recipients of Paul's letter in Philippi suffered the effects of Roman colonization. Colonizers had pushed aside established locals and occupied their land—the problem of access to land and its resources.[7] Three features made the area inviting for colonization. It stood on the important east-west land route built by the Romans in the second century BCE, the Via Egnatia. It was located close to gold and silver mines, and though they were depleted by the time of Philippians, they had enhanced the strategic location of the city.[8] Third, the land around Philippi was fertile, unusual in Greece where only 18 percent of the land was arable.[9] So after Antony and Octavian overcame Cassius and Brutus in the Battle of Philippi, Antony established a Roman colony there for his veterans and appropriated lands of established locals (42 BCE).[10] In a second stage of colonizing, after the Battle of Actium (30 BCE), Octavian parceled out more Philippian land to a cohort of military commanders. He also relocated to Philippi an additional number of Antony's military veterans whom he forced off their lands in Italy, which he then awarded to his veterans (Dio Cassius, *Hist. Rom.* 51.4.4–8). Thereafter prime lands and the civil administration of Philippi were in the hands of the colonizers.[11]

---

6. At times, however, philosophical presuppositions behind methods are incompatible.

7. Perry Anderson, *Lineages of the Absolutist State* (London: NLB, 1974), 31: "Land is a natural monopoly: it cannot be indefinitely extended, only redivided."

8. Commonly noted, e.g., James Leslie Houlden, *Paul's Letters from Prison: Philippians, Colossians, Philemon, and Ephesians* (Philadelphia: Westminster, 1977), 30–31.

9. Peter Oakes, *Philippians: From People to Letter*, SNTSMS 110 (Cambridge: Cambridge University Press, 2001), 19–20.

10. Ibid., 24–25.

11. Kathryn Lomas, "Roman Imperialism and the City in Italy," in *Cultural Iden-*

Assuming that the makeup of the assembly reflected something of the composition of the region, Peter Oakes demonstrates that a sizeable portion had been affected by colonial appropriation of their ancestral lands.[12] Loss of land was not merely a matter of economics; land also held familial, cultural, and religious significance. Loss of land devastated patrimonial and ethnic heritages and challenged the relationship of patron gods to the land. Though the primary Roman colonization occurred three generations before Paul's epistle, the colonized certainly carried the loss of land in their cultural memory. Some also likely suffered bad harvests that resulted in even more loss of land. Such losses compelled them to make practical adjustments in order to subsist, such as working land as tenants, becoming laborers on estates, or as unskilled artisans,[13] hired workers, or servants of the elite.[14]

Whereas in most *provincial* cities indigenous elite collaborators ruled in local affairs, *colonies* were ruled directly by Roman inhabitants.[15] Thus the colonized Philippians experienced discrimination under Romans who understood themselves to be culturally superior and took it as their imperial mandate to superimpose their supposedly advanced civilization upon "inferior" colonized peoples.[16] In spite of representations of Roman justice in statues of *Iustitia* holding the balances of judgment in her hand while blindfolded, the colonized knew that Roman citizens had clear advantages

---

tity in the Roman Empire, ed. Ray Laurence and Joanne Berry (London: Routledge, 1998), 64–78 (64).

12. Oakes develops a model of the Philippian population that accounts for social and economic status, by which he estimates the composition of the congregation (*Philippians*, 17, 44–63).

13. Gerhard Lenski, *Power and Privilege: A Theory of Social Stratification* (Chapel Hill: University of North Carolina Press, 1966), 278. Peasants who lost their land often became unskilled artisans. By contrast skilled artisans were closely allied with dominant powers.

14. On colonization as displacing local access to land, see Marchal, *Politics of Heaven*, 97.

15. Andrew Lintott, *Imperium Romanum: Politics and Administration* (London: Routledge, 1993), 130.

16. Benefactions of the (selective) kind constituted major tools in propagating Roman norms (Lomas, "Roman Imperialism and the City in Italy," 76; David Braund, "*Cohors*: The Governor and His Entourage in the Self-Image of the Roman Republic," in Laurence and Berry, *Cultural Identity*, 10–24 [10–11]).

before Roman magistrates.[17] Moreover, peace often meant coerced compliance under Roman administrators.

Further, the colonized Philippians lived daily under the gaze of urban institutions that propagated Rome's imperialism. Though the theater was a Greek institution built in the fourth century BCE, by the middle of the first century CE, it embodied Augustus's ideology for Roman social order.[18] A forum with Roman monuments, temples, and public buildings constructed under Claudius (41–54) put them in the shadow of Rome's grandeur.[19] In short, the city itself was an institution that intensified Roman domination. The imperial cult as well was hardly confined to Roman colonists. It was superimposed upon and transformed indigenous religions. A coin minted in Philippi under Claudius (virtually contemporary with Philippians) portrays Augustus on a pedestal with a traditional Philippian goddess[20] crowning him as *DIVVS AUG*.[21] Another portrays a Thracian equestrian, with the legend *RPCP* (*Res Publica Coloniae Philippensis*), bearing also the Latin *HEROI AULONITE*, which associates the very foundation of Philippi with an ancient Thracian hero cult; the verso portrays Augustus who is designated *DIVO AUGUSTO*.[22] This syncretism of the imperial cult with local religions meant that like social and political structures, religion also intensified domination over them.

---

17. Peter Garnsey, *Social Status and Legal Privilege in the Roman Empire* (Oxford: Clarendon, 1970).

18. Lomas, "Roman Imperialism and the City in Italy," 72–73; Peter Pilhofer similarly points to the prominence of theatrical performances in Latin (*Philippi I: Die erster christliche Gemeinde Europas*, WUNT 87 [Tübingen: Mohr Siebeck, 1995], 121).

19. Awesome constructions beyond peasants' means were products of power and displayed domination, both inspiring admiration and provoking trepidation (See Scott, *Domination and the Arts of Resistance*, 67). Oakes, *Philippians*, 34.

20. Archaeological evidence documents a variety of female deities at Philippi, including Diana, Isis, Magna Mater (Cybele), and Hecate, who may be candidates for the identity of the goddess on the coin (Holland Hendrix, "Philippi," *ABD* 5.316; Mark Nanos, "Paul's Reversal of Jews Calling Gentiles 'Dogs' [Philippians 3:2]: 1600 Years of an Ideological Tale of Wagging an Exegetical Dog?" *BibInt* 17 [2009]: 448–82 [458]).

21. Images of the coin are available at "Forum Ancient Coins," http://www.forumancientcoins.com.

22. Pilhofer, *Philippi I*, 93–98. An altar in Philippi is inscribed in Greek with Ἥρως Αὐλωνείτης, closely corresponding to the Latin associated with the equestrian on the coin (97 n. 20). Second century evidence that Roman *curatores* served as functionaries in this cult of the Thracian hero Αὐλωνείτης illustrates the syncretism (98–100).

But religious, social, and political dominance was acutely manifested in problems of access of the colonized to resources of the land. Without access to land, other means of subsistence were scarce.[23] From sheer percentages regarding distribution of goods in antiquity, the major portion of the recipients of Paul's letter must have stood at a low level of access to goods.[24] Those recipients of Philippians whose heritage was loss of land and its resources found themselves beholden to or servants of others. Although relative wealth is only one measure of how people fit into the social order, struggles to subsist aligned many members of the assembly with difficulties in city life as people of low standing, especially resonant in terms such as ταπεινόω, ταπεινοφροσύνη, and ταπείνωσις (2:3; 8; 3:21; 4:12).

Vanishing access to goods and a civil administration that privileged colonizers left displaced locals and their descendants with two apparent options: they could accommodate, acquiesce, ratify imperial ideology, and adopt its values and perspectives;[25] or they could resist in confrontational opposition.[26] The first would not only leave a bitter taste but leave them still in tenuous relationships with resources of the land, subservient to elites. Confrontational challenges would be a sure-fire way to be forced into compliance or to become sacrificial victims of the *pax Romana*. Was there an alternative? Could they build a creative community for themselves that would not depend on either acquiescence or confrontational opposition?[27] Could the Philippian assembly follow a way of life defined

---

23. Without land, people are separated from means of subsistence and must resort to labor and service to others higher up on the economic scale. See Robert Brenner, "The Social Basis of Economic Development," in *Analytical Marxism*, ed. John Roemer (Cambridge: Cambridge University Press, 1986), 23–53 (33). Brenner analyzes modern capitalism, but the point holds also for imperial society.

24. Steven Friesen, "Poverty in Pauline Studies: Beyond the New Consensus," *JSNT* 26 (2004): 323–61 (342–43, 347). Oakes, *Philippians*, 17, 44–54, 60–63.

25. On appearances of ratifying dominant ideology without genuine conformity, see Scott, *Domination and the Arts of Resistance*, 33. Moreover, the notion of acquiescence comes from hegemonic ideology (85).

26. W. E. B. Du Bois reflected similarly on the "double life" mindset of African Americans: "Double thoughts, double duties, and double social classes, must give rise to double words and double ideals, and tempt the mind to pretence (*sic*) or to revolt to hypocrisy or to radicalism" (*The Souls of Black Folk* [Oxford: Oxford University Press, 2007], 136).

27. Seldom was colonization an either/or of domination or resistance, but a complex relationship that nevertheless resulted in exploitation (Peter van Dommelen,

not by its relationship to hegemony, a way of life that was neither accommodation to nor confrontational opposition against local manifestations of Roman imperialism?

Roman domination lured the colonized to mimic its hegemony with enticements of a higher civilization and, ultimately, power.[28] Failure to move toward Roman ideology was to remain "uncivilized." But the recipients of Paul's letter revalued their own social and civil status as a creative space in which to form an alternative to hegemony. Persuaded by Paul and his coworkers, they joined together in an innovative assembly oriented toward the God of Israel and an Israelite named Jesus distinguished by his relationship to this God. This meant not merely opposing imperial systems, which would have defined them still by their conflict with Rome.[29] Rather, their marginal community provided a creative opportunity for them to develop their own reality.[30]

Identity and Agency in the Language of Address

The language of the assembly reflected significant features of their creative alternative. The congregation used insider language, part of which expressed the life and experiences of the congregation, such as ἅγιοι and εὐαγγέλιον. To be sure this is Paul's language, and we have no way of knowing that these terms were on the Philippians' tongues. But we can know that they recognized themselves and their roles in this language.

In addition, the letter contained ambiguous language that for outsiders said less than what it meant, but for insiders meant more than what it

---

"Punic Persistence: Colonialism and Cultural Identities in Roman Sardinia," in Laurence and Berry, *Cultural Identity*, 25–48 [33]).

28. Accepting domination with expectation of achieving power is a strong determinative for acquiescence (Scott, *Domination and the Arts of Resistance*, 20, 82).

29. For the problem of defining each by the other, see n. 3 above.

30. See R. S. Sugirtharajah, "Introduction: The Margin as a Site of Creative Revisioning," in *Voices from the Margin: Interpreting the Bible in the Third World*, ed. R. S. Sugirtharajah (Maryknoll, NY: Orbis, 1995), 2; Geoffrey Bennington, "Postal Politics and the Institution of the Nation," in *Nation and Narration*, ed. Homi K. Bhabha (London: Routledge, 1990), 121–37 (121). Max Weber notes special skills and originality among the subdominant (*Sociology of Religion* [Boston: Beacon, 1964], 126). Mikhail Bakhtin, *Speech Genres*, ed. Carol Emerson and Michael Holquist (Austin: University of Texas Press, 1986), 2: "the most intense and productive life of culture takes place on the boundaries."

said.[31] In a prison, Paul's writing (dictation) itself would have raised suspicion and would have been subject to scrutiny from authorities.[32] If he anticipated deliverance from his situation (Phil 1:19), he could hardly have afforded to unsettle his custodians. Likewise an alternative community in Philippi (e.g., "our citizenship is in heaven," Phil 3:20[33]) would have been subject to scrutiny.[34] Thus, a plausible reason for the semi-anonymous epithet γνήσιε σύζυγε (Phil 4:3) was to shield someone's identity against reprisals at the same time that he and the other recipients assuredly recognized who he was.

Belonging

Westerners today are on the wrong track if we superimpose modern individualism onto ancient culture. People in antiquity lived largely in positions that their community assigned to them. They were socialized to

---

31. Scott describes "the arts of resistance" as the discrepancy between public and hidden transcripts (*Domination and the Arts of Resistance*, 5, 62, 130–33). In her contribution to this volume, Angela Standhartinger identifies terms lacking elaboration as potential insider "codes." For N. T. Wright "safety" in 3:1 indicates language that is opaque for outsiders ("Paul's Gospel and Caesar's Empire," in *Paul and Politics: Ekklesia, Israel, Imperium, Interpretation; Essays in Honor of Krister Stendahl*, ed. Richard A. Horsley [Harrisburg, PA: Trinity Press International, 2000], 160–83, 175, 179–81).

32. For Dieter Georgi, sparse allusions to political propaganda in Philippians relative to other Pauline epistles indicates conditions under imprisonment and his "disguised affront," e.g. in declaring Jesus Lord (*Theocracy in Paul's Praxis and Theology* [Minneapolis: Fortress, 1991], 71–72). On prison conditions and scrutiny from custodians see Craig Wansink, *Chained in Christ: The Experience and Rhetoric of Paul's Imprisonments*, JSNTSup 130 (Sheffield: Sheffield Academic, 1996), 33–89. Standhartinger shows how Paul's imprisonment jeopardizes both the sender and receiver of the epistle (see her chapter).

33. "Citizenship in heaven" is an alternative to Roman systems (Pilhofer, *Philippi I*, 116). Alternatives to civil order were also evident in other associations that functioned as substitutes for the city but followed civic models for their functionaries (144). See also Richard A. Horsley, "General Introduction," in *Paul and Empire: Religion and Power in Roman Imperial Society*, ed. Richard A. Horsley (Harrisburg, PA: Trinity Press International, 1997), 1–8 (4, 8); Wright, "Paul's Gospel and Caesar's Empire," 161–62.

34. Rome used an "entire cadre of officials—*delatores*" to collect and report rumors of subversion (Ranajit Guha, *Elementary Aspects of Peasant Insurgency in Colonial India* [Delhi: Oxford, 1983], 251).

know who they were and what roles they should play.[35] Recipients of Paul's letter obviously recognized themselves when they internalized Paul's direct address. Personal names in Philippians are scarce: Epaphroditus, Euodia, Syntyche, Clement, and the semi-anonymous γνήσιε σύζυγε. Two of the five are women, whose prominence likely heightened the sense of belonging of other women in the assembly.[36] Although a few stood out as named, no recipients stood alone, because they belonged to communal networks. Living in a social order means that they were simultaneously embedded in multiple networks. They belonged to families in which they functioned as parents, siblings, and children or to networks of workers with whom they shared roles in crafts, labor, service, and management. They also belonged to the corporate residents of the city, so they knew themselves as belonging to "those who are in Philippi" (Phil 1:1). But because of belonging to an assembly of Christ followers, they also knew who they were as "the ἅγιοι in Christ Jesus."[37] The name itself already signified the assembly's autonomy with respect to outside systems.[38] Further, the recipients addressed as "you" (1:2) understood themselves—"I/we"—as embedded in the assembly.[39] Identity in terms of "I" or "we" meant self-identification as opposed to being identified by others. Because second person pronouns in Greek are not gendered, the address ὑμῖν (Phil 1:2) allowed for responses that included one's gender and also put recipients in the position of speaking for themselves.[40]

Both the syntax of Paul's address and the cultural context in Philippi are clues to how the assembly internalized who they were when addressed.

---

35. On ancient identity as a "reflex" of socialization see Jean-Claude Kaufmann, *L'invention de soi: Une théorie de l'identité* (Paris: Colin, 2004), 67–68.

36. See Kittredge, *Community and Authority*, 104.

37. Tensions in the congregation notwithstanding, Angela Standhartinger rightly calls "in Christ" an indication of solidarity ("Die paulinische Theologie im Spannungsfeld römisch-imperialer Machtpolitik: Eine neue Perspektive auf Paulus, kritisch geprüft anhand des Philipperbriefs," in *Religion, Politik und Gewalt*, ed. Friedrich Schweitzer, Europäischen Kongresses für Theologie 12 [Gütersloh: Gütersloher Verlagshaus, 2005], 364–82 [378]).

38. See Scott, *Domination and the Arts of Resistance*, 65.

39. Paul Ricoeur, *Oneself as Another* (Chicago: University of Chicago Press, 1992), 193.

40. See Monique Wittig, "The Mark of Gender," in *Poetics of Gender*, ed. Nancy K. Miller, Gender and Culture (New York: Columbia University Press, 1986), 63–73 (65–66).

That they were related to each other as the ἅγιοι in Christ Jesus also held for relationships with some singled out as ἐπίσκοποι and διάκονοι (1:1). First, as for the syntax, two attributive articles, one before ἅγιοι and the other before the participle of εἰμί, located both the Philippians and the ἐπίσκοποι and διάκονοι among the ἅγιοι. But the absence of an attributive article before ἐπίσκοποι and διάκονοι indicated that these were not offices but *corporate* functions—"looking out for and serving others."[41]

Second, evidence from the culture makes it plausible that terms such as ἐπίσκοπος originated in the congregation itself. Evidence from inscriptions demonstrates an uncommon phenomenon in the area of Philippi of publically naming functions of people both great and small.[42] Not only reputable or popular functions, such as those associated with military, theatrical, civil, or skilled positions were named, but even the smallest functions in the social hierarchy including those of slaves. Further, other local cultic assemblies named functionaries that have close parallels to titles in Philippians. The local cult of a Thracian hero (Ηρως Αὐλωνείτης) associated with a Thracian myth of origin had overseers named *procuratores* in Latin, closely corresponding to ἐπίσκοποι in Phil 1:1. To extend the evidence beyond ἐπίσκοπος in the address (1:1), Paul's naming of Epaphroditus as an ἀπόστολος and λειτουργός (2:25) not only attributes the titles to the Philippians (ὑμῶν ἀπόστολος καὶ λειτουργός), and the cult of the Almopian goddess in Macedonia also had functionaries with the title ἀπόστολοι.[43] Finally, this is the only use of ἐπίσκοπος in Paul, and its occurrence in the anarthrous plural means that it cannot be the later

---

41. The absence of the article notwithstanding, some interpreters take ἐπίσκοποι and διάκονοι as a later interpolation that named ecclesiastical offices. So Wolfgang Schenk, *Die Philipperbriefe des Paulus: Kommentar* (Stuttgart: Kohlhammer, 1984), 78–82, 334. No textual evidence directly supports a reading without ἐπίσκοποι and διάκονοι. T. C. Skeat, working with measurements of letters, lines, and columns conjectures that the damaged beginning of Philippians in P[46] lacks adequate space for *including* επισκοποις και διακονοις ("Did Paul Write to 'Bishops and Deacons' at Philippi? A Note on Philippians 1:1," *NovT* 37 [1995]: 12–15). An alternative reading of the *lectio continua* combines the preposition σύν with ἐπισκόποις = συνεπισκόποις (to "all the ἁγίοις co-superintendents and deacons"). On functions rather than offices see Martin Dibelius, *An die Thessaloniker I II: An die Philipper*, 3rd ed., HNT 11 (Tübingen: Mohr Siebeck, 1937), 62.

42. Pilhofer, *Philippi I*, 143–44. This is especially true in associations in Philippi that functioned as alternatives to the city (144–46).

43. Pilhofer, *Philippi I*, 145.

monarchic episcopal office.[44] Thus, it is plausible that Paul used *their term* for their functionaries.

Even if terms such as ἅγιοι, ἐπίσκοποι, διάκονοι, ἀπόστολος, and λειτουργός were not on the lips of the Philippians—and this is the crux— the addressees recognized themselves as members of the assembly and their functions under these titles. Belonging to a group and having functions in it are no insignificant phenomena for subaltern people.

Obstacles and Beneficences

The way ancients understood reality and their place in it tended to be stable. Changes in construing reality were rare. But when dramatic experiences collided with the way they construed reality, either because of obstacles or beneficence, change was possible. The recipients of Paul's letter knew something of both.

The nature of the Philippians's suffering mentioned in Phil 1:29 is beyond recovery. Because suffering is parallel to believing in Christ, Paul may have meant that fidelity incurs suffering from opposition in line with his imprisonment. But if specific suffering was in view, in all probability shared knowledge of the context made further explanation redundant. It was also possible that lack of elaboration allowed the language to remain innocuous under conditions of prison surveillance. Yet, Paul's encouragement in Phil 1:27 for the Philippians to live in the city in a way worthy of the good news of Christ and the opponents mentioned in Phil 1:28 imply difficulties with civil life under colonization as indicated above.[45] Whatever their suffering, Paul made it analogous to his imprisonment (Phil 1:30).

Significantly, in a world where voices of subaltern people were disregarded and seldom preserved, the recipients of Paul's letter communicated information about themselves. To begin with, Paul expects to hear from them (Phil 1:27). Granted, he stipulates what he wishes to hear, but in light of interchanges around the sending of Epaphroditus and his illness (Phil 2:25–26), it is also evident that the assembly engaged in communication

---

44. Ibid., 145–46. The local phenomenon of naming functions in all probability accounts for the only use of ἐπίσκοποι in the Pauline epistles. Standhartinger notes (above) that in sending Epaphroditus as the assembly's apostle to Paul in his imprisonment the assembly itself functioned as ἐπίσκοποι and διάκονοι.

45. Oakes, *Philippians*, 77–102, makes the case especially for economic suffering.

about experiences of struggles and concerns. In spite of hegemonic structures in which their stories were discounted, they nevertheless told their stories, and such stories were elements of "the arts of resistance." In particular narratives of struggles were pillars of *identity*, and this identity was not merely *cognitive* but bore fruit in *action*.[46] One action was telling their stories itself. They exercised agency in acting as narrators.

But the assembly also experienced striking beneficence. This was apparent in shared presumptions that underlay "coded" references. The letter presumed a common experience of "partnership in the grace of God" (Phil 1:7). Lack of explanation did not mean that "grace" was an abstract banality. On the contrary, it embodied common memories of concrete experiences. Somewhat similarly, in the context of the recipients' struggles, Paul's reference, without further explanation, to "life in the city that is worthy of the *good news* of Christ" (1:27)[47] likewise presumed shared presumptions of what the good news was.

Agency and Shared Perspectives and Values

Some of Paul's metaphors evoked mutual memories of roles that the Philippians played. Philippians 1:19 contained the shared presumption that praying was such a role. Praying was not separate from "assistance in the spirit of Jesus Christ" with which it was joined. Far from mere platitudes, praying and this spirit alluded to roles the recipients played. Here they were not passively submissive but took initiative to act. So they sent provisions to Paul the prisoner at the hands of their "apostle" (Phil 2:25). Paul also called this a "fragrant odor"[48] and a "sacrifice acceptable and pleasing to God" (Phil 4:18). The metaphors expressed concrete action of the Philippians to aid Paul. "Prayer and the assistance of the spirit of Jesus Christ" (Phil 1:19) were not two things but belonged together under one definite article as actions of the Philippians.

---

46. Adaptation of Ricoeur, *Oneself as Another*, 113, 190–91, and passim. Kaufmann (*Invention de soi*, 17) associates obstacles with narrative qualities of envisioning social roles.

47. Πολιτεύομαι has no other meaning than living in the city. See LSJ. Where one would expect ἀξίως τῆς πόλεως πολιτεύεσθε, 1:27 reads ἀξίως τοῦ εὐαγγελίου πολιτεύεσθε. Εὐαγγελίου occupies the place of the polis (Pilhofer, *Philippi I*, 136–37).

48. Prisons were notoriously malodorous.

Some of Paul's arguments (enthymemes) followed the form of syllogisms but differed from them, because the logic was so commonly accepted that it literally went without saying. Such logic reveals corporate understandings of reality rather than individual opinions. Premises composed of such presuppositions would have been invalid in formal logic, because they were based on cultural presumptions rather than empirical proof—social rather than objective facts.[49] Such logic works only when the writer and reader already share perspectives. What counts here is not the argument but the recognition of common assumptions that Paul and his readers shared about reality. A couple of instances follow.

Although the argument in Phil 1:9–10 is Paul's, it rests on a shared assumption—knowledge and discernment are bases for testing things that matter. A second premise is the corporate consensus that love made knowledge and discernment possible; the conclusion, therefore, was that love enabled testing things that matter. Paul's argument counts on a consensus with the Philippians about the potential of love for enlightenment.[50] Quite probably the assembly also concurred with the presumption that divine power could be manifested in experiences of strength in the midst of weakness. Contrary to many translations, Phil 4:13 made no claim to an ability to "do all things" (NRSV). The argument ran: "With respect to all [circumstances] I am strengthened by the one who empowers me."[51] The shared assumption behind the argument was that God was a source of strength for the weak and oppressed.

Retrieving Imprints of Philippian Initiatives and Actions in Paul's Account

In addition to sharing corporate presumptions, members of the assembly also acted in concert with each other. Their initiatives in narrating their

---

49. See Scott, *Domination and the Arts of Resistance*, 220. Scott uses the distinction between "objective facts" and "social logic" (such as a common belief among farm hands that land should be redistributed to laborers who actually work it) to explain the case of public defiance of domination (214–20).

50. This constituted a love epistemology: love enables knowing.

51. The accusative πάντα in verse 13 reiterates the dative of πᾶς with the preposition ἐν (2x) in verses 11–12. The prepositions ἐν with datives in Phil 4:11–12 function as datives of respect, and they are paralleled by the accusative πάντα in verse 13. Smyth documents an accusative of respect with πάντα (§1603c).

stories not only named their struggles but also identified others as objects of their concern who, thereby, became a part of their history.[52] Then they took initiative to act on their behalf.

(1) Against common assumptions that Euodia and Syntyche were in conflict with each other, the letter presented them as collaborative coworkers struggling together with Paul (Phil 4:2–3).[53] Moreover, they were coworkers alongside Clement, Paul, and other collaborators. Women in the assembly were leaders in its development.

(2) The assembly's support of Paul in Thessalonica left its mark in Paul's version of it (Phil 4:15–16). Frequently interpreters deduce from this that some in the congregation must have accumulated wealth.[54] This need not be the case in that 2 Cor 8:1–4 preserved memories of impressive generosity in the midst of "rock bottom poverty"[55] precisely among assemblies in Macedonia. The Philippians could also have told a narrative about this that focused not on suffering as such but on sharing resources for the sake of others. At least from his perspective, Paul identified their actions as sharing in tribulation (Phil 4:14), an indication of communal aspects of the people's history.

(3) In a close parallel, the assembly sent Epaphroditus to Paul with gifts (Phil 4:18). Ancient prisons were squalid and odorous; prison fare was paltry; and prisoners needed care and supplemental food from friends and family. But this was not without risks. Custodians were generally cruel and often demanded bribes, especially if supporters of prisoners appeared to be prosperous.[56] Such conditions likely provided reasons for Paul to play down both the gifts and his gratitude. In a similar vein, figurations

---

52. Ricoeur, *Oneself as Another*, 113, 190–91.

53. Kittredge interprets the women's relationship as collaborative, but then drives a wedge between them and Paul (*Community and Authority*, 105–8); similarly Marchal (*Politics of Heaven*, 102, 106, 172 n. 53). Markus Bockmuehl erroneously limits φρονεῖν here to a cognitive "attitude" of the women (*The Epistle to the Philippians*, BNTC [Peabody, MA: Hendrickson, 1998], 238). Kittredge points to a behavioral component in φρονεῖν, but her discussion still focuses on "thinking" (106). It means the entire orientation of life.

54. Gerhard Friedrich, *Der Brief an die Philipper*, in *Die kleineren Briefe des Apostles Paulus*, ed. H. W. Beyer et al., 9th ed., NTD 8 (Göttingen: Vandenhoeck & Ruprecht, 1962), 92–93.

55. Hans-Dieter Betz, *2 Corinthians 8 and 9: A Commentary on Two Administrative Letters of the Apostle Paul*, Hermeneia (Philadelphia: Fortress, 1985), 37.

56. Wansink, *Chained in Christ*, 33–89.

of these gifts in religious language of "sweet fragrance," "sacrifice pleasing to God," and "glory in Christ" (Phil 4:18–19) were hardly pious banalities. Rather, the metaphors referred concretely to the gifts that originated at the assembly's initiative.

(4) In a context where communication over distances required the travel of human envoys, the interchanges between the Philippians and Paul were lively. Exchanging news among Christ followers at some distance from each other signaled solidarity. Whatever the distance between Philippi and the place where Paul was, word traveled to Philippi that Paul was in prison. In response, the Philippians sent their ἀπόστολος and λειτουργός, Epaphroditus, to Paul with gifts (Phil 2:25). When Epaphroditus became ill, word traveled to Philippi, and finally news that his suffering sent ripples among the assembly traveled back to Epaphroditus. Philippians itself represented one more journey for communication.[57]

(5) The recipients of the letter also carried out actions in their life in the city, which obviously involved struggles in the imperial context (Phil 1:27). Their way of life in the city implicated not only individual members but the assembly itself. Some interpreters emphasize conflict in Philippians, either internal tensions or a group at odds with Paul. But evidence of solidarity is also strong, if only by virtue of belonging mutually to the ἅγιοι ἐν Χριστῷ Ἰησοῦ[58] but especially struggling together.

The sense of identity that the members had as a congregation, roles that they played, initiatives that they took in sharing and alleviating suffering, and communicating marked them as an assembly of insiders—an alternative to the dominant social order. Paul screened two images of the assembly as an alternative community. One was a beam of light shining in the midst of a crooked and distorted civilization (Phil 2:15). For modern Westerners the language may appear purely pious. But under the political realities of Philippi, it was an image of an alternative community in the midst of the dominant order. The second was the image of citizenship in

---

57. Communication indicates that the "hidden transcript" is a social product (Scott, *Domination and the Arts of Resistance*, 118–19).

58. Mutuality among the subordinate is itself an expression against domination (Scott, *Domination and the Arts of Resistance*, 118–19). Among members of the assembly, unity (e.g. μιᾷ ψυχῇ, 1:27) is revolutionary against imperial systems (Pilhofer, *Philippi I*, 137).

heaven in their *present time* (Phil 3:20).[59] These images envisaged a subaltern assembly that lived out a creative alternative to imperial systems.

Appropriating Paul's Letter in Oral Performances

Philippians was not only Paul's creation but at an early stage also a production of the assembly.[60] The epistle would hardly have survived had it not repeatedly met some of their needs, especially suffering, deprivation, and social marginalization.[61] It owed its existence not only to an author but also to recipients who performed it orally, not once but time and again.[62] These performances were not merely oral recitations featuring one person but an interactive event beyond speaking and hearing in which the entire assembly embodied a drama of their construct of their world.[63]

When the assembly performed the epistle, they dramatized a development from Israel's heritage, which in a context where Roman religion

---

59. Citizenship in heaven over against Roman citizenship is a formidable alternative to a Roman imperialism (Pilhofer, *Philippi I*, 125–32).

60. On the oral character of an emissary's presentation of Paul's letters, see Robert W. Funk, "The Apostolic Parousia: Form and Significance," in *Christian History and Interpretation: Studies Presented to John Knox*, ed. William R. Farmer, C. F. D. Moule, and Richard R. Niebuhr (Cambridge: Cambridge University Press, 1967), 249–68 (261); William G. Doty, *Letters in Primitive Christianity*, GBS (Philadelphia: Fortress, 1973), 45–46.

61. That repetition precedes canonicity is an axiom of canonical criticism (James Sanders, *Canon and Community: A Guide to Canonical Criticism* [Philadelphia: Fortress, 1984], 22). "Oral poetry" is particularly susceptible to repetition. See John Miles Foley, "Indigenous Poems, Colonialist Texts," in *Orality, Literacy, and Colonialism in Antiquity*, ed. Jonathan Draper, SemeiaSt 47 (Atlanta: Society of Biblical Literature, 2004), 9–36 (29). Polycarp, *Phil* 3.2 reminds the Philippians of their "study" and positive use of Paul's letters (*sic*) to them.

62. On oral performance, see David Rhoads, "Performing Events in Early Christianity: New Testament Writings in an Oral Context," in *The Interface of Orality and Writing*, ed. Annette Weissenrieder and Robert R. Coote, WUNT 260 (Tübingen: Mohr Siebeck, 2006), 166–93. In oral performance, composition and reception are mutually interactive (see Foley, "Indigenous Poems, Colonialist Texts," 9–35; what Foley calls a "voiced text" is incomplete without performance [17]; the performance is part of the meaning [31]).

63. David Rhoads, "Performing the Gospel of Mark," in *Body and Bible: Interpreting and Experiencing Biblical Narratives*, ed. Björn Krondorfer (Philadelphia: Trinity Press International, 1992), 107–8. Oral performance is "an experience" (Foley, "Indigenous Poems, Colonialist Texts," 28).

dominated and legitimated the empire, would in itself have been a thinly veiled alternative to living under imperial systems. Initially for gentiles to appeal to God as the father of an Israelite Jesus as well as their father must have appeared alien. Nevertheless, they dramatized adoption into kinship with this God as well as with a circle of siblings, both local and distant. They enacted their part in a movement that was the locus for creative activity for their alternative to the hegemonic social order.

A striking aspect of their performances was reiterating Paul's association of them with Israel's heritage: "We are the circumcision" (Phil 3:3). Against the virtually universal assumption that here the epistle usurped Israelite identity in favor of "Christian" identity separate from Israel, the assembly in Philippi must have dramatized this metonymy as linking them to Israel.[64] Simultaneously, they must have understood Paul's list of Israelite status markers (Phil 3:4–6) as relativizing rather than repudiating them. The dissonance of Paul's identification of himself as "of the tribe of *Benjamin*" rather than the Philippian Roman citizens' identification of themselves as "of the tribe of *Voltinia*" would have reinforced this.[65] Thus, the *positive* value of status markers that were surpassed enhanced all the more the value of knowing Christ.[66]

Each time the assembly performed the epistle, they highlighted another drama within their dramatization. In the middle, the discourse rolled into strophes that in all likelihood were already a part of the oral tradition of the Philippians with high affective value (Phil 2:6–11).[67] These lines were also peppered with elliptic allusions that reinforced their communal life "in Christ Jesus." Their performances dramatized relationships between Jesus, God, and the assembly, rehearsing not only Jesus's life and death but also a construal of his life and death in relation to God. For the

---

64. Nanos, "Paul's Reversal." Horsley appropriately asserts that Paul's gospel did not doom Judaism but the "rulers of this age" ("General Introduction," 6). See also the chapter by Nanos in this volume.

65. Pilhofer, *Philippi I*, 124–27.

66. William S. Campbell, "I Rate All Things as Loss: Paul's Puzzling Accounting System; Judaism as Loss or the Re-evaluation of All Things in Christ?" in *Unity and Diversity in Christ: Interpreting Paul in Context; Collected Essays* (Eugene, OR: Cascade, 2013), 203–23.

67. Kittredge, *Community and Authority*, 75–77. Oral tradition is especially apt for resistance because no author(ity) is accountable for it (Scott, *Domination and the Arts of Resistance*, 161); see also Jonathan Draper, "Orality, Literacy, and Colonialism in Antiquity," in Draper, *Orality, Literacy, and Colonialism in Antiquity*, 1–2.

vast majority of modern interpreters, the panegyric presented Jesus as an example for the Philippians to imitate.[68] But beyond that, performances dramatized the life of the assembly in relation to Jesus and God.

The communal character of their culture would have held the performers back from notions of individuals imitating Jesus. Further, the introduction to the panegyric in Phil 2:1–5 shaped their approach to Phil 2:6–11 along the lines of ancient Greek heritage oriented toward communal caring for one another. Anyone performing Phil 2:1–5 in Greek knew that at no place was an individual in view, with the one anomaly of someone who did not fit the orientation toward others (ἕκαστος, Phil 2:4).[69] The language of the lead-in to the encomium in verse 5 would have virtually required the same sort of corporate perspective: "Have the orientation among yourselves, which is the orientation that you have as those who are in Christ Jesus" (Phil 2:5).[70] Just before performing the panegyric, the assembly reenacted a call to care for one another. Their performances dramatized caring for one another in an alternative community as they were constituted "in the realm of jurisdiction established by … Christ."[71] Moreover, in the structure of the drama, the denouement involved something far beyond possibilities of any imitation. The dilemma of the drama

---

68. Bockmuehl opposes a "doctrinal reading" (being in Christ) with an "ethical reading" (*Epistle to the Philippians*, 122). He misses the metaethical questions of the source and motivation for ethics (but see 151–54). Belonging to the realm of Christ is a source and motivation for ethics beyond an example to imitate. A major part of Bockmuehl's interpretation arises from understanding φρονέω as "thinking." Φρονέω has to do rather with the orientation of life (see n. 69 below).

69. All nominatives are second-person plural, except ἕκαστος in 2:4, and it is used with the plural participle σκοποῦντες. It is a collective singular reiterated in the plural ἕκαστοι five words later. See Smyth, §951. The impact of 2:1–5 hangs on the verb φρονέω ([3x] in verses 2, 5). Translation with English verbal constructs is virtually impossible; conventionally translators resort to noun constructions such as "mind" or "mindset," construing the Greek in cognitive terms. "Right thinking" is an inadequate translation (as in Bockmuehl, *Epistle to the Philippians*, 23, 63, 108–9; in 2:5 he translates "attitude," p. 114). Φρονέω strongly connotes "orientation," mind and body (see the cognate noun φρήν,["midriff," "diaphragm"], inevitably the center of physical orientation), here the orientation of life.

70. Ernst Lohmeyer made a virtually airtight case that the τοῦτο introducing verse 5 refers to the preceding Phil 2:1–4 rather than to what follows: elsewhere in Paul τοῦτο always refers to what precedes (*Kyrios Jesus: Eine Untersuchung zu Phil. 2:5–11*, 2nd ed. [Heidelberg: Winter, 1961], 13).

71. Georgi, *Theocracy in Paul's Praxis and Theology*, 73.

was the seriously sober death of Jesus by crucifixion.[72] And this knot was untied by God's exaltation of the one who was crucified.

Further, this structure drew the Philippians who performed the encomium into a momentous development of Israel's traditions about the suffering of just persons. Fully one-half of the psalms had to do with suffering.[73] Among them and elsewhere in Israel's heritage, there was also a repetitive two-part pattern. The first part lamented persons who suffered, because they were poor, oppressed, or heeded God against injustice. The second part balanced the lament either by rescue or hope and anticipation of divine vindication.[74] When the Philippians performed these lines, they not only repeated the pattern of lament for Jesus as one who was oppressed, because he heeded God, but they also dramatized his vindication not as future but already in the past. What remained for the future in the drama was the incontestable recognition of God's vindication (2:11).

When the assembly performed the encomium, they also dramatized God as an actor in this drama that likewise was in continuity with Israelite traditions. Israel's traditions repeatedly portrayed God as championing the poor and oppressed: strangers; widows and orphans; the downtrodden. When the Philippians joined the assembly, they claimed their place in this tradition either as vanquished victims themselves or as acting with and for the downtrodden.

Although the vast majority of interpreters take the early part of the encomium as referring to Jesus's mythological preexistence, it far more likely alluded to his historical existence. Performances dramatized Jesus's life in history not only as one of the oppressed but one who was oppressed, because he heeded God, and this culminated in his *preeminently histori-*

---

72. "Death on a cross" (Phil 2:8) presents a stark reality whereas hegemony often uses euphemisms; compare "capital punishment" (see Scott, *Domination and the Arts of Resistance*, 53).

73. Karl Kleinknecht, *Der leidende Gerechtfertigte: Die altestamentlich-jüdische Tradition vom 'leidende Gerechte' und ihre Rezeption bei Paulus*, WUNT 2/13 (Tübingen: Mohr Siebeck, 1984), 75.

74. Lothar Ruppert traces the form over a period of a thousand years (*Der leidende Gerechte: Eine motivgeschichtliche Untersuchung zum Alten Testament und zwischentestamentlichen Judentum* [Würzburg: Echter, 1972], e.g. 182). In particular, Ruppert and Kleinknecht (n. 73 above) see strong resemblances between Phil 2:6–11 and Wis 2:12–20; 5:1–7, an original dyptich of an oppressed just person that predated its incorporation in Wisdom of Solomon, which separated it, and the inclusion of which in Wisdom of Solomon transformed it into the voice of the elite.

cal crucifixion. English translations notwithstanding, when the assembly performed the panegyric they could not have understood τὸ εἶναι ἴσα θεῷ (Phil 2:6) to mean Jesus's "equality with God." It meant "being like God."[75] Further, what they dramatized was qualified negatively, namely, Jesus's *refusal* to attempt to be like God. Rather than begin with Christ's preexistence and equality with God, performances of the panegyric dramatized his life in history as his *resistance to* being like God.

Allusions to Jesus's historical existence also dramatized his solidarity with others of low degree.[76] Performances of the encomium portrayed his place in the social order as a slave.[77] This quite probably evoked a double image. On the one hand, "slave" was a venerable figuration of commitment to God, such as Moses "my servant" (Num 12:7–8). Thus, Jesus heeded God to the point of being crucified. But with a cross, slave imagery would have shifted, because with rare exceptions, which were subject to severe criticism, crucifixion was reserved for unruly slaves and rebellious subjects of the empire who were not Roman citizens. Performing the encomium dramatized Jesus's comprehensive way of life that culminated in execution by crucifixion as if he were a slave.

When the assembly performed the end of the encomium, they linked themselves again to Israel's heritage by portraying a God of justice who champions the oppressed. They depicted this in the particular case of God's vindication of Jesus by exalting him—the exaltation of a just person

---

75. Interpreters often facilely assume an English equivalent "equality with God" (e.g., Bockmuehl, *Epistle to the Philippians*, 126, 129, 136). "To be equal with God" requires τὸ εἶναι ἴσος θεῷ. See BDF §434; BDAG, 481; J. Murphy-O'Connor, "Christological Anthropology in Philippians 2:6–11," *RB* 83 (1976): 39.

76. The phrase ἑαυτὸν ἐκένωσεν means "he emptied himself," not, as often assumed, "emptied himself [of something]." The parallel ἐταπείνωσεν ἑαυτόν connotes low status. The circumstantial participial phrase γενόμενος ὑπήκοος specifies that his low status is construed along with heeding God.

77. Sheila Briggs makes an astute analysis of Phil 2:6–11 as following a preconscious assumption of a slave-master social system ("Can an Enslaved God Liberate?" Hermeutical Reflections on Philippians 2:6–11," *Semeia* 47 [1989]: 137–53). She argues that Jesus as a slave obeying God as master reiterates the slave-master system. Marchal has a detailed analysis of patterns of domination and submission with particular emphases on a preconscious assumption of privileged male gender (*Politics of Heaven*, esp. 48–54). This proved true in history when Philippians was usurped in canonical and ecclesiastical debates. On the other hand, for the assembly as vanquished victims, I suggest alternatives in the discussion in the main text. See n. 85 below. The panegyric reflects harshly on imperial systems that crucify Jesus as if he were a slave.

of low degree. Because of Jesus's life and death, which they succinctly dramatized, "*therefore* God highly exalted him" (Phil 2:9).

Performances of the encomium then portrayed a universal significance of this particular case of God's exaltation of Jesus. They dramatized God's designation of Jesus as κύριος with universal implications (Phil 2:9–11). Given their historical status as Roman subjects, this language was hardly about a future inversion of power. The drama acclaimed that the name had been conferred. Thus, performances of this encomium indicted human powers who oppress others—a challenge to the emperor's claim to be the universal κύριος.[78]

Did this also invert imperial domination by a polar reversal of the lowly and exalted? Did performances of Philippians mimic imperial domination by acclaiming Jesus κύριος?[79] If the panegyric expressed resistance to imperial values, it is unlikely that performances endowed Jesus with imperial qualities. Rather, they dramatized Jesus's life of heeding God in terms of solidarity with people of low degree who himself was oppressed by imperial systems to the point of crucifixion. Consequently, performances construed images of both God and Jesus as agents of justice against powers of oppression. The God to be heeded was the champion of those whom hegemonic powers oppressed. And such a God vindicated Jesus against imperial systems that attempted to eliminate him from the social order by crucifying him. The panegyric defined κύριος in terms of Jesus's historical existence and God's vindication of him rather than let the emperor as κύριος define Jesus and God.

This happened in two ways. When the assembly performed the panegyric, they not only acclaimed Jesus Lord, they portrayed him as resisting attempts to be like God. From the time of Augustus designating someone ἴσα θεῷ was limited to the emperor alone (and perhaps his family).[80] The assembly, therefore, first dramatized Jesus's life as the inverse of imperial

---

78. Otfried Hofius, *Der Christushymnus Philipper 2:6–11* (Tübingen: Mohr Siebeck, 1976), 31–34.

79. Marchal suggests that Jesus was "kyriarch" on the basis of the title κύριος and that the panegyric was imperial mimicry, but he envisions the prospect of viewing it as counter-kyriarchal (*Politics of Heaven*, 51, 122).

80. Erik Heen, "Phil 2:6–11 and Resistance to Local Timocratic Rule: *Isa Theo* and the Cult of the Emperor in the East," in *Paul and the Roman Imperial Order*, ed. Richard A. Horsley (Harrisburg, PA: Trinity Press International, 2004), 123–53, esp. 128–34.

pretensions: he did not consider being ἴσα θεῷ something to be grasped. To reiterate, they dramatized his execution under imperial systems as if he were a slave. But in the second place, they also dramatized God's affirmation of Jesus as lord over all, because he resisted attempts to be ἴσα θεῷ. In effect, Jesus's lordship reduced imperial lordship to a vicious carnivalization of what Jesus demonstrated lordship to be.[81]

Further, the improbability of upward social mobility in antiquity implied the improbability of aspirations of the assembly to attain elite status.[82] In fact, people living at subsistence tended to resent accumulating accouterments of luxury that came at the expense of others.[83] They may well have desired the demise of imperial masters and the end of their marginalization, but they also wanted affirmation of their values, equitable access to the resources of the earth, and release from burdens and suffering.[84] Moreover, the panegyric did not end with the exaltation of Jesus but with its purpose: for the glory of a God who is like a parent.

"Glory" was hardly an abstract term. It had a referent. It meant the manifestation of God's power and eminence. Performances of the panegyric dramatized God's power and eminence as the exaltation of one who had the status of a slave and stood with God for justice to the point of death under imperial systems. In the same breath, however, the panegyric ended with a very masculine image of God as "father." To what extent was this patriarchal?[85] Two factors deserve mention. (1) "Father" appeared in the

---

81. Wright calls Caesar's lordship a "blasphemous parody" of Jesus's lordship ("Paul's Gospel and Caesar's Empire," 175, see also 173–74, 183). Parody trivializes; vicious carnivalization vitiates Caesar.

82. Wayne Meeks, *The First Urban Christians: The Social World of the Apostle Paul* (New Haven: Yale University Press, 1983), 13–14, 19–20.

83. Bruce Malina and Jerome Neyrey, "Honor and Shame in Luke-Acts: Pivotal Values of the Mediterranean World," in *The Social World of Luke-Acts: Models for Interpretation*, ed. Jerome Neyrey (Peabody, MA: Hendrickson, 1991), 25–65 (29); Halvor Moxnes, "Patron-Client Relations and the New Community in Luke-Acts," in Neyrey, *Social World of Luke-Acts*, 241–68 (255). Matthias Klinghardt documents that lower classes resisted reclining at meals as manifesting luxury and hautiness (*Gemeinschaftsmahl und Mahlgemeinschaft: Soziologie und Liturgie frühchristlicher Mahlfeiern* [Tübingen: Franke, 1996], 75). So Athenaeus, *Deipn.*, X.428B.

84. G. E. M. de St. Croix, *The Class Struggle in the Ancient Greek World: From the Archaic Age to the Arab Conquest* (Ithaca: Cornell University Press, 1981), 335.

85. Sheila Briggs perceptively notes that Roman patriarchal structures presupposed systems of slave and master that she contends are reproduced in Jesus's obedience to God ("Can an Enslaved God Liberate?" 143–46). Two qualifications deserve

genitive, generally obscured by English translations. Thus, the "father's" glory was still the manifestation of power and eminence in the exaltation of one who lived in solidarity with those of low degree and who heeded God to the point of crucifixion. (2) The image of father was hardly equated with elite patriarchal discourse but reflected communal values of common folk.[86] The image of father understood in the sense of a child's appeal to a parent was contracultural with respect to elite patriarchy.[87]

Finally, the exaltation of Jesus was extraordinarily anti-imperialistic in that it was the vindication of one who was executed as an extreme social deviant in imperial systems. First, performances of the panegyric dramatized this execution as imperial violence. Second, it portrayed this violence as an attempt to eliminate Jesus permanently. By way of contrast, performances of the panegyric dramatized Jesus as lord over against imperial systems, and the assembly participated proleptically in what the panegyric anticipated as the irrefutable recognition of Jesus as lord over against none other than Caesar.[88]

Conclusion

Under the name ἅγιοι, the recipients of Paul's letter understood themselves in a macrocosm of external history as well as in a microcosm of an assembly that identified itself as belonging to a realm of jurisdiction established by Christ. The vast majority of them occupied a place in the social order that was at least one rank removed from the hegemonic Roman ideology, and if their heritage was loss of lands through colonization or misfortune, they suffered economic, ethnic, familial, judicial, cultural, and religious disadvantages. Because few if any in the assembly were Roman citizens, the imperial situation dominated them culturally and politically. Unless they

---

mention: (1) God's paternity did not reproduce Roman patriarchialism but critiqued it. See the discussion that follows in the text and n. 87 below. (2) Jesus's obedience was not abstract submission but was embodied in his way of life against injustice that resulted in his crucifixion as a *rebellious* slave.

86. David G. Horrell, "From ἀδελφοί to οἶκος θεοῦ: Social Transformation in Pauline Christianity," *JBL* 120 (2001): 293–311 (298, 303).

87. E.g., the enthymeme in Luke 11:11 ("If your child asks for a fish, will [you] give a snake instead of a fish?") is built on cultural presumptions on the level of peasant values that critique abusive patriarchy.

88. Imagery of an ultimate future reversal is a negation of domination (see Scott, *Domination and the Arts of Resistance*, 199).

had direct access to the land and its resources, they were beholden to the elite as tenants, laborers, unskilled artisans, or servants in order to subsist. But evidence supports the history of an assembly that took their alienation from hegemony as a condition in which to form an alternative community. The traces of a coherent group by virtue of a specific identity under titles, and their actions with and for one another were already signs of resistance to hegemonic domination. They assembled together, took initiatives to narrate stories of their struggles, to communicate news good and bad with associates near and far, to care for one another, to share perspectives about reality, and to dramatize the possibility, source, and motivation for their life together. In this way they differentiated themselves as an alternative community from imperial systems. A part of their alternative community was their association with Israel's heritage in the form of the particular case of Jesus, all of which was literally foreign to their Roman colony.

Given the context of Roman imperialism, it was likely not the arrival of Paul that instigated difficulties with life in the colony. Nevertheless, when the assembly demonstrated that their alternative way of life involved heeding their vision of God by standing in solidarity against injustice especially for those of low degree, further difficulties with life in the city could hardly have come as a surprise. But there was also a feedback loop. Their experiences of struggles as a community and beneficence within the community enabled them to know who they were and how they fit into a reality that they construed anew.

DETERMINING WHAT IS BEST:
THE CAMPAIGN FOR FAIR FOOD
AND THE NASCENT ASSEMBLY IN PHILIPPI

Noelle Damico and Gerardo Reyes Chavez

Paul was a pivotal, but not the only, leader building an expansive social movement of poor, subjugated peoples in the cities of Greece and Asia Minor.[1] This-first century movement confronted the Roman imperial order with the very different power of God in Christ Jesus. What might considerations and challenges around the beginning and growing of such a movement suggest about how the assembly at Philippi was organized and the way leadership was developed and exercised? To explore these questions, we will reflect on our experiences within a twenty-first-century social movement, the Coalition of Immokalee Workers's Campaign for Fair Food. The Coalition of Immokalee Workers (CIW) is a community-based organization of approximately 5,000 Latino, Mayan Indian, and Haitian immigrants working in agriculture and other low-wage jobs throughout the state of Florida. Their Campaign for Fair Food brings farmworkers harvesting tomatoes in Florida and consumers from across the nation together to advance farmworkers' human rights, eliminate modern slavery, and ensure corporate accountability in the Florida tomato industry. The Fair Food Program through which farmworkers, growers, and major corporate buyers have successfully worked together to ensure dramatic

---

1. "The task before us is to explore the ways in which ordinary people whose lives were determined by the Roman imperial order formed communities and movements that spread and expanded into a significant historical force in late antiquity.... We are striving both to discover and reconstruct significant historical communities and movements and to explain them" (Richard A. Horsley, "Unearthing a People's History," in *Christian Origins*, vol. 1 of *A People's History of Christianity*, ed. Richard A. Horsley [Minneapolis: Fortress, 2005], 1–20 [4]).

human rights advances in the fields is now expanding beyond the Florida tomato industry to other crops and states.

Farmworkers and consumers have successfully pressed fast-food, food service, and supermarket corporations to pay a modest increase to improve wages and to purchase only from Florida tomato growers who uphold human rights standards for workers. As of September 2015, fourteen major corporate buyers (including Walmart, McDonald's, and Aramark) and Florida tomato growers representing over 90 percent of the state's tomato production participate in the CIW's Fair Food Program, which has produced a sea change in the industry—eliminating forced labor and sexual assault in the fields and establishing human rights for farmworkers—has been widely lauded by government and human rights organizations.[2] Winning major corporations to a new way of doing business and bringing about real change in the United States agricultural industry that has been marked by generations of abuse did not happen quickly or randomly. It happened because farmworkers organized themselves and then strategically reached out beyond Immokalee, Florida to consumers to engage the corporate food industry together.

For over a decade, the authors of this paper have worked side-by-side in the Campaign for Fair Food as a farmworker-leader and a national representative of the Presbyterian Church (U.S.A.) and the National Economic and Social Rights Initiative, which have been partners with the CIW throughout the Campaign. We have and continue to strategize and organize for the Campaign, teach in congregations and universities, organize and engage in mass direct action, forge agreements with major corporations, and labor together to implement and monitor reforms the Campaign has won. The Campaign and the implementation of the Fair Food Program are ongoing as more buyers are engaged and as the program expands beyond Florida and to other crops.

In preparing this chapter, we drew from this long and intense effort. Noelle Damico provided context from the People's History Working Group on Philippi to Gerardo Reyes Chavez. Reyes Chavez read Philippians in

---

2. Such recognition includes Robert F. Kennedy Memorial Human Rights Award (2003), Anti-Slavery International Award (2007), United States State Department's Trafficking in Persons "Hero" Award (2010), United Nation's Working Group on Business and Human Rights (2013), Roosevelt Institute's Four Freedoms Award (2013), Clinton Global Citizen Award (2014), and the Presidential Medal for Extraordinary Efforts to Combat Trafficking in Persons (2014).

Spanish translation. We discussed themes in the letter that struck us as important. The ideas simmered as Campaign activity continued to intensify, slavery investigations were pursued, and the Fair Food Program was implemented. We conversed directly and at a distance about these themes. Damico interviewed Reyes Chavez on specific work that CIW has done in slavery investigations and leadership development. She then wrote an outline to which Reyes Chavez gave input. Then she developed a draft that Reyes Chavez critiqued and improved. After receiving feedback from the People's History working group at the Society of Biblical Literature, we further refined our draft.[3]

Our primary work is in the field of human rights. We offer our perspectives as people who believe that biblical scholarship, particularly when done from a people's history perspective, has much to offer to social movements led by poor people, such as the Campaign for Fair Food. Further we believe that our on-the-ground experience can be helpful to scholars seeking to reconstruct "from below" the movement of Jesus loyalists in the first century of the Common Era.

We begin with a sketch of the people in Immokalee and Philippi and the social-economic context of both locales. We turn to Paul's letter to examine its contours and salient characteristics that point toward the context of the Philippian assembly. After discussing how the CIW-organized farmworkers in Immokalee and then the Campaign for Fair Food, we pose questions about how the assembly at Philippi might have gotten started, what influenced its development, what might have attracted people to it, and how it connected with the wider movement. Drawing on our experiences with corporate infiltration, slavery investigations, and the exercise of leadership within Immokalee and the Campaign for Fair Food, we highlight themes in Paul's letter that provide clues to the context and challenges facing the burgeoning assembly at Philippi.

We argue that because oral communication was dominant in antiquity and the context was dangerous, Paul's message was likely oral in delivery and composition as well. Noticing Paul's strategic use of hyperbole, we hypothesize that the Philippian assembly may have had local imperial

---

3. In addition to the text of Philippians and our own experiences, we have drawn from the scholarly work of Peter Oakes, Valerie Abrahamsen, Cynthia Briggs Kittredge, Angela Standhartinger, and Joseph Marchal (most of which are represented in this volume) to illumine the economic, social, and historical background of the assembly and Philippi in its imperial context.

infiltrators (or those with competing loyalties) within it. Finally, we examine Paul's references to leaders within the assembly in light of our own experience with the exercise of collective leadership. We recommend that the imperial/colonial manner in which Paul gives counsel should obscure neither the leadership of the Philippian assembly nor Paul's own understanding of the need to foster and share leadership within the Jesus movement. This chapter gives biblical scholars a window into organizing and building a social movement amid domination and intimidation and is an invitation to further exploration of the topics raised here.

Snapshot: Immokalee and Its People

Despite being separated across millennia, Jesus loyalists in Philippi and farmworkers in Immokalee share some interesting similarities. The populations of the town of Immokalee and the city of Philippi are both comprised of displaced people from different nations, living under domination. The agricultural town of Immokalee is located in southwest Florida about forty minutes due east of Fort Myers. It is the epicenter for fresh (hand-picked), domestic tomato production in the United States.[4] Mexican, Mayan, and Guatemalan small farmers who have lost their family land holdings due to NAFTA and the FTAA have migrated north, joining political refugees from Haiti and local Immokalee-born residents to pick in the tomato fields. Three principal languages are spoken in Immokalee: Spanish, English, and Haitian Creole, as well as dozens of indigenous languages like Mixtec, Kanjobal, Quiche, Tztotzil, and Mam. Most farmworkers have received minimal formal education; many possess only rudimentary reading and writing skills.

Immokalee is more a labor reserve than a town. From September to May each year the town of Immokalee becomes "home" to approximately 17,000 men and women who have come to work in the fields.[5] They have

---

4. "Today, Florida is the nation's largest producer of fresh tomatoes.... Florida produces virtually all the fresh-market, field-grown tomatoes in the US from October through June each year.... Total crop value at the farm level exceeds $619 million" (Florida Tomato Growers Exchange, "Tomato 101," http://www.floridatomatoes.org/wp-content/uploads/2013/01/Tomato_1011.pdf).

5. Immokalee is a Seminole word that means "my home." The CIW estimates that about ten thousand seasonal workers in Immokalee labor in the tomato fields and seven thousand in other crops.

few if any family connections in the United States. They are there to earn as much money as they can to support their families back home. To combat excessive rents of $1,200–2,000 a month for a trailer, they live with ten or twelve other farmworkers who they may not know. The men and women who harvest are day laborers who must seek work each morning. They are paid only for the buckets of tomatoes they pick. If they are not hired or if there is no work because of rain, they earn nothing. The crew leaders who supervise work in the fields are the ones who hire the workers. Until quite recently, these men wielded enormous power and controlled the workforce through insults, racial animus, and sometimes direct violence.

The vast majority of Florida tomato pickers are young men between the ages of sixteen and thirty. Thirty years ago there were more female pickers and farmworker families in the Immokalee region. The shift in the workforce is due to the stagnation of the piece rate. In real terms, per bucket, tomato pickers today actually earn about half of what they earned thirty years ago.[6] This means workers have to pick two and a half times as many buckets as they did in 1978 to earn the minimum wage. Still, about 10 percent of tomato pickers are women, and they have faced the additional challenge of confronting sexual violence and harassment in the fields.

Though farmworkers now have new rights due to the Fair Food Program, for generations Florida tomato pickers earned subpoverty wages, lacked basic labor protections, and, in extreme instances, harvested in conditions of forced labor (modern slavery). Between 1997 and 2012, nine major investigations and federal prosecutions in Florida agriculture freed over twelve hundred workers.[7] While such forced labor is not the norm, it

---

6. The piece rate is still at 45–50 cents per bucket outside the Fair Food Program (Coalition of Immokalee Workers, "Facts and Figures on Florida Farmworkers," http://ciw-online.org/wp-content/uploads/12FactsFigures_2.pdf).

7. United States v. Flores (1997); United States v. Cuello (1999); United States v. Tecum (2001); United States v. Michael Lee (2001); United States v. Ramos (2004); United States v. Ronald Evans (2007); United States v. Navarrete (2008); United States v. Bontemps (2010); United States v. Global Horizons (2010). While new cases continue to be investigated outside the Fair Food Program, within the Program, swift and severe market consequences, including corporate buyers suspending purchases, have eliminated forced labor and other serious abuses such as sexual assault. Tomato growers now have to be proactive in working to prevent these abusive conditions by upholding workers' rights and voice in the workplace lest their contracts with major buyers be suspended or terminated.

occurs along a continuum of abuse that can best be characterized as sweat-shop conditions.[8] These conditions can tip over into slavery, as unscrupulous bosses squeeze a little more profit out of already desperate people by holding them against their will and forcing them, through threats to them or their families or violence, to work for little to nothing. Retail food corporations (fast-food, food service, grocery) have a hand in creating these exploitative conditions through their high-volume, below market-cost purchasing from Florida growers. As an Oxfam America report explains, "Squeezed by the buyers of their produce, growers pass on the costs and risks imposed on them to those on the lowest rung of the supply chain: the farmworkers they employ."[9]

To change these conditions, farmworkers organized themselves into the CIW and then reached out to consumers to build the Campaign for Fair Food. The Campaign led to the development of the Fair Food Program that is now delivering some of the most significant human rights advances that farmworkers in the United States have ever seen, including eliminating forced labor on farms participating in the Fair Food Program.[10]

Snapshot: Philippi and Its People

Philippi was an important colony of the Roman Empire, located in Macedonia, nine miles from the sea port of Neapolis on the Aegean sea and situated on the Via Egnatia, the main trade route between Rome and the East. The Roman colonization of Philippi was brutal, dramatically disrupting the lives and livelihoods of the Greek small farmers on the area's lim-

---

8. Coalition of Immokalee Workers, "Slavery in the Fields and the Food We Eat," http://ciw-online.org/wp-content/uploads/12SlaveryintheFields.pdf.

9. Oxfam America, *Like Machines in the Fields: Workers without Rights in US Agriculture* (Boston: Oxfam America, 2004), 36, http://www.oxfamamerica.org/static/oa3/files/like-machines-in-the-fields.pdf.

10. For a comprehensive description of the dramatic wage increase and unparalleled rights established through the Fair Food Program (FFP), visit http://fairfoodprogram.org. For the FFP's operation and monitoring, as well as for a current list of participating corporations and Florida growers see www.fairfoodstandards.org. The Fair Food Standards Council estimates that the Fair Food Program positively impacts the working and living conditions of nearly 100,000 workers each year (Fair Food Standards Council, "The Coalition of Immokalee Workers Fair Food Program: Bringing Dignity and Justice to Florida's Tomato Fields," http://ciw-online.org/wp-content/uploads/FFP-brochure-Nov-2012.pdf).

ited, fertile land. Roman army veterans were rewarded for their service by being "given" land farmed by Philippian inhabitants, first in 42 BCE after Octavian and Anthony's defeat of Brutus and Cassius and again in 31 BCE after Octavian defeated his former ally, Antony, at Actium. Such displacement did not only happen in Philippi. Antony and Octavian's donation to their veterans of land from eighteen wealthy cities in Italy caused outrage and local rebellion. But the displacement at Philippi was different. As Peter Oakes describes it: "The victors could take whatever they wanted. Unlike Italy, there was no one to document the dispossession of Greek farmers at Philippi."[11] What happened to these displaced Philippian farmers? As Greeks, these former farmers were excluded from both Roman citizenship and Roman patronage.[12] Roman peasant colonists, who were themselves displaced as Roman elites consolidated their land holdings, might have become tenants of the new owner or switched to another town-based occupation such as craftwork. So Philippi is steeped in forced displacement and needful economic migration within the region.

Oakes argues that the Philippian assembly was economically poor, having fewer resources than other Christian communities. He notes how Paul underscores the Macedonian assemblies' "deep poverty" as he works to persuade the Corinthian assembly to contribute to the collection for Jerusalem (2 Cor 8:1–4), that the Philippians' donation to Paul appears to have been quite small (1 Thess 2:9), and that the probable makeup of the Philippian assembly was predominantly non-Roman craftworkers, tenant farmers, and slaves. "The Christian association at Philippi was not part of the town's Latin culture. It existed outside the locus of power, and because this was an embedded economy, this meant that the Christian group was also outside the main locus of economic success."[13] Further, the Philippian assembly was founded by and consisted mainly of women, accentuating the assembly's likely economic poverty as women generally had fewer resources and were financially dependent on men.

---

11. Peter Oakes, "The Economic Situation of the Philippian Christians," 66 in this volume.

12. Elsewhere Oakes suggests that a reasonable social model of the Christian assembly at Philippi would consist of "43 per cent service community, 25 per cent poor, 16 per cent slaves, 15 per cent colonist farmers, 1 per cent elite landowners." See Peter Oakes, *Philippians: From People to Letter*, SNTSMS 110 (Cambridge: Cambridge University Press, 2000), 60.

13. Oakes, "Economic Situation of the Philippian Christians," 69.

Women's participation in Greco-Roman cults was widespread in the region and encompassed women of all social standings, who exerted various kinds of influence depending on their role in the cult. As Valerie Abrahamsen explains, "Slave women and freedwomen (and their male counterparts) were members of religious associations along with upper-strata women and men and thus participated in association activities, even if they did not function as leaders."[14] The Philippian assembly may have been an alternative to these cults, distinctively offering leadership roles to slaves.[15] Still, when we imagine slaves and freed slaves as participants or leaders in the Philippian assembly, Joseph A. Marchal urges us to remember that this slave system is imperially gendered particularly in the ways that dynamics of gender, sexuality, and status are refracted through slave-owning perspectives and the treatment of slaves.[16] Even the few slaves who were able to save up money and purchase their freedom were still bound to their former owners who were now their patrons.[17] As Marchal argues, "attitudes about slave (and other socially subordinate) bodies are conditioned by elite imperial male (or kyriarchal) concerns about the proper use of pleasure, χρῆσις ἀφροδισίων."[18] It was taken for granted that slaves are available for their masters' "use" sexually and that "the treatment of social subordinates like slaves does not 'count' as ethically or socially significant, showing in turn the lesser significance of slaves in general."[19] That the assembly was likely founded and led by Euodia and Syntche thus becomes more remarkable even as we must guard against importing easy notions of equality or freedom into such ancient leadership.

---

14. Valerie Abrahamsen, "Priestesses and Other Female Cult Leaders at Philippi in the Early Christian Era," 51 in this volume.

15. Marchal suggests that Euodia and Syntche may have been slaves or manumitted women. Joseph A. Marchal, *The Politics of Heaven: Women, Gender, and Empire in the Study of Paul*, Paul in Critical Context (Minneapolis: Fortress, 2008), 108.

16. Joseph A. Marchal, "Slaves as Wo/men and Unmen: Reflecting upon Euodia, Syntyche, and Epaphroditus in Philippi," in this volume.

17. See a fuller discussion of manumission and how it functioned to further domination (rather than freedom) and freedpersons' obligations to their former masters in Sheila Briggs, "Paul on Bondage and Freedom in Imperial Roman Society," in *Paul and Politics: Ekklesia, Israel, Imperium, Interpretation; Essays in Honor Krister Stendahl*, ed. Richard A. Horsley (Harrisburg, PA: Trinity Press International, 2000), 110–23.

18. Marchal, "Slaves as Wo/men and Unmen," 156–57.

19. Ibid., 159.

Few in the Philippian assembly would have spoken Latin, the language of the Roman elite.[20] How many would have been able to read Greek is difficult to determine. But if we follow Oakes in his contention that many were from among the poorest nonfarmers, it is reasonable to imagine that these members would have had minimal to no reading and writing skills. The vast majority of people in the Roman Empire were nonliterate, and there was only 10 to 15 percent literacy in cities.[21] Yet, it was from among poor and subjugated persons in this Roman colony of Philippi that a social movement of Jesus followers was born that would challenge the legitimacy and operation of the empire.

Farmworkers in Immokalee and members of the assembly at Philippi both found themselves in a subjugated position relative to powerful interests that determined their lives: the corporate food industry and the Roman Empire. Living over and against such domination is risky business. Building a movement beyond an individual locale to change such circumstances is profoundly difficult. It requires the ability to connect disempowered, poor, nonliterate people across cultures, languages, and geography and unite them in concerted effort, while not getting eviscerated by the forces you are combating or becoming domesticated by powerful entities or individuals that believe accommodation within structures of domination is the best way forward.

Contours, Characteristics, and the Dangerous Context of Paul's Letter to the Philippian Assembly

Following his salutation, Paul insists that his prayer is "to help you to determine what is best, so that on the day of Christ you may be pure and blameless, having produced the harvest of justice that comes through Jesus Christ for the glory and praise of God" (Phil 1:10–11).[22] Reading Philippians from within a contemporary social movement whose members have faced violence, intimidation, and threats, surveillance and attempts at co-

---

20. See, for instance, the discussion in Oakes, "Economic Situation of the Philippian Christians," 69–70.

21. William V. Harris, *Ancient Literacy* (Cambridge: Harvard University Press, 1991). For an extended discussion of orality, see Richard A. Horsley with Jonathan Draper, *Whoever Hears You Hears Me: Prophets, Performance, and Tradition in Q* (Harrisburg, PA: Trinity Press International, 1999).

22. Unless otherwise indicated, all biblical translations follow that of the NRSV.

optation, we believe that the central objective of Paul's letter is to empower the Philippian assembly[23] to determine how to live faithfully amidst opposition and danger.

Paul's message to the assembly in Philippi was composed from jail. He and his message were perceived as a threat by the Roman Empire. In his letters, he describes torture, hunger, nakedness, beatings, and more. He has evidently experienced severe persecution. It is intense suffering.[24] Paul expounds on how his suffering in jail is actually a proclamation of Christ who had been crucified. Indeed, Paul encourages the assembly to stand strong in the face of opposition *and their own suffering* (in Phil 1:28–30). Given the Roman imperial context, *pistis* (in Phil 1:27, 29) must be translated not as "believing in" but as "loyalty to." *Pistis* (in Latin, *fides*) was what Roman rulers demanded of their subjects: loyalty. Paul exhorts the Philippians to pledge their loyalty to Christ, not Rome.

Because we consider Paul to be a primary leader among other leaders within a larger social movement, it is important not only to attend to the circumstances under which Paul composed his message (suffering, from jail) but also to the context of the assembly in Philippi which received his message. In Phil 1:30, Paul likens the suffering of the Philippian assembly to his own. Whatever this suffering may have encompassed, such as "deep poverty," we dare not overlook the fact that Paul is concretely suffering from imprisonment, torture, and malnourishment in the Roman jail from which he composes the message. Assembly members may have been similarly persecuted or be facing persecution for the first time. Epaphroditus, who was sent by the assembly at Philippi to aid Paul, almost died, according to Paul, "risking his life to make up for those services that you could not give me" (Phil 2:30b). Could the guards have suspected Epaphroditus as a coconspirator and tortured or jailed him for information? Whether or not Philippian leaders themselves were facing

---

23. Although we will continue to use the word *assembly* to denote Christ-followers in Philippi, we urge the reader to think of this assembly as scattered in multiple urban and countryside locations rather than in one place in downtown Philippi, which will be discussed later in the chapter.

24. Angela Standhartinger, "Letter from Prison as Hidden Transcript: What It Tells Us about the People at Philippi," in this volume. Significantly, Standhartinger distinguishes how Paul's imprisonment is portrayed in the book of Acts from the historical conditions faced by nonelites within Roman prisons, conditions likely experienced by Paul and perhaps described by him in his letters.

or had done jail time, these are dangerous times for Paul, the leaders in Philippi, and the assembly's emissary.

That Paul communicates from jail with the assembly at Philippi and links the counterimperial pledge of *pistis* to the gospel with standing firm against opponents also suggests that the assembly itself may have already been a "known entity" to specific "opponents" affiliated with Rome, under intimidation, experiencing surveillance, or at further risk. Given Paul's reference to the hostility of Roman officials toward those proclaiming the lordship of Jesus Christ, whose name "is above every name" at which every knee in heaven and on earth should bend (Phil 2:9–11), it is not unreasonable to consider the degree to which local magistrates who were looking to clamp down on dissent and improve their status may have kept tabs on those members of the Jesus movement who were based in assemblies in Philippi, Corinth, Rome, Jerusalem, and elsewhere. Attending to the safety of the Philippian leaders receiving his message would arguably have been of paramount concern to Paul. His own words demonstrate his affection and concern for his friends and coworkers to whom he was writing: Paul addresses the Philippian assembly as "brothers and sisters" (in Phil 1:12; 3:1, 17; 4:1, 8) and his "beloved" (Phil 2:12; 4:1), even combining these descriptions as those "whom I love and long for, my joy and crown" (Phil 4:1).

Further we notice that the letter makes use of hyperbole: the whole imperial guard knows that Paul is imprisoned for Christ (Phil 1:12–13), while Paul regards everything as loss for the value of knowing Christ (Phil 3:7–9). Why use such hyperbole? Is it merely a form of encouraging the assembly? Or could there be an additional purpose? Paul also gives cautionary advice couched within metaphorical language to the assembly, "Beware of the dogs, beware of the evil workers, beware of those who mutilate the flesh!" (Phil 3:2). If Paul is concerned enough to warn the assembly, why not speak more directly about these opponents? What is gained by being opaque? Finally, Paul spends a great deal of the letter discussing particular leaders and coworkers among Jesus followers in Philippi. He empowers leaders to "work out your own salvation with fear and trembling" (Phil 2:12). He exhorts them to "hold fast to the word of life" (Phil 2:16), "be of the same mind" (Phil 3:15), and to "join in imitating me" (Phil 3:17). Paul's use of hyperbole and opaque speech as well as his call to discernment, steadfastness, and unity by assembly leaders comes into better focus when considered against the backdrop of building a social movement "from below" to challenge powerful, dominating forces.

Organizing and Developing a Community and a Movement in Immokalee

We now turn to examine critical aspects of CIW's organizing in Immokalee to explore opportunities, resources, and challenges faced when organizing the assembly in Philippi. Learning from other movements of collective resistance to oppression, the CIW built unity, community, and power
through

- collective, participatory leadership;
- popular education;
- nonviolent action; and
- meeting survival needs and needs of the human spirit.

These four aspects of CIW's organizing reinforce each other and serve as
the foundation for connecting with others beyond Immokalee.[25]

In 1993, a handful of day laborers gathered in a small room in Our
Lady of Guadalupe Catholic Church on South Ninth Street in Immokalee.
Together they discussed the beatings and threats with guns that were commonplace in the fields surrounding Immokalee, the push by growers to
lower wages, and widespread wage theft by crew leaders. But they did not
come empty-handed to that discussion. Those who gathered were indigenous Mexicans from Chiapas, Guatemalans, and Salvadorans who had
fled civil war and attacks on rural organizations and political refugees who
had escaped Haiti after a military coup unseated President Jean Bertrand
Aristide. Some of the Haitians were trained organizers from the Mouvman
Peyizan Papay (MPP), Haiti's largest peasant movement that wrested participatory democracy from the corruption and violence of the regime run
by "Baby Doc" Duvalier and the dreaded Tounton Macoute. These men
and women brought the tools of popular education, collective action, and
survival strategies to bear on what seemed intractable, endemic problems
in their new North American context. The farmworkers' own analysis has
grounded and shaped the CIW's efforts from its earliest days. Founders
of the CIW pooled their knowledge and experience to shape a powerful,

---

25. A full history of CIW's early organizing may be found in Greg Asbed, "¡Gol-
pear a Uno Es Golpear a Todos!" in *Bringing Human Rights Home: A History of Human
Rights in the United States*, ed. Cynthia Soohoo, Catherine Albisa, and Martha Davis
(Santa Barbara, CA: Greenwood, 2008), 3:1–23.

egalitarian model for collective, critical reflection by farmworkers upon their experience in the fields.

The nonhierarchical approach that characterizes organizing from Latin America and the Caribbean is different from traditional community or union organizing in the United States. Such broad-based organizing is fueled by and aims for the full realization of human dignity and rights, rather than incremental, measurable organizing goals. It features popular education and mass nonviolent direct action, rather than, for example, bringing legal cases or lobbying for policy to win a particular goal. Most importantly, the organizers are not professional organizers from the outside, they are farmworkers living and working in the fields while working to change their conditions with their neighbors. CIW leaders understand themselves as *los animadores* (literally, "animators"). This Haitian and Latin American term refers to those who help someone find purpose, joy, and meaning through participation.

Collective Leadership and Leadership Development

The CIW does not have one leader but many leaders. There are twelve farmworker staff members who share decision-making and strategic responsibilities.[26] Key directions are refined and affirmed through the community's participation in weekly and annual meetings. All CIW staff earn the same wage as their counterparts harvesting in the fields, and most of the staff continue to work in the fields during the summer months. New leaders are constantly being developed, and athough they are not staff, they have the opportunity to be trained and lead in organizing efforts, fundraising, and communication. Because of CIW's flat organizational structure, interested farmworkers who have been in town but a few weeks can get involved; they bring their own specific skills and creativity as well. Given the rapid turnover in the farmworker population, such leadership development makes a virtue out of necessity, even as it transfers skills that allow additional sharing of responsibility. Further, the CIW's women's group focuses particularly on women's rights and empowerment. This collective leadership approach of many staff and leaders, combined with constant development of new leaders, not only provides a greater capacity for organizing and

---

26. This number is expanding as the work expands. Currently one third of the staff are women.

educating; it is also tactical, ensuring that the movement can always keep progressing if a given leader cannot continue in his or her role. From its inception, the CIW has always had collective leadership. Such collectivity is not only possible; it is indeed, quite desirable.

Popular Education

From its inception, the CIW paired collective leadership with participatory, critical reflection upon the conditions in the fields through popular education, continually drawing more workers into conversation and interactive analysis of their situation. Using *teatro* (people's theatre), story, song, and political drawings, they stimulate conversation and involve newly arrived workers as well as their more seasoned counterparts. The *teatros*, in particular, recreate situations from farmworkers' experiences in the field and present them in an entertaining way that involves everyone. Through these critical conversations, farmworkers break their isolation and begin to tap their own experiences as a resource for understanding and changing their circumstances.

Nonviolent Direct Action

In 1995, two years after farmworkers began this process of critical reflection, one of the growers decided to pay less than the minimum wage. Even though this was in violation of the law, the grower did not expect the farmworkers to do anything.[27] But the CIW led several thousand workers in a five-day work stoppage, the first in Immokalee's history. They occupied the Pantry Shelf parking lot, the recruitment spot where they would face the barrage of ridicule from crew leaders as they sought work each day. The grower relented, and workers experienced their first sense of collective power. A year later a seventeen-year-old boy who asked for a drink of water while harvesting in the tomato fields was beaten brutally and stumbled into the CIW's office wearing his blood-stained shirt. CIW leaders sat down to talk with the crew leader (and his bodyguards), who basically shrugged. That night over five hundred farmworkers marched to

---

27. For the ineffectiveness of the Department of Labor and Legal Aid in addressing these concerns in an adequate, timely way, see John Bowe, *Nobodies: Modern American Slave Labor and the Dark Side of the New Global Economy* (New York: Random House, 2007), 28–29, 54–56.

the offending crew leader's house, bearing the bloody shirt before them, shouting in Spanish, Mam, and Creole that "an injury to one is an injury to all." The next day not a soul turned up to work for that crew leader. Days turned into weeks, and as word continued to spread of his brutality, the crew leader found that he could no longer recruit workers and ceased operating entirely.

For years workers had not reported abuses such as this beating, not because they were not happening, but because they knew it was likely that nothing would be done and that they would lose their job for complaining. While this could be true in any industry, earning subpoverty wages in an industry where crew leaders and growers held all the power and could easily retaliate intensified their situation. Workers were faced with a choice: do I defend my dignity, or do I choose to put food on the table for my child? But with the coming of the CIW, workers began to risk together what made no sense to risk alone. The consciousness that, if they stood together, they could indeed change the dynamics in the fields, was electrifying and generative.

Then in December of 1997, six farmworkers undertook a hunger strike that went on for a month, in order to draw public attention to human rights abuses in tomato fields. The hunger strike was reported across the nation, and farmworkers ceased the strike at the entreaty of former President Jimmy Carter, who promised growers would come to the table to talk. One grower did and raised wages slightly, but the real victory was that the hunger strikers' sacrifice strengthened the resolve of the farmworker community and for the first time drew the attention of the wider world to the problems they were confronting.

Survival Needs and Needs of the Human Spirit

After the first work stoppage, the CIW rented a small office on Third Street.[28] This office provided a crucial, farmworker-defined space that was essential for the growth of the CIW, and it was the site where workers began gathering weekly for popular education meetings on Wednesday nights and for cultural activities throughout the week. Meanwhile, the CIW was gaining access (sometimes by court order) to labor camps

---

28. CIW reached out to churches and human rights institutions for small grants to enable them to get started. One of the earliest grants came from the PC(USA)'s Self Development of People program.

located far away from town in the fields, meeting with workers who were isolated and conversing in these settings about workers' experience, analysis, and ideas. The office also housed the farmworkers' co-op, an essential project of survival. For years, the grocery store in Immokalee had been price gouging because it was the only game in town. The CIW's co-op changed the terrain. By buying in bulk and selling at cost, the CIW ensured farmworkers and their families could get the lowest possible prices for basic goods from rice to laundry detergent, while simultaneously building a sense of community among people who were otherwise separated by language, culture, and daily competition among themselves as day laborers. Plus the co-op carried a few favorite foods from Latin America (such as *pacaya*, a Guatemalan cactus) that were hard to find anywhere else. The grocery store was forced to lower its prices accordingly in order to compete.[29] Only by working together through the co-op did this change happen, and it benefited everyone.

The CIW's organizing also involves many communal and cultural points of entry. They created the Day of the Worker (a huge street party), projected fun movies onto the side of the community center, established *Radio Conciencia* on its low-power FM radio station (the hub for the best mix of Latin American music as well as human rights programming), and invested in two marimbas so people can make music together. Such "entry point" activities are not lures. There is no "bait and switch." The movies, music, and parties are things that everyone needs: to laugh, to sing, to celebrate, to encounter one another, to be, in short, human. They are as essential as the co-op or a march. And they are part of the movement, because the movement is about the life of the people.

Beyond Immokalee: Building a Movement

The CIW recognized it needed to move beyond direct engagements of growers to take on the corporate buyers that had the power and resources to change conditions in the fields. To do this, it was necessary for farmworkers to link with consumers across the nation whose patronage of these corporations provided a critical point of leverage. The CIW first reached out to students and people of faith as they launched the first initiative in

---

29. Now the co-op is larger and operates like a small grocery store that makes no profit. It sells nonfood items at a small 10 percent profit in order to sell food items and communication items (telephone cards) at cost.

the Campaign for Fair Food: the Taco Bell Boycott in 2001. Students (eighteen to twenty-four years old) were both farmworkers' peers and the target market of Taco Bell (and other fast-food corporations). People of faith had supported the CIW from the time of its earliest work stoppages, hunger strikes, and marches. Farmworkers did deep organizing by crisscrossing the country on Truth Tours, speaking in universities and churches and holding protests with newly empowered allies. This first, pivotal engagement in the Campaign for Fair Food ended successfully in March 2005 when Yum! Brands (Taco Bell's parent company and the largest fast-food company in the world) signed a fair food agreement with CIW.

Even as the CIW grew in numbers and in strength over the years and launched a movement involving hundreds of thousands of consumers nationwide to successfully change conditions in the fields, they stayed focused on organizing their community: Immokalee.[30] This was imperative for remaining accountable to tomato pickers in an industry with rapid turnover. Every season, new men and women would arrive and others would depart. Many who departed went to work in fields in other states and carried their knowledge of rights and organizing as well as a connection to the CIW with them. Indeed, these men and women have subsequently helped identify people in situations of slavery in other states, as well as returned back to their countries of origin with accurate information about conditions in the United States agricultural industry and the ability to guide others who might in turn make this journey for economic survival. Some former CIW leaders have returned to Guatemala and Mexico to buttress burgeoning efforts for rights there.[31]

Early Organizing in Philippi

While Paul may have been a persuasive public preacher, the extent to which the Jesus movement took root, grew, and flourished in diverse settings compels us to challenge the simple "preacher on a street corner" model. We do not think Paul and his coworkers came to Philippi and saw the people there as means to some political/religious end. Rather, we expect

---

30. To give a sense of the scope and public impact of this movement, the CIW's website (http://ciw-online.org) received approximately 3 million hits a month in 2015.

31. Coalition of Immokalee Workers, "Injustice Anywhere: Farmworker Strike in Mexico Underscores Urgent Need for Human Rights Protections on Both Sides of the Border," http://ciw-online.org/blog/2015/04/injustice-anywhere/.

that Paul, who strove "to be all things to all people," invited people to fulfilling life in covenant community. He was not a narrow political activist; he organized in a deep way that understood the needs of the human spirit and body.

We suspect there may have already been various projects of survival afoot among poor displaced communities of people in Philippi. For example, burial societies helped the poorest people ensure a dignified burial. Particularly for anyone who might have lost family relationships (such as widows, orphans, women who had been divorced by their husbands, migrants from other cities who have not yet established themselves in craftwork, or freedpersons whose relationship with their patron has been disrupted), finding a community to which to belong would have been essential for survival. If early assemblies did grow from or begin such efforts, they would have been attractive to the poor people we believe did form the core of these assemblies. Paul and his coworkers may have been building upon communities that had already organized themselves for survival needs and communication. Is this the sort of work in which Euodia and Syntyche might have already been engaged when they met Paul? Groups organized around projects of survival would already have had their own form of leadership, ways of making decisions, apportioning resources, and sharing information. If such groups existed, did any have anti-imperial leanings?

Projects of survival address fundamental material needs through empowerment and collective action. They are projects developed by and sustained by poor communities. Given our experience in how essential projects of survival are if poor communities are to organize to change conditions, we believe such projects would have been at the heart of the early assemblies in Philippi and elsewhere. The collection for the poor saints in Jerusalem (2 Cor 8; Rom 15) itself may be understood as a project of survival that builds relationship and unity across the predominantly poor members of the early assemblies. Paul's discussion of and collection of that offering (Rom 15; 1 Cor 16; 2 Cor 8; and Gal 2) underscores the value and leadership of the poorest members of the burgeoning movement of Christ-followers in Macedonia. While the collection for the poor saints in Jerusalem came from both poor and marginally less poor communities like Corinth, Paul emphasizes that poor people are in the lead of sending financial support to other poor people. Here we have an example of poor Macedonians supporting the poor in Jerusalem. While most commentators focus on connecting Jew and Gentile, it should be noted that this is an instance of poor people sharing with poor people so that everyone survives.[32]

In the Corinthian correspondence, Paul discusses a "fair balance," in other words, reciprocal giving (2 Cor 8:12–14). Some are poor now; you may be poor later. You entrust your survival to one another's care by giving what you can as you can and even beyond what you can. This dislocates certain relatively less poor members of the Corinthian assembly from a potential position of charity or patronage toward others in the movement, as well as undermines a (false) sense of economic security, demanding that they consider that they might also be recipients of financial help in the future. By lifting up the Macedonians as giving from the midst of their "extreme poverty," Paul affirms how the destitute poor understand that reciprocal sharing, which is at the heart of the gospel, is necessary for their survival and the flourishing of the movement and therefore willingly sacrifice to contribute.

Sze-kar Wan has argued that the point of the offering is not "merely economic"—it is about incorporating other subject peoples into the movement as equals.[33] The offering is an example of a project of survival that shifts kinship or identity from a person's particular ethnicity or family or patron or even assembly to the new network of assemblies loyal to Jesus. But it is the monetary sharing itself that constructs the equality, unity, and interdependency necessary for building a movement. Paul and coworkers brought a connection to other communities elsewhere in the eastern Roman Empire who were creating alternative, resistant patterns of life together. Individual assemblies were not alone, therefore, but part of a larger network that provided mutual support for its adherents through offerings, communication, and shared practices.

Paul was a pivotal but not exclusive leader, whose creativity, courage, and commitment catalyzed and connected other leaders within and among the assemblies of the Jesus movement. This happened because of Paul and,

---

32. See also Richard A. Horsley, "1 Corinthians: A Case Study of Paul's Assembly as an Alternative Society," in *Paul and Empire: Religion and Power in Roman Imperial Society*, ed. Richard A. Horsley (Harrisburg, PA: Trinity Press International, 1997), 242–52; Horsley, *Covenant Economics: A Biblical Vision of Justice for All* (Louisville: Westminster John Knox, 2009); and James C. Scott, *The Moral Economy of the Peasant: Rebellion and Subsistence in Southeast Asia* (New Haven: Yale University Press, 1977).

33. Sze-kar Wan, "Collection for the Saints as Anticolonial Act: Implications of Paul's Ethnic Reconstruction," in Horsley, *Paul and Politics*, 191–215 (195).

sometimes, in spite of him as we will see. These other leaders rightfully were thinking and acting out of their own contexts and experiences on an ongoing basis in Rome, Antioch, Corinth, and Philippi. The test of the movement's staying power was its ability to harness analyses, strength, and experience toward a new way of life together in Rome's shadow.

As we consider CIW's own organizing experience, these are some of the questions that interest us about the nascent assembly in Philippi and the growing Jesus movement in the first century.

- What social movements were afoot in the first century among displaced people among non-Jewish *ethne* that may have influenced how the assembly at Philippi and the Jesus movement itself developed?[34]

- If we assumed collective leadership was a part of the Philippian assembly from the very start (Phil 4:2–3), how might that change our understanding of authority within the community and between the community and Paul? We will explore this later in the chapter.

- If there were multiple assemblies spread across Corinth and its suburb, what if we considered the Philippian "assembly" as having multiple locations, where people would gather, similar to the way in which the CIW would go to labor camps to meet with workers who could not physically come to Wednesday meetings in town? This would open the possibility of broader organizing beyond the city that could have included tenant farmers living on the outskirts of town, slaves working in mines and fields, women serving in cults located in the countryside, despite or even because of their distance and isolation from the city. It may have even been easier to organize without observation or interference in these places.[35]

---

34. For a comprehensive study of Jewish movements and direct action at this time, see Horsley, *Jesus and the Spiral of Violence: Popular Jewish Resistance in Roman Palestine* (Minneapolis: Fortress, 1993).

35. Sheila Briggs argues that Paul and contemporary biblical scholars focus "on the urban and upwardly mobile slave" and would not have had contact with these isolated slave populations ("Paul on Bondage and Freedom," 115). However, if we begin thinking of the assembly as having many leaders and perhaps, like Corinth, scattered assemblies throughout the city and surrounding suburbs, this assertion should be revisited by further rhetorical analysis of Paul's letters, as well as by looking for any extant manuscripts or artifacts for signs of this possibility.

- Where were the places where day laborers and others gathered to seek work? Did specific populations of displaced persons live or labor in particular areas? How accessible were these places? What did tenant farming look like? Was the housing clumped together in certain areas or spread out? Was there a section of Philippi where craftworkers lived? These areas seem likely spots for Paul and other coworkers to have organized.

- Philippi was on the Via Egnatia, the main trade route between Rome and the East. What were the migration patterns? Might there have been turnover in the membership of the assembly due to the need to migrate for work, whether slave or free? How could (or did) migration assist and challenge the burgeoning assemblies and the movement as a whole?

- How might organizing have grown out of existing groups in the Philippian countryside such as the Dionysiac mysteries discussed by Abrahamsen?[36] Could some assembly sites have begun as alternatives to such cults?

- How would our interpretation of the Christ hymn change if we imagined it functioning as a political drawing, inviting Philippians (and others) to analyze power relations through singing and reflecting critically together?

- How would thinking about the sharing of a message from Paul or instruction on the Lord's Supper be changed if we conceived of it as more "popular theatre" and less "depository learning" or even "ritual practice"? What kinds of give and take might have taken place as a community acted out these instructions and communications?

- What "divides" were in play within Philippi and within the wider movement?[37] Were there divides of geography, ethnicity, and

---

36. "Priestesses and Other Female Cult Leaders."

37. Davina Lopez, through a "gender-critical reimagination," examines the interconnectivity of status, race, gender, and sexuality in Roman images and challenges us to a complex, material understanding of gentiles as the many conquered *ethne* of Rome. She writes, "What the Gentiles look like, literally and ideologically, is underexplored in New Testament interpretation that reconsiders the Roman Empire as the religious-political context for Paul's life and mission, as well as the overall emergence of earliest Christianity" (Davina C. Lopez, *Apostle to the Conquered: Reimagining Paul's Mission*, Paul in Critical Contexts [Minneapolis: Fortress, 2008], 124). We wonder, what were the particular ethnic barriers or hostilities among the scores of "conquered

social standing, the kinds of divides that the Immokalee actions moved beyond in order to build the Campaign for Fair Food? How might gathering together and taking up the offering have been a step toward building unity across such divides?

Of course, as assemblies, organizations, and movements grow in power and numbers, so do the challenges. We now turn to explore some of the challenges of organizing in a dangerous context and exercising leadership that we believe are salient to understanding the Philippian assembly, its context, and Paul's particular communication we know as the letter to the Philippians.

Infiltration of the Campaign for Fair Food and, perhaps, of the Philippian Assembly

In the Campaign for Fair Food's engagement of corporations, farmworkers with basically no rights, little income, and few protections united with consumers from the student and religious communities to challenge multibillion dollar corporations that are not necessarily inclined either to know or desire to be accountable for human rights violations against farmworkers in their supply chain. Corporations want to protect their brand's image. If they sense their brand's reputation is being tarnished, they will move swiftly to correct that, sometimes going to extraordinary lengths.

In 2008, Burger King hired Diplomatic Tactical Services (DTS) to infiltrate Student Farmworker Alliance (SFA), the national student network that works in partnership with the CIW. DTS employees carry weapons.[38] Burger King's goal in hiring DTS to infiltrate the student group was to gain information about a mass, peaceful protest and, ostensibly, to prevent it from either being carried out or carried out successfully. An employee of DTS posed as a student from a Florida college who was interested in learning more and getting involved in a protest being planned at Burger King's headquarters. She contacted one of the coordinators of SFA, and

---

peoples" themselves that would need to be surmounted in order to effectively organize resistance "from the bottom" among diverse populations?

38. Two employees were wanted on outstanding warrants in a murder case in Miami. A subcontractor was facing murder charges in United States District Court in Miami for his role in allegedly executing four crew members of a charter fishing boat and then dumping their bodies at sea. See Coalition of Immokalee Workers, "Burger King Campaign Comes to an End with Historic Press Conference, Signing Ceremony at U.S. Capitol," http://ciw-online.org/BK_campaign_archive.html.

they began an email exchange. Her email and phone conversations seemed "off" to suspicious student organizers who were able to match her telephone number and name to the owner of DTS. As she was slated to be on a planning call for an upcoming protest, the student organizers informed the other members of the call and decided to throw off the infiltrator and the company by exaggerating anticipated attendance into the thousands to draw out more information from *her*. Meanwhile, they contacted journalist Eric Schlosser, who assembled evidence and wrote an op-ed in the *New York Times* exposing the company's ploy.[39] Burger King is now working as a partner with the CIW, but this example of infiltration is not isolated in the history of the Campaign.

In his letter, Paul refers several times to opponents within the Philippian community (Phil 1:15–18, 3:2) and outside of the assembly (Phil 3:18–19). Some scholars have suggested that these are people whose practice may be critical of or who simply posed alternatives to those of Paul.[40] We would suggest another possibility: there may have been infiltrators (or those with competing loyalties) in the assembly who viewed the assembly's practice as threatening to local Roman rule. It has been our experience that when powerful interests are threatened, they usually fight back. Being able to get inside the opponent's "camp" is a tactical advantage. It gives a window into your opponent's disposition (both mental and material) and analysis (what they think are effective triggers for moving you, how they think you will respond) as well as provides advance notice of engagements, giving time for the adversary to deflect or redirect impact or to try and squash a particular effort or group as a whole. But infiltrated groups who are aware can also gather intelligence from such interlopers.

Paul has been jailed for his activities, which leads us to believe that he and his message were viewed as a threat (or at least as opposed) to Roman control. Would local Roman magistrates in Philippi have worried enough about a fledgling Jesus-following assembly to infiltrate it? Or would people variously attracted or even partially attached to the assembly have a range of views of the empire or local imperial authorities (complacent, complicit, sympathetic, aligned, or even employed)? While it is impossible to answer definitively, we immediately noticed Paul's use of hyperbole, because it is

---

39. Eric Schlosser, "Burger With a Side of Spies," *New York Times*, May 7, 2008, http://www.nytimes.com/2008/05/07/opinion/07schlosser.html?_r=2&oref=slogin.

40. M. Eugene Boring and Fred B. Craddock, *The People's New Testament Commentary* (Louisville: Westminster John Knox, 2009).

one tactic for misdirecting those who represent powerful interests. Paul opens his letter with brash statements calculated to illustrate that he is not in any way intimidated by his opponents and to imply that neither should the Philippian assembly (Phil 1:12–14). Not only is the *whole imperial guard* hearing the gospel, but *most of the brothers and sisters* (presumably within and without of jail) are emboldened. Such an opening salvo in the first person sends a strong message while keeping the focus off the Philippian assembly itself. Through hyperbole, he is deftly irritating any imperially aligned or affiliated hearers who may be within the assembly, while not endangering any of the other Philippian assembly members.

That this blustery pronouncement comes within the first twelve verses is also significant. He may also be warning the Philippian assembly that infiltrators (or those with competing loyalties) may be present, if they do not already suspect as much. How might Paul know things about the Philippian assembly that they themselves do not know? The answer is he may not know specifically what is going on, but he may have strong suspicions based on his experience with other assemblies and because of his personal experience tangling with Rome's power. We should also remember the Philippian assembly sent Epaphroditus to Paul. Epaphroditus may have shared information about dynamics or situations within the assembly that raised Paul's concern. Once you have experienced infiltration, you start to notice the signs. The more varied experiences you have, the more adept you become at picking up the clues. Immediately after this opening salvo, Paul then proceeds to deflate any who are particularly affiliated with or loyal to the empire who think that they can succeed by posing as a member of the assembly but having its demise as their goal. He does not name names, which could be a way of further dismissing his opponents' significance. Rather he insists "What does it matter? Just this, that Christ is proclaimed in every way, whether out of false motives or true; and in that I rejoice" (1:18). The message to Rome: the movement is not crumbling; we will succeed because the power of God cannot be defeated!

Paul's caution for the community to beware of "dogs," "evil workers," and "those who mutilate the flesh" in 3:2 is an intensification of his earlier discussion of opponents. These general terms do not easily translate into comments directed against "Judaizers."[41] These derogatory, yet nonspecific

---

41. See Mark D. Nanos, "Out-Howling the Cynics: Reconceptualizing the Concerns of Paul's Audience from His Polemic in Philippians 3," in this volume.

epithets could help Paul force the hand of Roman or Roman-affiliated collaborators, without naming names that might place the Philippian assembly leaders themselves in jeopardy. Imagine that you are an infiltrator (or one with significant imperial loyalties) in such a situation, and you hear Paul's words first about unnamed opponents and then these epithets in 3:2. You may be the target of these terms, but you cannot be sure; you do not know whether you are exposed or not. Such uncertainty of standing leads inexperienced infiltrators to expose themselves through reaction and can make experienced infiltrators cut their losses and pull out, lest they become unreliable conduits of information. As was clear in the example of infiltration within the SFA, it can be useful to let infiltrators continue to operate while factoring in their presence. Paul may have had similar concerns in mind.

Throughout the letter to the Philippians, Paul and the messenger faced the daunting task of deftly juggling the sharing of instruction and encouragement to the assembly while sending strong messages to any overhearing opponents within the assembly at Philippi.

The Centrality of Oral Communication

Oral communication is central to the CIW's efforts to build community among diverse, dispossessed, immigrant farmworkers and their ability to navigate dangerous situations as they investigate potential cases of slavery. Again, most farmworkers have minimal reading and writing skills, although they may speak multiple languages. Face-to-face conversations, dialogue on *Radio Consciencia*, and *teatros* at the Wednesday night meetings are immediate and flexible as oral communications, promoting responsive dialogue and the participation of those gathered in shaping the message itself. While there is certainly information conveyed, the information is conveyed in a way that asks people to probe their own experience, test and see what is true, and elaborate by sharing their insights, ideas, and experiences. In such settings, communication is not fixed; it is fluid, and in that fluidity lays its power to speak specifically and urgently and to knit people together in common community.

In its work against modern slavery, the CIW is a long-standing partner of the United States Department of Justice and the Federal Bureau of Investigation. One of the roles of the farmworker organization is to undertake preliminary investigations when abuses are suspected. As farmworkers who know the fields and collectively speak multiple languages and come from different cultures, they play the dual role of messenger and investigator, a role that it is difficult if not impossible for law enforcement themselves to play. Aside from issues of language and culture,[42] they have only the most basic idea of the work setting in the fields (manner of work, modes of communication, norms of expected behavior), making it almost impossible for them to successfully navigate and investigate the circumstances. As one can imagine, this is precarious, dangerous work. Forced labor cases in Florida agriculture have been marked by extreme violence, including shootings, pistol whipping, beatings, and rape.

When the CIW is investigating a slavery case, they do not go to the worksite but rather to the trailers where farmworker crews are living. Once there, they assess where the crew leaders and their families live. The place where the CIW chooses to deliver its message is not a public space; it is private, but not confidential. With CIW's slavery investigations, the message is tailored and adjustments are made in the moment depending on their sense of the room, whether there are informants present, and how freely workers are speaking. In one slavery case, CIW investigators timed their visit to coincide with Palm Sunday church services, because the slavers attended church faithfully. They were confident the principal actors would not be present and their cellphones would be turned off, slowing down any potential communication between the guards onsite and the slavers in church. This exploration of CIW's oral communication reminds us to be sensitive to the context in which a message is received and to imagine that context in the fullest way. Where and when (seasons/times) might it have been performed? What are the different ways that the gathered community may have received this message depending on whether they were a slave, a craftsperson, a woman, or an "infiltrator?"

Due to its sensitive themes, it is likely that Paul's message was delivered orally to small groups within domiciles of the assembly members or other more private settings.[43] These would have been somewhat secluded places,

---

42. Finding a Mam-speaking young man who is familiar with indigenous Guatemalan culture, has worked harvesting produce, and is also an Federal Bureau of Investigation agent is a long-shot, for example.

43. See David Rhoads, "Performance Events in Early Christianity: New Testament Writings in an Oral Context," in *The Interface of Orality and Literacy: Speaking, Seeing, Writing in the Shaping of New Genres*, ed. Annette Weissenreider and Robert B. Coote (Tübingen: Mohr Siebeck, 2010), 166–93, for a discussion of the many places performances of the gospels and Paul's letters may have taken place and the impor-

apart from the public and attended by those understood to be Christ loyalists. They were private, but not necessarily confidential spaces. Further, it may have been delivered in different houses to different groups from the assembly that had gathered at different times. Each of these "places" may have had different features, such as proximity to opponent's homes or imperial spaces or particular times of meeting that would have needed to be taken into consideration. An oral message is a flexible message, capable of being adjusted by the messenger according to circumstances that present themselves. Particularly in dangerous or uncertain settings, the messenger performing the message plays an active, critical role in delivering the message in such a way that it does not jeopardize the hearers, provides space for the hearers to respond, and best transmits the distinctive content of the original message. Trust in the messenger *and* the flexibility of the message is paramount. The messenger delivering Paul's words to the Philippian assembly could have adjusted the message depending on who was in the room for any number of reasons (safety, local customs, to respond to a question, or to take into account changes in practice or understanding in the community since the message was sent) so that it communicated most effectively in the presented context.

In the letter, Paul claims that his imprisonment is a proclamation of the gospel (Phil 1:7, 12–26; 3:7–16) and repeatedly refers to his suffering. Such discourse may well serve as credentialing to a community he only knows intermittently, a community that itself may well have faced jail or worse. Further, Paul's discussion of his imprisonment or his own suffering at the hands of opponents may also be used by the messenger to test the room, to see how people respond. Are they fearful? Do they begin to talk about members of the Philippian assembly who are facing harassment or jail? We only have one side of the message—we do not know how the Philippian assembly responded. But one can imagine that with pauses in the delivery of the message came discussion, pushback or, more ominously, absolute silence.[44]

---

tance of imagining the conditions under which such performances would have taken place. Rhoads wonders, "what danger might the Roman prisoner Paul have been inviting for the Philippians when he wrote a contra-imperial letter to a Christian community in this Roman military colony?" (190).

44. An oral message would have allowed leaders who did not read and write (the majority in ancient society, not only the Philippian assembly) the ability to participate fully in receiving and analyzing Paul's message and on equal footing with other lead-

Of course, what we have in hand is a written document which scholarly consensus attributes to Paul. At some point, this message was put into writing by Paul or someone else. But given the principally nonliterate make-up of the Philippian assembly and its potentially dangerous context, we argue that we should interpret this letter first and foremost as an oral message rather than as a manuscript.[45] Antoinette Clark Wire, David Rhoads, and Richard Horsley are among those scholars who have pioneered the recent movement within biblical studies to shift the academy's fundamental paradigm of scripture from that of writing to orality (in composition, performance, reception, and representation). Such a focus on orality opens exciting horizons such as the collective composition of the Gospel of Mark over time in performance that Wire has proposed.[46] Such scholarly work resonates with our experience on the ground both in organizing as well as in the priority of oral communications, particularly in dangerous situations where messages must be dynamically tailored to the audience and context as new information is gleaned.

---

ers in the assembly (if there *were* any who were literate themselves). As the "letter" is performed, we should presume that there were pauses in delivery of the message so that the Philippian assembly leaders could discuss, comment, or object to what Paul was saying. See this discussion of letter reception in Rhoads, "Performance Events in Early Christianity."

45. If the letter began as an oral communication, what prompted someone to write it down? When might this have happened? The letter has specific references to the community that do not seem to be references "for all time," such as Paul discussing sending Timothy and Epaphroditus to Philippi (Phil 2:19, 25), the disagreement between Paul and Euodia and Syntyche or between the women themselves in which Paul asks a "loyal companion" to "help these women" (Phil 4:2–3), and Paul's thanksgiving for resources sent through Epaphroditus (Phil 4:15–20). This seems to us to point toward the letter moving, within the near term, from oral to written medium. We also wondered if there might be some who gained preeminence in the Philippian community (perhaps the "loyal companion" in 4:3) that sought to solidify their own power by writing down what they remembered of Paul's communication. For a discussion of signs of orality within written texts, see Jonathan Draper, "Recovering Oral Performance from Written Text in Q," in Horsley and Draper, *Whoever Hears You Hears Me*, 175–94. Our argument is that we should presume the "letter" is actually an oral communication, at the very least in the message's composition and initial performance(s), because of the lack of literacy in the ancient world and the need to adjust the message in changing or dangerous contexts.

46. Antoinette Clark Wire, *The Case for Mark Composed in Performance*, Biblical Performance Criticism 3 (Eugene, OR: Cascade Books, 2011).

Paul sent this message from jail to the assembly in Philippi. We do not know for certain where Paul was imprisoned, but we do know something about Roman prisons. Given Paul's imprisonment, it is unlikely that the apostle is seated at a desk, quill in hand, scribing his thoughts in the mode of medieval illuminations. While visitors to prison offered food and encouragement, would a helper such as Epaphroditus actually have been able to come into the prison and hand Paul easy means of communication? While it may have been possible (bribing the guards, smuggling papyrus), stakes were high. If Paul was bound or shackled, someone else would have needed to write. Beyond the practical considerations of writing such a letter, any letter composed in prison would need to be secured and handled by a trusted, if not literate, courier. Even given such a courier, a document could be lost or confiscated and never reach its intended audience. If confiscated by prison guards, these guards could, if literate, read the letter or pass it on to superiors for review, placing Paul and Epaphroditus, for example, in further jeopardy. Angela Standhartinger argues that Paul has taken Roman officials' reading into account within the letter, suggesting that this letter is a public transcript that contains within it a hidden transcript, understandable only to the dominated community to which it is addressed.[47] But how "hidden" is the refrain "so that at the name of Jesus every knee should bend, in heaven and on earth and under the earth, and every tongue should confess that Jesus Christ is Lord?" (Phil 2:10–11)

We would like to suggest a far more straightforward alternative. Paul composed and delivered this "letter" orally to a messenger who would have remembered and then recounted this message to others orally.[48] We suggest that the "letter" was an oral message, not only because the communication environment of the Roman Empire was oral and Paul's situation in prison was perilous, but also because the situation of the assembly in Philippi was precarious.

---

47. See Standhartinger, "Letter from Prison as Hidden Transcript." For definition and discussion of public and hidden transcripts, see James C. Scott, *Domination and the Arts of Resistance* (New Haven: Yale University Press, 1990).

48. As Horsley argues, "Since not only the Israelite popular tradition(s) generally but also the great tradition in its cultivation even by scribal teachers was oral, we are led to a major recognition that biblical studies, devoted as it is to the interpretation of sacred texts, has been resisting for some time: that the communication environment of Palestine in particular and Hellenistic Roman antiquity in general was oral" (Horsley and Draper, *Whoever Hears You Hears Me*, 5).

Leadership Models and Challenges

Leadership, Accountability, and Authority within the CIW and the Campaign for Fair Food

As discussed earlier, the CIW's leadership is collective and participatory. CIW leaders who are staff have specific responsibilities for decision-making, strategy, organizing, and involving the farmworker community. At meetings and assemblies, these plans are tested, refined, and initiated. There have not been major disagreements about the commitment and direction of the Campaign as a whole, although there have, of course, been disagreements at times about how to carry out a particular action and where that fits in overall strategy. This lack of conflict is not surprising because of the rigorously participatory way that CIW developed and continues to function. CIW staff, "at large" leaders, and members have great respect for one another's experience and appreciation for their varied skills. As the farmworkers grew the Campaign for Fair Food, involving students, faith communities, unions, human rights organizations, and sustainable food groups, it was especially important to develop leaders who knew the culture, commitments, processes, structures, and resources from within each of these different sectors. For example, the CIW did not give advice on how to bring an overture at a church national assembly or even whether that was the best strategy. They trusted allied religious leaders to *lead*, knowing they shared with CIW a common goal. Yet, while there are many leaders *in* the movement, the farmworkers still remain the leaders *of* the movement, and it is to them that the movement must maintain accountability to ensure real and lasting change on the ground.

Easy affirmations such as "we are all leaders" in contemporary social movements can serve to mask the real power held and exercised by some over others. Too often, multistakeholder initiatives gloss over the real inequalities of power under the banner of inclusion of everyone at the table. In the Campaign for Fair Food, the farmworkers are the primary stakeholders; they are the leaders at the forefront of the movement. This distinction is important for reasons of ethics as well as efficacy. It is farmworkers who have experienced abuses in the fields, not religious leaders, not NGO program coordinators, not student activists. Farmworkers have unique knowledge of the material configuration of how dominating power is exercised on a daily basis in the agricultural fields. They are distinctively placed to determine what needs to change, to develop and test new approaches, and to see whether remedies are actually effective. The result of ensuring such accountability in the movement has led to the creation of the Fair Food Program, the first truly collaborative, sustainable, and comprehensive program among farmworkers, growers, and corporations that has dramatically reshaped the tomato industry, securing and protecting farmworkers' human rights. The advances are possible, because all parties are at the table as equals; the Fair Food Standards Council holds all parties accountable to the Fair Food standards; and the advances are ultimately guaranteed by a conscious, mobilized consumer base.

In the Campaign, allies and farmworkers must work side by side to be successful. But navigating the trajectories of power, position, and assumptions can at times be difficult. There are plenty of people who come to Immokalee with good intentions, who begin as allies but can get so bound up in their way of seeing the world and their need to be the hero or savior or expert that they have the potential to do damage. Nonprofits who believe in and fund the work at times overreach in ways that can eclipse the CIW's priorities and need to be confronted. Religious institutions, whose members often include both farmworkers and CEOs, can at times become nervous about how hard and how fast to push even as they agree on the goals. With CIW's help, however, faith bodies have played a critical role in creating spaces where farmworkers and executives could meet on equal footing. Crusading individuals or groups may want to push for certain objectives that are not priorities for the CIW, viewing farmworkers' demands as insufficient, while lacking an appreciation of the CIW's history of successful organizing to change exploitative circumstances. Other individuals or organizations began supporting the CIW but are not willing to sacrifice their position of influence within corporations or endure suffering as a result of push-back from them. Sometimes this is rectified by further communication. Other times allies walk away or may turn to work against the movement's gains. Of course, some academics that come to study "farmworkers" or "the problems of agricultural labor" or "patterns of domination" can forget that it is the farmworkers and not they who have the expertise in this particular instance. At other times, academics have put their expertise in history, or the Bible, or human rights at the disposal of the movement, broadening the movement's reach and serving as critical sounding boards for the development of key provisions for change.

Through shared conversation and analysis with the CIW, allies work with the CIW to change the system using the power and resources uniquely available to each. We are different people, all working toward the same, common goal. The process of forging relationships of dignity and equality does not happen overnight; it happens over time.

Leadership, Accountability, and Authority in Philippi and the Jesus Movement

Historically, biblical scholarship has not paid much attention to the members of the assemblies to which Paul wrote, other than to assume that Paul chastised them or encouraged them according to how well their theology and practice accorded with Paul's own. Feminist and postcolonial biblical approaches have critiqued such efforts, insisting that we must also pay attention to the communities to which Paul wrote and not simply to Paul.[49] Our experience leads us to affirm Paul as a pivotal but not the only leader within the movement. Paul's authority rests on persuasion, not position. Further, we believe the simple yet compelling fact that this social movement of Jesus followers survived is itself testimony to strong collective leadership in Philippi and beyond.

Paul's salutation is significant: "Paul and Timothy, servants of Christ Jesus, To all the saints in Christ Jesus who are in Philippi, with the bishops and deacons" (Phil 1:1). The "letter" is from Paul *and Timothy*. Although the letter quickly moves into the first person singular by 1:3, it is important that the message is from both men, not simply Paul. Further, note how both Paul and Timothy are situated as leaders who are servants of Christ Jesus. It is Christ Jesus who is the leader of this movement. Paul and Timothy view themselves as ultimately accountable to Christ, just as all other leaders in the movement are accountable to Christ (Phil 2:5). It is a nod not only to the fact that there *are* other leaders in the movement, but presses toward the idea of equality among the all leaders, because they are all accountable to Christ.

However, Paul also employs the imperial language of "subjection." Examining Paul's rhetoric in 1 Corinthians, Cynthia Briggs Kittredge argues that "Paul uses imperial language to both subvert and reinscribe the imperial system."[50] Looking at Paul's rhetoric in the letter to the Philippians through postcolonial and feminist lenses, Marchal contends, "If Paul

---

49. For a comprehensive review and development of feminist and postcolonial approaches, see Marchal, *Politics of Heaven*.

50. Cynthia Briggs Kittredge, "Corinthian Women Prophets and Paul's Argumentation in 1 Corinthians," in Horsley, *Paul and Politics*, 103–9 (104).

is arguing in terms of a divine empire, then it seems that he is positioning himself as a provincial governor or colonial administrator for the divine *imperator*."[51] Paul passionately, even arrogantly, argues that the Philippian assembly should "join in imitating me" (Phil 3:17), corrects the assembly on behavior (Phil 2:3), urges obedience (Phil 2:12), and gives advice (Phil 2:14). But we view this as Paul arguing hard. His standing is not necessarily higher, just different than that of other leaders, and his social standing was not high at all. Paul refers to himself as a "tent maker" and while in Corinth, "because he was of the same trade, he stayed with them (Aquila and Priscilla), and they worked together—by trade they were tentmakers" (Acts 18:3). His travels might have been necessary economic migrations that he used to spread the gospel rather than vice versa. Perhaps Paul was more like one farmworker organizing other farmworkers in Immokalee, one tent maker organizing other tent makers and reaching out. Thus, if Paul *is* of lesser status than once believed (e.g. not a Roman citizen, not literate), would the assembly have heard his use of imperial imagery in the same way?

Still, Paul has stature and influence within the Jesus movement. He is a leader. To some Paul may have been *the* leader who stood *for* the very movement itself. As Paul speaks, perhaps he is not innovating so much as speaking aloud the shared understanding among people conquered by the empire that, until now, has not been spoken. James C. Scott argues that such a leader's role

> in this case is to a large extent scripted in advance offstage by all members of the subordinate group, and the individual who fills that role is that one who somehow—through anger, courage, a sense of responsibility, or indignation—summons the wherewithal to speak on behalf of others to power.[52]

Paul therefore may be a leader not because he has been formally declared such by himself or by the assemblies, but because in his speech, subordinated peoples genuinely recognize themselves; he quite genuinely speaks for them and, we would underscore, is one of them. Yet Paul's letters do not simply rest on his authority; they are part of how he develops his authority

---

51. Marchal, *Politics of Heaven*, 51.
52. Scott, *Domination and the Arts of Resistance*, 222.

as Kittredge reminds us.[53] Others beside Paul may well have functioned as leaders in the way Scott describes in their own assemblies in Philippi, Rome, Corinth, or Galatia.

There are real stakes in how the Philippian assembly lives during dangerous times, and Paul is arguing with all his might. The assembly may see those stakes differently than he. They may end up being moved by Paul's pleas to act differently. He may end up being moved by their response. It may well be that Paul is trying to gain more control and influence over the Philippian assembly. Interestingly, Paul himself may have become aware of the barriers he could be creating. Throughout the letter Paul's imperious advising is tempered by his reference to the Philippian assembly and to others who are a part of the Jesus movement as "brothers and sisters" (Phil 1:14; 3:1, 17; and 4:1). All are children of God, including Paul himself. Further, Paul spends a significant portion of his letter discussing and commending leaders within the Jesus following movement who are based in Philippi.

The Philippian assembly also encouraged Paul in his own leadership (Phil 1:7–8; 2:25). Is Paul the senior leader in the relationship? Not necessarily. Paul has much experience, and his ability to travel has brought him vast and specialized knowledge of other cities, assemblies, and jails across the Roman Empire. That Paul has suffered for the gospel, that he has been tortured, experienced deprivation, and been imprisoned gives him a set of experiences that other leaders may not yet have encountered or about which they are just now encountering and wondering as they consider their own next steps. But local leaders rooted in their own towns also had their own experiences and would likely have had their own priorities in mind when developing the movement within their home area. Some may have even suffered as Paul has suffered. At its core, collective leadership is about harnessing experience and sharing experience. Paul would not have been the "expert" in what works best in Philippi. How could he have been? For that local leaders were required. That they were based in Philippi and not traveling to the corners of the empire does not mean they were lesser than Paul. Rather, they brought knowledge of how the movement was growing in a particular context, a history and understanding of social relationships

---

53. Kittredge, "Corinthian Women Prophets," 104; referencing the work of Wire, Elisabeth Schüssler Fiorenza, Elizabeth Castelli, and other feminist scholars.

(kin, patronage, and other), as well as their own unique experiences as a community trying to live amidst and in resistance to imperial power.

Of course, conflicts and differences of opinion will emerge, personalities will irritate, serious debates about strategy will occur, and compromises will sometimes have to be made. Real movements have all of these factors always going on. Such pushing and pulling was happening either inside the Philippian assembly or between assembly leaders Euodia and Syntyche and Paul. If the disagreement was internal, Paul's exhortation for Euodia and Syntyche to "be of the same mind" (Phil 4:2) can be seen as a practical comment from a leader outside of Philippi (Paul) who brings his perspective of the whole movement. We do not know what the women were struggling about, but they are veteran leaders in the movement. Paul acknowledges their "time in" as well as their unimpeachable standing as coworkers together with him and Clement (Phil 4:2–3). If this is an internal conflict within the assembly, it could be an example of how leadership challenges actually play out on the ground when there is a nonhierarchical, collective approach among the leaders. While Paul calls upon his "loyal companion" to "help" these women leaders, such help need not be understood as censure or as "taking them in hand." The involvement of this loyal companion could indicate a desire that Euodia and Syntyche each be heard fully by one another and perhaps by the whole assembly, so that a collective way forward can be forged. We do not read Paul's calls for "unity" or "being of the same mind" (Phil 1:27; 2:2) as squelching disagreement but as reminding leaders what they already know—if they are going to be successful, they need to get there together. His call for unity should be read against his prayer for the Philippian assembly to "determine what is best" (Phil 1:10).

Alternatively, several feminist scholars have argued that Euodia and Syntyche were not in conflict with each other; they were in conflict with Paul.[54] The women had been working together for a long time with Paul

---

54. See, for example, the work of Mary Rose D'Angelo, "Women Partners in the New Testament," *JFSR* 6 (1990): 65–86; D'Angelo, "Euodia," in *Women in Scripture: A Dictionary of Named and Unnamed Women in the Hebrew Bible, the Apocryphal/Deuterocanonical Books, and the New Testament*, ed. Carol Meyers, Toni Craven, and Ross S. Kraemer (Grand Rapids: Eerdmans, 2000), 79; D'Angelo, "Syntyche," in Meyers, Craven, and Kraemer, *Women in Scripture*, 159; Cynthia Briggs Kittredge, *Community and Authority: The Rhetoric of Obedience in the Pauline Tradition*, HTS 45 (Harrisburg, PA: Trinity Press International, 1998), 90–94, 105–10; Joseph A. Marchal,

or as an independent missionary pair. Kittredge specifically speaks about their possible leadership role among the *diakonoi* and *episkopoi* greeted at the letter's opening.[55] Perhaps Euodia and Syntyche agreed with Paul but faced constraints due to their status as enslaved or manumitted women.[56] Or perhaps they disagreed with Paul on strategy due to what they knew of Philippi and the particular exigencies of that context. How might Paul's call for unity then be received?

In some ways, we are stuck, because we do not know what happened next. While Paul's writings remain, we have not discovered correspondence from the various assemblies to Paul. So it is doubly important we remember that there *is* two-way communication going on: from Philippi to Paul and from Paul to Philippi (the latter, in this "letter"). The Philippian leaders may have first heard of Jesus from Paul. But it was they, not Paul, who had the responsibility for seeding and cultivating the Jesus movement in Philippi. In doing so, they would have had important information to share with him. They may have wanted more accountability from Paul; after all they had supported him financially as well (Phil 4:15–20)! Indeed, the Philippian assembly sent Epaphroditus as their messenger/apostle (Phil 2:25) to Paul. Scholars have noted that Epaphroditus ministered to Paul on behalf of the Philippian assembly, but as a messenger he may well have been carrying a *message* (oral most likely) to Paul *from* Philippi. Paul then discusses "sending" Epaphroditus back to Philippi (Phil 2:25). While we do not know the content of the message, in Paul's view, Epaphroditus risked his life in this mission to communicate with and aid Paul (Phil 2:30). Epaphroditus may even have ended up imprisoned himself with Paul—the text is not clear. He became gravely ill (Phil 2:27), whether that was from time in prison or something else remains a mystery. But such two-way communication between the assembly and Paul points toward the assembly's strength. Like Paul, they have things to communicate—analyses, news, perspectives—as well as material resources to share.

Hierarchy, Unity, and Imitation: A Feminist Rhetorical Analysis of Power Dynamics in Paul's Letter to the Philippians, Academia Biblica 24 (Atlanta: Society of Biblical Literature, 2006); and Marchal, *Politics of Heaven*.

55. Kittredge, *Community and Authority*, 101–10.

56. See Marchal, *Politics of Heaven*, 108.

Conclusion

Paul opens his letter by lauding the Philippian assembly saying, "all of you share in God's grace with me, both in my imprisonment and in the defense and confirmation of the gospel" (Phil 1:7). He is buoyed by their support even as he offers his own support to them. His prayer is that they be able to "determine what is best" at this juncture in their life together (Phil 1:10). And that was an act of faith (or loyalty, *pistis*). It was also an act of faith for farmworkers to pursue the dignity and rights they knew should be theirs and to believe they could use collective power to bring about these changes. They imagined the goal, but they still had to break through society's seeming indifference to build relationships and to construct a new model of worker-driven corporate responsibility that had never existed, let alone been tested. "In this sense, I feel a kinship with Paul and the assembly in Philippi," said Reyes Chavez, "because, I can imagine, like us, they knew the necessity of the goal but were not sure how they would actually get there or precisely what it would look like in practice; there was no blueprint. Loyalty to one another and to that vision of a new day is all you have. But, in the end, it is enough."

By reading Philippians against the backdrop of a contemporary social movement, we hope that we have provided a window into some concrete considerations of movement building as well as stimulated biblical scholars to further explore a range of ideas: the possibility of infiltrators (or those with competing loyalties) in the assembly at Philippi, the oral primacy and flexibility of Paul's message, and the significance and benefit of having many leaders in building and growing the social movement of Christ loyalists in the first century.

Response: A Component Community of an Alternative Society

Richard A. Horsley

A decade ago some historians of Christianity persuaded a few of us in New Testament studies to explore a "people's history" approach to the early Jesus movements and Christ loyalists. We recognized right away that those who formed the earliest communities and movements (that later developed into what came to be known as Christianity) were subordinated and largely impoverished people. Our exploration of "history from below" entailed a departure from standard procedure in New Testament studies as well as in the related fields of classics and ancient history. In such fields, research has usually been conducted by the modern cultural elite, has focused mainly on the ancient political-economic elite, and has drawn on sources from the ancient cultural elite. "History from below," however, seems particularly appropriate for the movement(s) that emerged and expanded in response to the events surrounding the mission of Jesus of Nazareth, which were comprised almost exclusively of ordinary people, such as peasants and poor urbanites, including slaves.[1]

Our collective attempt to discern and understand the ordinary people involved in the Jesus movements and communities of Christ loyalists also involved a sharp break with some of the standard assumptions and concepts in New Testament studies that appeared to block discernment and understanding of the sources for and the dynamics of those movements. In a field deeply rooted in Protestant theology, our mentors taught us that the mission of the apostle Paul "among the gentiles" catalyzed the origin of a more universal and spiritual religion of Christianity that broke

---

1. See the provisional attempt to outline such an approach in Richard A. Horsley, "Unearthing a People's History," in *Christian Origins*, vol. 1 of *A People's History of Christianity*, ed. Richard A. Horsley (Minneapolis: Fortress, 2005), 1–20.

away from the more parochial religion of Judaism. They read Paul's letters primarily as statements of nascent Christian theology in the context
of a synthesized and largely elite Hellenistic culture, even after ostensibly recognizing that they were ad hoc letters to particular communities.
Recent work on Paul, however, had recognized that the Roman Empire
was the determining context of all subordinated peoples, whether Judeans,
Samaritans, and Galileans in Palestine, diaspora Jewish communities, or
the people(s) among whom assemblies loyal to Jesus Christ were formed.[2]
Historians of the Roman Empire, moreover, were pointing out that each
city and province of the Empire was distinctive in its history, mix of peoples, and culture(s).[3]

In discussions in the Society of Biblical Literature Paul and Politics Group, we realized that since Paul's letters were ad hoc arguments
addressed to particular communities, it was only appropriate to investigate each assembly in its distinctive political and cultural context. The
"working groups" we formed for this purpose recognized that collaborative investigation would involve bringing together whatever information might be available on the ordinary people of particular cities, such
as Philippi, and whatever clues might be gleaned from a close (rhetorical) critical reading of Paul's arguments to a particular assembly. In the
working groups, we deliberately focused our approach as investigations
of "people's history." The working group on the assembly (of Christ loyalists) in Philippi, under the energetic leadership of Joseph A. Marchal,
was purposely formed of colleagues with a variety of (overlapping) perspective and expertise, such as rhetorical criticism, archaeology, sociology, political analysis, feminist criticism, and direct engagement in labor
organizing. Each contribution to our annual working sessions brought

---

2. See Neil Elliott, *Liberating Paul: The Justice of God and the Politics of the Apostle*
(Maryknoll, NY: Orbis, 1994); Richard A. Horsley, ed., *Paul and Empire: Religion and
Power in Roman Imperial Society* (Harrisburg, PA: Trinity Press International, 1997);
Horsley, with Neil Asher Silberman, *The Message and the Kingdom: How Jesus and
Paul Ignited a Revolution and Transformed the Ancient World* (Minneapolis: Fortress,
2002); and, from different angles, Davina C. Lopez, *Apostle to the Conquered: Rei-
magining Paul's Mission*, Paul in Critical Contexts (Minneapolis: Fortress, 2008); and
Joseph A. Marchal, *The Politics of Heaven: Women, Gender, and Empire in the Study of
Paul*, Paul in Critical Contexts (Minneapolis: Fortress, 2008).

3. See, for example, Susan E. Alcock, *Graecia Capta: Landscapes of Roman Greece*
(Cambridge: Cambridge University Press, 1993); and Stephen Mitchell, *Anatolia:
Land, Men, and Gods in Asia Minor*, 2 vols. (Oxford: Clarendon, 1993).

important information and critical perspective to our collective inquiry into the people who formed the assembly in Philippi with whom Paul communicated in his letter.

The essays by Robert L. Brawley, Mark D. Nanos, and Noelle Damico and Gerardo Reyes Chavez all bring significant insights to particular aspects of the assembly of Christ loyalists in Philippi. Having engaged in intensive discussions of earlier drafts of these articles in our working sessions, I will be able to focus only on some of the fundamental issues they raise in this brief response.

Determinative for the situation of people living in Philippi in mid-first century CE would have been the establishment of two successive colonies of Roman military veterans on the site roughly eighty years before. The Philippians were pushed off their land, which was parceled out to the Roman veterans.[4] It also entailed the displacement of the previous Greek-speaking Philippian culture by Roman civic institutions and Latin language and culture, as mentioned by Brawley. Concepts typical of modern American sociology, such as "loss of status" or "social deviance," however, are hardly adequate to indicate the subordination to which the Philippians were subjected. Although by no means a direct analogy, the more seriously displaced and exploited people in Immokalee, Florida, in the account by Damico and Reyes Chavez, provide a contemporary comparison that enables us to appreciate the displacement and domination that the ancient Philippians would have experienced.

It is thus tempting for us to surmise that the gospel of Christ that Paul and his coworkers had communicated among the Philippians and around which a community had coalesced was particularly compelling for such economically and culturally displaced people. Once we recognize that Roman imperial conquest and rule were the context of the mission of Jesus in Galilee and his crucifixion by the Romans, (ostensibly) as a leader of insurrection in Jerusalem, it seems clear that the gospel of Christ was a story rooted in the history of a people subjected by the Romans. As another subject people, those who formed the assembly among the Philippians may well have responded readily to the gospel of Christ. Judging from the other letters of Paul, the gospel of Christ focused on the three

---

4. See the discussion by Peter Oakes, "The Economic Situation of the Philippian Christians," in this volume; and Joseph A. Marchal, *Hierarchy, Unity, and Imitation: A Feminist Rhetorical Analysis of Power Dynamics in Paul's Letter to the Philippians*, Academia Biblica 24 (Atlanta: Society of Biblical Literature, 2006), 53–62, 99–112.

"eschatological" events of the crucifixion, resurrection, and parousia, was about the fulfillment of history, which had been running through the people of Israel, not through Rome. Through the crucifixion and resurrection, the fulfillment of God's promise made to Abraham, the ancestor of Israel, was now available to all peoples (see Paul's argument in Gal 3–5). Those who had responded and formed "assemblies" of Christ loyalists were now awaiting the final "coming" of their Lord in "the day of Christ." That this is the gospel that Paul and coworkers had presented and around which the Philippians had formed a community is evident in several steps in Paul's argument (e.g., Phil 1:3–11; 3:17–21).

It is impossible to discern from Paul's argument(s) to the Philippians, however, the extent to which they had come to identify themselves as "the saints" of Christ and the fulfillment of Israelite tradition, so that they were eagerly awaiting the imminent "day of Christ." In the formation of his argument, Paul evidently assumes that his focus on the current struggle that the Philippians, like himself, were undergoing would have some resonance among them. In this regard a reading of the letter "with the grain" (as Brawley does) rather than "against the grain" seems indicated.

Of course, it is unlikely that in the course of their "resocialization" under Paul's and his coworkers' teaching they would have come to spout "Pauline" language in the same way he did. As he formulates his argument from prison, he dramatically plays up his own heroic identification with Christ's suffering (he may well have been experiencing a genuine anticipation of possible martyrdom for the gospel; 1:12–14, 19–26; 2:17). It seems clear that the Philippians are experiencing opposition of some sort from others in Philippi (1:28; that Paul frames as analogous to his own suffering). This would appear to be a main reason for his letter, to encourage them to conduct their community life in the midst of the hostile wider civic (imperial) order in a way that was "worthy of the gospel of Christ," "standing firm in one spirit," in solidarity in their loyalty to the gospel, whatever suffering it might entail (1:27–30). His citation and application of the "Christ hymn" appear to reinforce the same exhortation to remaining in solidarity, in "one mind," in the midst of a hostile situation (2:1–18). The image of the Philippians' own vindication as potential martyrs for their solidarity with Christ, as they would "shine like stars in the world" (1:15, cf. his own "depart and be with Christ," 1:23), could be one indication that the gospel in which they are thus to persist (amidst a "crooked and perverse generation") is (understood as) the fulfillment of history running through Israel. Paul must have already taught such imagery to the Philippians, imagery that we know mainly from earlier Judean scribes' anticipation of their martyrdom for remaining faithful to Israelite tradition, especially the promises and demands of God (Dan 12:3; 1 En. 104:2, 6).

It is difficult to tell from Paul's arguments and imagery (Phil 1:27–30; 2:14–18) whether those who were opposing the Philippian assembly were simply keeping them under surveillance or directly harassing them in more invasive ways. The Roman imperial order was maintained mainly through local officials and self-appointed local guardians of civic discipline. In the crowded circumstances of an ancient city, the very formation of a new community may have appeared threatening—all the more so if some members were the servants, slaves, or otherwise in some close power relationship to social "superiors." The account of organizing the Immokalee workers by Damico and Reyes Chaves again provides a helpful comparison for what may have been happening in ancient Philippi. The workers' organizing against exploitative circumstances was seriously threatening to the growers, who already had a repressive system in place. The organizers thus had to use extreme caution not to bring violent reprisals down on themselves and the workers. The local power-holders and their networks even attempted to infiltrate the organization. This enables us to reckon with the potential for similar measures of surveillance, intimidation, or conflict with those who opposed the Christ loyalists in ancient Philippi.

To imagine that the assembly of Philippians being "of one mind" was "revolutionary" against the Roman imperial system is surely hyperbole. But Brawley's concept of "alternative society" seems apt. The end of the argument in Phil 3:2–4:1 makes this clear after the intimations in "sharing in the gospel" and "standing firm in one mind." "Our (alternative) polity/ politics are in heaven, from where we await a(n) (alternative) Savior, the Lord Jesus Christ" (3:20). The "Lord" and "Savior" in the empire was, of course, Caesar, whose presence pervaded local civic space in the various honors to the emperor, whose lordship was now being challenged by the new assemblies loyalty to an alternative "Lord." We do not know whether the Philippians were already familiar with just such language (such as πολιτεύεσθε) from the teaching of Paul and coworkers. Presumably Paul assumed that they would understand this bold assertion. It certainly resembles his assertions in 1 Corinthians and Romans of Jesus Christ as the (alternative) Lord and fits the community living by anticipation of the future fulfillment at "the day of Christ" earlier in the letter. Brawley's discussion parallels what I argued some years ago on the basis of statements in 1 Corinthians: that Paul (at least) understood the assemblies as local communities in an (interpeople) alternative social order living under, but separate from the Roman imperial order.[5] The orientation is to the imminent future fulfillment. But the community is to be already conducting its affairs (πολιτεύεσθε) in anticipation of its polity (πολίτευμα) that is already established in (heaven in anticipation of) God's governance of historical life. We can hardly be sure about the extent to which the Philippians shared this understanding. That the community had supported Paul's mission earlier in Thessalonica (4:16) and were more recently supporting him in prison (4:18), however, suggests that they did in some way.

The recognition that the Roman imperial order was the determinative context of the mission of Paul and his coworkers and that the communities that came together formed an alternative society (however inauspicious at the time) offers a historically credible alternative to the old Christian theological scheme of Paul (and "justification through faith") in opposition to "Judaism" (and "works righteousness"). In a series of recent articles, Nanos has effectively "laid to rest" the previously dominant reading of Phil 3:2–4:1 and other key texts in terms of Paul's battle with "Judaizers." In Paul's polemic to the Philippians, Nanos argues, "the dogs, workers of evil, and mutilation of the flesh" are references to Cynic philosophers.[6]

Nanos suggests a further implication for Paul's exhortation to the Philippians. Insofar as the primary opposition in Paul's gospel was between Christ and Roman imperial rule (not Christ and "Judaism") and the nascent assemblies of Christ were the fulfillment of the history of Israel (not "Christianity" versus "Judaism"), he suggests that when Paul exhorts the Philippians to stand firm in opposition to the dominant culture, he is urging them to live according to Jewish traditions. This is the clear implication of the statement near the beginning of the argument in 3:2–4:1: "For

---

5. See Richard A. Horsley, *1 Corinthians*, ANTC (Nashville: Abingdon, 1998); Horsley, "Rhetoric and Empire—and 1 Corinthians," in *Paul and Politics: Ekklesia, Israel, Imperium, Interpretation; Essays in Honor of Krister Stendahl*, ed. Richard A. Horsley (Harrisburg, PA: Trinity Press International, 2000), 72–102.

6. Mark D. Nanos, "Paul's Reversal of Jews Calling Gentiles 'Dogs' (Philippians 3:2): 1600 Years of an Ideological Tale Wagging an Exegetical Dog?" *BibInt* 17 (2009): 448–82; Nanos, "Paul's Polemic in Philippians 3 as Jewish-Subgroup Vilification of Local Non-Jewish Cultic and Philosophical Alternatives," *Journal for the Study of Paul and His Letters* 3 (2013): 47–92; and his chapter in this volume.

it is we [that is, the assembly in Philippi, including himself and coworkers, and the other assemblies] who are the circumcision, who worship in the Spirit of God and boast in Christ Jesus" (3:3). It is difficult to articulate this, since we lack a modern concept for how Paul seems to understand the assemblies as the extra-Israelite peoples now included in the fulfillment of the history of Israel as the result of the Christ events. Moreover, even though he was clear that observance of the law/torah was not the condition of participation in this fulfillment for extra-Israelite peoples, he and his coworkers taught the assemblies the traditions of Israel and then he appealed to them in his later letters (e.g., of exodus and wilderness tradition, 1 Cor 8–10). Even though it was not necessary for the Galatians and other peoples to become physically circumcised (Gal 3–5), the maintenance of justice in Paul's exhortations evidently meant basically the maintenance of torah, broadly speaking.

The term *Judaism* may not be the appropriate term for this, insofar as what we moderns think of as Judaism (a religious-ethnic group/people, heavily influenced by the rabbis of late antiquity) had not yet emerged. We do not know from Paul's arguments whether or the extent to which the Philippians (or other assemblies) had begun to "identify" themselves as Israelites (would they themselves have declared "*we are* the circumcision"?). In responding to the gospel of Christ and forming a local assembly in the wider movement of Christ loyalists, however, the Philippians were identifying in a significant way with the tradition (history) of Israel, another people subject to Roman imperial rule.

Directly or indirectly, by implication, all three of the articles raise the question of the social form assumed by the community of Christ loyalists in Philippi. Judging from the terms in which Paul addresses them (as a collective, with "political" language such as πολιτεύεσθε, πολίτευμα), they had formed a cooperative community of some sort. The community probably built on already existing social networks, such as kinship, friendships, and neighborhood (the traditional wider social or "civic" network had probably disintegrated from the impact of the Roman colonization). Paul's letter, however, gives no indication of subassemblies such as those that emerged in the much larger urban area of Corinth. It seems doubtful that we should imagine the emergence of a hierarchy of officers—"bishops and deacons"—already in the early assembly of Philippians. These terms probably came into written manuscripts of the letter to the Philippians, originally intended for oral performance, in the course of its subsequent copying.

That the assemblies in Philippi and elsewhere took the form of "associations" has been discussed widely in recent scholarship.[7] Various kinds of associations met for meals and sociability in honor of some hero, god, or benefactor: guilds of artisans such as cobblers, dyers, and stone-masons, or social clubs of bankers or physicians. It may well be that the social form in Greek cities that the assemblies most resembled locally was some sort of an association. If the assemblies of Christ loyalists bore some similarities to some of the associations, however, they were more than associations. They were local communities of a wider interpeople movement of assemblies in other Greek cities with a link to the people of Israel who were also living under Roman rule. Although Paul does not mention it in his letter to the Philippians, it would appear from his references in other letters that the Philippian community was included in the "collection for the poor" (among the saints) in Jerusalem. That is, as Damico and Reyes Chavez point out, the poor in one city were sharing resources with the poor in another city subject to the empire. As noted already, moreover, members of the assembly in Philippi had been supporting the work of movement leaders in Thessalonica.

In summation, the essays by Brawley, Damico and Reyes Chavez, and Nanos offer valuable new angles on the people beside Paul in the assembly of Philippi. These essays help us understand the particular configuration and enforcement of the Roman imperial order in the Roman colonial city of Philippi. These investigations of "history from below" move well beyond the way that scholars of the previous generation applied concepts of "social stratification" (borrowed from Western structural-functional sociology) to the Hellenistic urban world in general. They pursue an approach more appropriate to the distinctive situations of the assemblies of Christ loyalists in particular cities of the eastern Roman Empire. Moreover, they strongly confirm and reinforce the recognition that the mission of Paul and his coworkers and the communities that formed in different cities were not opposed to "Judaism," as previously imagined in a history of interpretation rife with Christian anti-Judaism. The assemblies in Philippi and other cities were, rather, local communities in a wider

---

7. See, for instance, Richard S. Ascough, *Paul's Macedonian Associations: The Social Context of Philippians and 1 Thessalonians*, WUNT 2/61 (Tübingen: Mohr Siebeck, 2003); John S. Kloppenborg and Ascough, *Achaia, Central Greece, Macedonia, Thrace*, vol. 1 of *Greco-Roman Associations: Texts, Translations, and Commentary*, BZNW 181 (Berlin: de Gruyter, 2011).

interpeople movement that formed an alternative to the Roman imperial order. While not as intensively as Paul himself, they had evidently found in the crucified and resurrected (and returning) Christ a "Lord" who was an alternative to the lord who reigned over the Roman imperial order in Philippi and elsewhere. They now also had an alternative politics or social order in the assembly of the wider movement. While they retained their social identity as Philippians in subjection to the Roman imperial order, in joining this movement they had (to some extent at least) identified with another subject people (and their Israelite/Judean tradition) among whom the followers of Jesus had acclaimed him as the Messiah who had been crucified by the Romans but vindicated by God.

Bibliography

Abrahamsen, Valerie. "Christianity and the Rock Reliefs at Philippi." *BA* 51 (1988): 46–56.

———. "Evidence for a Christian Goddess: The Bendis-Zodiac Relief at Philippi." *Forum* 3 (2007): 97–112.

———. "The Honoring of Livia at Philippi." Paper presented for discussion in the Philippi/Philippians Working Group, Society of Biblical Literature Annual Meeting, Washington, DC, 17 November 2006.

———. *Women and Worship at Philippi: Diana/Artemis and Other Cults in the Early Christian Era*. Portland, ME: Astarte Shell, 1995.

———. "Women at Philippi: The Pagan and Christian Evidence." *JFSR* 3 (1987): 17–30.

Agosto, Efrain, *Servant Leadership: Jesus and Paul*. St. Louis: Chalice, 2005.

Alcock, Susan E. *Graecia Capta: Landscapes of Roman Greece*. Cambridge: Cambridge University Press, 1993.

Alföldy, Géza. "The Crisis of the Third Century as Seen by Contemporaries." *GRBS* 15 (1974): 89–111.

Anderson, Perry. *Lineages of the Absolutist State*. London: NLB, 1974.

Apollonius Sophista. *Lexicon Homericum*. Edited by J. C. Molini. Vol. 2. Paris: Molini, 1773.

Arnove, Anthony. *Voices of a People's History of the United States*. New York: Seven Stories Press, 2005.

Asbed, Greg. "¡Golpear a Uno Es Golpear a Todos!" Pages 1–23 in vol. 3 of *Bringing Human Rights Home: A History of Human Rights in the United States*. Edited by Cynthia Soohoo, Catherine Albisa, and Martha Davis. Santa Barbara, CA: Greenwood, 2008.

Ascough, Richard S. *Lydia: Paul's Cosmopolitan Hostess*. Paul's Social Network: Brothers and Sisters in the Faith. Collegeville, MN: Liturgical Press, 2009.

———. *Paul's Macedonian Associations: The Social Context of Philippians and 1 Thessalonians*. WUNT 2/161. Tübingen: Mohr Siebeck, 2003.

Attridge, Harold W. *First-Century Cynicism in the Epistles of Heraclitus.* HTS 29. Missoula, MT: Scholars Press for the Harvard Theological Review, 1976.

Aune, David Edward. *Prophecy in Early Christianity and the Ancient Mediterranean World.* Grand Rapids: Eerdmans, 1983.

Austin, Norman J. E., and N. Boris Rankov. *Exploratio: Military and Political Intelligence in the Roman World from the Second Punic War to the Battle of Adrianople.* London: Routledge, 1995.

Bagnall, Roger, and Raffaella Cribiore. *Women's Letters from Ancient Egypt 300 BC–AD 800.* Ann Arbor: University of Michigan Press, 2006.

Bain, Katherine. *Women's Socioeconomic Status and Religious Leadership in Asia Minor in the First Two Centuries C.E.* Emerging Scholars. Minneapolis: Fortress, 2014.

Bakhtin, Mikhail. *Speech Genres.* Edited by Carol Emerson and Michael Holquist. Austin: University of Texas Press, 1986.

Bakirtzis, Charalambos. "Paul and Philippi: The Archaeological Evidence." Pages 37–48 in *Philippi at the Time of Paul and after His Death.* Edited by Charalambos Bakirtzis and Helmut Koester. Harrisburg, PA: Trinity Press International, 1998.

Bakirtzis, Charalambos, and Helmut Koester, eds. *Philippi at the Time of Paul and after His Death.* Harrisburg, PA: Trinity Press International, 1998.

Barclay, John. "Poverty in Pauline Studies: A Response to Steven Friesen." *JSNT* 26 (2004): 363–66.

Barker, Kenneth L., ed. *The NIV Study Bible*, UK ed. London: Hodder & Stoughton, 1987.

Barrett, Anthony. *Livia: First Lady of Imperial Rome.* New Haven: Yale University Press, 2002.

Barth, Karl. *Erklärung des Philipperbriefs.* 6th ed. Zollikon: Evangelischer Verlag, 1947.

Bass, Diana Butler. *A People's History of Christianity: The Other Side of the Story.* New York: HarperOne, 2009.

Baumann, Richard. *Crime and Punishment in Ancient Rome.* London: Routledge, 1996.

Baur, Ferdinand Christian. *Paulus, der Apostel Jesu Christi.* Leipzig: Fues, 1867.

Beard, Mary, John A. North, and S. R. F. Price, *Religions of Rome.* 2 vols. Cambridge: Cambridge University Press, 1998.

Bennington, Geoffrey. "Postal Politics and the Institution of the Nation."

Pages 121–37 in *Nation and Narration*. Edited by Homi K. Bhabha. London: Routledge, 1990.

Bett, Richard. *Sextus Empiricus, Against the Ethicists (Adversus Mathematicos XI)*. Oxford: Clarendon, 1997.

Betz, Hans-Dieter. *2 Corinthians 8 and 9: A Commentary on Two Administrative Letters of the Apostle Paul*. Hermeneia. Philadelphia: Fortress, 1985.

———. *Der Apostel Paulus in Rom*. Julius-Wellhausen-Vorlesung 4. Berlin: de Gruyter, 2013.

———. *Religion in Geschichte und Gegewart*. 4th ed. Tübingen: Mohr Siebeck, 1998–2007.

———. *Studies in Paul's Letter to the Philippians*. WUNT 343. Tübingen: Mohr Siebeck, 2015.

Bitzer, Lloyd F. "The Rhetorical Situation," *Philosophy and Rhetoric* 1 (1968): 1–14.

Blass, Friedrich, Albert Debrunner, and Robert W. Funk. *A Greek Grammar of the New Testament and Other Early Christian Literature*. Chicago: University of Chicago Press, 1961.

Bloomquist, L. Gregory. *The Function of Suffering in Philippians*. JSNTSup 78. Sheffield: JSOT Press, 1993.

———. "Subverted by Joy: Suffering and Joy in Paul's Letter to the Philippians." *Int* 61 (2007): 270–83.

Bockmuehl, Markus. *The Epistle to the Philippians*. BNTC. Peabody, MA: Hendrickson, 1998.

Bonz, Marianne Palmer. "Differing Approaches to Religious Benefaction: The Late Third-Century Acquisition of the Sardis Synagogue." *HTR* 86 (1993): 139–54.

Boring, M. Eugene, and Fred B. Craddock. *The People's New Testament Commentary*. Louisville: Westminster John Knox, 2009.

Bormann, Lukas. *Philippi: Stadt und Christengemeinde zur Zeit des Paulus*. NovTSup78. Leiden: Brill, 1995.

Bornkamm, Günther. "Der Philipperbrief als paulinische Briefsammlung." Pages 195–205 in vol. 2 of *Geschichte und Glaube*. Munich: Kaiser 1971.

Boulding, Elise. *The Underside of History*. Rev. ed. Newbury Park: Sage, 1992.

Bowe, John. *Nobodies: Modern American Slave Labor and the Dark Side of the New Global Economy*. New York: Random House, 2007.

Bowker, John. *The Complete Bible Handbook*. New York: DK Publishing, 1998.

Boyle, Leonard E. *A Short Guide to St. Clement's Rome*. Rome: Collegio San Clemente, 1989.

Bradley, Keith. *Slavery and Society at Rome*. Key Themes in Ancient History. Cambridge: Cambridge University Press, 1994.

Branham, Robert Bracht, and Marie-Odile Goulet-Cazé, eds. *The Cynics: The Cynic Movement in Antiquity and Its Legacy*. Berkeley: University of California Press, 1996.

Braund, David. "*Cohors*: The Governor and His Entourage in the Self-Image of the Roman Republic." Pages 10–24 in *Cultural Identity in the Roman Empire*. Edited by Ray Laurence and Joanne Berry. London: Routledge, 1998.

Brélaz, Cédric. *Corpus des inscriptions grecques et latines de Philippes*. Vol. 2: *La colonie romaine*. Part 1, *La vie publique de la colonie*. Études épigraphiques 6. Athènes: École française d' Athènes, 2014.

Bremen, Riet van. *The Limits of Participation: Women and Civic Life in the Greek East in the Hellenistic and Roman Periods*. Dutch Monographs on Ancient History and Archaeology. Amsterdam: Gieben, 1996.

Brenk, Beat. *Die Christianisierung der spätromischen Welt*. Spätantike-Frühes Christentum-Byzanz B: Studien und Perspektiven 10. Wiesbaden: Reichert, 2003.

Brenner, Robert. "The Social Basis of Economic Development." Pages 23–53 in *Analytical Marxism*. Edited by John Roemer. Cambridge: Cambridge University Press, 1986.

Brewer, R. R. "The Meaning of πολιτεύεσθε in Phil 1:27." *JBL* 73 (1954): 76–83.

Briggs, Sheila. "Can an Enslaved God Liberate? Hermeneutical Reflections on Philippians 2:6–11." *Semeia* 47 (1989): 137–53.

———. "Paul on Bondage and Freedom in Imperial Roman Society." Pages 110–23 in *Paul and Politics: Ekklesia, Israel, Imperium, Interpretation; Essays in Honor of Krister Stendahl*. Edited by Richard A. Horsley. Harrisburg, PA: Trinity Press International, 2000.

———. "Slavery and Gender." Pages 171–92 in *On the Cutting Edge: The Study of Women in Biblical Worlds; Essays in Honor of Elisabeth Schüssler Fiorenza*. Edited by Jane Schaberg, Alice Bach, and Esther Fuchs. New York: Continuum, 2003.

Briones, David. "Paul's Intentional 'Thankless Thanks' in Philippians 4.10–20." *JSNT* 34 (2011): 47–60.

Brooten, Bernadette J. *Love Between Women: Early Christian Responses to Female Homoeroticism*. The Chicago Series on Sexuality, History, and Society. Chicago: University of Chicago Press, 1996.

Brooten, Bernadette J., with Jacqueline L. Hazelton, eds. *Beyond Slavery: Overcoming Its Religious and Sexual Legacies*. Black Religion, Womanist Thought, Social Justice. New York: Palgrave Macmillan, 2010.

Brown, Raymond E., Karl P. Donfried, Joseph A. Fitzmyer, and John Reumann, eds. *Mary in the New Testament*. Philadelphia: Fortress, 1978.

Bruce, F. F. *Philippians*. A Good News Commentary. San Francisco: Harper & Row, 1983.

Brunt, Peter A. *Italian Manpower: 225 BC–AD 14*. Oxford: Oxford University Press, 1987.

Buchholz, Hans-Günter. *Methymna: Archäologische Beiträge zur Topographie und Geschichte von Nordlesbos*. Mainz: von Zabern, 1975.

Burke, Peter, ed. "Overture: The New History; Its Past and Its Future." Pages 1–24 in *New Perspectives on Historical Writing*. Edited by Peter Burke. 2nd ed. University Park: Pennsylvania State University Press, 2001.

———. *Popular Culture in Early Modern Europe*. London: Harper & Row, 1978.

Burkert, Walter. *Ancient Mystery Cults*. Cambridge: Harvard University Press, 1987.

Byrne, Janet, ed. *The Occupy Handbook*. New York: Back Bay Books, 2012.

Cadwallader, Alan H. *Beyond the Word of a Woman: Recovering the Bodies of the Syrophoenician Women*. ATF Biblical Series 1. Adelaide, Australia: ATF Press, 2008.

Callahan, Allen Dwight. "Paul, *Ekklēsia*, and Emancipation in Corinth: A Coda on Liberation Theology." Pages 216–23 in *Paul and Politics: Ekklesia, Israel, Imperium, Interpretation; Essays in Honor of Krister Stendahl*. Edited by Richard A. Horsley. Harrisburg, PA: Trinity Press International, 2000.

Callahan, Allen Dwight, Richard A. Horsley, and Abraham Smith, eds. *Slavery in Text and Interpretation*. Semeia 83–84. Atlanta: Society of Biblical Literature, 1998.

Campbell, William S. " 'I Rate All Things as Loss': Paul's Puzzling Accounting System; Judaism as Loss or the Re-evaluation of All Things in Christ?" Pages 39–61 in *Celebrating Paul: Festschrift in Honor of Jerome Murphy O'Connor O.P. and Joseph Fitzmyer S.J.* Edited by Peter Spitaler. CBQMS 48. Washington, DC: Catholic Biblical Association of America, 2011. Repr. as pages 203–23 in *Unity and Diversity in Christ: Interpreting Paul in Context; Collected Essays.* Eugene, OR: Cascade, 2013.

Carter, Warren. "Matthew's People." Pages 138–61 in *Christian Origins.* Vol. 1 of *A People's History of Christianity.* Edited by Richard A. Horsley. Minneapolis: Fortress, 2005.

Cassidy, Richard J. *Paul in Chains: Roman Imprisonment and the Letters of Paul.* New York: Crossroad Press, 2001.

Castelli, Elizabeth A. *Imitating Paul: A Discourse of Power.* Literary Currents in Biblical Interpretation. Louisville: Westminster John Knox, 1991.

Coalition of Immokalee Workers. "Burger King Campaign Comes to an End with Historic Press Conference, Signing Ceremony at U.S. Capitol." http://ciw-online.org/BK_campaign_archive.html.

———. "Facts and Figures on Florida Farmworkers." http://ciw-online.org/wp-content/uploads/12FactsFigures_2.pdf.

———. "Injustice Anywhere: Farmworker Strike in Mexico Underscores Urgent Need for Human Rights Protections on Both Sides of the Border." http://ciw-online.org/blog/2015/04/injustice-anywhere/.

———. "Slavery in the Fields and the Food We Eat." http://ciw-online.org/wp-content/uploads/12SlaveryintheFields.pdf.

Cohen, Shaye J. D. *The Beginnings of Jewishness: Boundaries, Varieties, Uncertainties.* HCS 31. Berkeley: University of California Press, 1999.

Colange, Jean-François. *The Epistle of Saint Paul to the Philippians.* Translated by A. W. Heathcote. London: Epworth, 1979.

Cole, Susan Guettel. *Theoi Megaloi: The Cult of the Great Gods at Samothrace.* EPRO 96. Leiden: Brill, 1984.

Collart, Paul. "Inscriptions de Philippes." *BCH* 57 (1933): 360–62.

———. *Philippes: Ville de Macédoine: Depuis ses origins jusqu'à la fin de l'époque romaine.* Travaux et Mémoires 5. Paris: École Française d'Athènes, 1937.

———. "Le sanctuaire des dieux égyptiens à Philippes." *BCH* 53 (1929): 82–87.

Collins, Adela Yarbro. *The Combat Myth in the Book of Revelation.* Missoula, MT: Scholars Press, 1976.

Connelly, Joan Breton. *Portrait of a Priestess: Women and Ritual in Ancient Greece.* Princeton: Princeton University Press, 2007.

Connolly, Joy. "Mastering Corruption: Constructions of Identity in Roman Oratory." Pages 130–51 in *Women and Slaves in Greco-Roman Culture: Differential Equations*. Edited by Sandra R. Joshel and Sheila Murnaghan. London: Routledge, 1998.

Cotter, Wendy. "Women's Authority Roles in Paul's Churches: Countercultural or Conventional?" *NovT* 36 (1994): 350–72.

Cowley, J. M. S., and K. Maresch. *Urkunden des Politema der Juden von Herakleopolis*. Edited by Papyrologia Coloniensia 29. Wiesbaden: Westdeutscher Verlag, 2001.

Cross, F.L., and E.A. Livingstone, eds. *The Oxford Dictionary of the Christian Church*. 3rd ed. Oxford: Oxford University Press, 1997.

Cullmann, Oscar. "Infancy Gospels." *NTApoc* 1:353–401.

Dabashi, Hamid. *The Arab Spring: The End of Postcolonialism*. London: Zed Books, 2012.

Dahl, Nils A. "Euodia and Syntyche and Paul's Letter to the Philippians." Pages 3–15 in *The Social World of the First Christians: Essays in Honor of Wayne A. Meeks*. Edited by L. Michael White and O. Larry Yarbrough. Minneapolis: Fortress, 1995.

D'Angelo, Mary Rose. "Euodia." Page 79 in *Women in Scripture: A Dictionary of Named and Unnamed Women in the Hebrew Bible, The Apocryphal/Deuterocanonical Books, and the New Testament*. Edited by Carol Meyers, Toni Craven, and Ross S. Kraemer. Grand Rapids: Eerdmans, 2000.

———. "Syntyche." Page 159 in *Women in Scripture: A Dictionary of Named and Unnamed Women in the Hebrew Bible, The Apocryphal/Deuterocanonical Books, and the New Testament*. Edited by Carol Meyers, Toni Craven, and Ross S. Kraemer. Grand Rapids: Eerdmans, 2000.

———. "Women Partners in the New Testament." *JFSR* 6 (1990): 65–86.

Danker, Frederick W., Walter Bauer, William F. Arndt, and F. Wilbur Gingrich. *Greek-English Lexicon of the New Testament and Other Early Christian Literature*. 3rd ed. Chicago: University of Chicago Press, 2000.

Deissmann, Adolf. *Bibelstudien*. Marburg: Elwert, 1895.

———. *Bible Studies: Contributions, Chiefly from Papyri and Inscriptions, to the History of the Language, the Literature, and the Religion of Hellenistic Judaism and Primitive Christianity*. Translated by Alexander Grieve. Edinburgh: T&T Clark, 1901.

———. *Licht vom Osten*. Tübingen: Mohr Siebeck, 1923.

Depeyrot, Georges. "Crise économique, formation des prix, et politique monétaire au troisème siecle après J.-C." *Histoire & Mesure* 3 (1988): 235–47.

DeWitt, Norman Wentworth. *St. Paul and Epicurus.* Minneapolis: University of Minnesota Press, 1954.

Dexter, Miriam Robbins. *Whence the Goddesses: A Source Book.* The Athene Series. New York: Pergamon, 1990.

DeYoung, Curtiss Paul, Wilda C. Gafney, Leticia A. Guardiola-Sáenz, George "Tink" Tinker, and Frank M. Yamada, eds. *The Peoples' Bible: New Revised Standard Version, with the Apocrypha.* Minneapolis: Fortress, 2008.

———. *The Peoples' Companion to the Bible.* Minneapolis: Fortress, 2010.

Dibelius, Martin. *An die Thessaloniker I–II: An die Philipper.* 3rd ed. HNT 11. Tübingen: Mohr Siebeck, 1937.

Dimitrova, Nora M. *Theoroi and Initiates in Samothrace: The Epigraphical Evidence.* Hesperia Supplement 37. Athens: American School of Classical Studies, 2008.

Dittenberger, Wilhelm, ed. *Sylloge inscriptionum graecum.* 4 vols. 3rd ed. Leipzig: Hirzel, 1915–1924.

Dodd, Brian J. *Paul's Paradigmatic "I": Personal Example as Literary Strategy.* JSNTSup 177. Sheffield: Sheffield Academic, 1999.

Dommelen, Peter van. "Punic Persistence: Colonialism and Cultural Identities in Roman Sardinia." Pages 25–48 in *Cultural Identity in the Roman Empire.* Edited by Ray Laurence and Joanne Berry. London: Routledge, 1998.

Donfried, Karl P., and I. Howard Marshall. *The Theology of the Shorter Pauline Letters.* New Testament Theology. Cambridge: Cambridge University Press, 1993.

D'Orta, Piemme, and Enrika D'Orta. *Together in Pompeii.* Pompeii: Falanga Edizioni Pompeiane, 1985.

Doty, William G. *Letters in Primitive Christianity.* GBS. Philadelphia: Fortress, 1973.

Downing, Francis Gerald. *Cynics and Christian Origins.* Edinburgh: T&T Clark, 1992.

———. *Cynics, Paul, and the Pauline Churches.* London: Routledge, 1998.

Draper, Jonathan. "Orality, Literacy, and Colonialism in Antiquity." Pages 1–6 in *Orality, Literacy, and Colonialism in Antiquity.* Edited by Jonathan Draper. SemeiaSt 47. Atlanta: Society of Biblical Literature, 2004.

——. "Recovering Oral Performance from Written Text in Q." Pages 175–94 in Richard A. Horsley and Jonathan Draper, *Whoever Hears You Hears Me: Prophets, Performance, and Tradition in Q*. Harrisburg, PA: Trinity Press International, 1999.

Droogers, Andre. "Towards the Concerned Study of Religion: Exploring the Double Power-Play Disparity." *Religion* 40 (2010): 227–38.

duBois, Page. *Slaves and Other Objects*. Chicago: University of Chicago Press, 2003.

Du Bois, W. E. B. *The Souls of Black Folk*. Oxford: Oxford University Press, 2007.

Ducrey, Pierre. "The Rock Reliefs of Philippi." *Arch* 30 (1977): 102–7.

Dunant, Christiane and Jean Pouilloux. *Recherches sur l'histoire et les cultes de Thasos*. Volume 2. Paris: Ecole Française d'Athènes, 1958.

Ecole Française d'Athènes. *Guide de Thasos*. Paris: de Boccard, 1968.

Eder, Walter. "Prison Sentence." *Brill's New Pauly*. Edited by Hubert Cancik and Helmuth Schneider. http://www.encquran.brill.nl/entries/brill-s-new-pauly/prison-sentence-e420370.

Edson, Charles. "Cults of Thessalonica." Pages 886–940 in *ΘΕΣΣΑΛΟΝΙΚΗ ΦΙΛΙΠΠΟΥ ΒΑΣΙΛΙΣΣΑΝ* [Studies on Ancient Thessalonica]. Edited by Polyxeni Adam-Veleni. Thessaloniki: Archaeological Museum, 1985.

——. "Double Communities in Roman Macedonia." Pages 97–102 in *Essays in Memory of Basil Laourdas*. Edited by C. Edson et al. Thessalonica: Laourda, 1975.

Elliott, Neil. *Liberating Paul: The Justice of God and the Politics of the Apostle*. Maryknoll, NY: Orbis, 1994.

Elliott, Susan M. *Cutting Too Close for Comfort: Paul's Letter to the Galatians in Its Anatolian Cultic Context*. JSNTSup 248. London: T&T Clark, 2003.

Ellis, E. Earle. "Paul and His Opponents: Trends in Research." Pages 263–98 in *Christianity, Judaism and Other Greco-Roman Cults: Studies for Morton Smith at Sixty*. Edited by Jacob Neusner. Leiden: Brill, 1975.

Etienne, Robert. *Pompeii: The Day a City Died*. Discoveries Series. New York: Abrams, 1992.

Fair Food Standards Council. "The Coalition of Immokalee Workers Fair Food Program: Bringing Dignity and Justice to Florida's Tomato Fields." http://ciw-online.org/wp-content/uploads/FFP-brochure-Nov-2012.pdf.

Fears, J. Rufus. "Ruler Worship." Pages 1009–25 in vol. 2 of *Civilization of the Ancient Mediterranean: Greece and Rome*. Edited by Michael Grant and Rachel Kitzinger. New York: Scribner, 1988.

Fee, Gordon D. *Paul's Letter to the Philippians*. NICNT. Grand Rapids: Eerdmans, 1995.

———. *Philippians*. Intervarsity Press New Testament Commentary Series 11. Downers Grove, IL: Intervarsity Press, 1999.

Feissel, Denis. *Recueil des inscriptions chrétiennes de Macédoine, du IIIe an VIe siècle*. Paris: de Boccard, 1983.

Finley, Moses I. *Ancient Slavery and Modern Ideology*. New York: Viking Press, 1980.

Florida Tomato Growers Exchange. "Tomato 101." http://www.floridatomatoes.org/wp-content/uploads/2013/01/Tomato_1011.pdf.

Foley, John Miles. "Indigenous Poems, Colonialist Texts." Pages 9–36 in *Orality, Literacy, and Colonialism in Antiquity*. Edited by Jonathan Draper. SemeiaSt 47. Atlanta: Society of Biblical Literature, 2004.

Fortna, Robert T. "Philippians: Paul's Most Egocentric Letter." Pages 220–34 in *The Conversation Continues: Festschrift for J. Louis Martyn*. Edited by Robert T. Fortna and Beverly R. Gaventa. Nashville: Abingdon, 1990.

Foucault, Michel. *The Use of Pleasure*. Vol. 2 of *The History of Sexuality*. Translated by Robert Hurley. New York: Vintage, 1990.

Fowl, Stephen E. *Philippians*. The Two Horizons New Testament Commentary. Grand Rapids: Eerdmans, 2005.

Frederickson, David E. "Natural and Unnatural Use in Romans 1:24–27: Paul and the Philosophic Critique of Eros." Pages 197–222 in *Homosexuality, Science, and the "Plain Sense" of Scripture*. Edited by David Balch. Grand Rapids: Eerdmans, 2000.

Fredriksen, Paula. "Judaizing the Nations: The Ritual Demands of Paul's Gospel." *NTS* 56 (2010): 232–52.

Frend, W. H. C. *The Rise of Christianity*. Philadelphia: Fortress, 1984.

Friedrich, Gerhard. "Der Briefe an die Philipper." Pages 92–93 in *Die kleineren Briefe des Apostels Paulus*. Edited by H. W. Beyer et al. 9th ed. NTD 8. Göttingen: Vandenhoeck & Ruprecht, 1962.

———. "Der Briefe eines Gefangenen." *Montatsschrift für Pastoraltheologie* 44 (1955): 270–80.

Friesen, Steven J. "Poverty in Pauline Studies: Beyond the So-Called New Consensus." *JSNT* 26 (2004): 323–61.

Friesen, Steven J., Daniel N. Schowalter, and James C. Walters, eds. *Corinth in Context: Comparative Studies on Religion and Society*. Leiden: Brill, 2010.

Friesen, Steven J., Sarah A. James, and Daniel N. Schowalter. "Inequality in Corinth." Pages 1–13 in *Corinth in Contrast: Studies in Inequality*. Edited by Steven J. Friesen, Sarah A. James, and Daniel N. Schowalter. NovTSup 155. Leiden: Brill, 2014.

Funk, Robert W. "The Apostolic Parousia: Form and Significance." Pages 249–68 in *Christian History and Interpretation: Studies Presented to John Knox*. Edited by William R. Farmer, C. F. D. Moule, and Richard R. Niebuhr. Cambridge: Cambridge University Press, 1967.

Garland, David. "The Composition and Unity of Philippians: Some Neglected Literary Factors." *NovT* 27 (1985): 141–73.

Garnsey, Peter. *Ideas of Slavery from Aristotle to Augustine*. Cambridge: Cambridge University Press, 1996.

———. *Social Status and Legal Privilege in the Roman Empire*. Oxford: Clarendon, 1970.

Geoffrion, Timothy C. *The Rhetorical Purpose and the Political and Military Character of Philippians: A Call to Stand Firm*. Lewiston: Mellen, 1993.

Georgi, Dieter. *Theocracy in Paul's Praxis and Theology*. Minneapolis: Fortress, 1991.

Gizewski, Christian. "Maiestas." *Brill's New Pauly*. Edited by Hubert Cancik and Helmuth Schneider. http://brillonline.nl/entries/brill-s-new-pauly/maiestas-e718120.

Glancy, Jennifer A. *Slavery in Early Christianity*. Minneapolis: Fortress, 2006.

Gnilka, Joachim. *Der Philipperbrief*. HTKNT 10.3. Freiburg: Herder, 1968.

Goodblatt, David. *Elements of Ancient Jewish Nationalism*. Cambridge: Cambridge University Press, 2006.

Gosline, Sheldon L. *Archaeogender: Studies in Gender's Material Culture*. Marco Polo Monographs 2. Warren Center, PA: Shangri-La, 1999.

Goulet-Cazé, Marie-Odile. "Religion and the Early Cynics." Pages 47–80 in *The Cynics: The Cynic Movement in Antiquity and Its Legacy*. Edited by Robert Bracht Branham and Marie-Odile Goulet-Cazé. Berkeley: University of California Press, 1996.

Gounaris, G. G. *The Bathhouse and the Northern Outhouses of the Octagon at Philippi* [Greek]. Bibliotheke tes en Athenais Archaiologikes Hetaireias 112. Athens: Athenais Archaiologike Hetaireia, 1990.

Gounaris, G. G., and E. Gounari. *Philippoi: Archaiologikos hodēgos* [Greek]. Thessaloniki: University Studio Press, 2004.

Grayston, Kenneth. "The Opponents in Philippians 3." *ExpTim* 97 (1986): 170–72.

Grether, Gertrude, "Livia and the Roman Imperial Cult," *AJP* 67 (1946): 222–52.

Griffin, Miriam. "Cynicism and the Romans: Attraction and Repulsion." Pages 190–202 in *The Cynics: The Cynic Movement in Antiquity and Its Legacy*. Edited by Robert Bracht Branham and Marie-Odile Goulet-Cazé. Berkeley: University of California Press, 1996.

Guha, Ranajit. *Elementary Aspects of Peasant Insurgency in Colonial India*. Delhi: Oxford, 1983.

Gunther, John J. *St. Paul's Opponents and Their Background: A Study of Apocalyptic and Jewish Sectarian Teachings*. NovTSup 35. Leiden: Brill, 1973.

Hallett, Judith P., and Marilyn B. Skinner, eds. *Roman Sexualities*. Princeton: Princeton University Press, 1997.

Halperin, David M. *How to Do the History of Homosexuality*. Chicago: University of Chicago Press, 2002.

———. *One Hundred Years of Homosexuality: And Other Essays on Greek Love*. New York: Routledge, 1990.

Halperin, David M., John J. Winkler, and Froma I. Zeitlin, eds. *Before Sexuality: The Construction of Erotic Experience in the Ancient Greek World*. Princeton: Princeton University Press, 1990.

Hamilton, Edith. *Mythology: Timeless Tales of Gods and Heroes*. Chicago: Mentor, 1942.

Haraguchi, Takaaki. "Das Unterhaltsrecht des frühchristlichen Verkündigers: Eine Untersuchung Hirschfeld zur Bezeichnung ἐργάτης im Neuen Testament." *ZNW* 84 (1993): 178–95.

Hardt, Michael, and Antonio Negri. *Multitude: War and Democracy in the Age of Empire*. New York: Penguin, 2004.

Harland, Philip A. *Associations, Synagogues, and Congregations: Claiming a Place in Ancient Mediterranean Society*. Minneapolis: Fortress, 2003.

Harrill, J. Albert. *The Manumission of Slaves in Early Christianity*. HUT 32. Tübingen: Mohr Siebeck, 1995.

———. "Paul and Slavery." Pages 575–607 in *Paul in the Greco-Roman World: A Handbook*. Edited by J. Paul Sampley. Harrisburg, PA: Trinity Press International, 2003.

———. *Slaves in the New Testament: Literary, Social, and Moral Dimensions.* Minneapolis: Fortress, 2006.

Harris, William V. *Ancient Literacy.* Cambridge: Harvard University Press, 1991.

Hawthorne, Gerald F. *Philippians.* WBC 43. Waco, TX: Word, 1983.

Hawthorne, Gerald F., and Ralph P. Martin. *Phillipians.* Revised by Ralph P. Martin. WBC 43. Nashville: Nelson, 2004.

Heen, Erik M. "Phil 2:6–11 and Resistance to Local Timocratic Rule: *Isa Theō* and the Cult of the Emperor in the East." Pages 125–53 in *Paul and the Roman Imperial Order.* Edited by Richard A. Horsley. Harrisburg, PA: Trinity Press International, 2004.

Hellerman, Joseph H. *Reconstructing Honor in Roman Philippi: Carmen Christi as Cursus Pudorum.* SNTSMS 132. New York: Cambridge University Press, 2005.

Hemberg, Bengt. *Die Kabiren.* Upssala: Almquist & Wiksell, 1950.

Hendrix, Holland L. "Philippi." *ABD* 5:313–17.

Henrichs, Albert. *Die Phoinikika des Lollianos: Fragmente eines neuen griechischen Romans.* Papyrologische Texte und Abhandlungen 14. Bonn: Habelt, 1972. •

Hesychius of Alexandria. *Lexicon.* Edited by Kurt Latte. Vol. 2. Copenhagen: Ejnar Munksgaard, 1953.

Heubeck, A. "Personennamen (A)." Page 2268 in *Lexikon der Alten Welt.* Edited by C. Andresen et al. Zürich: Artemis, 1965.

Heyob, Sharon Kelly. *The Cult of Isis Among Women in the Graeco-Roman World.* Leiden: Brill, 1975.

Hirschfeld, Otto. "Die Sicherheitspolizei im römischen Kaiserreich." Pages 577–623 in *Kleine Schriften.* Berlin: Weidmannsche Buchhandlung, 1913.

Hock, Ronald F. "Infancy Gospels." Pages 367–96 in *The Complete Gospels.* Edited by Robert J. Miller. Sonoma: Polebridge, 1994.

Hofius, Otfried. *Der Christushymnus Philipper 2:6–11.* Tübingen: Mohr Siebeck, 1976.

Höistad, Ragnar. *Cynic Hero and Cynic King: Studies in the Cynic Conception of Man.* Uppsala: Lund, 1948.

Holladay, Carl R. "Paul's Opponents in Philippians 3." *ResQ* 12 (1969): 77–90.

Hopkins, Keith. *Conquerors and Slaves.* Sociological Studies in Roman History 1. Cambridge: Cambridge University Press, 1978.

Horrell, David G. "From ἀδελφοί to οἶκος θεοῦ: Social Transformation in Pauline Christianity." *JBL* 120 (2001): 293–311.

Horsley, Richard A. *1 Corinthians.* ANTC. Nashville: Abingdon, 1998.

———. "1 Corinthians: A Case Study of Paul's Assembly as an Alternative Society." Pages 242–52 in *Paul and Empire: Religion and Power in Roman Imperial Society.* Edited by Richard A. Horsley. Harrisburg, PA: Trinity Press International, 1997.

———. *Covenant Economics: A Biblical Vision of Justice for All.* Louisville: Westminster John Knox, 2009.

———, ed. *Hidden Transcripts and the Arts of Resistance: Applying the Work of James C. Scott to Jesus and Paul.* SemeiaSt 48. Atlanta: Society of Biblical Literature, 2004.

———. *Jesus and the Spiral of Violence: Popular Jewish Resistance in Roman Palestine.* Minneapolis: Fortress, 1993.

———, ed. *Paul and Empire: Religion and Power in Roman Imperial Society.* Harrisburg, PA: Trinity Press International, 1997.

———, ed. *Paul and Politics: Ekklesia, Israel, Imperium, Interpretation; Essays in Honor of Krister Stendahl.* Harrisburg, PA: Trinity Press International, 2000.

———, ed. *Paul and the Roman Imperial Order.* Harrisburg, PA: Trinity Press International, 2004.

———. "Rhetoric and Empire—and 1 Corinthians." Pages 72–102 in *Paul and Politics: Ekklesia, Israel, Imperium, Interpretation; Essays in Honor of Krister Stendahl.* Edited by Richard A. Horsley. Harrisburg, PA: Trinity Press International, 2000.

———. "Unearthing a People's History." Pages 1–20 in *Christian Origins.* Vol. 1 of *A People's History of Christianity.* Edited by Richard A. Horsley. Minneapolis: Fortress, 2005.

Horsley, Richard A., and Jonathan Draper. *Whoever Hears You Hears Me: Prophets, Performance, and Tradition in Q.* Harrisburg, PA: Trinity Press International, 1999.

Horsley, Richard A., and Neil Asher Silberman. *The Message and the Kingdom: How Jesus and Paul Ignited a Revolution and Transformed the Ancient World.* New York: Grossett/Putnam, 1997.

Houlden, James Leslie. *Paul's Letters from Prison: Philippians, Colossians, Philemon, and Ephesians.* Philadelphia: Westminster, 1977.

Hurley, Donna. "Livia (Wife of Augustus)." *De Imperatoribus Romanis: An Online Encyclopedia of Roman Emperors.* http://www.roman-emperors.org/livia.htm.

Huttunen, Perrti. *The Social Strata in the Imperial City of Rome: A Quantitative Study of the Social Representation in the Epitaphs Published in the Corpus Inscriptionum Latinarum Volumen VI.* Oulu: University of Oulu, 1974.

Jaccottet, Anne-Françoise. *Choisir Dionysos: Les Associations Dionysiaques ou La Face Cachée du Dionysisme.* Vol. 2. Zurich: Akanthus, 2003.

Jäggi, Carola. "Archäologische Zeugnisse für die Anfänge der Paulus-Verehrung." Pages 306–22 in *Biographie und Persönlichkeit des Paulus.* Edited by Eve-Marie Becker and Peter Pilhofer. WUNT 187. Tübingen: Mohr Siebeck, 2005.

Janz, Denis R., ed. *A People's History of Christianity.* 7 vols. Philadelphia: Fortress, 2005–2008.

Jaschik, Scott. "Daniels vs. Zinn, Round II." Inside Higher Ed. http://www.insidehighered.com/news/2013/07/18/mitch-daniels-renews-criticism-howard-zinn#sthash.CUFSIof5.dpbs.

Jewett, Robert. "Conflicting Movements in the Early Church as Reflected in Philippians." *NovT* 12 (1970): 362–90.

Johnson-DeBaufre, Melanie, and Laura Nasrallah. "Beyond the Heroic Paul: Toward a Feminist and Decolonizing Approach to the Letters of Paul." Pages 161–74 in *The Colonized Apostle: Paul through Postcolonial Eyes.* Edited by Christopher D. Stanley. Paul in Critical Contexts. Minneapolis: Fortress, 2011.

Jones, Siân and Sarah Pearce, eds. *Jewish Local Patriotism and Self-Identification in the Graeco-Roman Period.* JSPSup 31. Sheffield: Sheffield Academic, 1998.

Joshel, Sandra R. *Work, Identity, and Legal Status at Rome: A Study of the Occupational Inscriptions.* Oklahoma Studies in Classical Culture 11. Norman: University of Oklahoma Press, 1992.

Joshel, Sandra R., and Sheila Murnaghan, eds. *Women and Slaves in Greco-Roman Culture: Differential Equations.* London: Routledge, 1998.

Kahl, Brigitte. *Galatians Re-imagined: Reading with the Eyes of the Vanquished.* Paul in Critical Contexts. Minneapolis: Fortress, 2010.

Karwiese, Stefan. "The Church of Mary and the Temple of Hadrian Olympios." Pages 311–19 in *Ephesos: Metropolis of Asia.* Edited by Helmut Koester. Valley Forge, PA: Trinity Press International, 1995.

Kaufmann, Jean-Claude. *L'invention de soi: Une théorie de l'identité.* Paris: Colin, 2004.

Keppie, Lawrence. *Colonisation and Veteran Settlement in Italy: 47–14 B.C.* London: British School at Rome, 1983.

Kilpatrick, George D. "ΒΛΕΠΕΤΕ, Philippians 3.2." Pages 146–48 in *In Memorium Paul Kahle*. Edited by Matthew Black and George Fohrer. Berlin: Alfred Töpelmann, 1968.

Kittredge, Cynthia Briggs. *Community and Authority: The Rhetoric of Obedience in the Pauline Tradition*. HTS 45. Harrisburg, PA: Trinity Press International, 1998.

———. "Corinthian Women Prophets and Paul's Argumentation in 1 Corinthians." Pages 103–9 in *Paul and Politics: Ekklesia, Israel, Imperium, Interpretation; Essays in Honor of Krister Stendahl*. Edited by Richard A. Horsley. Harrisburg, PA: Trinity Press International, 2000.

———. "Reconstructing 'Resistance' or Reading to Resist: James C. Scott and the Politics of Interpretation." Pages 145–55 in *Hidden Transcripts and the Arts of Resistance: Applying the Work of James C. Scott to Jesus and Paul*. Edited by Richard A. Horsley. SemeiaSt 48. Atlanta: Society of Biblical Literature, 2004.

———. "Rethinking Authorship in the Letters of Paul: Elisabeth Schüssler Fiorenza's Model of Pauline Theology." Pages 318–33 in *Walk in the Ways of Wisdom: Essays in Honor of Elisabeth Schüssler Fiorenza*. Edited by Shelly Matthews, Cynthia Briggs Kittredge, and Melanie Johnson-Debaufre. Harrisburg, PA: Trinity Press International, 2003.

Klauck, Hans-Josef. *The Religious Context of Early Christianity: A Guide to Graeco-Roman Religions*. Minneapolis: Fortress, 2003.

Kleiner, Diana E. E. *Roman Group Portraits: The Funerary Reliefs of the Late Republic and Early Empire*. New York: Garland, 1977.

Kleinknecht, Karl. *Der leidende Gerechtfertigte: Die altestamentlich-jüdische Tradition vom 'leidende Gerechte' und ihre Rezeption bei Paulus*. WUNT 2/13. Tübingen: Mohr Siebeck, 1984.

Klijn, A. F. J. "Paul's Opponents in Philippians iii." *NovT* 7 (1964): 278–84.

Klinghardt, Matthias. *Gemeinschaftsmahl und Mahlgemeinschaft: Soziologie und Liturgie frühchristlicher Mahlfeiern*. Tübingen: Franke, 1996.

Kloppenborg, John S. "Collegia and *Thiasoi*: Issues in Function, Taxonomy, and Membership." Pages 16–30 in *Voluntary Associations in the Graeco-Roman World*. Edited by Kloppenborg and Stephen G. Wilson. New York: Routledge, 1996.

Kloppenborg, John S., and Richard S. Ascough. *Attica, Central Greece, Macedonia, Thrace*. Vol. 1 of *Greco-Roman Associations: Texts, Translations, and Commentary*. BZNW 181. Berlin: de Gruyter, 2011.

Klutz, Todd. *The Exorcism Stories in Luke-Acts: A Sociostylistic Reading.* SNTSMS 129. Cambridge: Cambridge University Press, 2004.

Knapp, Robert. *Invisible Romans.* Cambridge: Harvard University Press, 2011.

Koester, Helmut. *Einführung in das Neue Testament.* Berlin: de Gruyter, 1980.

———. "The Purpose of the Polemic of a Pauline Fragment." *NTS* 8 (1961–1962): 317–32.

Kolb, Anne. "Cryptography." *Brill's New Pauly.* Edited by Hubert Cancik and Helmuth Schneider. http://referenceworks.brillonline.com/entries/brill-s-new-pauly/cryptography-e623760.

Koukouli-Chrysantaki, Chaido. "Colonia Iulia Augusta Philippensis." Pages 5–35 in *Philippi at the Time of Paul and after His Death.* Edited by Charalambos Bakirtzis and Helmut Koester. Harrisburg, PA: Trinity Press International, 1998.

———. "Κήπια—Ακροβούνι." *Archaiologikon deltion* 40 (1985): 263–36.

Krause, Jens-Uwe. *Gefängnisse im Römischen Reich.* Heidelberger althistorische Beiträge und epigraphische Studien 23. Stuttgart: Steiner, 1996.

Krentz, Edgar M. "Military Language and Metaphors in Philippians." Pages 105–27 in *Origins and Method: Towards a New Understanding of Judaism and Christianity; Essays in Honour of John. C. Hurd.* Edited by Bradley H. McLean. JSNTSup 86. Sheffield: Sheffield Academic, 1993.

———. "Paul, Games, and the Military." Pages 344–83 in *Paul in the Greco-Roman World: A Handbook.* Edited by J. Paul Sampley. Harrisburg, PA: Trinity Press International, 2003.

Krueger, Derek. "The Bawdy and Society: The Shamelessness of Diogenes in Roman Imperial Culture." Pages 222–39 in *The Cynics: The Cynic Movement in Antiquity and Its Legacy.* Edited by Robert Bracht Branham and Marie-Odile Goulet-Cazé. Berkeley: University of California Press, 1996.

Lampe, Peter. "Paul, Patrons, and Clients." Pages 488–523 in *Paul in the Greco-Roman World: A Handbook.* Edited by Paul Sampley. Harrisburg, PA: Trinity Press International, 2003.

Lazarides, Demetrios. "Philippi." Pages 704–5 in *Princeton Encyclopedia of Classical Sites.* Edited by Richard Stillwell. Princeton: Princeton University Press, 1976.

———. "Philippoi." *Archaeologikon Deltion* 16 (1960): 218–19.

Lehmann, Karl. "The *Epopteia* and the Function of the Hieron." Pages 3–50 in *The Hieron*. Vol. 3.2 of *Samothrace*. Edited by Phyllis Williams Lehmann. Princeton: Princeton University Press, 1969.

———. *Samothrace: A Guide to the Excavations and the Museum*. Thessaloniki: Akamatis, 1998.

Lemerle, Paul. *Philippes et la Macédoine orientale à l'époque chrétienne et byzantine*. Bibiothèque des écoles Françaises d'Athènes et de Rome 158. Paris: de Boccard, 1945.

Lenski, Gerhard. *Power and Privilege: A Theory of Social Stratification*. Chapel Hill: University of North Carolina Press, 1966.

Leveau, Philippe. *Caesarea de Maurétanie: Une Ville Romaine et ses Campagnes*. Collection de l'école française de Rome 70. Rome: École Fr., 1984.

Levick, Barbara. *Roman Colonies in Southern Asia Minor*. Oxford: Clarendon, 1967.

Lewis, Naphtali. *The Ancient Literary Sources*. Vol. 1 of *Samothrace*. London: Routledge & Kegan Paul, 1959.

Lidell, Henry George, Robert Scott, and Henry Stuart Jones. *A Greek-English Lexicon*. 9th ed. with revised supplement. Oxford: Clarendon, 1996.

Liew, Tat-Siong Benny. *What Is Asian American Hermeneutics? Reading the New Testament*. Honolulu: University of Hawai'i Press, 2008.

Lightfoot, J. B. *St. Paul's Epistle to the Philippians: A Revised Text with Introduction, Notes and Dissertations*. 12th ed. 4 vols. J. B. Lightfoot's Commentary on the Epistles of St. Paul. Peabody, MA: Hendrickson, 1995.

Lightfoot, J. B., and J. R. Harmer. *The Apostolic Fathers*. Grand Rapids: Baker Books, 1889.

Lintott, Andrew. *Imperium Romanum: Politics and Administration*. London: Routledge, 1993.

Livesey, Nina. *Circumcision as a Malleable Symbol*. WUNT 2/295. Tübingen: Mohr Siebeck, 2010.

LoBianco, Tom. "Mitch Daniels Wanted to Replace Historian's Teachings in Favor of Bill Bennett's Conservative Review." Indystar. http://www.indystar.com/story/news/education/2013/08/18/mitch-daniels-wanted-to-replace-liberal-historians-teachings-in-favor-of-bill-bennetts-conservative-review/2669093/

Lohmeyer, Ernst. *Die Briefe an die Philipper, an die Kolosser und Philemon*. KEK 9. 13th ed. Göttingen: Vandenhoeck & Ruprecht, 1964.

———. *Kyrios Jesus: Eine Untersuchung zu Phil. 2:5–11.* 2nd ed. Heidelberg: Winter, 1961.

Lomas, Kathryn. "Roman Imperialism and the City in Italy." Pages 64–78 in *Cultural Identity in the Roman Empire.* Edited by Ray Laurence and Joanne Berry. London: Routledge, 1998.

Long, A. Anthony. "The Socratic Tradition: Diogenes, Crates, and Hellenistic Ethics." Pages 28–46 in *The Cynics: The Cynic Movement in Antiquity and Its Legacy.* Edited by Robert Bracht Branham and Marie-Odile Goulet-Cazé. Berkeley: University of California Press, 1996.

Lopez, Davina C. *Apostle to the Conquered: Reimagining Paul's Mission.* Paul in Critical Contexts. Minneapolis: Fortress, 2008.

Luz, M. "A Description of the Greek Cynic in the Jerusalem Talmud." *JSJ* 20 (1989): 49–60.

MacDonald, Margaret Y. "Slavery, Sexuality, and House Churches: A Reassessment of Colossians 3.18–4.1 in Light of New Research on the Roman Family." *NTS* 53 (2007): 94–113.

Malherbe, Abraham, ed. *The Cynic Epistles.* Resources for Biblical Study. Missoula, MT: Scholars Press, 1977.

———. *Paul and the Popular Philosophers.* Minneapolis: Fortress, 1989.

Malina, Bruce and Jerome Neyrey. "Honor and Shame in Luke-Acts: Pivotal Values of the Mediterranean World." Pages 25–65 in *The Social World of Luke-Acts: Models for Interpretation.* Edited by Jerome Neyrey. Peabody, MA: Hendrickson, 1991.

Marchal, Joseph A. *Hierarchy, Unity, and Imitation: A Feminist Rhetorical Analysis of Power Dynamics in Paul's Letter to the Philippians.* Academia Biblica 24. Atlanta: Society of Biblical Literature, 2006.

———. " 'Making History' Queerly: Touches across Time through a Biblical Behind." *BibInt* 19 (2011): 373–95.

———. "Military Images in Philippians 1–2: A Feminist Rhetorical Analysis of Scholarship, Philippians, and Current Contexts." Pages 265–86 in *Her Master's Tools? Feminist and Postcolonial Engagements of Historical-Critical Discourse.* Edited by Caroline Vander Stichele and Todd Penner. GPBS 9. Atlanta: Society of Biblical Literature, 2005.

———. *Philippians: Historical Problems, Hierarchical Visions, Hysterical Anxieties.* Phoenix Guides to the New Testament 11. Sheffield: Sheffield Phoenix, 2014.

———. *The Politics of Heaven: Women, Gender, and Empire in the Study of Paul.* Paul in Critical Contexts. Minneapolis: Fortress, 2008.

————. "Queer Approaches: Improper Relations with Paul's Letters." Pages 209–27 in *Studying Paul's Letters: Contemporary Perspectives and Methods*. Edited by Joseph A. Marchal. Minneapolis: Fortress, 2012.

————, ed. *Studying Paul's Letters: Contemporary Perspectives and Methods*. Minneapolis: Fortress, 2012.

————. "The Usefulness of an Onesimus: The Sexual Use of Slaves and Paul's Letter to Philemon." *JBL* 130 (2011): 373–95.

Martin, Clarice J. "The Eyes Have It: Slaves in the Communities of Christ-Believers." Pages 221–39 in *Christian Origins*. Vol. 1 of *A People's History of Christianity*. Edited by Richard A. Horsley. Minneapolis: Fortress, 2005.

————. "The Rhetorical Function of Commercial Language in Paul's Letter to Philemon (Verse 18)." Pages 321–37 in *Persuasive Artistry: Studies in New Testament Rhetoric in Honor of George A. Kennedy*. Edited by Duane F. Watson. JSNTSup 50. Sheffield: JSOT Press, 1992.

Mason, Steve. "Jews, Judaeans, Judaizing, Judaism: Problems of Categorization in Ancient History." *JSJ* 38 (2007): 457–512.

McGinn, Thomas A. J. *The Economy of Prostitution in the Roman World: A Study of Social History and the Brothel*. Ann Arbor: University of Michigan Press, 2004.

————. *Prostitution, Sexuality, and the Law in Ancient Rome*. New York: Oxford University Press, 1988.

McGowan, Andrew. *Ascetic Eucharist: Food and Drink in Early Christian Ritual Meals*. Oxford: Clarendon, 1999.

McManus, Barbara. "Livia: *Princeps Femina*." *Augustus and Tiberius: Historical Background*. http://www.vroma.org/~bmcmanus/livia.html.

Meeks, Wayne A. *The First Urban Christians: The Social World of the Apostle Paul*. New Haven: Yale University Press, 1983.

Mentzos, Aristoteles. "Questions of the Topography of Ancient Philippi" [Greek]. *Egnatia* 9 (2005): 101–49.

Merk, Otto. *Handeln aus Glauben: Die Motivierung der Paulinischen Ethik*. Marburger Th St 5. Marburg: Elwert, 1968.

Meyer, Heinrich August Wilhelm. *Critical and Exegetical Handbook to the Epistles to the Philippians and Colossians, and to Philemon*. Translated by J. C. Moore and William P. Dickson. 6th ed. H. A. W. Meyer's Commentary on the New Testament. Peabody, MA: Hendrickson, 1983.

Michaelis, Wilhelm. *Der Brief des Paulus an die Philipper*. THKNT 11. Leipzig: Deichert, 1935.

————. "Die Gefangenschaftsbriefe des Paulus und antike Gefangenenbriefe." *NKZ* 36 (1925): 586–95.

Mikaelian, Allen. "The Mitch Daniels Controversy: Context for the AHA Statement." American Historical Association. https://www.historians.org/publications-and-directories/perspectives-on-history/september-2013/the-mitch-daniels-controversy-context-for-the-aha-statement.

Miller, E. C. "πολιτεύεσθε in Phil. 1.27: Some Philological and Thematic Observations." *JSNT* 15 (1982): 86–96.

Mitchell, Stephen. *Anatolia: Land, Men, and Gods in Asia Minor*. 2 vols. Oxford: Clarendon, 1993.

Moles, John. "Cynic Cosmopolitanism." Pages 105–20 in *The Cynics: The Cynic Movement in Antiquity and Its Legacy*. Edited by Robert Bracht Branham and Marie-Odile Goulet-Cazé. Berkeley: University of California Press, 1996.

————. "'Honestius Quam Ambitiosius'? An Exploration of the Cynic's Attitude to Moral Corruption in His Fellow Men." *JHS* 103 (1983): 103–23.

Montserrat, Dominic. *Sex and Society in Greco-Roman Egypt*. New York: Kegan Paul, 1996.

Moore, Stephen D. *God's Beauty Parlor: And Other Queer Spaces in and around the Bible*. Contraversions: Jews and Other Differences. Stanford, CA: Stanford University Press, 2001.

————. "Que(e)rying Paul: Preliminary Questions." Pages 249–74 in *Auguries: The Jubilee Volume of the Sheffield Department of Biblical Studies*. Edited by David J. A. Clines and Stephen D. Moore. JSOTSup 269. Sheffield: Sheffield Academic, 1998.

Moxnes, Halvor. "Patron-Client Relations and the New Community in Luke-Acts." Pages 241–68 in *The Social World of Luke-Acts: Models for Interpretation*. Edited by Jerome Neyrey. Peabody, MA: Hendrickson, 1991.

Müller, Ulrich B. *Der Brief des Paulus an die Philipper*. 2nd ed. THKNT 11.1. Leipzig: Evangelische Verlagsanstalt, 2003.

Murphy-O'Connor, Jerome. "Christological Anthropology in Philippians 2:6–11." *RB* 83 (1976): 25–50.

Nanos, Mark D. "How Inter-Christian Approaches to Paul's Rhetoric Can Perpetuate Negative Valuations of Jewishness—Although Proposing to Avoid That Outcome." *BibInt* 13 (2005): 255–69.

————. *The Irony of Galatians: Paul's Letter in First-Century Context.* Minneapolis: Fortress, 2002.

————. "Paul and Judaism: Why Not Paul's Judaism?" Pages 117–60 in *Paul Unbound: Other Perspectives on the Apostle.* Edited by Mark D. Given. Peabody, MA: Hendrickson, 2010.

————. "Paul and the Jewish Tradition: The Ideology of the *Shema.*" Pages 62–80 in *Celebrating Paul: Festschrift in Honor of Jerome Murphy-O'Connor, O.P., and Joseph A. Fitzmyer, S.J.* Edited by Peter Spitaler. CBQMS 48. Washington, DC: Catholic Biblical Association of America, 2012.

————. "Paul's Non-Jews Do Not Become 'Jews,' But Do They Become 'Jewish'? Reading Romans 2:25–29 within Judaism, alongside Josephus." *Journal of the Jesus Movement in its Jewish Setting* 1 (2014): 26–53.

————. "Paul's Polemic in Philippians 3 as Jewish-Subgroup Vilification of Local Non-Jewish Cultic and Philosophical Alternatives." *Journal for the Study of Paul and His Letters* 3 (2013): 47–92.

————. "Paul's Reversal of Jews Calling Gentiles 'Dogs' (Philippians 3:2): 1600 Years of an Ideological Tale Wagging an Exegetical Dog?" *BibInt* 17 (2009): 448–82.

Nanos, Mark D., and Magnus Zetterholm, eds. *Paul within Judaism: Restoring the First-Century Context to the Apostle.* Minneapolis: Fortress, 2015.

Nasrallah, Laura S., Charalambos Bakirtzis, and Steven J. Friesen, eds. *From Roman to Early Christian Thessalonike: Studies in Religion and Archaeology.* HTS 64. Cambridge: Harvard University Press, 2010.

Navia, Luis E. *Diogenes of Sinope: The Man in the Tub.* Contributions in Philosophy. Westport, CT: Greenwood, 1998.

Nicholson, John. "The Delivery and Confidentiality of Cicero's Letters." *CJ* 90 (1994): 33–63.

Nippel, Wilfried. *Public Order in Ancient Rome.* Key Themes in Ancient History. Cambridge: Cambridge University Press, 1995.

Noethlichs, Karl Leo. "Der Jude Paulus: Ein Tarser oder Römer?" Pages 53–84 in *Rom und das himmlische Jerusalem: Die frühen Christen zwischen Anpassung und Ablehnung.* Edited by Raban von Haehling. Darmstadt: Wissenschaftliche Buchgesellschaft, 2000.

Norman, Edward. *The House of God: Church Architecture, Style, and History.* London: Thames & Hudson, 1990.

Oakes, Peter S. "Constructing Poverty Scales for Graeco-Roman Society: A Response to Steven Friesen's 'Poverty in Pauline Studies.'" *JSNT* 26 (2004): 367–71.

———. "Economic Approaches: Scarce Resources and Interpretive Opportunities." Pages 72–91 in *Studying Paul's Letters: Contemporary Perspectives and Methods*. Edited by Joseph A. Marchal. Minneapolis: Fortress, 2012.

———. "Methodological Issues in Using Economic Evidence in Interpretation of Early Christian Texts." Pages 9–34 in *Engaging Economics: New Testament Scenarios and Early Christian Reception*. Edited by Bruce W. Longenecker and Kelly D. Liebengood. Grand Rapids: Eerdmans, 2009.

———. *Philippians: From People to Letter*. SNTSMS 110. Cambridge: Cambridge University Press, 2001.

———, ed. *Rome in the Bible and the Early Church*. Grand Rapids, MI: Paternoster/Baker Academic, 2002.

Oakman, Douglas E. "The Countryside in Luke-Acts." Pages 151–79 in *The Social World of Luke-Acts*. Edited by Jerome H. Neyrey. Peabody, MA: Hendrickson, 1991.

O'Brien, Peter. *The Epistle to the Philippians*. NIGTC. Grand Rapids: Eerdmans, 1991.

Oldfather, C. H. *Diodorus of Sicily III*. Cambridge: Harvard University Press, 1970.

Omerzu, Heike. *Der Prozess des Paulus: Eine exegetische und rechtshistorische Untersuchung der Apostelgeschichte*. BZNW 115. Berlin: de Gruyter, 2002.

———. "Spurensuche: Apostelgeschichte und Paulusbriefe als Zeugnis einer ephesischen Gefangenschaft des Paulus." Pages 295–326 in *Die Apostelgeschichte im Kontext antiker und frühchristlicher Historiographie*. Edited by Jörg Frei, Clare K. Rothschild, and Jens Schröter. BZNW 162. Berlin: de Gruyter, 2009.

Onfray, Michel. *Cynismes: Portrait du philosophe en chien*. Paris: Bernard Grassett, 1990.

Oropeza, B. J. *Jews, Gentiles, and the Opponents of Paul: The Pauline Letters*. Apostasy in the New Testament Communities 2. Eugene, OR: Cascade, 2011.

Osiek, Carolyn L. "Family Matters." Pages 201–20 in *Christian Origins*. Vol. 1 of *A People's History of Christianity*. Edited by Richard A. Horsley. Minneapolis: Fortress, 2005.

————. "Female Slaves, *Porneia*, and the Limits of Obedience." Pages 255–74 in *Early Christian Families in Context: An Interdisciplinary Dialogue*. Edited by David L. Balch and Carolyn Osiek. Grand Rapids: Eerdmans, 2003.

————. *Philippians, Philemon*. ANTC. Nashville: Abingdon, 2000.

Osiek, Carolyn L., and David L. Balch, eds. *Early Christian Families in Context: An Interdisciplinary Dialogue*. Religion, Marriage, and Family. Grand Rapids: Eerdmans, 2003.

————. *Families in the New Testament World: Households and House Churches*. The Family, Religion, and Culture. Louisville: Westminster John Knox Press, 1997.

Oxfam America. *Like Machines in the Fields: Workers without Rights in US Agriculture*. Boston: Oxfam America, 2004. http://www.oxfamamerica.org/static/oa3/files/like-machines-in-the-fields.pdf.

Pagnol, Marcel. *Manon des sources: L'Eau des collines*. Paris: Editions Flammarion, 1995.

Parenti, Michael. *The Assassination of Julius Caesar: A People's History of Ancient Rome*. New York: New Press, 2003.

Parkin, Michael. *Economics*. 7th ed. Boston: Addison Wesley, 2005.

Patterson, Orlando. *Slavery and Social Death: A Comparative Study*. Cambridge: Harvard University Press, 1982.

Pelekanides, Stylianos. "ΑΝΑΣΚΑΦΑΙ ΟΚΤΑΓΩΝΟΥ ΦΙΛΙΠΠΩΝ." *Praktika tes en Athinais Archaiologikes Hetaireias* 15 (1960): 76–94.

————. "Kultprobleme im Apostel-Paulus-Oktogon von Philippi im Zusammenhang mit einem älteren Heroenkult." Pages 393–99 in vol. 2 of *Atti del IX Congresso Internazionale di Archeologia Cristiana*. Rome: Pontificio Istituto di Archeologia Cristiana, 1978.

Perdrizet, Paul. "Inscriptions de Philippes: Les Rosalies." *BCH* 24 (1900): 304–5.

Pervo, Richard I. *Acts: A Commentary*. Hermeneia. Minneapolis: Fortress, 2009.

Peterman, Gerald W. *Paul's Gift from Philippi: Conventions of Gift Exchange and Christian Giving*. SNTSMS 92. Cambridge: Cambridge University Press, 1997.

Petersen, Norman R. *Rediscovering Paul: Philemon and the Sociology of Paul's Narrative World*. Philadelphia: Fortress, 1985.

Picard, Charles. "Un texte nouveau de la correspondance entre Abgar D'Osroène et Jésus-Christ gravé sur une porte de ville, à Philippes (Macédoine)." *BCH* 44 (1920): 41–69.

Pilhofer, Peter. "Einer der 5984072? Zum römischen Bürgerrecht des Paulus." Pages 63–75 in *Neues aus der Welt der frühen Christen*. BWANT 195. Stuttgart: Kohlhammer, 2011.

———. *Philippi I: Die erste christliche Gemeinde Europas*. WUNT 87. Tübingen: Mohr Siebeck, 1995.

———. *Philippi II: Katalog der Inschriften von Philippi*. 2nd ed. WUNT 119. Tübingen: Mohr Siebeck, 2009.

Poland, Franz. *Geschichte des griechischen Vereinswesens*. Leipzig: Teubner, 1909.

Polanyi, Karl, et al. *Trade and Market in the Early Empires*. Chicago: Henry Regnery, 1971.

Portefaix, Lilian. *Sisters Rejoice: Paul's Letter to the Philippians and Luke-Acts as Received by First-Century Philippian Women*. ConBNT 20. Stockholm: Almqvist & Wiksell, 1988.

Pottier, Edmond, and Amédée Hauvette-Besnault. "Inscriptions d' Érythrées et de Téos." *BCH* 4 (1880): 153–82.

Preisigke, Friedrich. *Wörterbuch der griechischen Papyrusurkunden*. Vol. 1. Wiesbaden: Harrassowitz, 1925.

Preisigke, Friedrich, et al. *Sammelbuch griechischer Urkunden aus Aegypten*. 21 vols. Wiesbaden: Harrassowitz, 1915–2002.

Räisänen, Heikki. *The Rise of Christian Beliefs: The Thought World of Early Christians*. Minneapolis: Fortress, 2010.

Rappe, Sarah. "Father of the Dogs? Tracking the Cynics in Plato's Euthydemus." *CP* 95 (2000): 291–93.

Rapske, Brian. *The Book of Acts and Paul in Roman Custody*. Grand Rapids: Eerdmans, 1994.

———. "The Importance of Helpers to the Imprisoned Paul in the Book of Acts." *TynBul* 42 (1991): 3–30.

Rawson, Beryl, ed. *The Family in Ancient Rome: New Perspectives*. Ithaca, NY: Cornell University Press, 1986.

Reed, Jeffrey T. *A Discourse Analysis of Philippians: Method and Rhetoric in the Debate over Literary Integrity*. JSNTSup 136. Sheffield: Sheffield Academic, 1997.

Reilly, L. C. *Slaves in Ancient Greece: Slaves from Greek Manumission Inscriptions*. Chicago: Ares, 1978.

Reumann, John. *Philippians: A New Translation with Introduction and Commentary*. AB 33B. New Haven: Yale University Press, 2008.

Rhoads, David. "Performing Events in Early Christianity: New Testament Writings in an Oral Context." Pages 166–93 in *The Interface of Orality and Writing.* Edited by Annette Weissenrieder and Robert R. Coote. WUNT 260. Tübingen: Mohr Siebeck, 2006.

———. "Performing the Gospel of Mark." Pages 102–17 in *Body and Bible: Interpreting and Experiencing Biblical Narratives.* Edited by Björn Krondorfer. Philadelphia: Trinity Press International, 1992.

Richardson, Cyril R., ed. *Early Christian Fathers.* New York: Macmillan, 1978.

Richlin, Amy. *The Garden of Priapus: Sexuality and Aggression in Roman Humor.* Rev. ed. New Haven: Yale University Press, 1992.

———. "Pliny's Brasserie." Pages 197–220 in *Roman Sexualities.* Edited by Judith P. Hallett and Marilyn B. Skinner. Princeton: Princeton University Press, 1997.

Ricoeur, Paul. *Oneself as Another.* Chicago: University of Chicago Press, 1992.

Rieger, Joerg, and Kwok Pui-lan. *Occupy Religion: Theology of the Multitude.* Religion in the Modern World. Lanham: Rowman & Littlefield, 2012.

Riepl, Wolfgang. *Das Nachrichtenwesen des Altertums mit besonderer Rücksicht auf die Römer.* Leipzig: Teubner, 1913.

Rist, J. M. *Stoic Philosophy.* Cambridge: Cambridge University Press, 1969.

Robbins, Lionel. *Essay on the Nature and Significance of Economic Science.* London: Macmillan, 1932.

Roebuck, Carl. *The World of Ancient Times.* New York: Scribner, 1966.

Romano, David G. "Urban and Rural Planning in Roman Corinth." Pages 25–59 in *Urban Religion in Roman Corinth: Interdisciplinary Approaches.* Edited by Daniel Schowalter and Steven J. Friesen. HTS 53. Cambridge: Harvard University Press, 2005.

Romm, James. "Dog Heads and Noble Savages: Cynicism before the Cynics?" Pages 121–35 in *The Cynics: The Cynic Movement in Antiquity and Its Legacy.* Edited by Robert Bracht Branham and Marie-Odile Goulet-Cazé. Berkeley: University of California Press, 1996.

Ruden, Sarah. *The Aeneid: Virgil.* New Haven: Yale University Press, 2008.

———. *Aristophanes: Lysistrata.* Cambridge, MA: Hackett, 2003.

———. *Homeric Hymns.* Cambridge, MA: Hackett, 2005.

———. *Paul among the People: The Apostle Reinterpreted and Reimagined in His Own Time.* New York: Image Books, 2010.

———. *Petronius: Satyricon.* Cambridge, MA: Hackett, 2000.

Runesson, Anders. "Inventing Christian Identity: Paul, Ignatius, and Theodosius I." Pages 59–92 in *Exploring Early Christian Identity*. Edited by Bengt Holmberg. WUNT 226. Tübingen: Mohr Siebeck, 2008.

Ruppert, Lothar. *Der leidende Gerechte: Eine motivgeschichtliche Untersuchung zum Alten Testament und zwischentestamentlichen Judentum*. Würzburg: Echter, 1972.

Russell, Frank Santi. *Information Gathering in Classical Greece*. Ann Arbor: University of Michigan Press, 1999.

Sampley, J. Paul. *Pauline Partnership in Christ: Christian Community and Commitment in Light of Roman Law*. Philadelphia: Fortress, 1980.

———, ed. *Paul in the Greco-Roman World: A Handbook*. Harrisburg, PA: Trinity Press International, 2003.

Sanders, E. P. "Paul on the Law, His Opponents, and the Jewish People in Philippians 3 and 2 Corinthians 11." Pages 75–90 in *Anti-Judaism in Early Christianity: Paul and the Gospels*. Edited by Peter Richardson and David M. Granskou. Waterloo: Wilfrid Laurier University Press, 1986.

Sanders, James. *Canon and Community: A Guide to Canonical Criticism*. Philadelphia: Fortress, 1984.

Sandnes, Karl Olav. *Belly and Body in the Pauline Epistles*. SNTSMS 120. Cambridge: Cambridge University Press, 2002.

Scheid, John, and Janet Lloyd. *An Introduction to Roman Religion*. Bloomington: Indiana University Press, 2003.

Schenk, Wolfgang. *Die Philipperbriefe des Paulus: Kommentar*. Stuttgart: Kohlhammer, 1984.

Schmithals, Walter. *Paul and the Gnostics*. Translated by John E. Steely. Nashville: Abingdon, 1972.

Schmitz, Otto. *Aus der Welt eines Gefangenen: Der Philipperbrief*. Giessen: Brunnen Verlag, 1988.

Schneemelcher, Wilhelm. "Acts of Paul." *NTApoc* 2:322–90.

Schüssler Fiorenza, Elisabeth. *Bread Not Stone: The Challenge of Biblical Interpretation*. 10th Anniversary Edition. Boston: Beacon, 1995.

———. *But She Said: Feminist Practices of Biblical Interpretation*. Boston: Beacon, 1992.

———. *In Memory of Her: A Feminist Theological Reconstruction of Christian Origins*. New York: Crossroad, 1983; 10th anniversary edition, 1994.

———. *Jesus: Miriam's Child, Sophia's Prophet; Critical Issues in Feminist Christology*. New York: Continuum, 1994.

———. "Paul and the Politics of Interpretation." Pages 40–57 in *Paul and Politics: Ekklesia, Israel, Imperium, Interpretation; Essays in Honor of Krister Stendahl*. Edited by Richard A. Horsley. Harrisburg, PA: Trinity Press International, 2000.

———. *The Power of the Word: Scripture and the Rhetoric of Empire*. Minneapolis: Fortress, 2007.

———. *Rhetoric and Ethic: The Politics of Biblical Studies*. Minneapolis: Fortress, 1999.

———. *Wisdom Ways: Introducing Feminist Biblical Interpretation*. Maryknoll, NY: Orbis, 2001.

Schwartz, Daniel R. *Judeans and Jews: Four Faces of Dichotomy in Ancient Jewish History*. Toronto: University of Toronto Press, 2014.

———. "'Judaean' or 'Jew'? How Should We Translate *Ioudaios* in Josephus?" Pages 3–27 in *Jewish Identity in the Greco-Roman World*. Edited by Jörg Frey, Daniel R. Schwartz, and Stephanei Gripentrog. Ancient Judaism and Early Christianity 71. Leiden: Brill, 2007.

Schwyzer, Eduard, and Albert Debrunner. *Syntax und syntaktische Stilistik*. Vol. 2 of *Griechische Grammatik*. 5th edition. Handbuch der Altertumswissenschaft 2.1.2. Munich: Beck, 1988.

Scott, James C. *Domination and the Arts of Resistance*. New Haven: Yale University Press, 1990.

———. *The Moral Economy of the Peasant: Rebellion and Subsistence in Southeast Asia*. New Haven: Yale University Press, 1977.

Scroggs, Robin. "Paul the Prisoner: Political Asceticism in the Letter to the Philippians." Pages 187–207 in *Asceticism and the New Testament*. Edited by Leif E. Vaage and Vincent L. Wimbush. New York: Routledge, 1999.

Seeley, David. "The Background of the Philippians Hymn (2:6–11)." *Journal of Higher Criticism* 1 (1994): 49–72.

Segovia, Fernando F., and Mary Ann Tolbert, eds. *Social Location and Biblical Interpretation in the United States*. Vol. 1 of *Reading from This Place*. Minneapolis: Fortress, 1995.

———. *Social Location and Biblical Interpretation in Global Perspective*. Vol. 2 of *Reading from This Place*. Minneapolis: Fortress, 1995.

Seiber, Jakob "Der Geheimdienst Alexanders des Grossen (336–325 v. Chr.)." Pages 21–33 in *Geheimdienste in der Weltgeschichte*. Edited by Wolfgang Krieger. Cologne: Anaconda, 2007.

Sève, Michel. *Guide du forum de Philippes*. Sites et Monuments 18. Athènes: École Française, 2012.

———. "Un monument honorifique au forum de Philippes." *BCH* 112 (1988): 467–79.

———. "De la naissance à la mort d'une ville: Philippes en Macédoine; IVᵉ siècle av. J.-C.-VIIᵉ siècle ap. J.-C." *Histoire Urbaine* 1 (2000): 187–204.

Sève, Michel, and Patrick Weber. "Le côté nord du forum de Philippes," *BCH* 110 (1986): 531–81.

Shapiro, H. Alan, and Tonio Hölscher. "Homonoia/Concordia." *LIMC* 5 (1990): 479–98.

Sharpe, Jim. "History from Below." Pages 25–41 in *New Perspectives on Historical Writing*. Edited by Peter Burke. 2nd ed. University Park: Pennsylvania State University Press, 2001.

Sheldon, Rose Mary. *Intelligence Activities in Ancient Rome*. London: Frank Cass, 2005.

Sherwin-White, Adrian N. *The Roman Citizenship*. 2nd ed. Oxford: Clarendon, 1973.

Skeat, T.C. "Did Paul Write to 'Bishops and Deacons' at Philippi? A Note on Philippians 1:1." *NovT* 37 (1995): 12–15.

Skinner, Marilyn B. "Introduction: *Quod multo fit aliter in Graeci...*" Pages 3–25 in *Roman Sexualities*. Edited by Judith P. Hallett and Marilyn B. Skinner. Princeton: Princeton University Press, 1997.

Smith, Jonathan Z. *Drudgery Divine: On the Comparison of Early Christianities and the Religions of Late Antiquity*. CSJH. Chicago: University of Chicago Press, 1990.

Smyth, Herbert Weir. *Greek Grammar*. Revised by Gordon M. Messing. Cambridge: Harvard University Press, 1920.

Spawforth, A. J. S. "Roman Corinth: The Formation of a Colonial Elite." Pages 167–82 in *Roman Onomastics in the Greek East: Social and Political Aspects*. Edited by A. D. Rizakis. Meltēmata 21. Athens: Research Center for Greek and Roman Antiquity. Paris: de Boccard, 1996.

Spelman, Elizabeth. *Inessential Woman: Problems of Exclusion in Feminist Thought*. Boston: Beacon, 1988.

Spitaler, Peter, ed. *Celebrating Paul: Festschrift in Honor of Jerome Murphy O'Connor O.P. and Joseph Fitzmyer S.J.* CBQMS 48. Washington, DC: Catholic Biblical Association of America, 2011.

Spivak, Gayatri Chakravorty. "Can the Subaltern Speak?" Pages 271–313 in *Marxism and the Interpretation of Culture*. Edited by Cary Nelson and Lawrence Grossberg. Urbana: University of Illinois Press, 1988.

St. Croix, G. E. M. de. *The Class Struggle in the Ancient Greek World: From the Archaic Age to the Arab Conquest.* Ithaca, NY: Cornell University Press, 1981.

Standhartinger, Angela. "Eintracht in Philippi: Zugleich ein Beitrag zur Funktion von Phil 2,6–11 im Kontext." Pages 149–75 in *Paulus—Werk und Wirkung: Festschrift für Andreas Lindemann zum 70. Geburtstag.* Edited by Paul-Gerhard Klumbies and David DuToit. Tübingen: Mohr Siebeck, 2013.

———. " 'Join in Imitating Me' (Philippians 3.17): Towards an Interpretation of Philippians 3." *NTS* 54 (2008): 417–35.

———. "Die paulinische Theologie im Spannungsfeld römisch-imperialer Machtpolitik: Eine neue Perspektive auf Paulus, kritisch geprüft anhand des Philipperbriefs." Pages 364–82 in *Religion, Politik und Gewalt.* Edited by Friedrich Schweitzer. Europäischen Kongresses für Theologie 12. Gütersloh: Gütersloher Verlagshaus, 2005.

Stark, Rodney. *Discovering God: The Origins of the Great Religions and the Evolution of Belief.* New York: HarperOne, 2007.

———. *The Rise of Christianity: A Sociologist Reconsiders History.* Princeton: Princeton University Press, 1996.

Stegemann, Wolfgang. "War der Apostel Paulus ein römischer Bürger." *ZNW* 78 (1987): 200–229.

Stoler, Ann Laura. *Along the Archival Grain: Epistemic Anxieties and Colonial Common Sense.* Princeton: Princeton University Press, 2009.

Stowers, Stanley K. "Friends and Enemies in the Politics of Heaven: Reading Theology in Philippians." Pages 105–121 in *Thessalonians, Philippians, Galatians, Philemon.* Vol. 1 of *Pauline Theology.* Edited by Jouette M. Bassler. Minneapolis: Augsburg Fortress, 1991.

Stumpp, Bettina Eva. *Prostitution in der römischen Antike.* Berlin: Akademie, 1998.

Sugirtharajah, R. S. "Convergent Trajectories? Liberation Hermeneutics and Postcolonial Biblical Criticism." Pages 103–23 in *Postcolonial Criticism and Biblical Interpretation.* Oxford: Oxford University Press, 2002.

———. "Introduction: The Margin as a Site of Creative Re-visioning." Pages 1–10 in *Voices from the Margin: Interpreting the Bible in the Third World.* Edited by R. S. Sugirtharajah. Maryknoll, NY: Orbis, 1995.

Sumney, Jerry L. *"Servants of Satan," "False Brothers" and Other Opponents of Paul.* JSNTSup 188. Sheffield: Sheffield Academic, 1999.

Sylburg, Frederic, ed. *Etymologicum magnum.* Leipzig: Wiegel, 1816.

Tajra, H. W. *The Martyrdom of St. Paul*. WUNT 2/67. Tübingen: Mohr Siebeck, 1994.

Theissen, Gerd. *The Social Setting of Pauline Christianity: Essays on Corinth*. Translated by John H. Schütz. Philadelphia: Fortress, 1982.

Thistlethwaite, Susan B. *#OccupytheBible: What Jesus Really Said (and Did) about Money and Power*. New York: Astor + Blue, 2012.

Thomas, Christine M. "On Not Finding Small Finds: Spatial Discourse in Early Christianity at Ephesos and Elsewhere." Paper presented at the Annual Meeting of the Society of Biblical Literature. Boston, 23 November 1999.

Tsalampouni, Ekaterini. *Makedonia in the New Testament Period* [Greek]. Bibliotheca Biblica 23. Thessaloniki: Pournaras, 2002.

Tsitouridou, Anna. "Ena anaglupho apo tous Philippous me parastaseis apo to zodiako kuklo." *Résumés des communications*. Thessaloniki: Xe Congres International d'Archéologie Chrétienne, 1980.

Tyson, Joseph B. "Paul's Opponents at Philippi." *PRSt* 3 (1976): 82–95.

Tzanavari, Katerina. "The Worship of Gods and Heroes in Thessaloniki." Pages 177–262 in *Roman Thessaloniki*. Edited by D. V. Grammenos. Thessaloniki: Archaeological Museum, 2003.

Ulonska, H. "Gesetz und Beshneidung: Überlegungen zu einem paulinish-cen Ablösungskonflikt." Pages 314–31 in *Jesus Rede von Gott*. Edited by D. Koch. Gütersloh: Gütersloher Verlag Mohn, 1989.

Vaage, Leif E. "Like Dogs Barking: Cynic Parrêsia and Shameless Asceticism." *Semeia* 57 (1992): 25–39.

Vander Waerdt, Paul A. "Zeno's Republic and the Origins of Natural Law." Pages 300–301 in *The Socratic Movement*. Edited by Vander Waerdt. Ithaca, NY: Cornell University Press, 1994.

Verhoef, Eduard. "Christians Reacted Differently to Non-Christian Cults." *HTS Teologiese Studies* 67 (2011): 265–71.

———. *Philippi: How Christianity Began in Europe; The Epistle to the Philippians and the Excavations in Philippi*. London: Bloomsbury, 2013.

———. "Syncretism in the Church of Philippi." *HTS Teologiese Studies* 64 (2008): 697–714.

Veyne, Paul. "Homosexuality in Ancient Rome." Pages 26–35 in *Western Sexuality: Practice and Precept in Past and Present Times*. Edited by Philippe Ariès and Andre Béjin. Oxford: Oxford University Press, 1985.

Vincent, Marvin R. *Critical and Exegetical Commentary on the Epistles to the Philippians and to Philemon*. ICC: Edinburgh, 1897.

Vos, Craig S. de. *Church and Community Conflicts: The Relationships of the Thessalonian, Corinthian, and Philippian Churches with Their Wider Civic Communities.* SBLDS 168. Atlanta: Scholars Press, 1999.

Walker, Barbara G. *The Woman's Dictionary of Symbols and Sacred Objects.* San Francisco: Harper & Row, 1988.

———. *The Woman's Encyclopedia of Myths and Secrets.* San Francisco: Harper & Row, 1983.

Walker, Susan, and Andrew Burnett. *Augustus: Handlist of the Exhibition.* Occasional Paper 16. London: British Museum Publications, 1981.

Walter, Nikolaus, et al. *Die Briefe an die Philipper: Thessalonicher und an Philemon.* NTD 8.2. Göttingen: Vandenhoeck & Ruprecht, 1998.

Walters, James. "Civic Identity in Roman Corinth and Its Impact on Early Christians." Pages 397–417 in *Urban Religion in Roman Corinth.* Edited by Steven J. Friesen and Daniel N. Schowalter. HTS 53. Cambridge: Harvard University Press, 2005.

Walters, Jonathan. "Invading the Roman Body: Manliness and Impenetrability in Roman Thought." Pages 29–43 in *Roman Sexualities.* Edited by Judith P. Hallett and Marilyn B. Skinner. Princeton: Princeton University Press, 1997.

———. " 'No More Than a Boy': The Shifting Construction of Masculinity from Ancient Greece to the Middle Ages." *Gender and History* 5 (1991): 20–33.

Walton, Steve. "Paul, Patronage and Pay: What Do We Know about the Apostle's Financial Support?" Pages 220–33 in *Paul as Missionary: Identity, Activity, Theology, and Practice.* Edited by Travor J. Burke and Brian S. Rosner. London: T&T Clark, 2001.

Wan, Sze-kar. "Collection for the Saints as Anticolonial Act: Implications of Paul's Ethnic Reconstruction." Pages 191–215 in *Paul and Politics: Ekklesia, Israel, Imperium, Interpretation: Essays in Honor of Krister Stendahl.* Edited by Richard A. Horsley. Harrisburg, PA: Trinity Press International, 2000.

Wansink, Craig S. *Chained in Christ: The Experience and Rhetoric of Paul's Imprisonments.* JSNTSup 130. Sheffield: Sheffield Academic, 1996.

Weaver, P. R. C. *Familia Caesaris: A Social Study of the Emperor's Freedmen and Slaves.* Cambridge: Cambridge University Press, 1972.

Weber, Max. *Sociology of Religion.* Boston: Beacon, 1964.

Wedderburn, A. J. M. *Baptism and Resurrection: Studies in Pauline Theology against Its Graeco-Roman Background.* WUNT 44. Tübingen: Mohr Siebeck, 1987.

White, L. Michael. "Morality between Two Worlds: A Paradigm of Friendship in Philippians." Pages 201–15 in *Greeks, Romans, and Christians: Essays in Honor of Abraham J. Malherbe*. Edited by David L. Balch, Everett Ferguson, and Wayne A. Meeks. Minneapolis: Fortress, 1990.

———. "Paul and *Pater Familias*." Pages 457–87 in *Paul in the Greco-Roman World: A Handbook*. Harrisburg, PA: Trinity Press International, 2003.

Wild, Robert. *Water in the Cultic Worship of Isis and Sarapis*. Leiden: Brill, 1981.

Williams, Craig A. *Roman Homosexuality: Ideologies of Masculinity in Classical Antiquity*. New York: Oxford University Press, 1999.

Williams, Margaret H. "The Meaning and Function of *Ioudaios* in Graeco-Roman Inscriptions." *ZPE* 116 (1997): 249–62.

Wimbush, Vincent L. "Interpreters: Enslaving/Enslaved/Runagate." *JBL* 130 (2011): 5–24.

Wimbush, Vincent L., with Rosamond C. Rodman, eds. *African-Americans and the Bible: Sacred Texts and Social Structures*. New York: Continuum, 2000.

Winkes, Rolf. *Livia, Octavia, Iulia: Porträts und Darstellungen*. Archaeologia Transatlantica 13. Louvain-la-Neuve: Département d'archéologie et d'histoire de l'art Collège Erasme, 1995.

Winter, Bruce W. *Seek the Welfare of the City: Christians as Benefactors and Citizens*. First-Century Christians in the Graeco-Roman World. Carlisle: Paternoster, 1994.

Wire, Antoinette Clark. *The Case for Mark Composed in Performance*. Biblical Performance Criticism 3. Eugene, OR: Cascade, 2011.

———. *The Corinthian Women Prophets: A Reconstruction through Paul's Rhetoric*. Minneapolis: Fortress, 1990.

Witt, Rex. "The Egyptian Cults in Ancient Macedonia." Pages 324–33 in *Ancient Macedonia*. Edited by B. Laourdas. Thessaloniki: Institute for Balkan Studies, 1970.

———. "The Kabeiroi in Ancient Macedonia." Pages 964–77 in *ΘΕΣΣΑΛΟΝΙΚΗ ΦΙΛΙΠΠΟΥ ΒΑΣΙΛΙΣΣΑΝ* [Studies on Ancient Thessalonica]. Edited by Polyxeni Adam-Veleni. Thessaloniki: Archaeological Museum, 1985.

Wittig, Monique. "The Mark of Gender." Pages 63–73 in *Poetics of Gender*. Edited by Nancy K. Miller. Gender and Culture. New York: Columbia University Press, 1986.

Wood, Susan. "Diva Augusta: Images of Imperial Women in Roman Art." *Text for Exhibition*. Sackler Museum. Cambridge: Harvard University: 1986.

Wright, N. T. "Paul's Gospel and Caesar's Empire." Pages 160–83 in *Paul and Politics: Ekklesia, Israel, Imperium, Interpretation: Essays in Honor of Krister Stendahl*. Edited by Richard A. Horsley. Harrisburg, PA: Trinity Press International, 2000.

Writers for the 99%. *Occupy Wall Street: The Inside Story of an Action That Changed America*. Chicago: Haymarket Books, 2012.

Zahn, Theodor. *Einleitung in das Neue Testament*. Vol. 1. Leipzig: Deichert, 1906.

Zinn, Howard. *A People's History of the United States*. New York: Harper & Row, 1980.

CONTRIBUTORS

Valerie A. Abrahamsen holds master's and doctoral degrees in New Testament and Early Christian Origins from Harvard Divinity School. Her primary research interests are women in antiquity and New Testament archaeology. She is the author of *Goddess and God: A Holy Tension in the First Christian Centuries* (2006), *Women and Worship at Philippi* (1995), and numerous articles. Her current project is an examination of evidence for the survival of the individual soul after death. Abrahamsen is a member of the Society of Biblical Literature and the Archaeological Institute of America and an active Episcopalian.

Richard Ascough is full Professor and the Director at the School of Religion at Queen's University in Kingston, Canada, where he teaches undergraduate and graduate courses in religious studies. His research focuses on the history of early Christianity and Greco-Roman religious culture, on which he has published more than thirty articles and nine books, including *Associations in the Greco-Roman World* (with John Kloppenborg and Philip Harland, 2012) and *1 and 2 Thessalonians: Encountering the Christ Group at Thessalonike* (2014).

Robert Brawley is McGaw Professor of New Testament Emeritus at McCormick Theological Seminary. He also taught at La Comunidad Reformada de Estudios Superiores in Mexico and Memphis Theological Seminary. He is the author of numerous publications in New Testament studies including the commentary on Luke in the Fortress Commentary on the Bible and the editor-in-chief of *The Oxford Encyclopedia of Bible and Ethics*.

Noelle Damico is a Senior Fellow at the National Economic and Social Rights Initiative. An ordained minister in the United Church of Christ, she has worked side-by-side with the Coalition of Immokalee Workers for fifteen years, organizing institutional and grassroots support for the farm-workers' Campaign for Fair Food. Noelle serves on the Board of Directors of the Fair Food Standards Council. She has lectured on the advances made by the Fair Food Program at universities, the Organization for Security and Cooperation in Europe, the US Department of Justice National Conference on Human Trafficking, and other national and international forums.

Richard A. Horsley was the Distinguished Professor of Liberal Arts and the Study of Religion at the University of Massachusetts, Boston. He is the author and editor of numerous works that challenge traditional approaches to the study of Paul's letters, including *Paul and Empire* (1997), *Paul and Politics* (2000), *Paul and the Roman Imperial Order* (2004), and *A People's History of Christianity: Christian Origins* (2005).

Joseph A. Marchal is Associate Professor of Religious Studies (and Affiliated Faculty in Women's and Gender Studies) at Ball State University and the author of *Hierarchy, Unity, and Imitation: A Feminist Rhetorical Analysis of Power Dynamics in Paul's Letter to the Philippians* (2006), *The Politics of Heaven: Women, Gender, and Empire in the Study of Paul* (2008), and *Philippians: Historical Problems, Hierarchical Visions, Hysterical Anxieties* (2014). He is also the editor of *Studying Paul's Letters: Contemporary Perspectives and Methods* (2012).

Mark D. Nanos holds a Ph.D. from the University of St. Andrews. He is a lecturer at the University of Kansas and author of *The Mystery of Romans: The Jewish Context of Paul's Letter* (1996), which won the National Jewish Book Award for Christian-Jewish Relations. He also authored *The Irony of Galatians* (2002), edited *The Galatians Debate* (2002), and coedited *Paul Within Judaism* (2015). A Jewish specialist on the New Testament, he is a frequent speaker on how to interpret Paul within Judaism and has contributed many essays to a variety of journals and edited volumes on the subject.

Peter Oakes is Greenwood Senior Lecturer in the New Testament at the University of Manchester, UK. His previous publications include: *Philippians: From People to Letter* (2001); *Reading Romans in Pompeii: Paul's Letter at Ground Level* (2009); *Galatians* (2015); "Methodological Issues in Using Economic Evidence in Interpretation of Early Christian Texts," in Bruce

W. Longenecker and Kelly D. Liebengood's *Engaging Economics* (2009); and "Economic Approaches: Scarce Resources and Interpretive Opportunities," in Joseph A. Marchal's *Studying Paul's Letters* (2012).

Gerardo Reyes Chavez is a senior staff member with the award-winning human rights organization, the Coalition of Immokalee Workers (CIW). Reyes is a farmworker and has worked in the fields since age eleven, first as a peasant farmer in Mexico and then in the fields of Florida picking oranges, tomatoes, blueberries, and watermelon. Reyes has worked with consumer allies to organize national actions in the Campaign for Fair Food. As part of the implementation of the Fair Food Program, Reyes conducts workers' rights education with thousands of farmworkers on participating tomato farms.

Angela Standhartinger is Professor of New Testament Studies at Philipps-Universität Marburg, Germany. She is author of *Das Frauenbild im Judentum der hellenistischen Zeit: Ein Beitrag anhand von 'Joseph und Aseneth'* (1995) and *Studien zur Entstehungsgeschichte und Intention des Kolosserbriefs* (1999) and editor of *Doing Gender—Doing Religion: Fallstudien zur Intersektionalität im frühen Judentum, Christentum und Islam* (2013). She is currently preparing a commentary on Philippians in the series *Handbuch zum Neuen Testament.*

Eduard Verhoef used to be a minister of the Dutch Protestant church. He also taught New Testament Studies at Bryn Mawr College in 1982–1983. His publications include books and articles on the Pauline epistles to the Thessalonians, the Galatians, and the Philippians. He has also published on the problem of the authenticity of the Paulines. Verhoef's most recent books are *Philippi: How Christianity Began in Europe* (2013) and his Dutch translation of the Qur'an (2015). He has a keen interest in the points of connection between early Christianity and contemporary mystery cults.

Antoinette Clark Wire is Professor Emerita at San Francisco Theological Seminary and the Graduate Theological Union. Her research has focused on the theology and practice of women in the communities to whom Paul wrote. In 1990 she published *The Corinthian Women Prophets: A Reconstruction through Paul's Rhetoric,* and she is now writing a feminist commentary on 2 Corinthians for Liturgical Press's Wisdom Series. Her work on pre-Gospel oral traditions appeared in *Mark Composed in Performance*

(2011) and *Holy Lives, Holy Deaths: A Close Hearing of Early Jewish Storytellers* (2002).

Author Index

Subject Index

acropolis, of Philippi 21–22, 39–43, 46–47

Acts of the Apostles 7, 22, 51, 53–54, 61, 65, 67, 74–75, 77, 81, 87, 103, 108–13, 117–19, 121, 123, 129–32, 143, 177, 193–94, 201, 207, 215, 256, 279

Apollo, 39, 50, 124, 194, 207

apostle(s) 10, 93, 108, 110, 112, 114, 118, 121, 123, 132–33, 135–36, 138–39, 179, 184, 223–24, 233–34, 256, 270, 274–75, 282, 285

    Epaphroditus as an apostle, 123, 132–33, 223–24, 233–34, 237, 256, 270, 274, 282

archaeological resources 16, 21–22, 25–48, 50, 53–54, 56, 59–62, 86, 107, 200, 207, 227, 286. *See also* coins; inscriptions; monuments; statues

Artemis 26, 34–37, 39–42, 48, 50–51, 53, 55, 59–62, 83, 89, 96, 227

assembly community, at Philippi 1, 5, 10, 14–17, 20–28, 33–34, 49–88, 92–108, 114, 123–24, 130–40, 142–51, 156, 162–81, 183–202, 208–11, 213–221, 223–47, 249–250, 253–57, 263–75, 278–83, 286–93

Augustus 4, 27, 29–32, 34–36, 54, 125, 127, 135, 194, 227, 243

Campaign for Fair Food 18, 20, 23, 247–52, 258–63, 268–69, 271–72, 276–78, 283

church buildings 44, 83–87, 94–98

church community, at Philippi. *See* assembly community

circumcision 188–90, 195–99, 205, 218, 239, 291

citizens, Roman 5, 8, 31, 38, 49–50, 62, 68, 70–73, 109–11, 121, 130, 155, 212, 226–27, 238–39, 242, 245, 253, 279, improbability of Paul's Roman citizenship 5, 109–10, 279

civil wars, Roman 4–5, 8, 10, 66, 142

Claudius 28, 31, 227, 236, 281

Clement 51, 69, 71, 81, 141, 180, 231

Coalition of Immokalee Workers 247–52, 258–63, 266, 268–69, 271–72, 276–78, 283, 289

coins 30–34, 43, 86, 207, 227

colonization 2–5, 16, 22–23, 49–50, 53, 66–68, 70–73, 81, 107, 142–44, 147–48, 154, 156, 170, 173, 176, 225–29, 233, 245, 250, 252–53, 279, 292. *See also* Roman Empire

contact zone 52–53, 83, 87, 96, 144

Corinthians, First 13–14, 110, 120–21, 130, 132, 144, 166, 178, 180, 264, 278, 289, 290–91

Corinthians, Second 65, 71, 76–78, 81, 100–101, 110, 114, 117–18, 120–21, 123, 130–33, 135–37, 180, 236, 253, 264–65

Constantine 59, 83, 95, 129

coworkers 13, 51–53, 118, 120, 165–67, 229, 236, 257, 263–64, 267, 281, 287–92

craftworkers 49, 68, 71–74, 76, 81, 99, 231, 253, 264, 267, 272

Cybele 194, 199–200, 206, 227

Cynics 23, 193, 200, 203–18, 221

CPSIA information can be obtained at www.ICGtesting.com
Printed in the USA
LVOW06s0431301015

460349LV00001B/6/P

9 781628 370966